IMMORTAL RAIN

VOLUME 3

BY
KAORI OZAKI

HAMBURG // LONDON // LOS ANGELES // TOKYO

Immortal Rain Vol. 3
Created by Kaori Ozaki

Translation - Michael Wert
English Adaptation - Sam Stormcrow Hayes
Copy Editors - Peter Ahlstrom and Hope Donovan
Retouch and Lettering - Rubina Chabra
Production Artist - Haruko Furukawa
Cover Design - Anna Kernbaum

Editor - Bryce P. Coleman
Digital Imaging Manager - Chris Buford
Pre-Press Manager - Antonio DePietro
Production Managers - Jennifer Miller and Mutsumi Miyazaki
Art Director - Matt Alford
Managing Editor - Jill Freshney
VP of Production - Ron Klamert
President and C.O.O. - John Parker
Publisher and C.E.O. - Stuart Levy

A **TOKYOPOP** Manga

TOKYOPOP Inc.
5900 Wilshire Blvd. Suite 2000
Los Angeles, CA 90036

E-mail: info@TOKYOPOP.com
Come visit us online at www.TOKYOPOP.com

ISBN: 1-59182-724-8

First TOKYOPOP printing: October 2004
10 9 8 7 6 5 4 3 2 1
Printed in the USA

OUR STORY SO FAR...

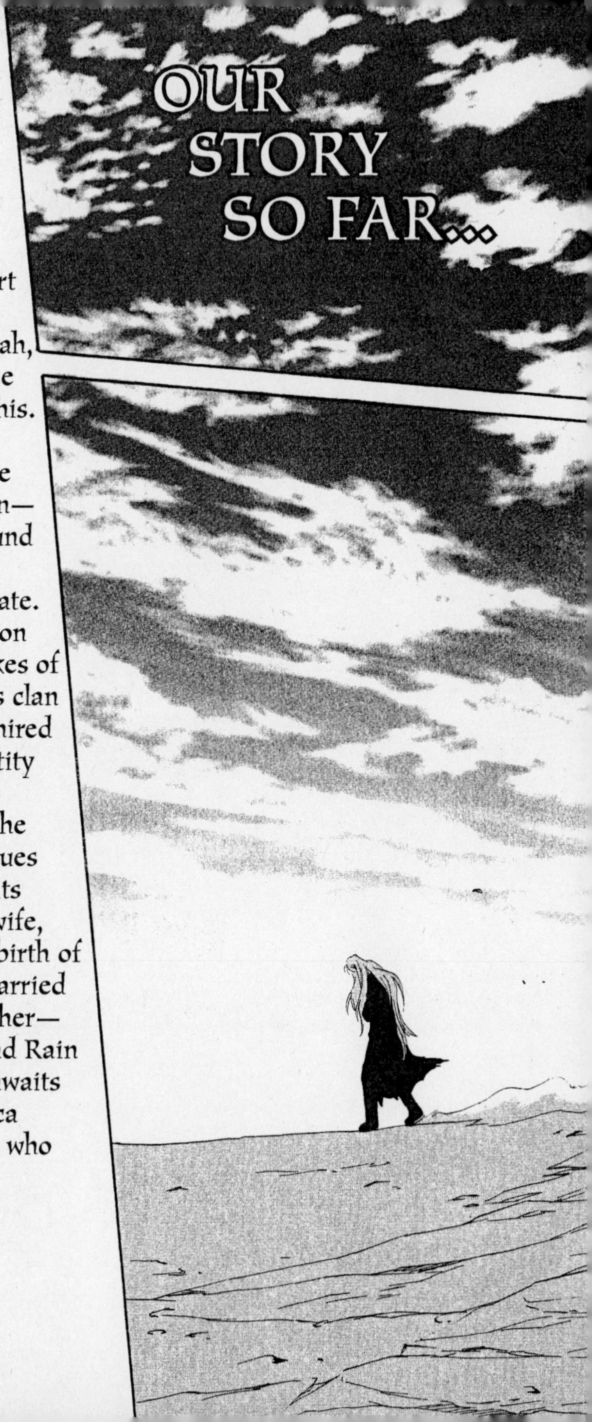

As he endlessly wanders through wastelands of desert and ice, Rain, The Immortal Methuselah, searches for a peace that may never be his. Accompanied by Machika—who once swore death to Rain—they have been bound together by circumstance and fate. Together, they are on the run from the likes of Eury Evans and his clan of Desert Pirates, hired by the shadowy entity known as "The Corporation." As The Corporation continues the hunt for Rain, its president and his wife, Sharem, await the birth of their child, being carried by a surrogate mother—Sharem's sister. And Rain waits as well. He awaits the "rebirth" of Yuca Collabell...the man who cursed him with immortality.

IMMORTAL RAIN

CONTENTS

THERE IS NO ETERNITY...

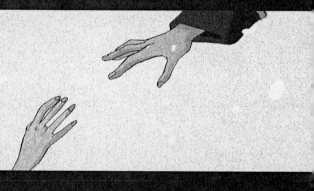

LOOK, AGAIN TODAY...

...YOU WILL LOSE ANOTHER...

°°°Cross 11 °°°

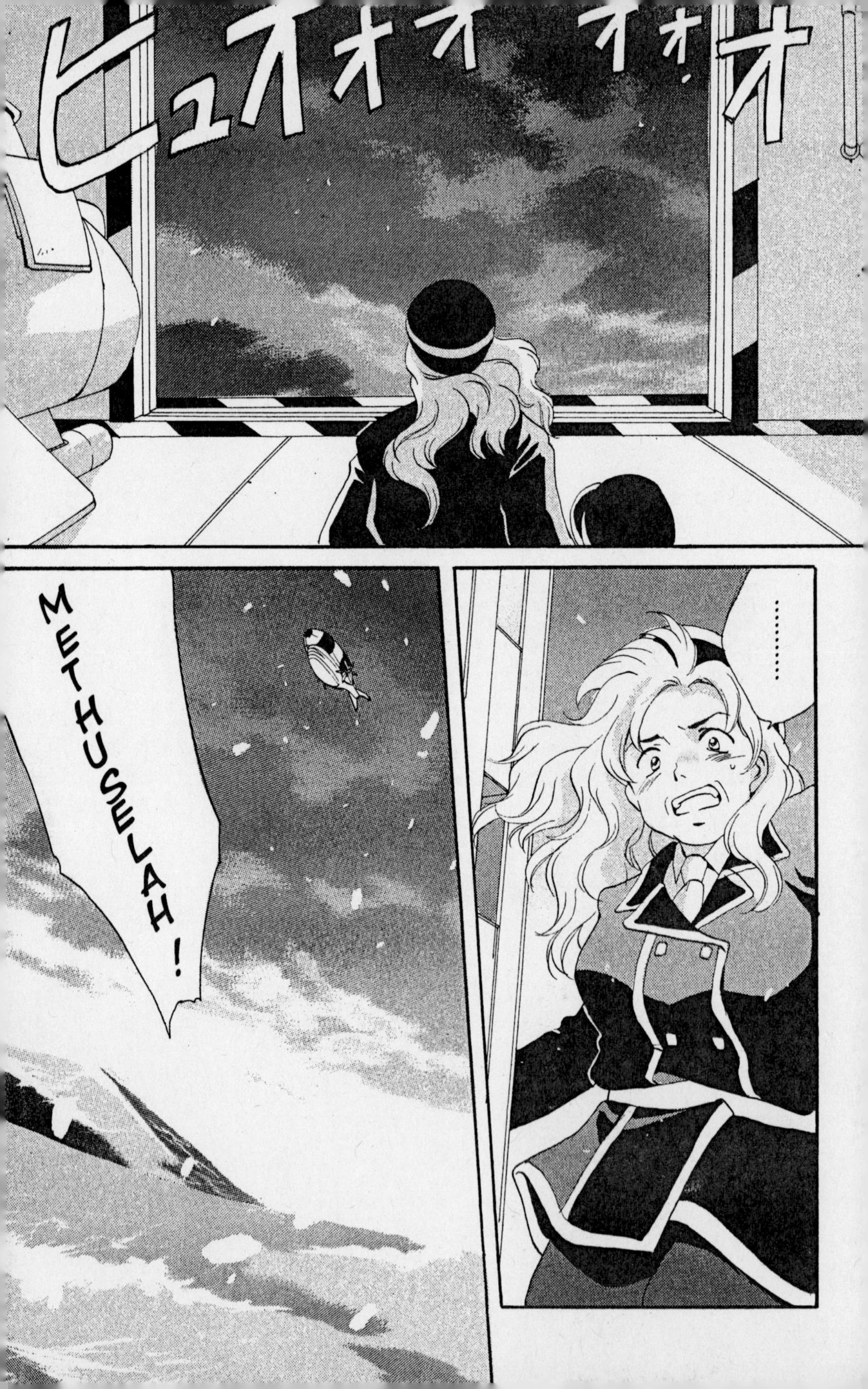
ヒュオオオ オオオ
......
METHUSELAH!

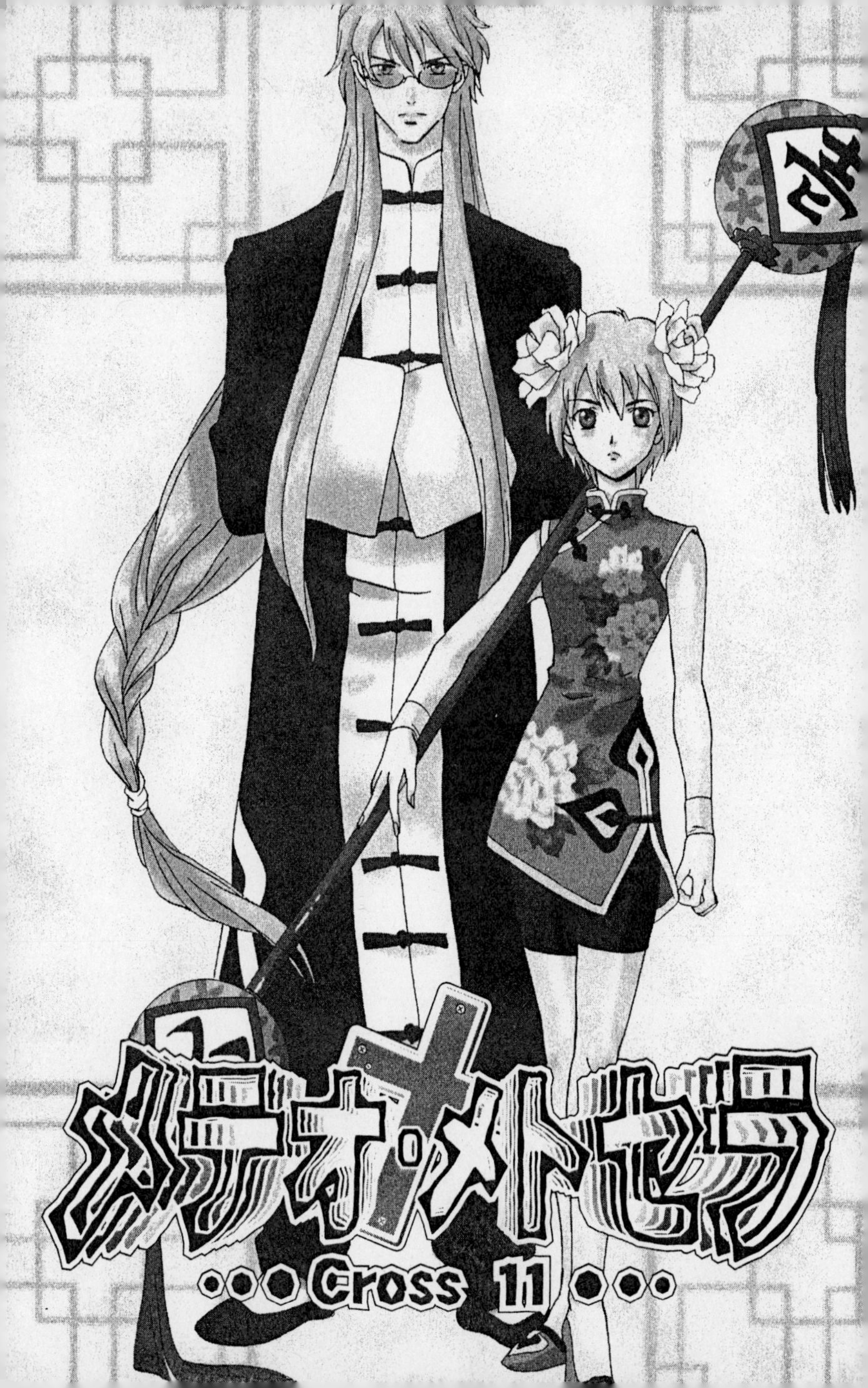

Cross 11

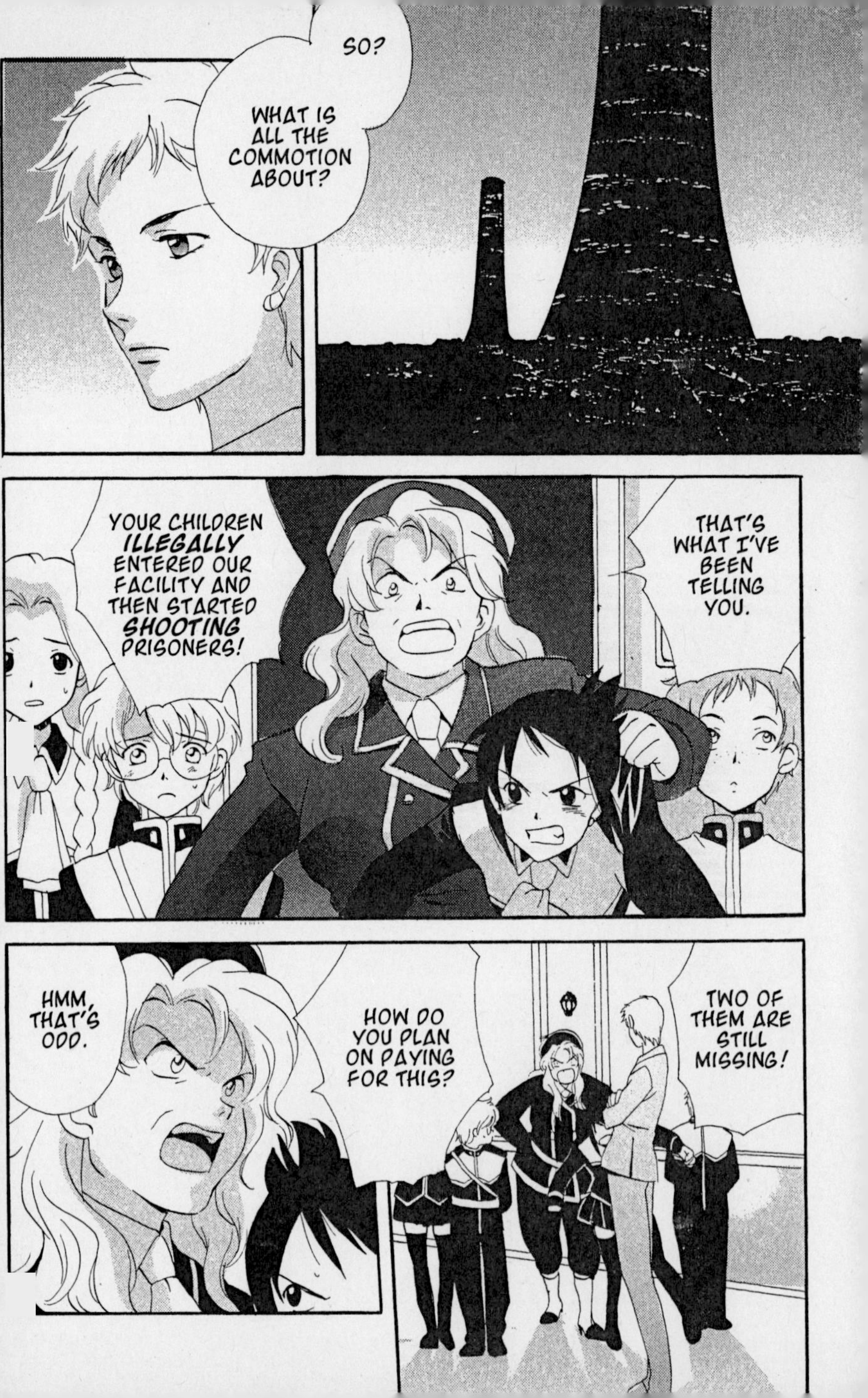
SO?
WHAT IS ALL THE COMMOTION ABOUT?
THAT'S WHAT I'VE BEEN TELLING YOU.
YOUR CHILDREN **ILLEGALLY** ENTERED OUR FACILITY AND THEN STARTED **SHOOTING** PRISONERS!
TWO OF THEM ARE STILL MISSING!
HOW DO YOU PLAN ON PAYING FOR THIS?
HMM, THAT'S ODD.

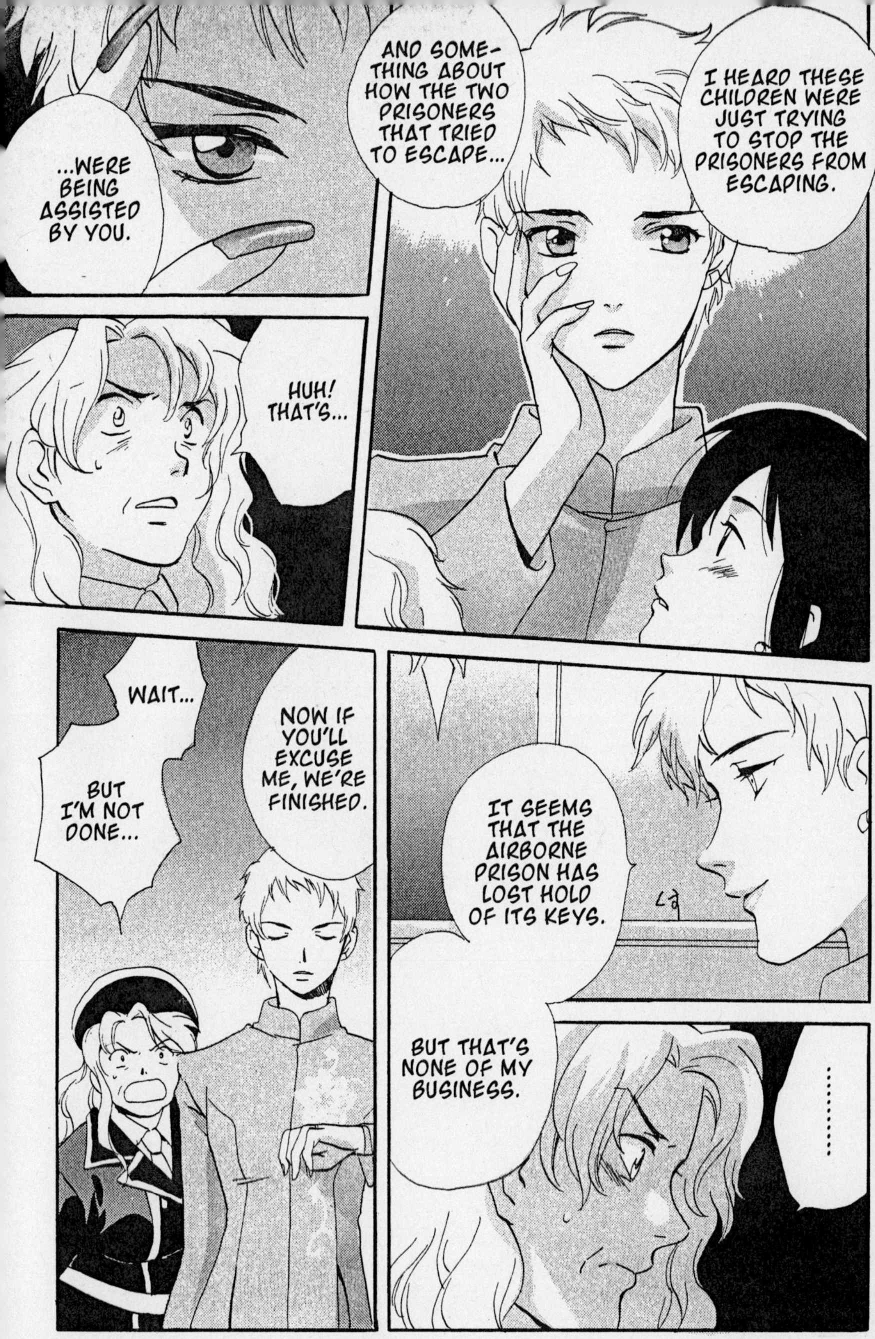
I HEARD THESE CHILDREN WERE JUST TRYING TO STOP THE PRISONERS FROM ESCAPING.
AND SOMETHING ABOUT HOW THE TWO PRISONERS THAT TRIED TO ESCAPE...
...WERE BEING ASSISTED BY YOU.
HUH! THAT'S...
IT SEEMS THAT THE AIRBORNE PRISON HAS LOST HOLD OF ITS KEYS.
BUT THAT'S NONE OF MY BUSINESS.
....
NOW IF YOU'LL EXCUSE ME, WE'RE FINISHED.
WAIT...
BUT I'M NOT DONE...

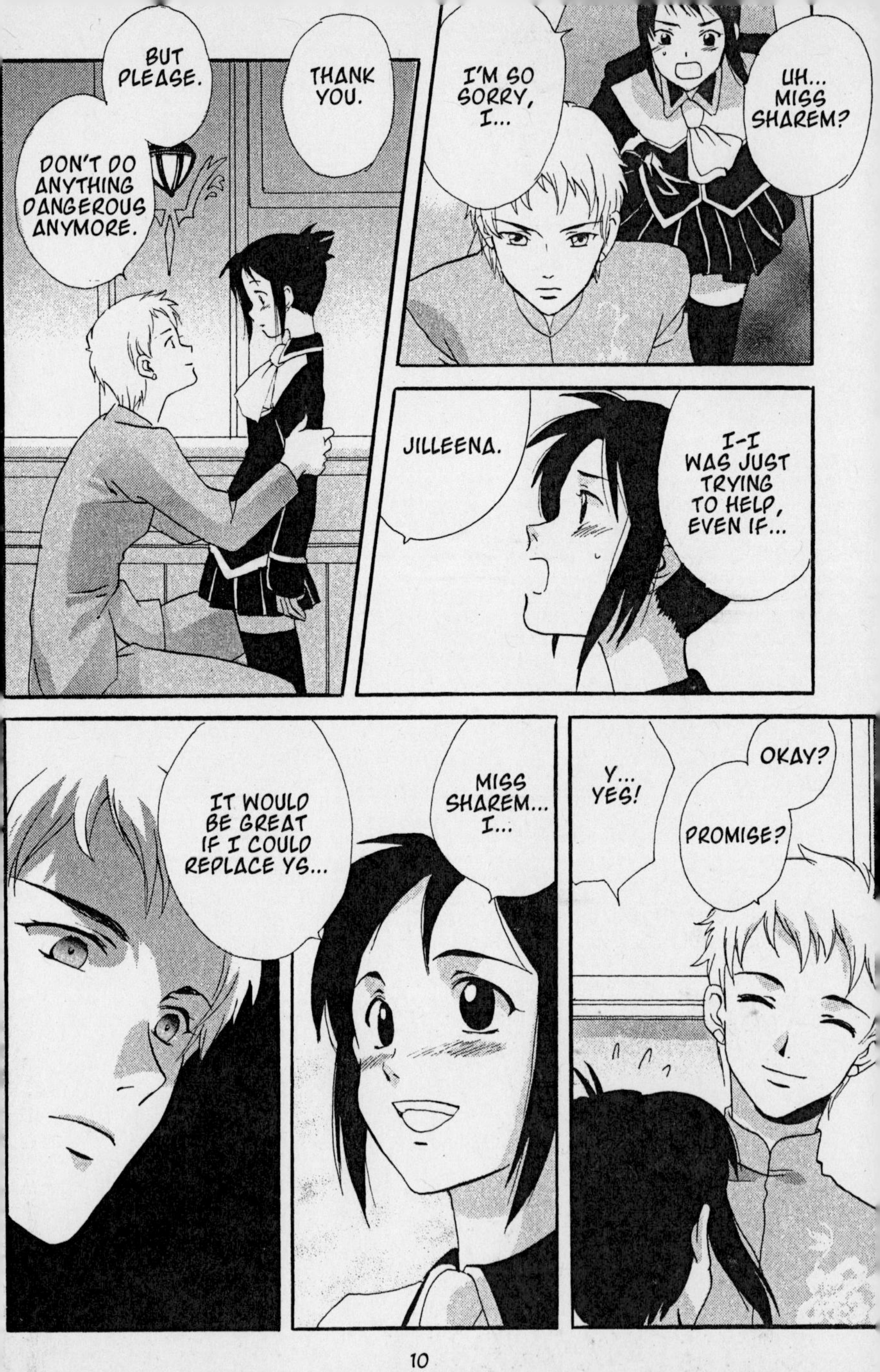
UH... MISS SHAREM?
I'M SO SORRY, I...
I-I WAS JUST TRYING TO HELP, EVEN IF...
JILLEENA.
THANK YOU.
BUT PLEASE.
DON'T DO ANYTHING DANGEROUS ANYMORE.
OKAY?
PROMISE?
Y... YES!
MISS SHAREM... I...
IT WOULD BE GREAT IF I COULD REPLACE YS...

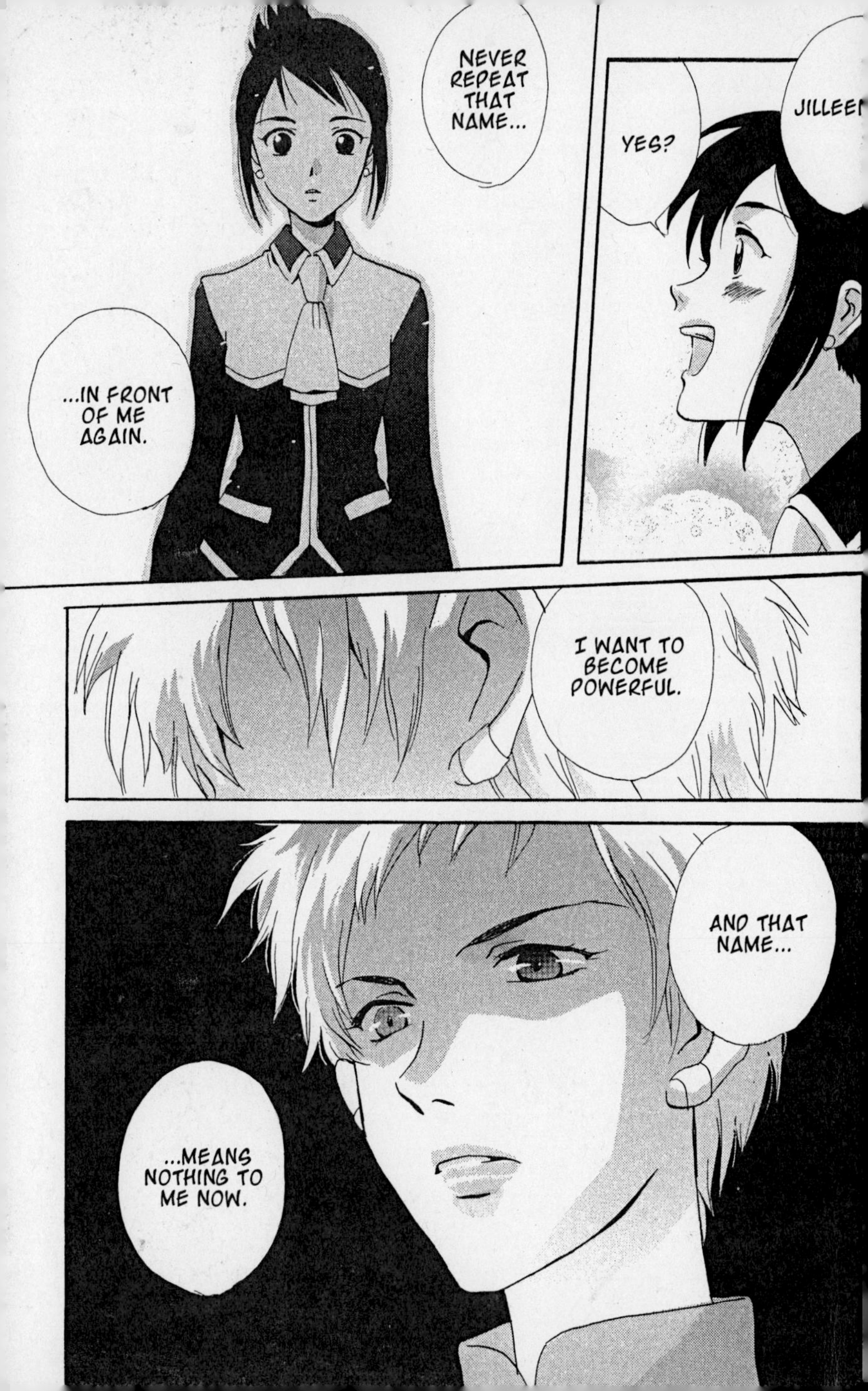
JILLEEI
YES?
NEVER REPEAT THAT NAME...
...IN FRONT OF ME AGAIN.
I WANT TO BECOME POWERFUL.
AND THAT NAME...
...MEANS NOTHING TO ME NOW.

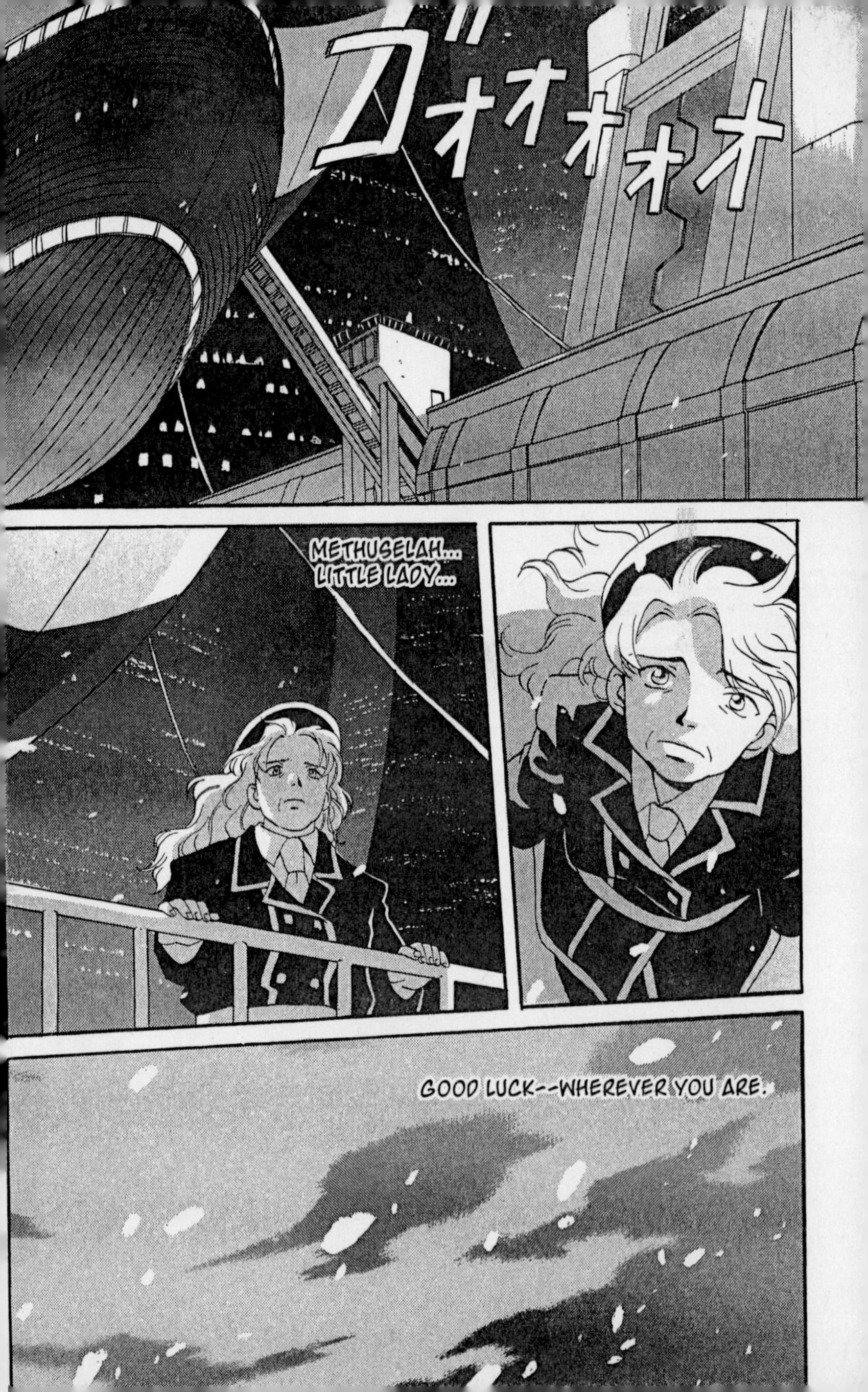
ゴォオオォオ
METHUSELAH... LITTLE LADY...
GOOD LUCK--WHEREVER YOU ARE.

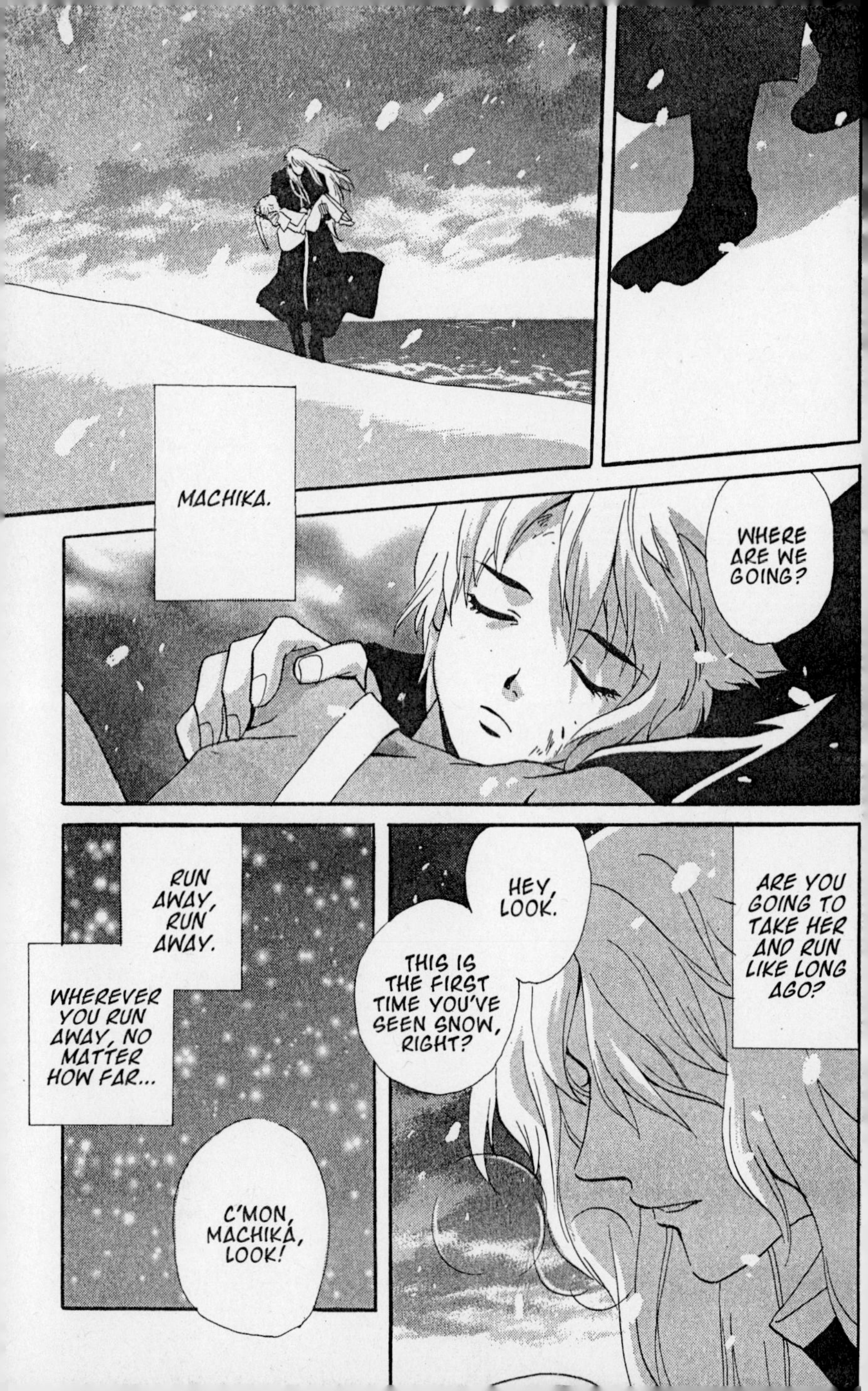
MACHIKA.
WHERE ARE WE GOING?
ARE YOU GOING TO TAKE HER AND RUN LIKE LONG AGO?
HEY, LOOK.
THIS IS THE FIRST TIME YOU'VE SEEN SNOW, RIGHT?
RUN AWAY, RUN AWAY.
WHEREVER YOU RUN AWAY, NO MATTER HOW FAR...
C'MON, MACHIKA, LOOK!

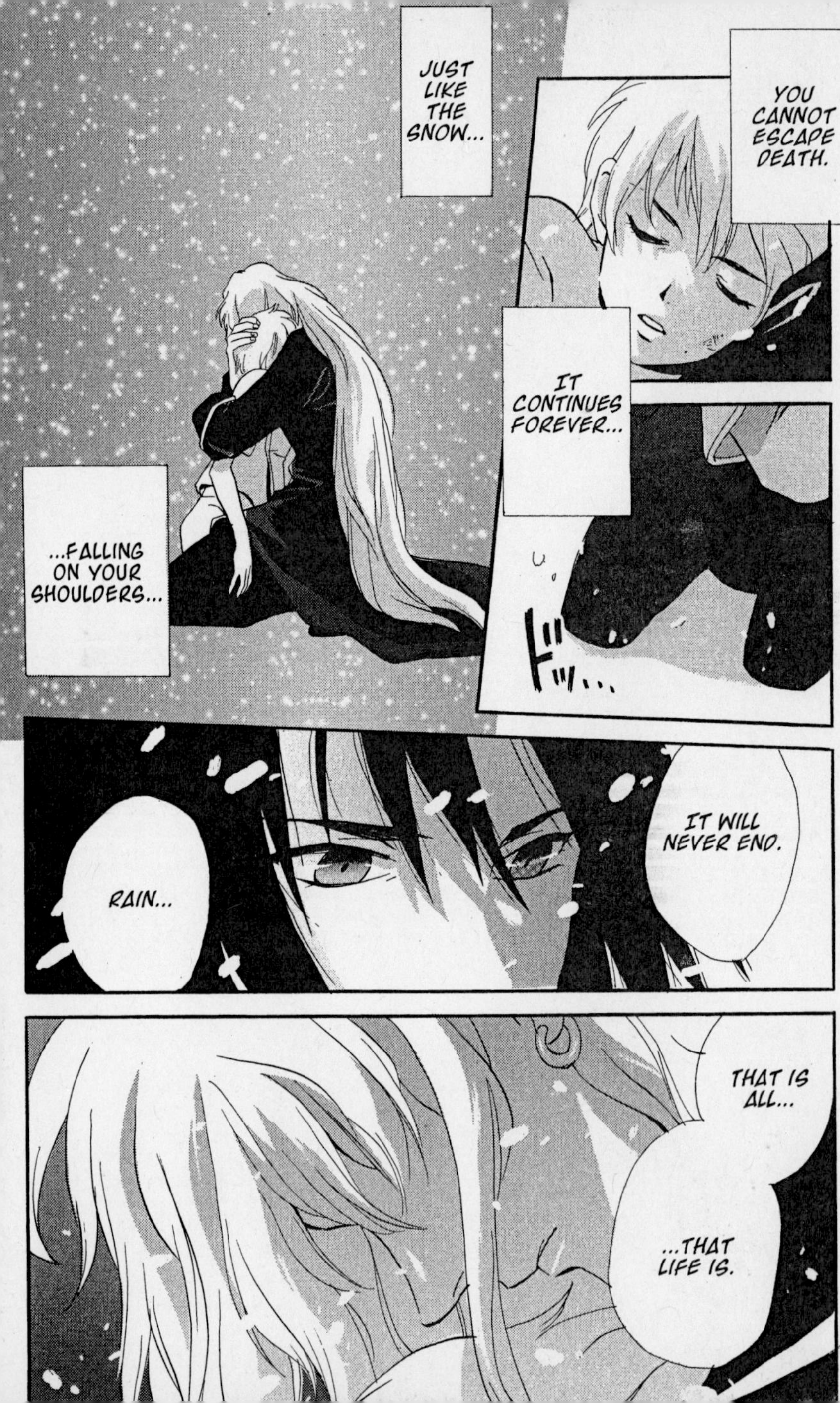

YOU CANNOT ESCAPE DEATH.
IT CONTINUES FOREVER...
ドッ...
JUST LIKE THE SNOW...
...FALLING ON YOUR SHOULDERS...
IT WILL NEVER END.
RAIN...
THAT IS ALL...
...THAT LIFE IS.

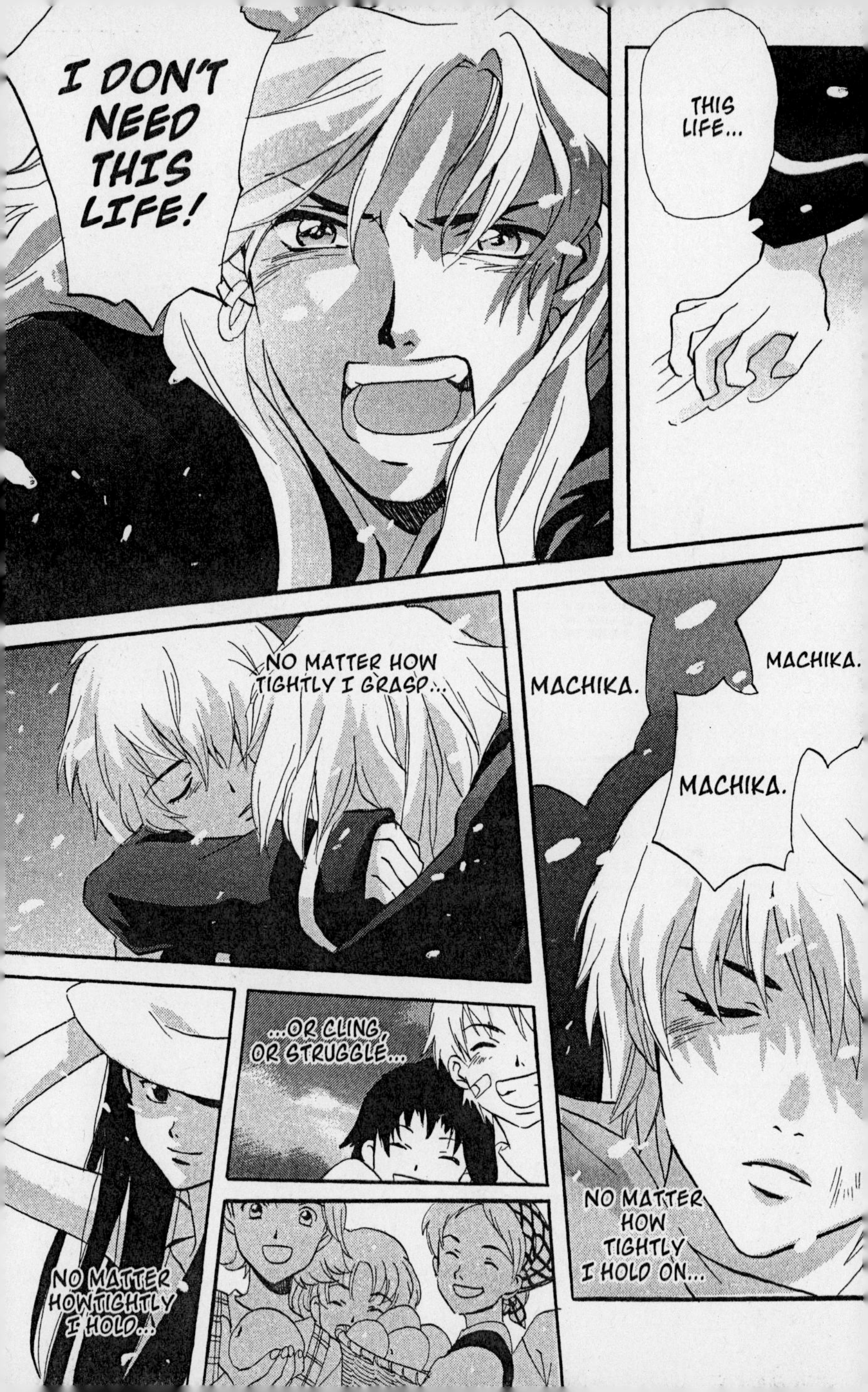
THIS LIFE...
I DON'T NEED THIS LIFE!
MACHIKA.
MACHIKA.
MACHIKA.
NO MATTER HOW TIGHTLY I HOLD ON...
NO MATTER HOW TIGHTLY I GRASP...
...OR CLING, OR STRUGGLE...
NO MATTER HOWTIGHTLY I HOLD...

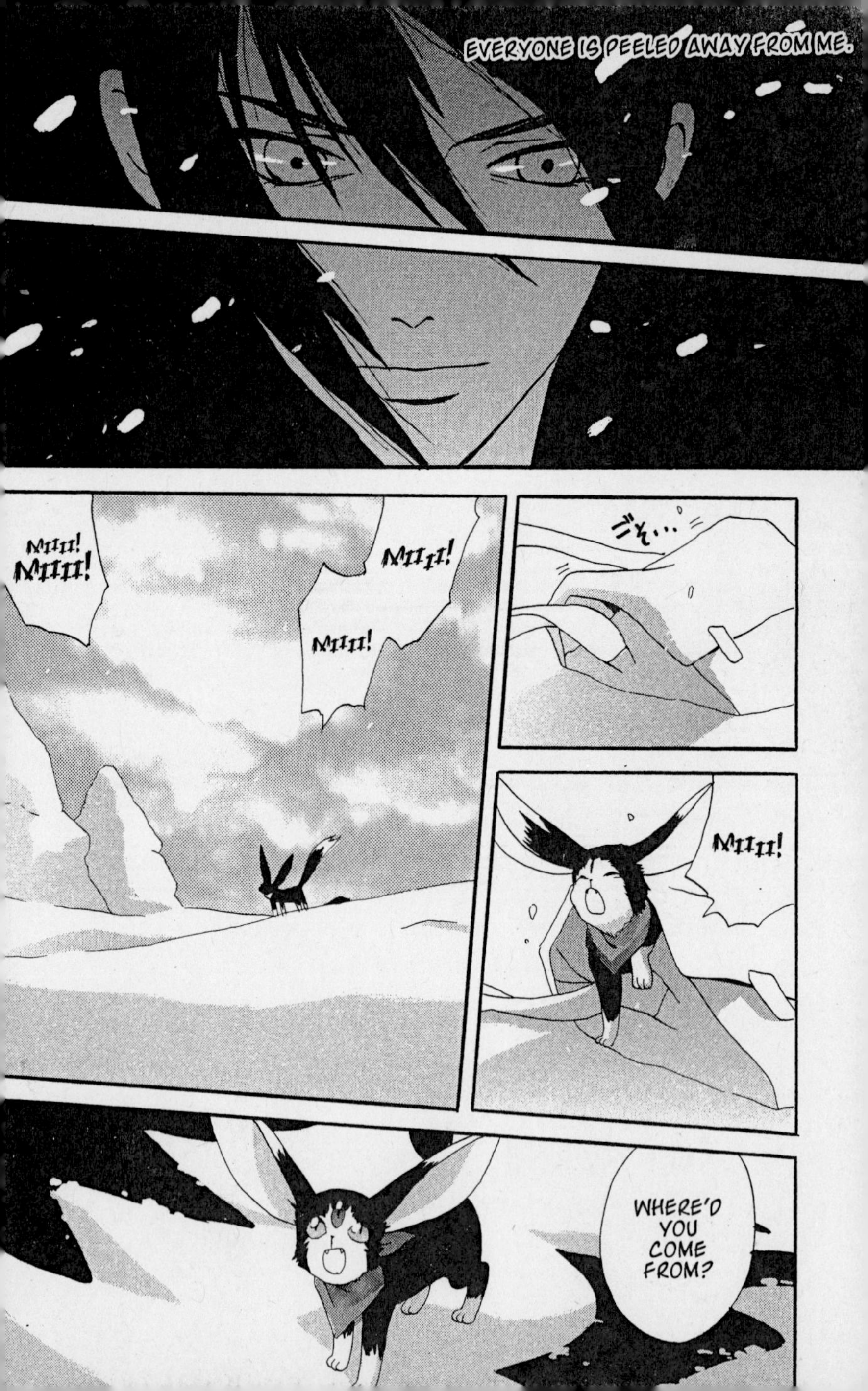
EVERYONE IS PEELED AWAY FROM ME.
ごそ…
MIIII!
MIIII!
MIIII!
MIIII! MIIII!
WHERE'D YOU COME FROM?

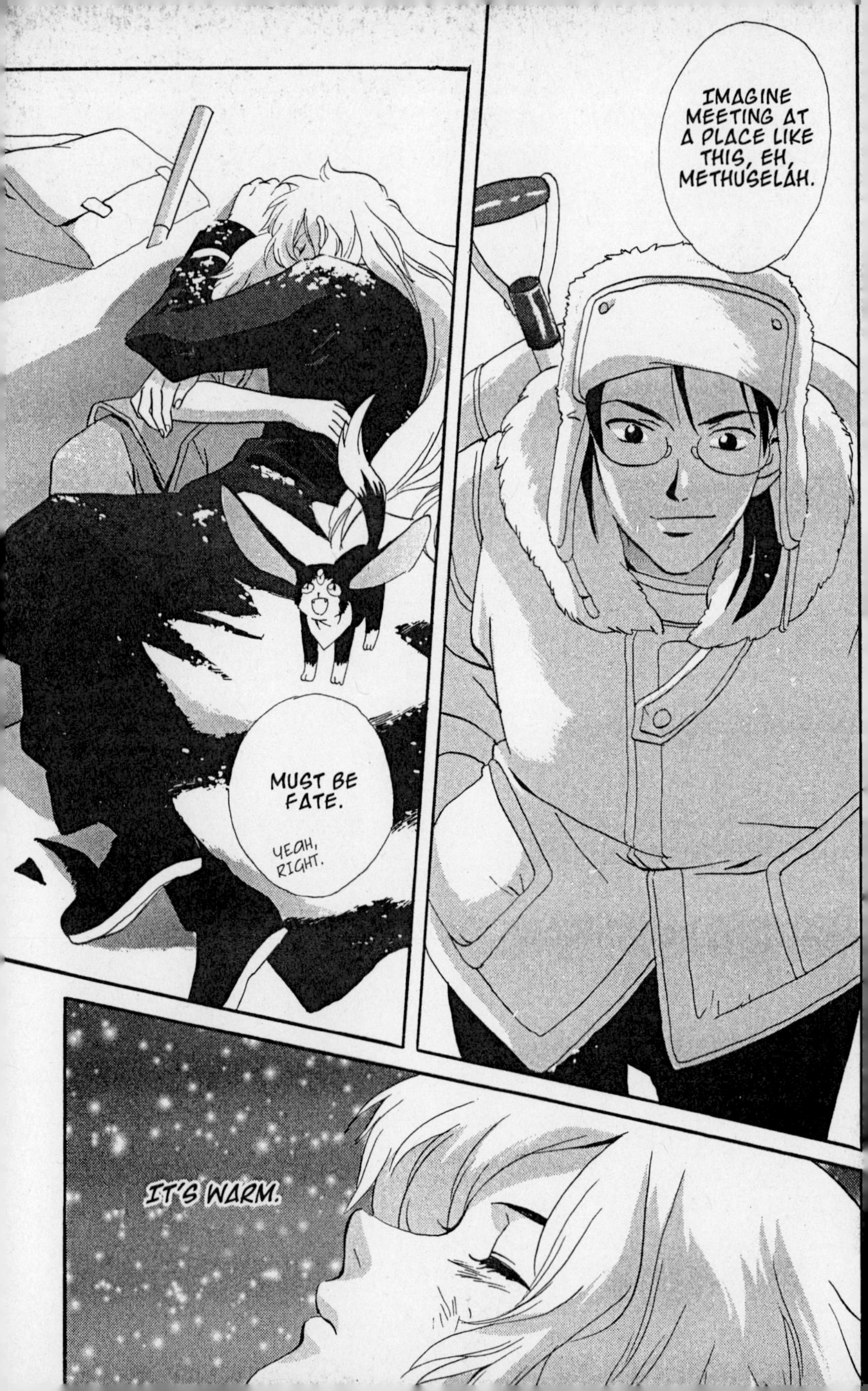
IMAGINE MEETING AT A PLACE LIKE THIS, EH, METHUSELAH.
MUST BE FATE.
YEAH, RIGHT.
IT'S WARM.

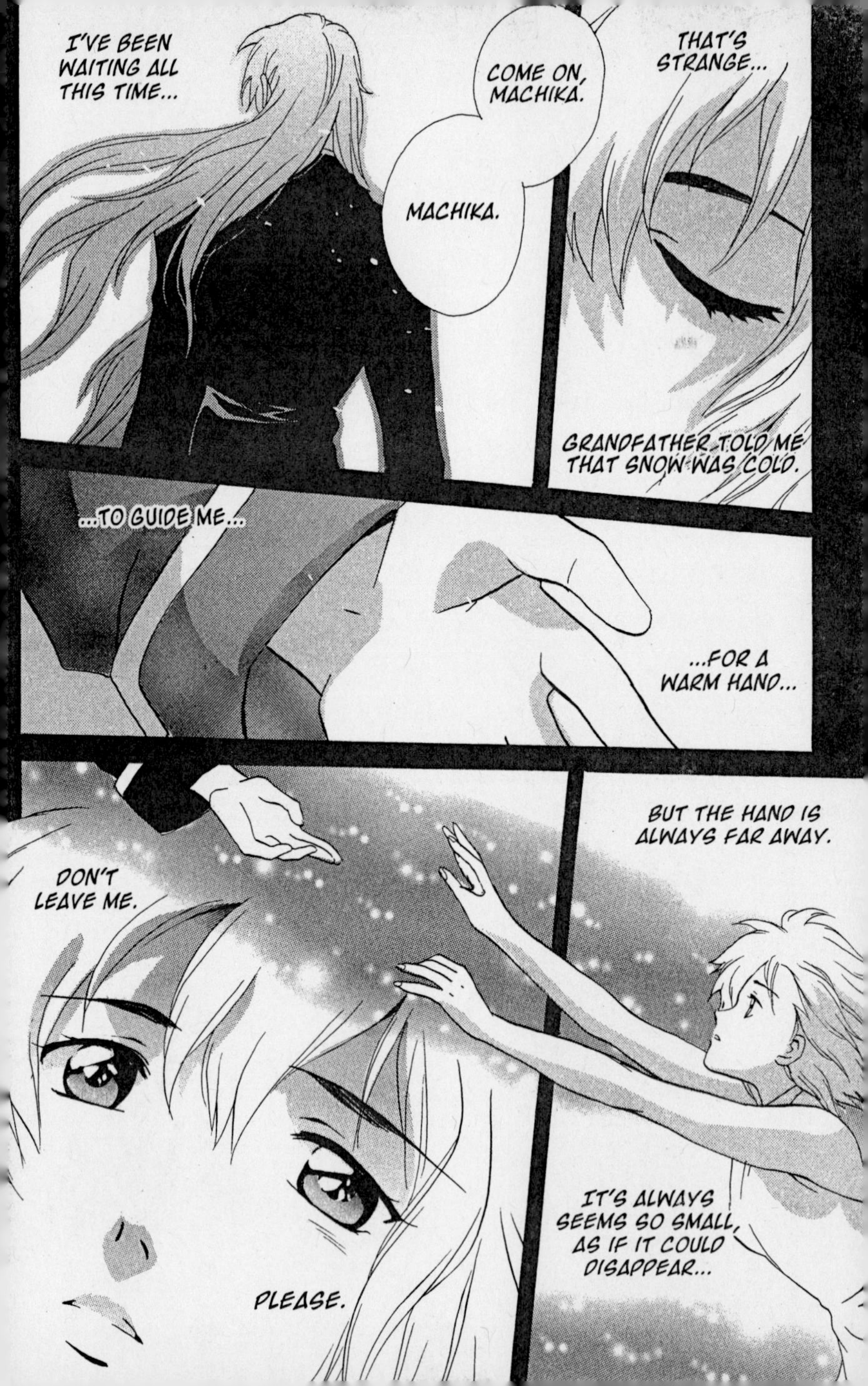
THAT'S STRANGE...
GRANDFATHER TOLD ME THAT SNOW WAS COLD.
COME ON, MACHIKA.
MACHIKA.
I'VE BEEN WAITING ALL THIS TIME...
...TO GUIDE ME...
...FOR A WARM HAND...
BUT THE HAND IS ALWAYS FAR AWAY.
IT'S ALWAYS SEEMS SO SMALL, AS IF IT COULD DISAPPEAR...
DON'T LEAVE ME.
PLEASE.

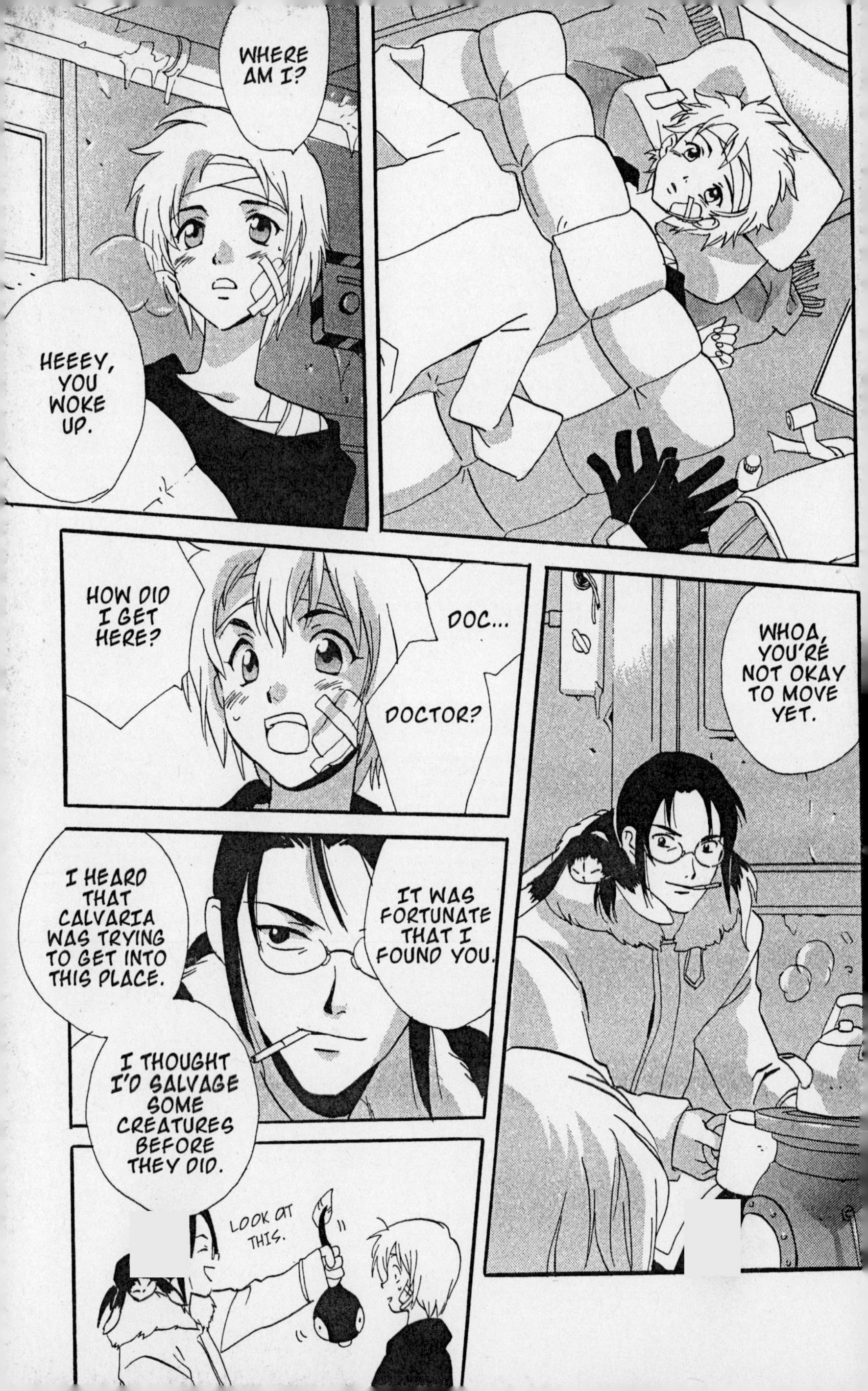
WHERE AM I?
HEEEY, YOU WOKE UP.
WHOA, YOU'RE NOT OKAY TO MOVE YET.
DOC...
DOCTOR?
HOW DID I GET HERE?
IT WAS FORTUNATE THAT I FOUND YOU.
I HEARD THAT CALVARIA WAS TRYING TO GET INTO THIS PLACE.
I THOUGHT I'D SALVAGE SOME CREATURES BEFORE THEY DID.
LOOK AT THIS.

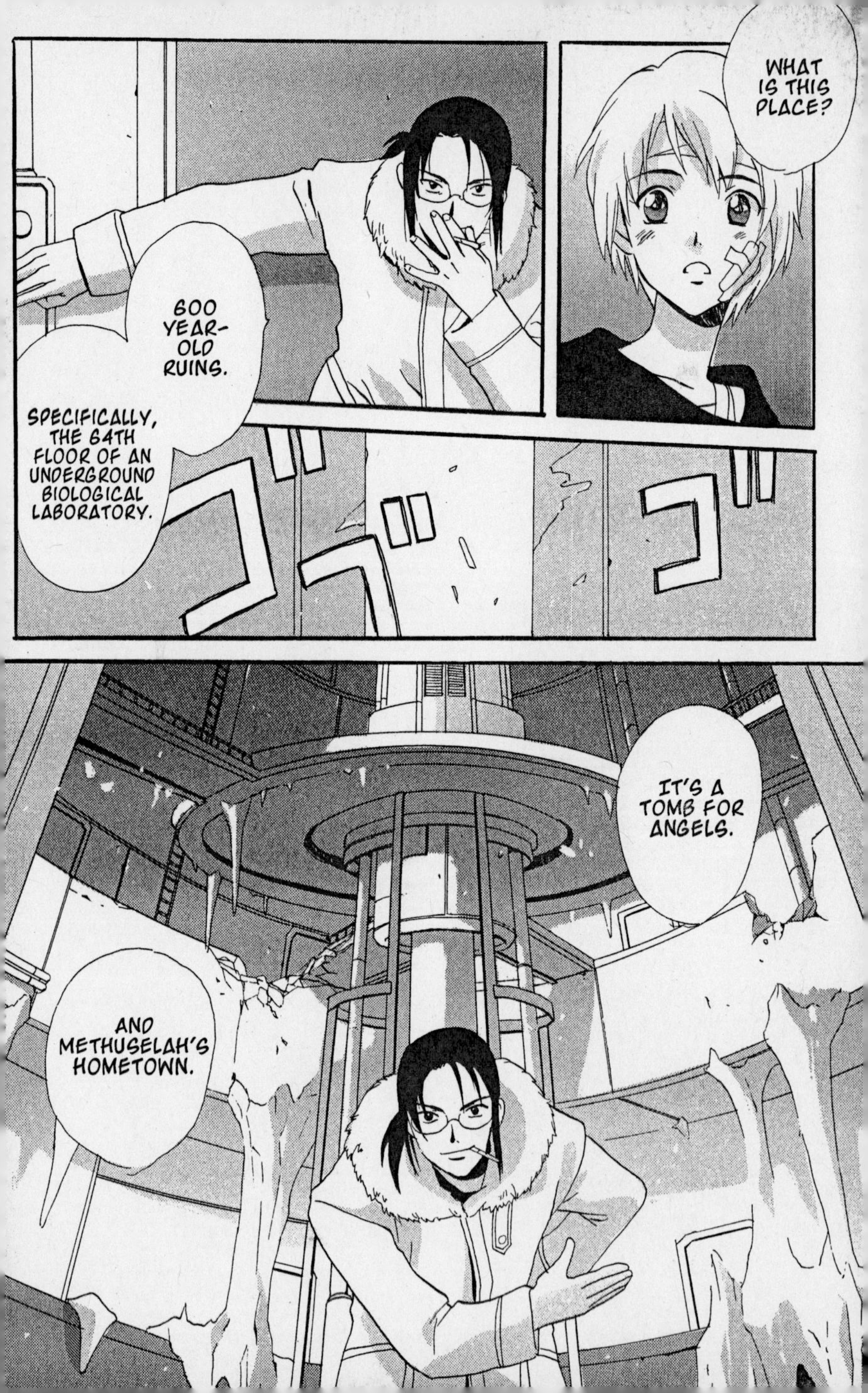
WHAT IS THIS PLACE?
600 YEAR-OLD RUINS.
SPECIFICALLY, THE 64TH FLOOR OF AN UNDERGROUND BIOLOGICAL LABORATORY.
ゴゴゴ
IT'S A TOMB FOR ANGELS.
AND METHUSELAH'S HOMETOWN.

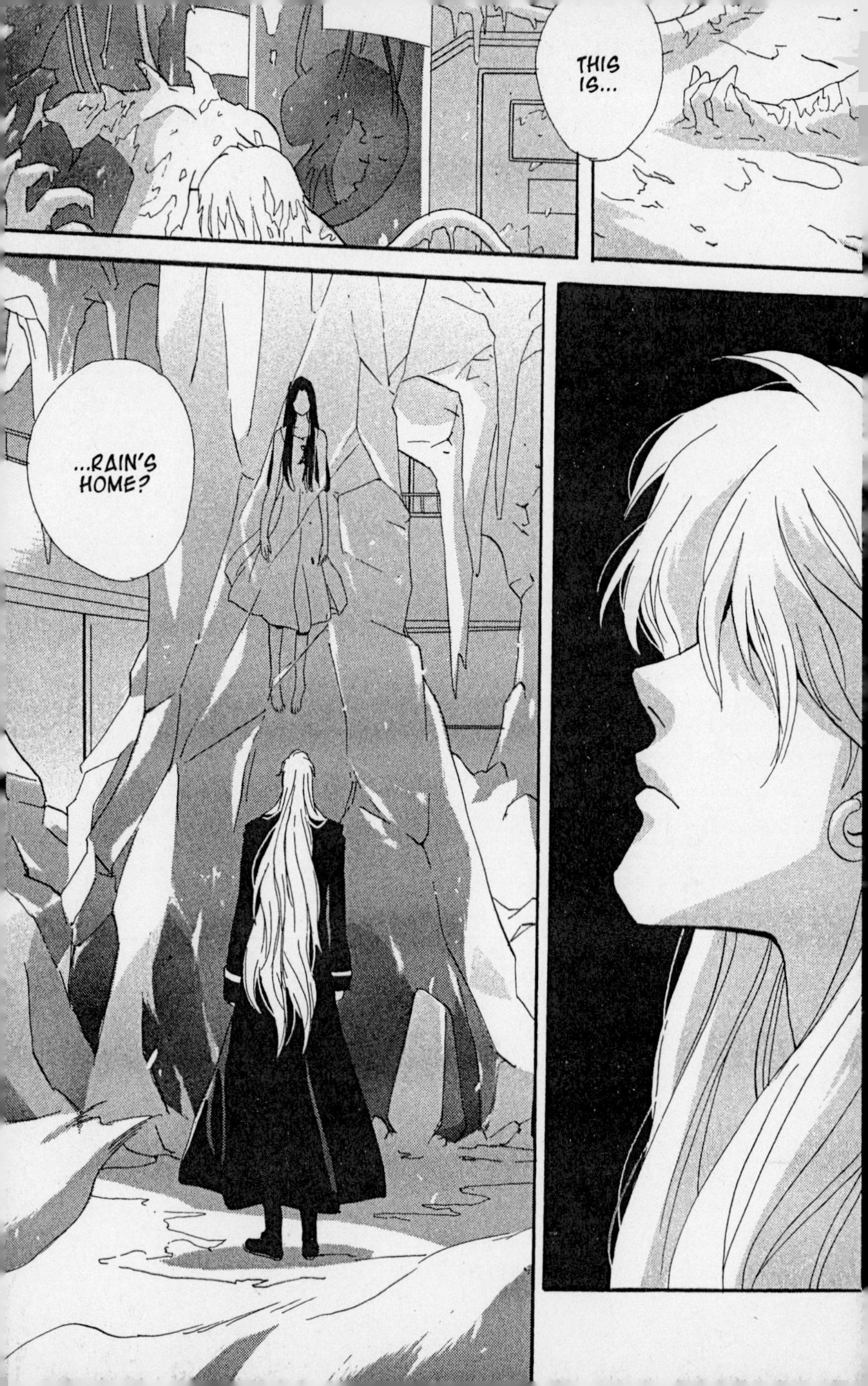
THIS IS...
...RAIN'S HOME?

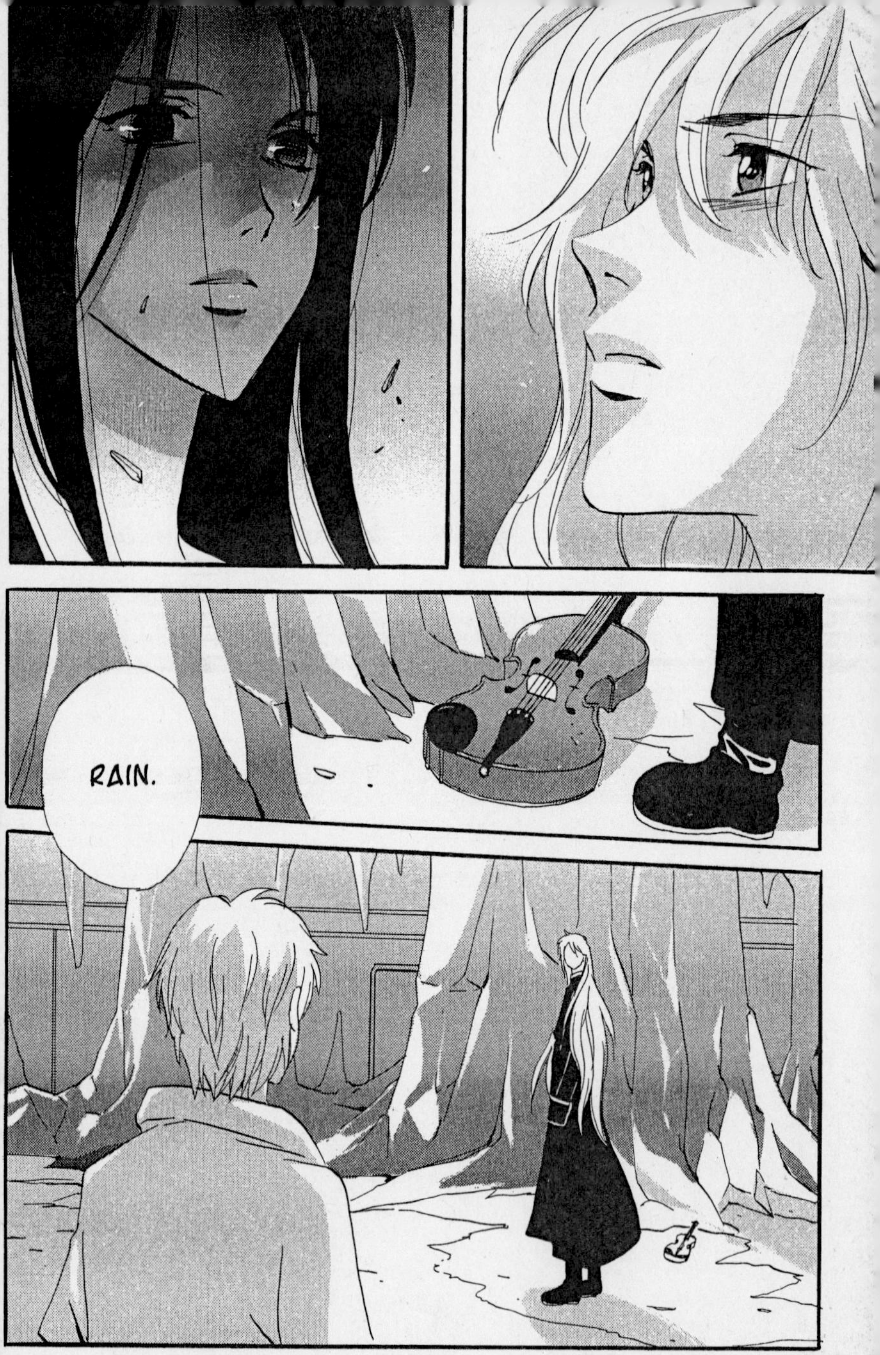
RAIN.

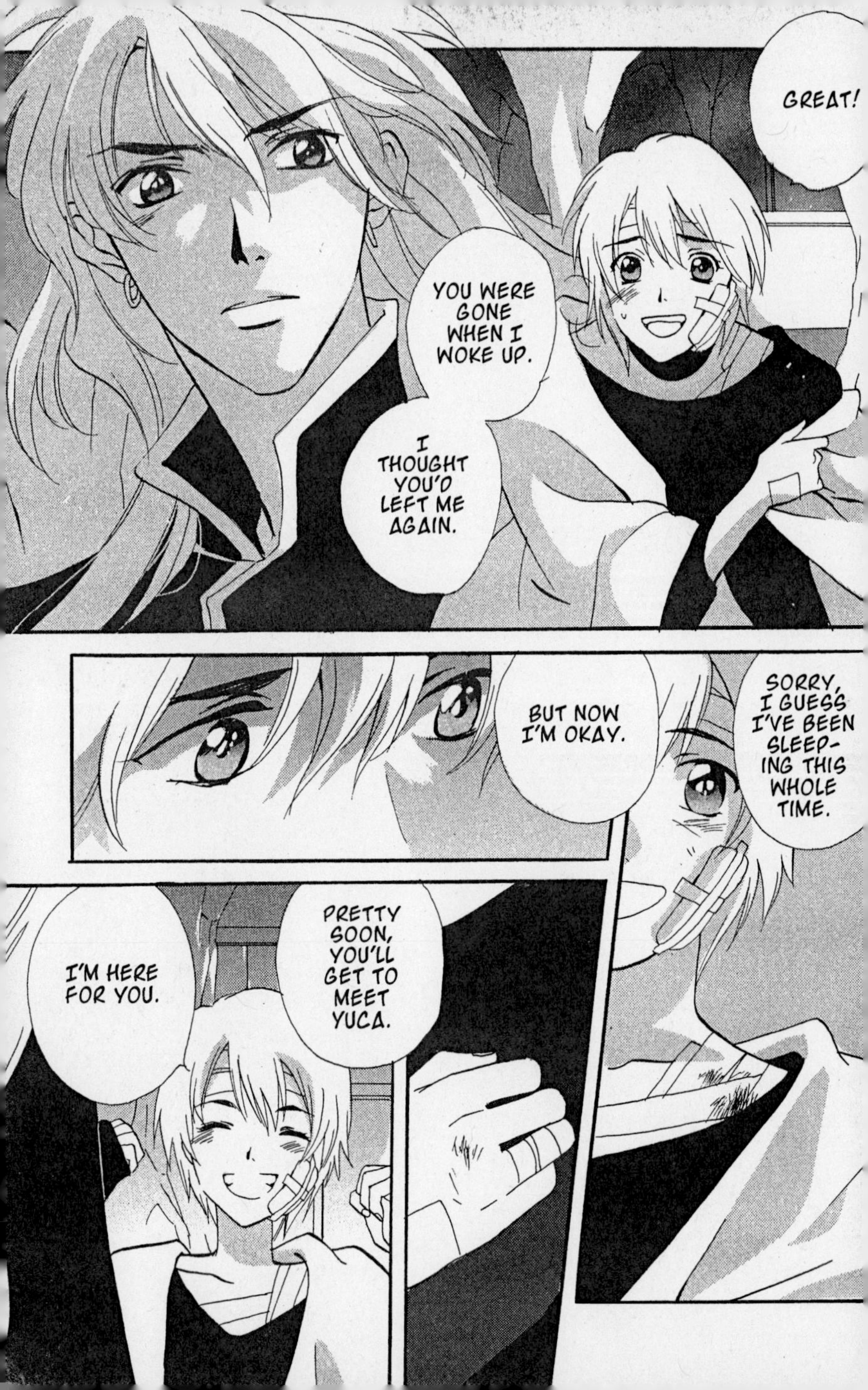
GREAT!
YOU WERE GONE WHEN I WOKE UP.
I THOUGHT YOU'D LEFT ME AGAIN.
SORRY, I GUESS I'VE BEEN SLEEP-ING THIS WHOLE TIME.
BUT NOW I'M OKAY.
PRETTY SOON, YOU'LL GET TO MEET YUCA.
I'M HERE FOR YOU.

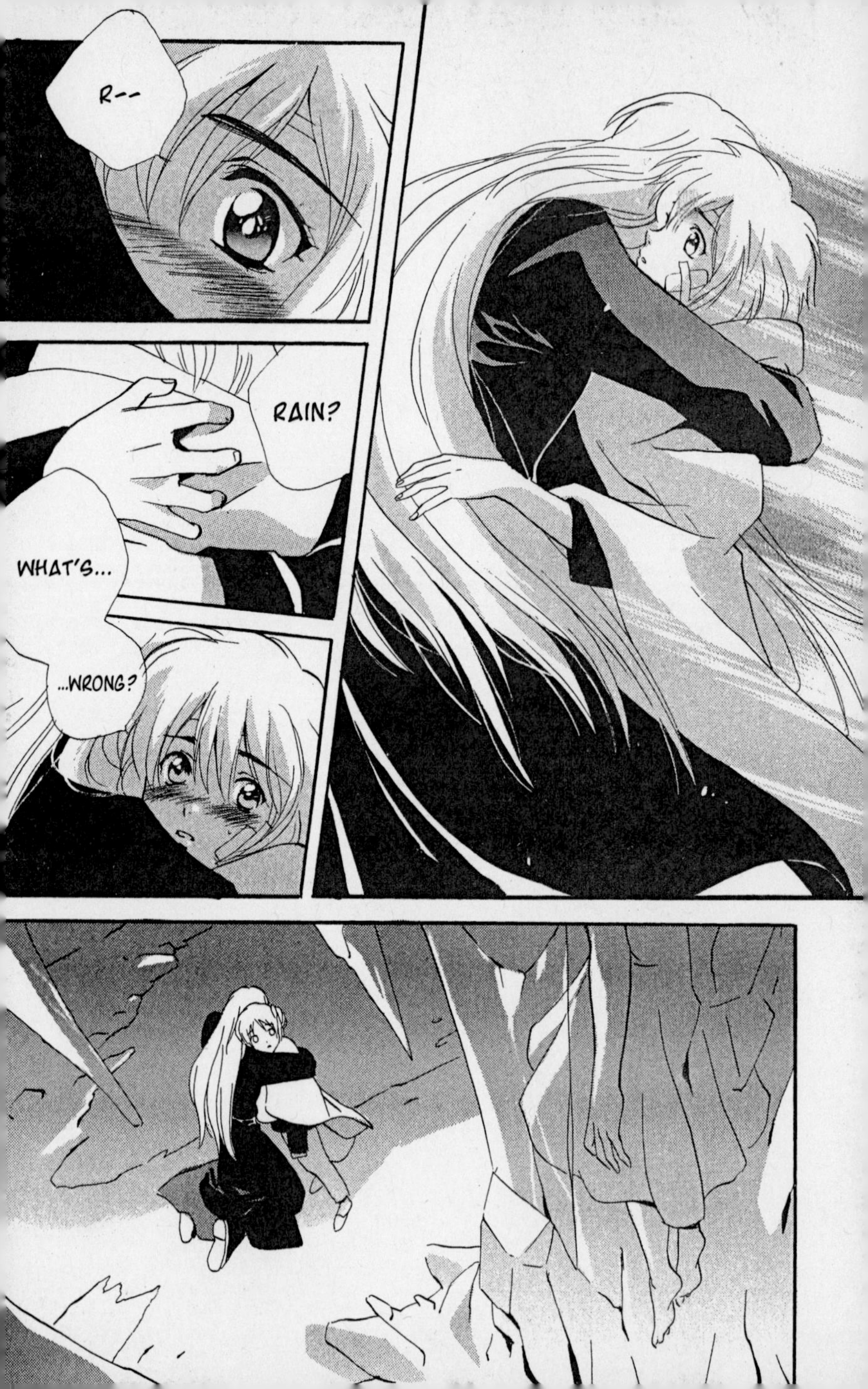
R--
RAIN?
WHAT'S...
...WRONG?

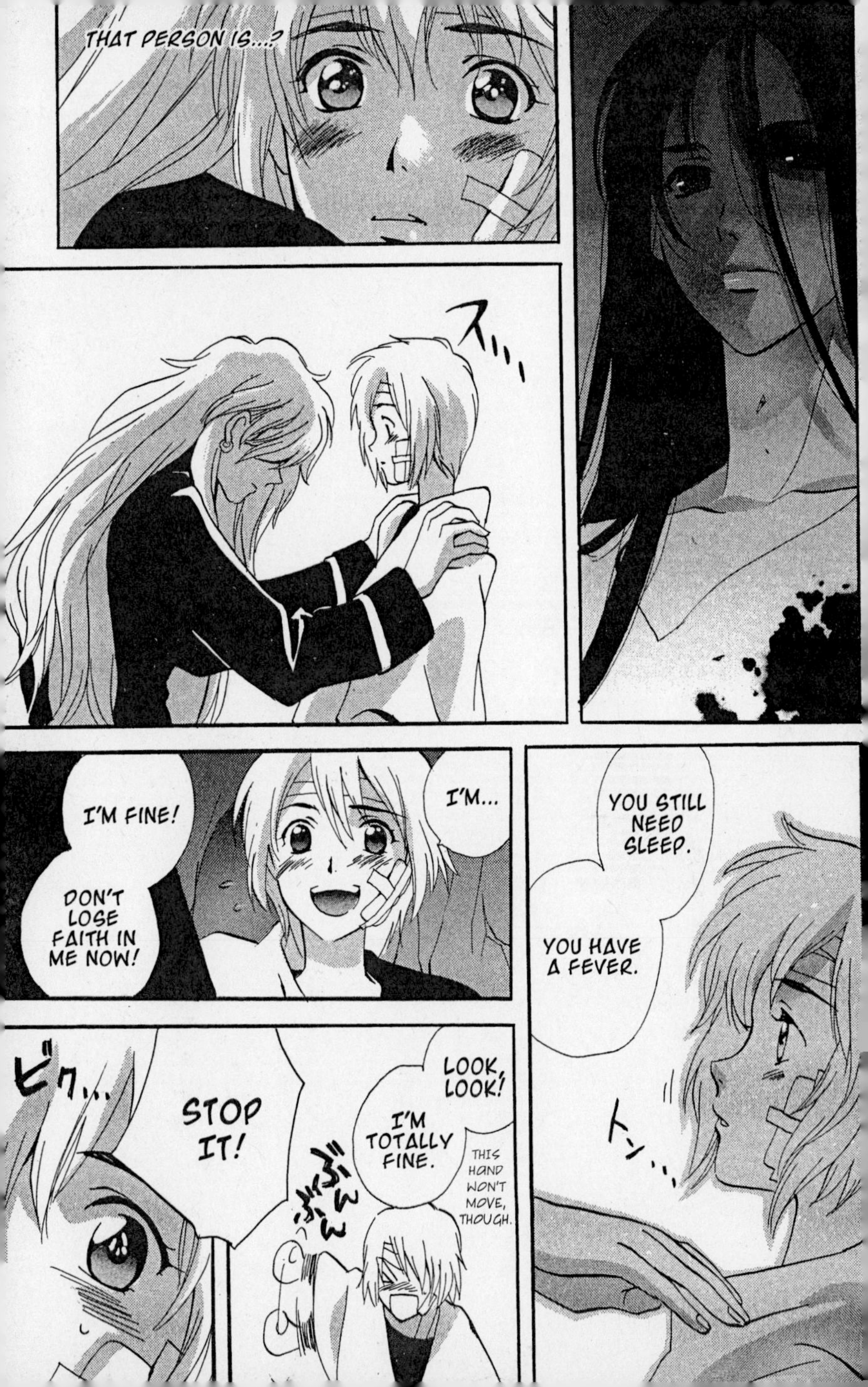
THAT PERSON IS...?
ス...
YOU STILL NEED SLEEP.
YOU HAVE A FEVER.
トン...
I'M...
I'M FINE!
DON'T LOSE FAITH IN ME NOW!
LOOK, LOOK!
I'M TOTALLY FINE.
THIS HAND WON'T MOVE, THOUGH.
ぶんぶん
STOP IT!
ビク...

I CAUSED YOU TO GET HURT.

I'M SORRY.

RAIN?

WHY ARE YOU APOLOGIZING?

. . . . .

THAT'S NOT YOUR FAULT.

IS SHE...

...THE OWNER OF THE VIOLIN?

. . . .

RAIN.

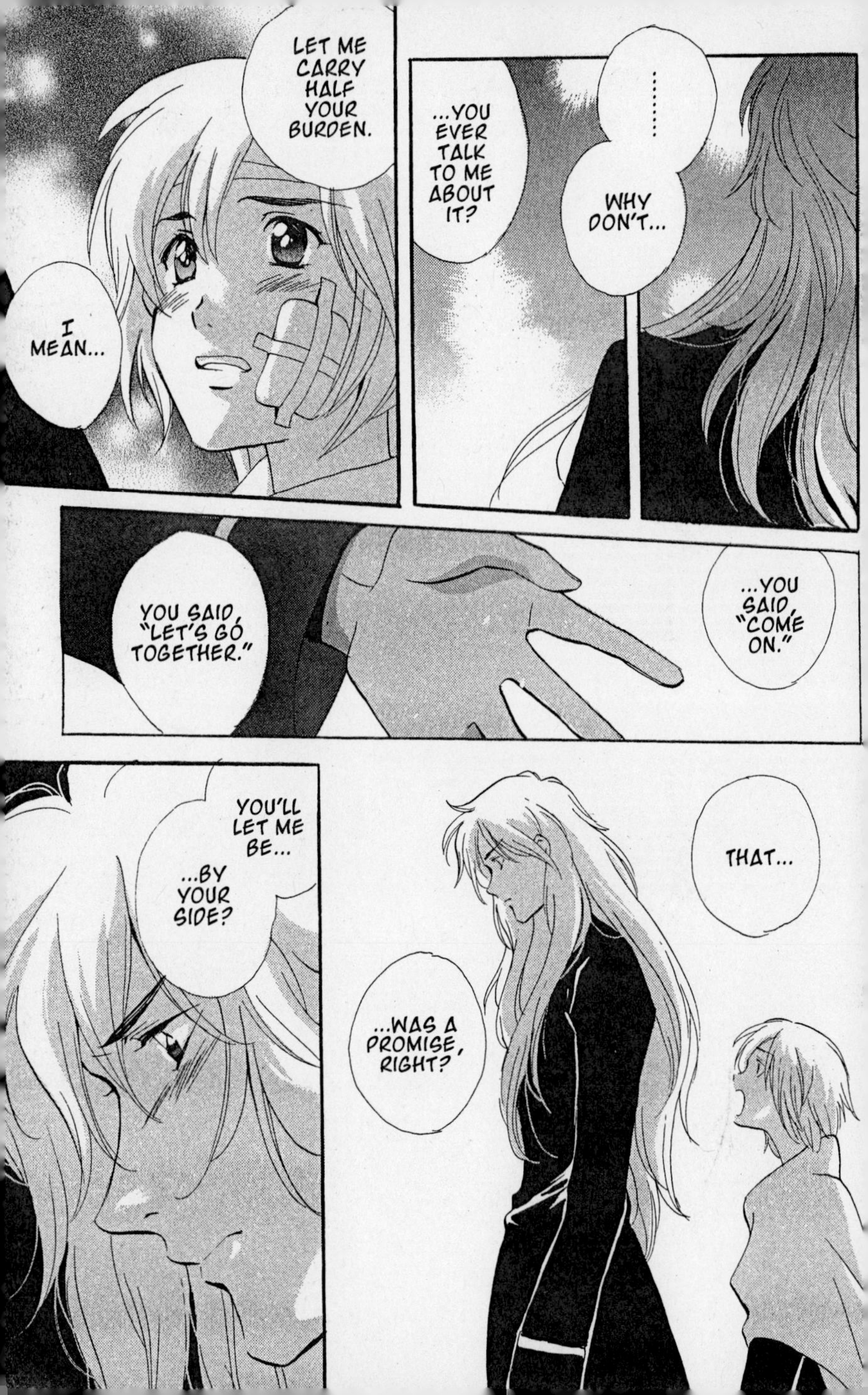
......
WHY DON'T...
...YOU EVER TALK TO ME ABOUT IT?
LET ME CARRY HALF YOUR BURDEN.
I MEAN...
...YOU SAID, "COME ON."
YOU SAID, "LET'S GO TOGETHER."
THAT...
...WAS A PROMISE, RIGHT?
YOU'LL LET ME BE...
...BY YOUR SIDE?

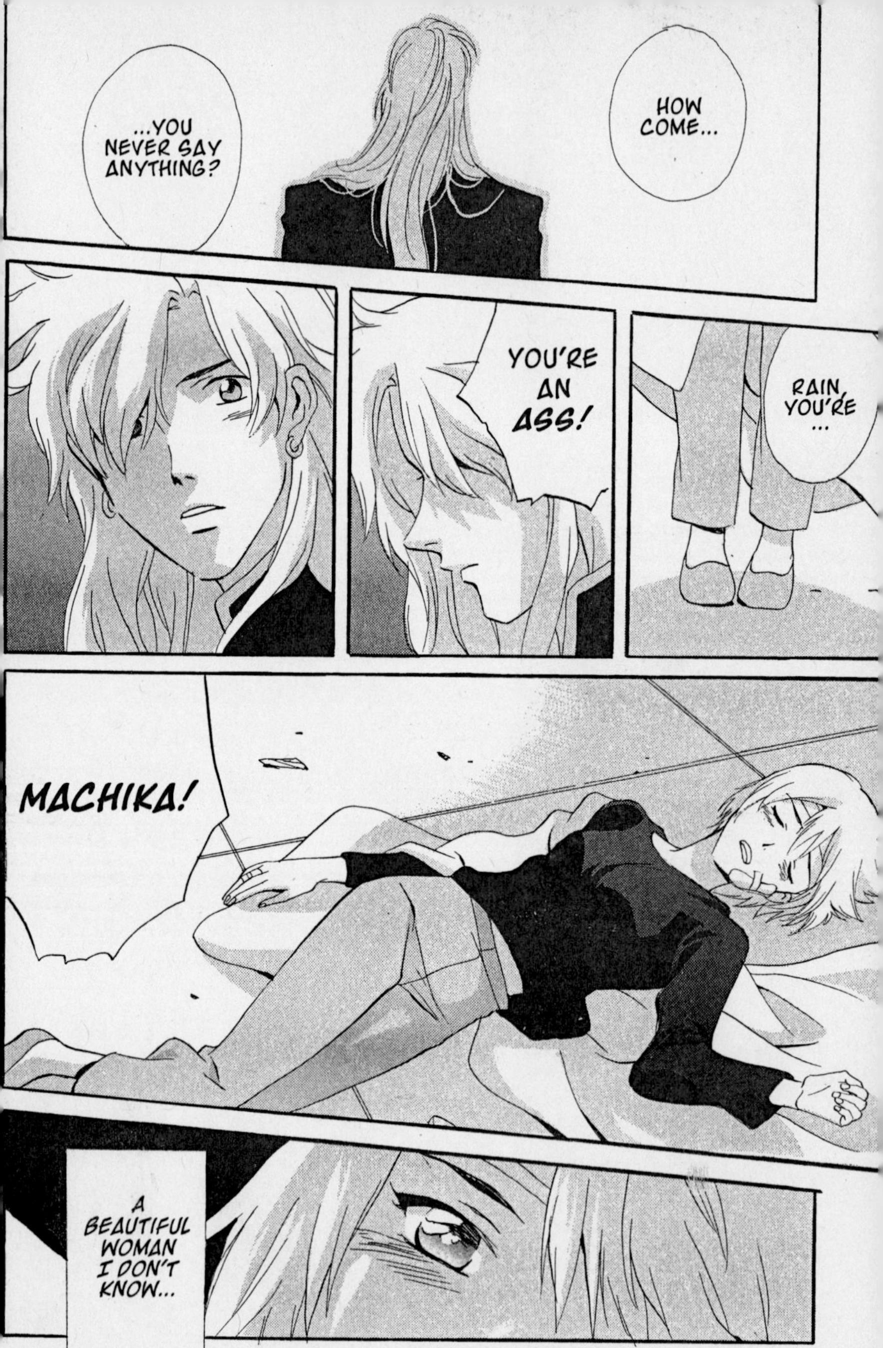
HOW COME...
...YOU NEVER SAY ANYTHING?
RAIN, YOU'RE ...
YOU'RE AN ASS!
MACHIKA!
A BEAUTIFUL WOMAN I DON'T KNOW...

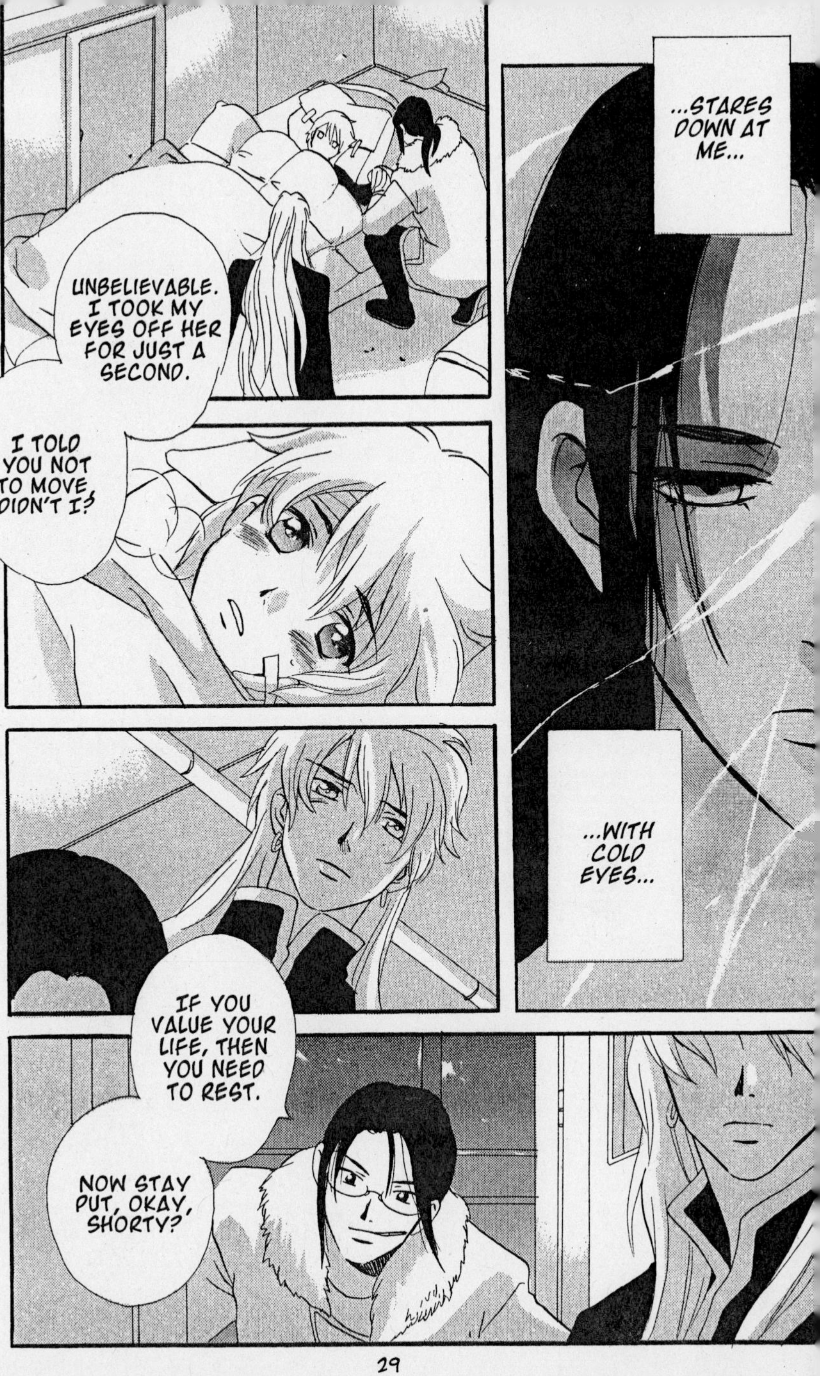
...STARES DOWN AT ME...
...WITH COLD EYES...
UNBELIEVABLE. I TOOK MY EYES OFF HER FOR JUST A SECOND.
I TOLD YOU NOT TO MOVE, DIDN'T I?
IF YOU VALUE YOUR LIFE, THEN YOU NEED TO REST.
NOW STAY PUT, OKAY, SHORTY?

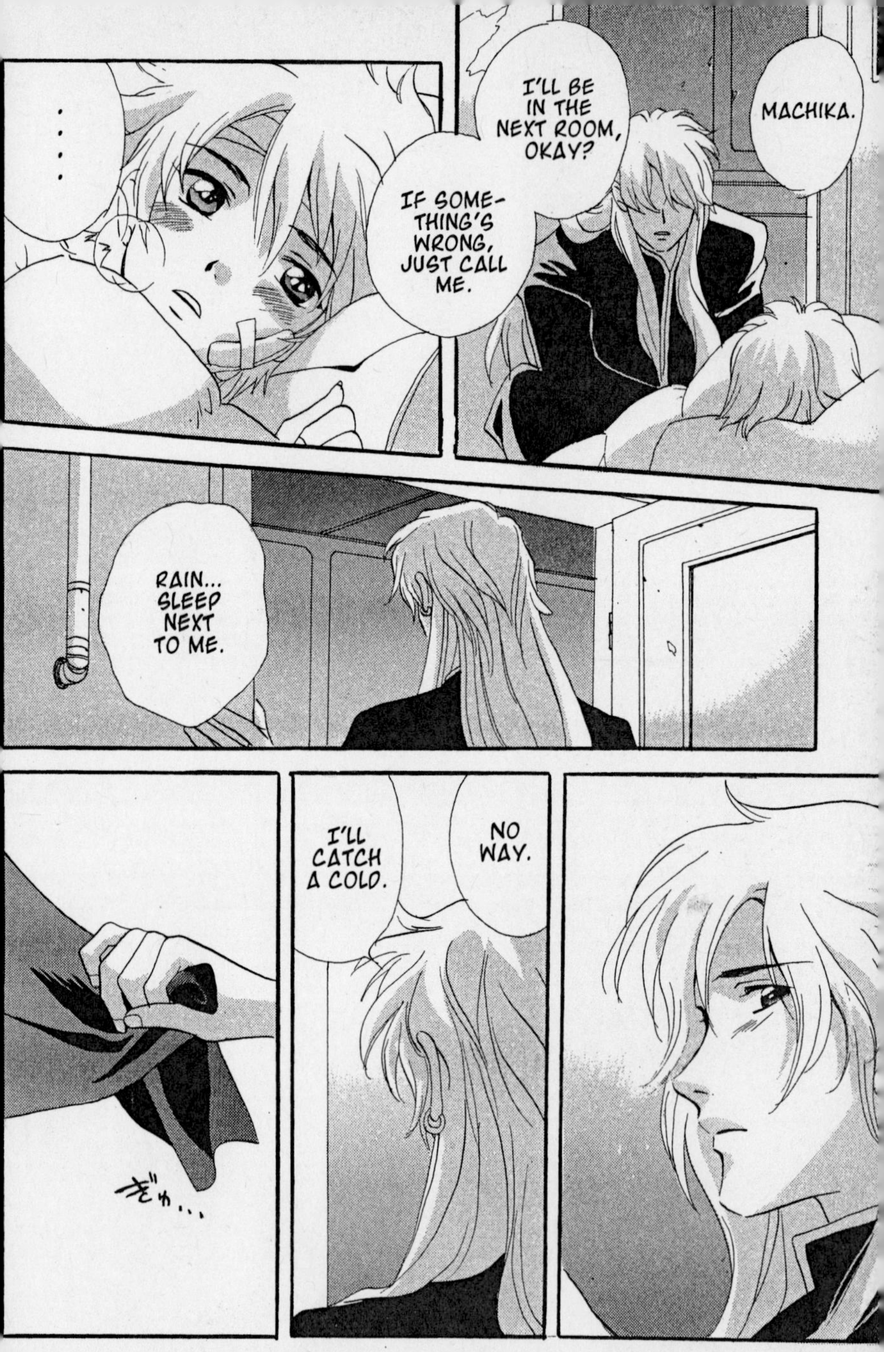
MACHIKA.
I'LL BE IN THE NEXT ROOM, OKAY?
IF SOMETHING'S WRONG, JUST CALL ME.
. . . .
RAIN... SLEEP NEXT TO ME.
NO WAY.
I'LL CATCH A COLD.
ぎゅ...

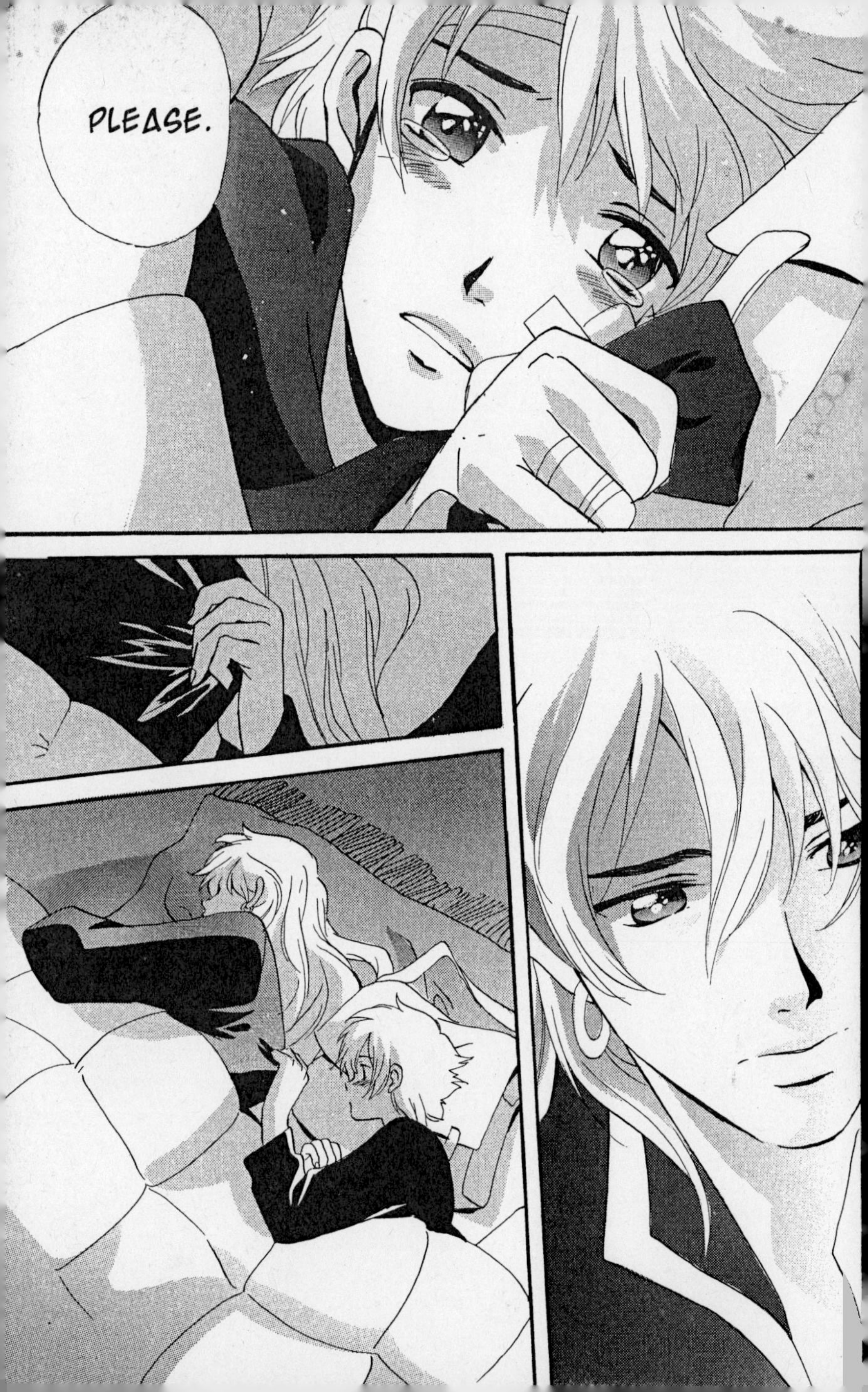
PLEASE.

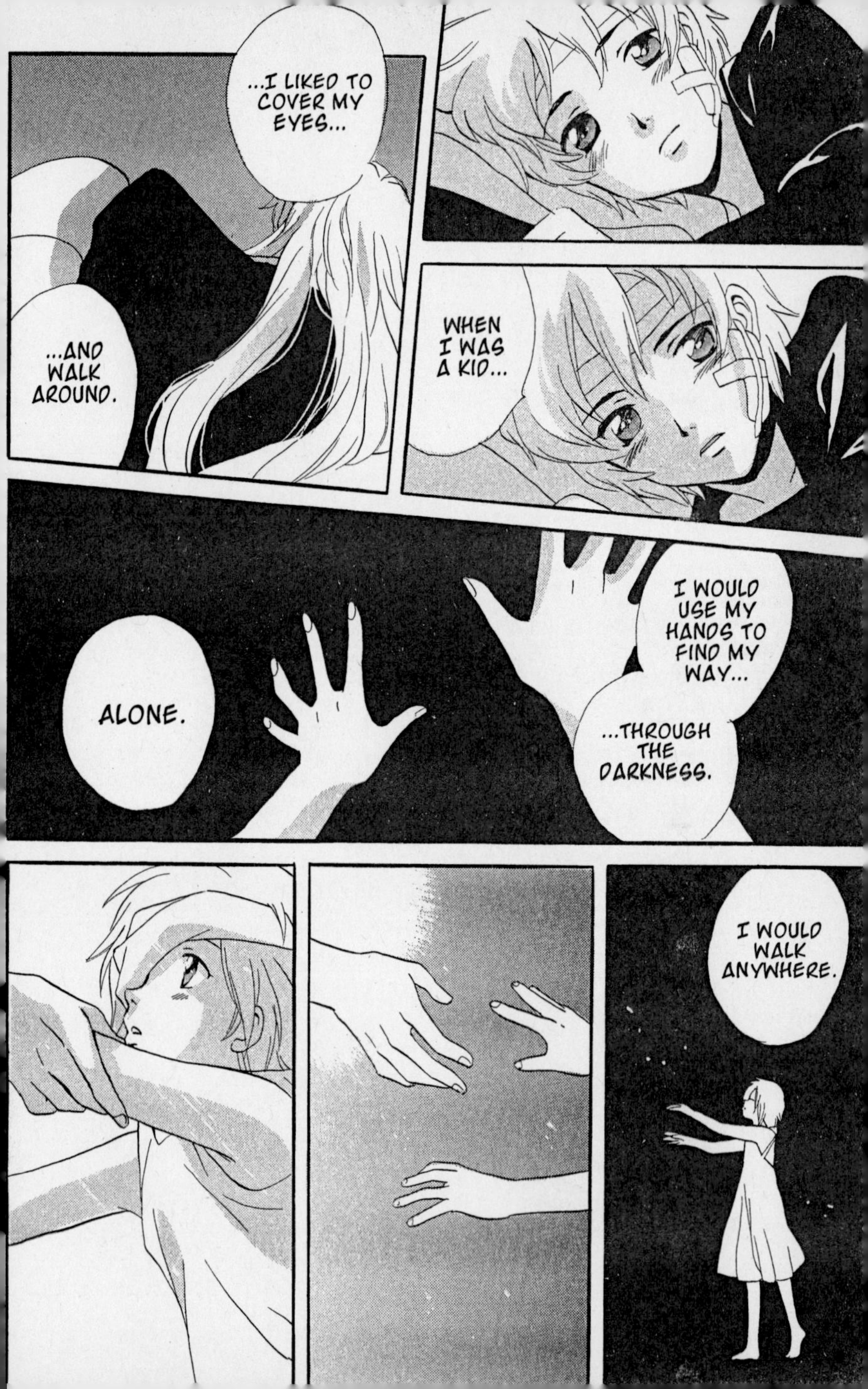
WHEN I WAS A KID...
...I LIKED TO COVER MY EYES...
...AND WALK AROUND.
I WOULD USE MY HANDS TO FIND MY WAY...
...THROUGH THE DARKNESS.
ALONE.
I WOULD WALK ANYWHERE.

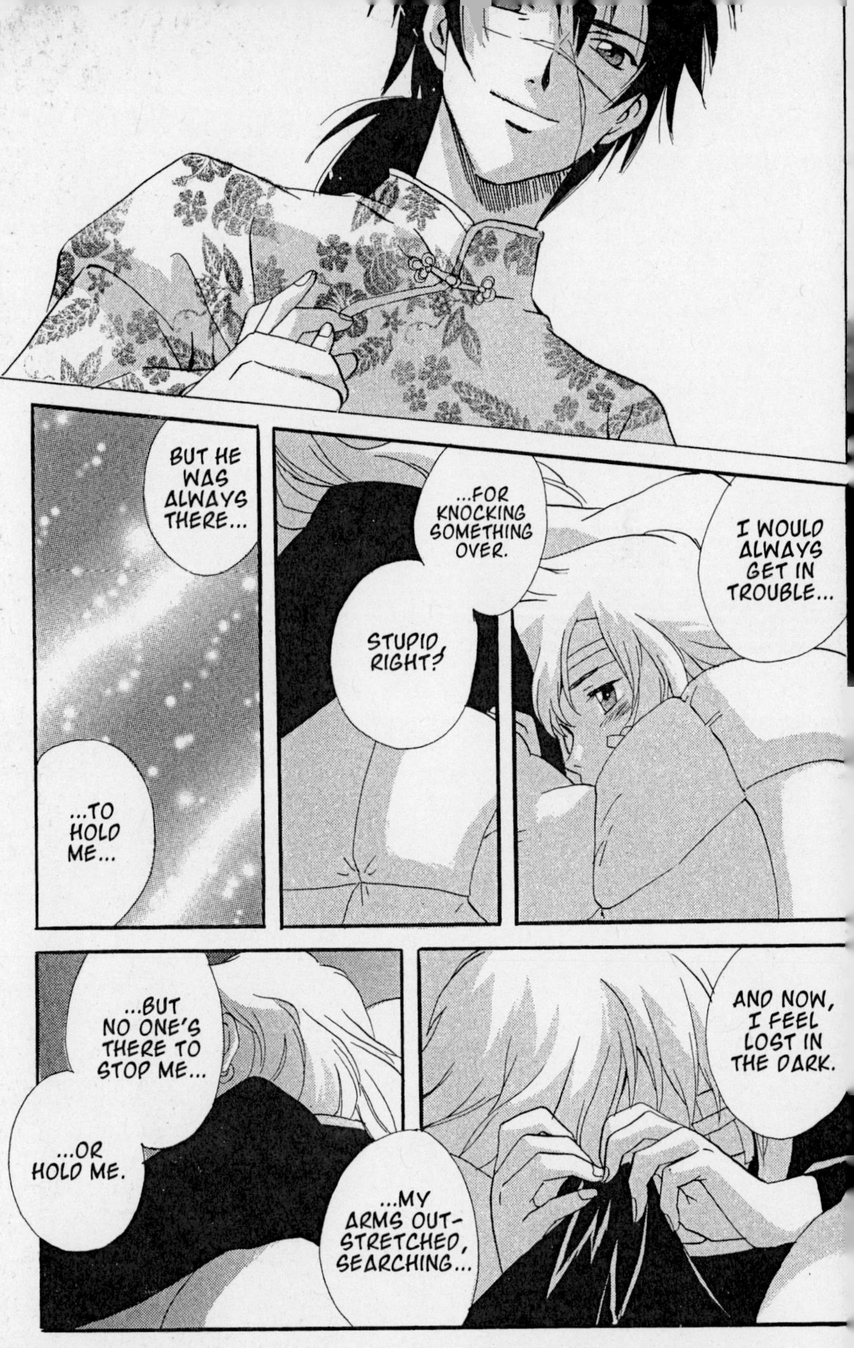
I WOULD ALWAYS GET IN TROUBLE...
...FOR KNOCKING SOMETHING OVER.
STUPID RIGHT?
BUT HE WAS ALWAYS THERE...
...TO HOLD ME...
AND NOW, I FEEL LOST IN THE DARK.
...MY ARMS OUT-STRETCHED, SEARCHING...
...BUT NO ONE'S THERE TO STOP ME...
...OR HOLD ME.

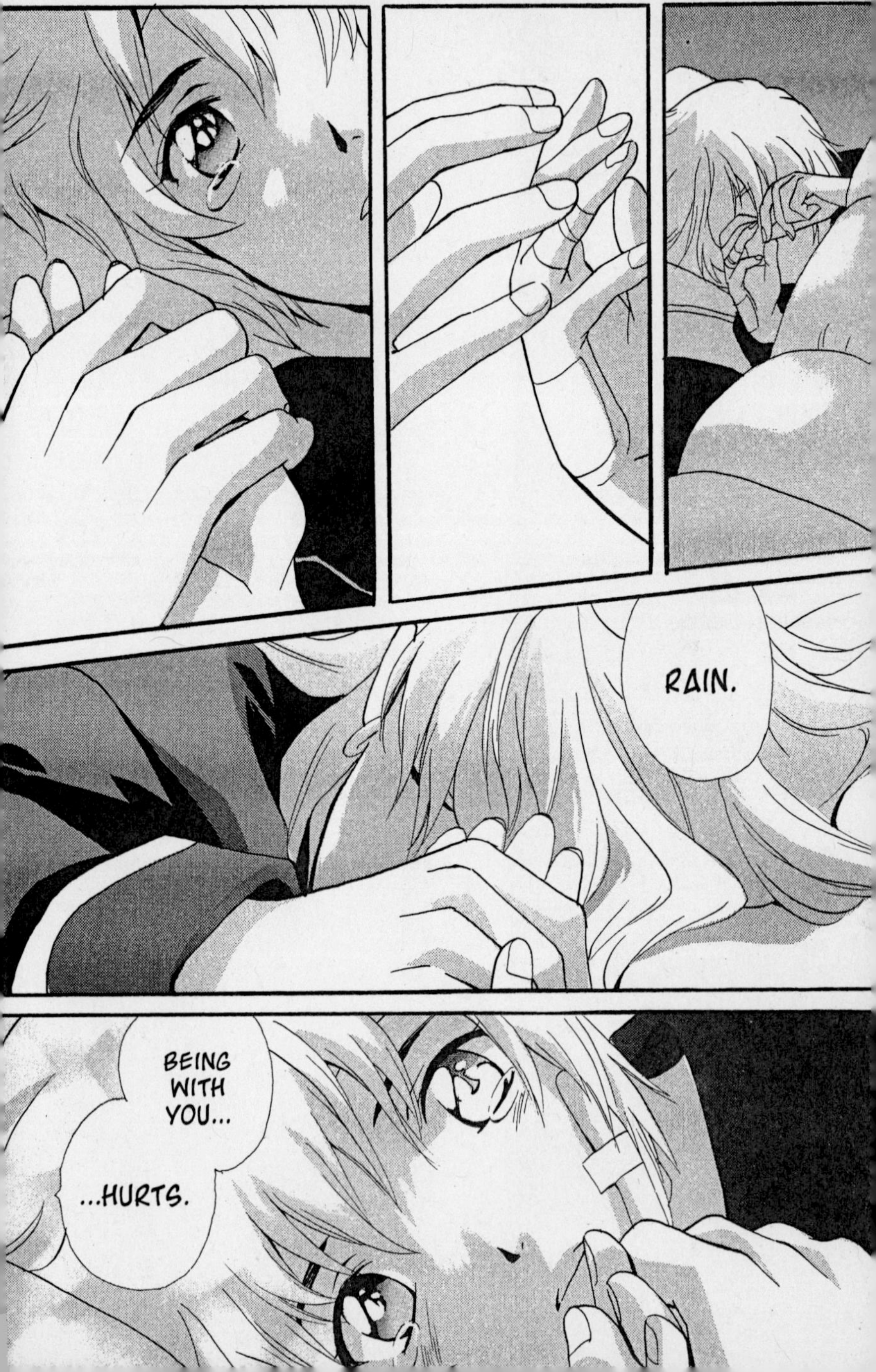
RAIN.
BEING WITH YOU...
...HURTS.

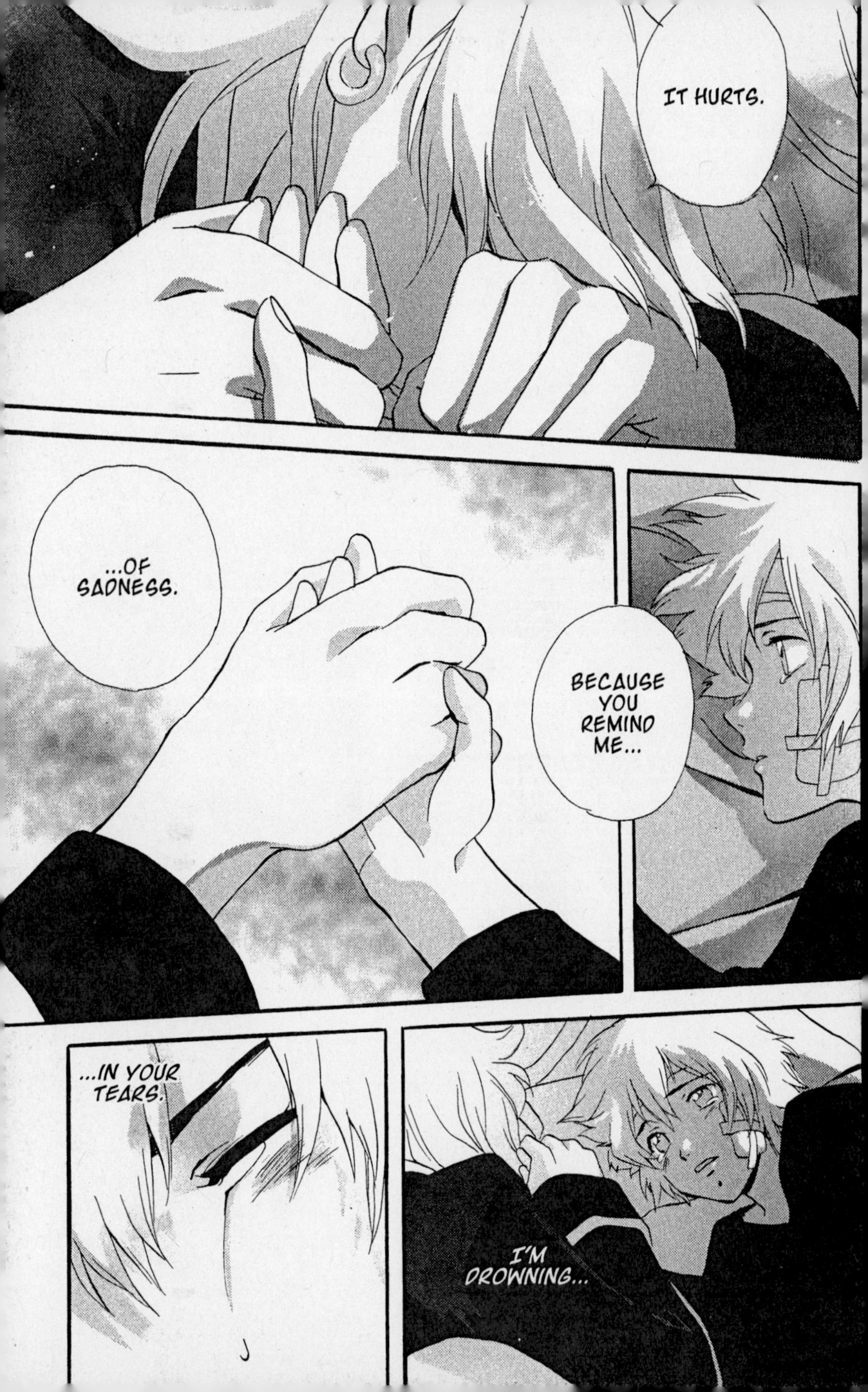
IT HURTS.
BECAUSE YOU REMIND ME...
...OF SADNESS.
I'M DROWNING...
...IN YOUR TEARS.

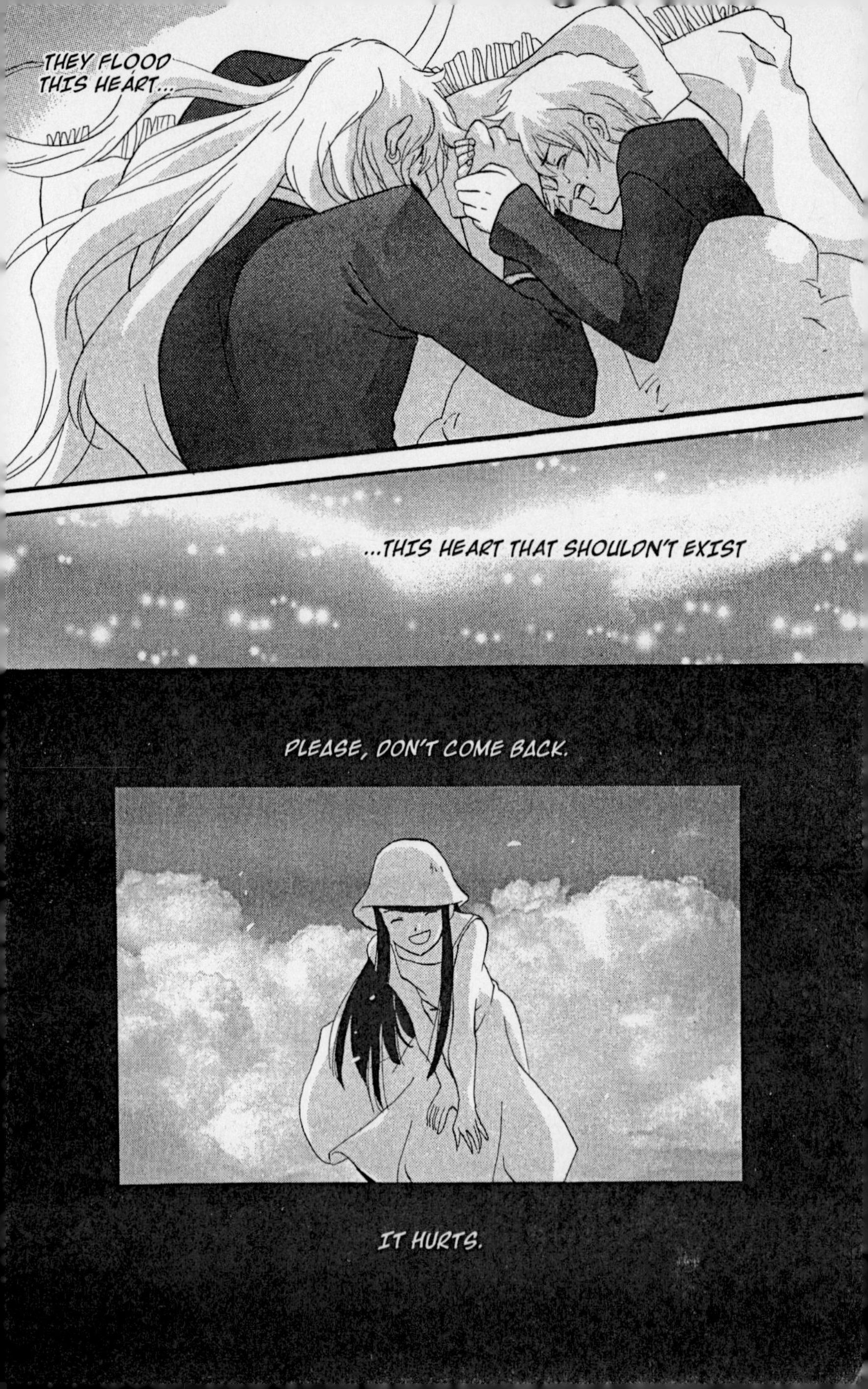
THEY FLOOD THIS HEART...
...THIS HEART THAT SHOULDN'T EXIST
PLEASE, DON'T COME BACK.
IT HURTS.

Jilleena Lacot

Age:15
Height:156cm
Blood type:A

Command:
Fight
Brawl
Flee

LV:.................14
HP:.....242/242
Offense
Strength:......60
Defense
Strength:......38
Speed:..........60
Cleverness:..21
Luck:............31

Equipment
Weapon: Tonfa/offense strength +23
Armor: Uniform/defense strength +11
Accessory: Loyalty as strong as iron
Performs 100% of the commands

Death Blow Technique Command
Knee Smash ⇨Ⓚ
Sharem Heel ⇦Ⓚ+Ⓖ
Combination Spiral ⓅⓅⓅ⇧ⓀⓀ

She will only obey Sharem's commands and goes berserk whenever Sharem isn't around. She is also quite gullible.

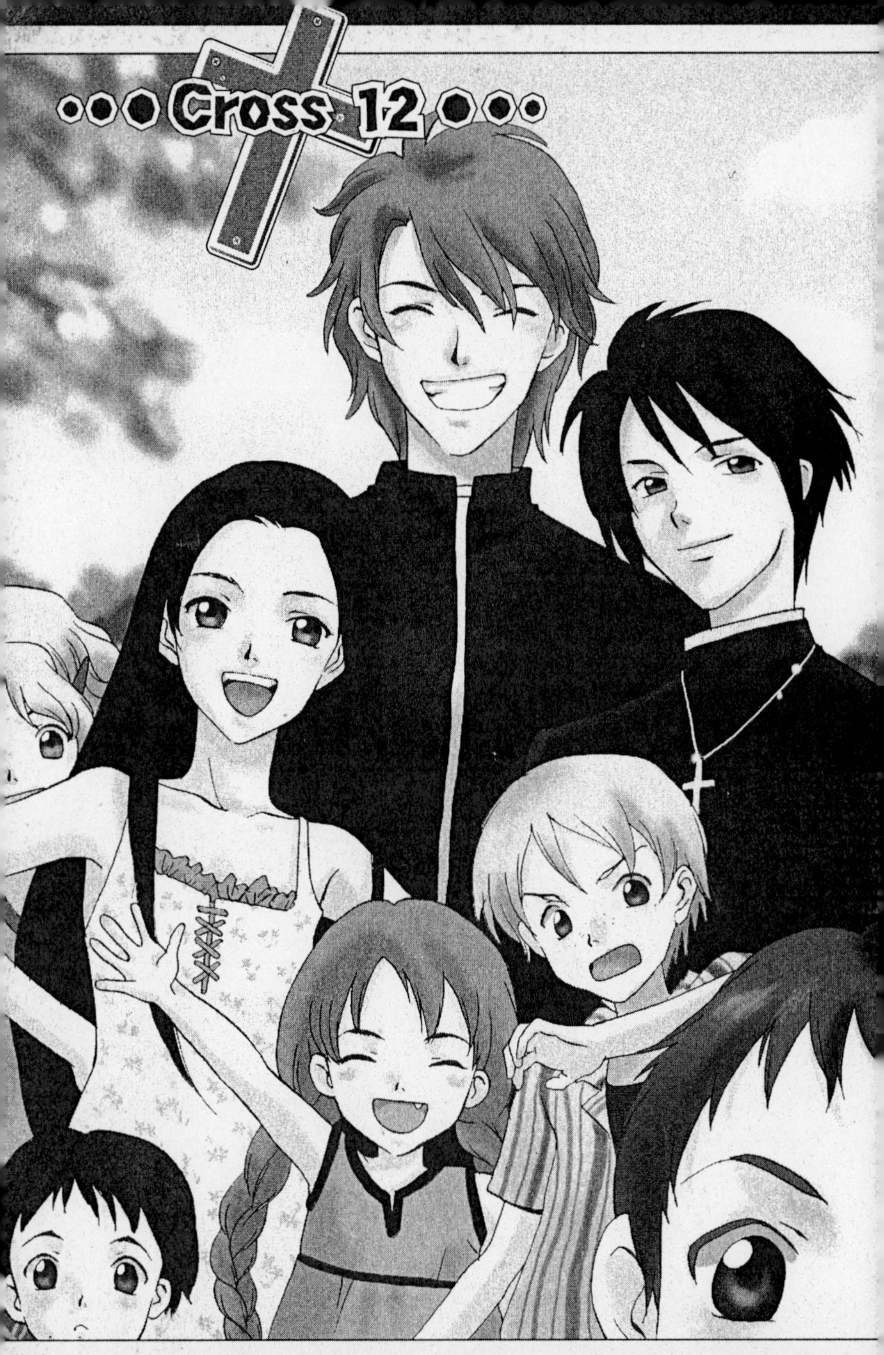
Cross 12

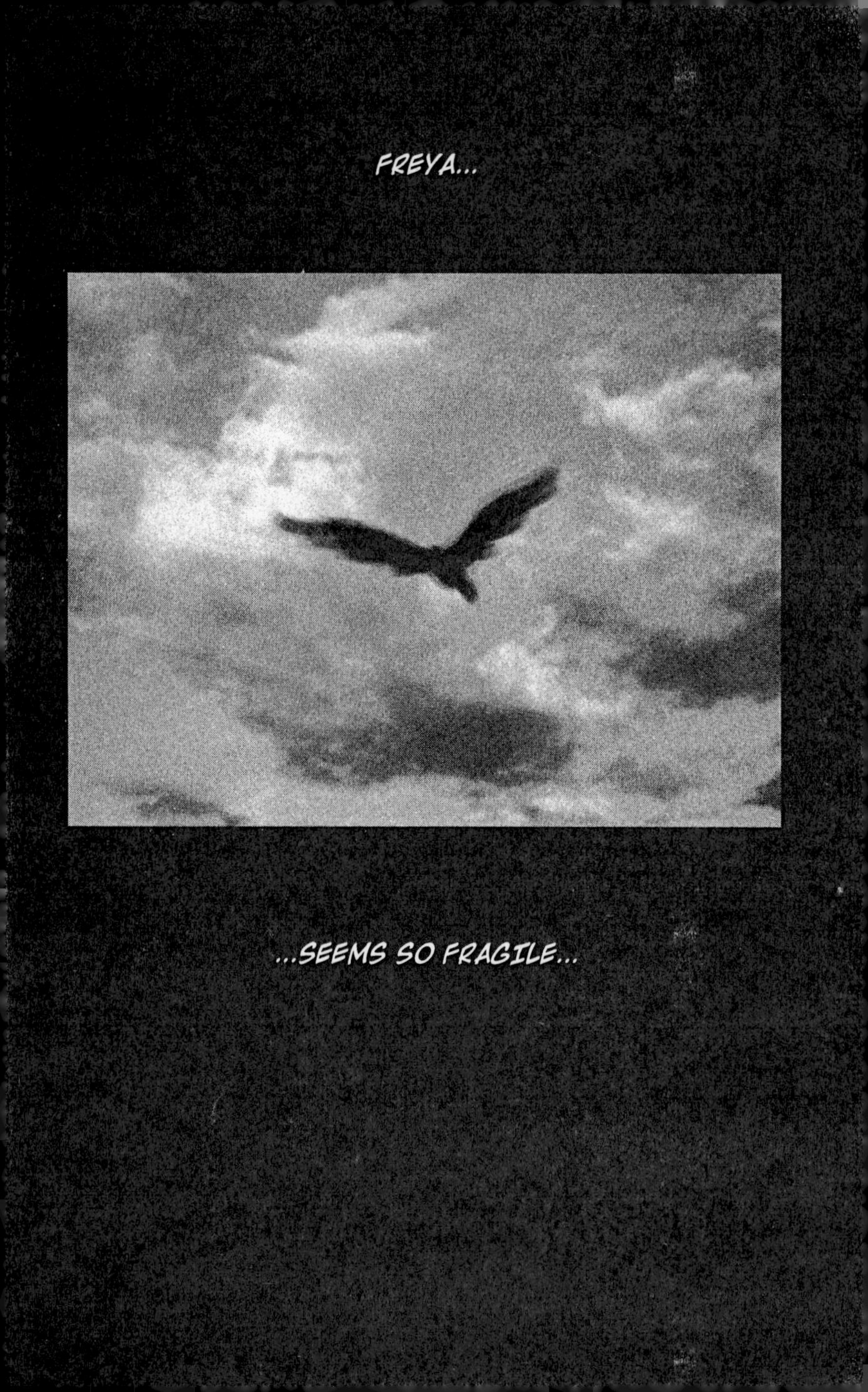
FREYA...
...SEEMS SO FRAGILE...

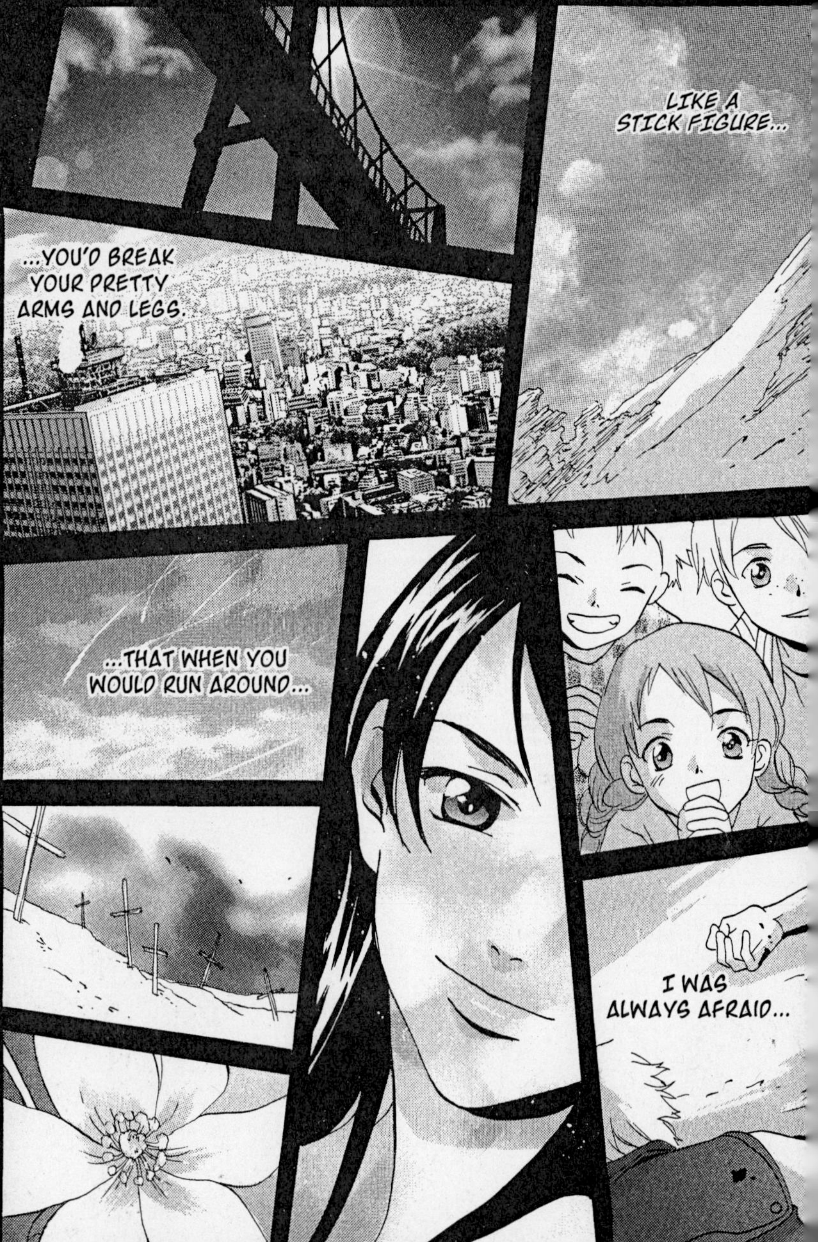
LIKE A STICK FIGURE...
...YOU'D BREAK YOUR PRETTY ARMS AND LEGS.
I WAS ALWAYS AFRAID...
...THAT WHEN YOU WOULD RUN AROUND...

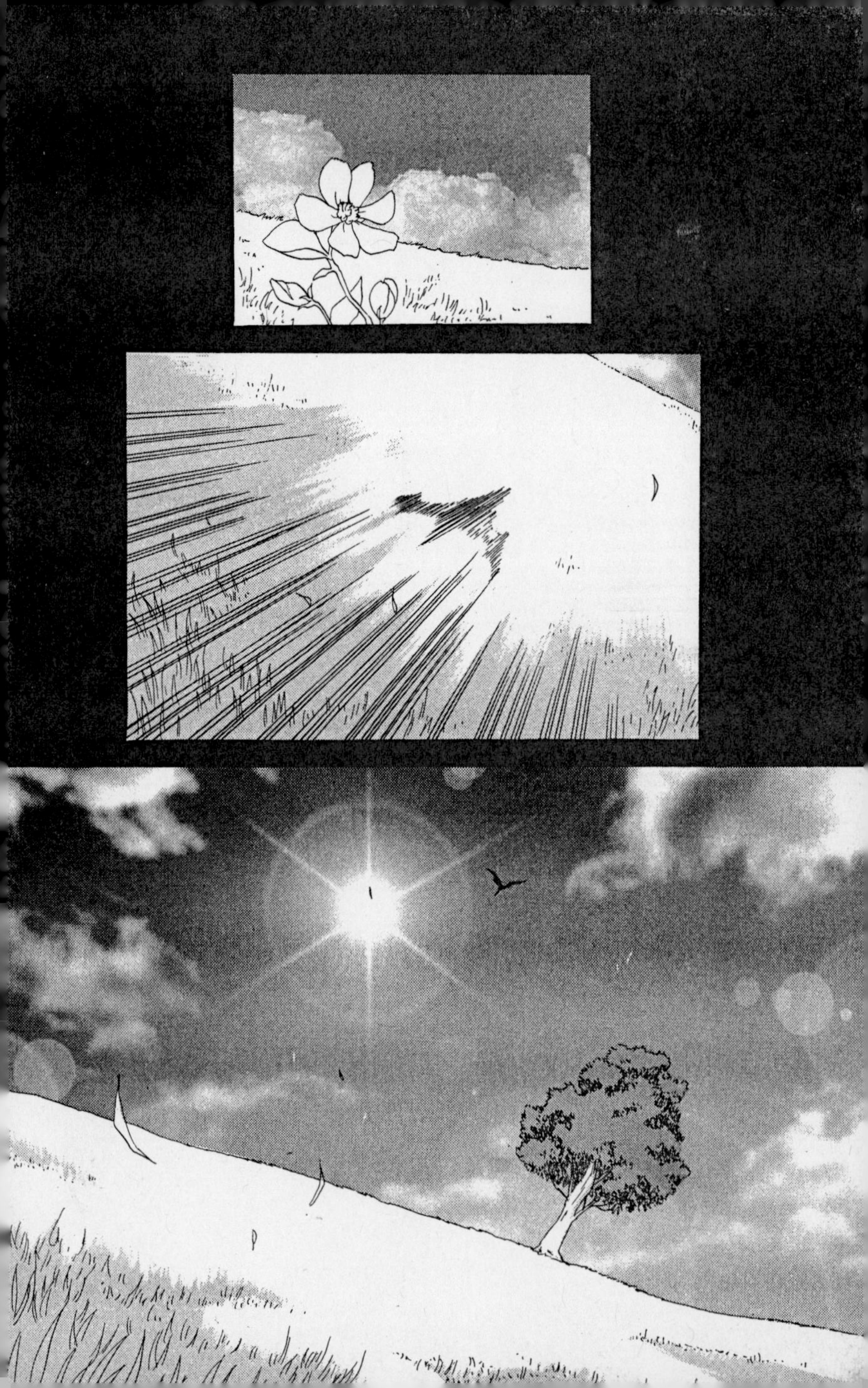

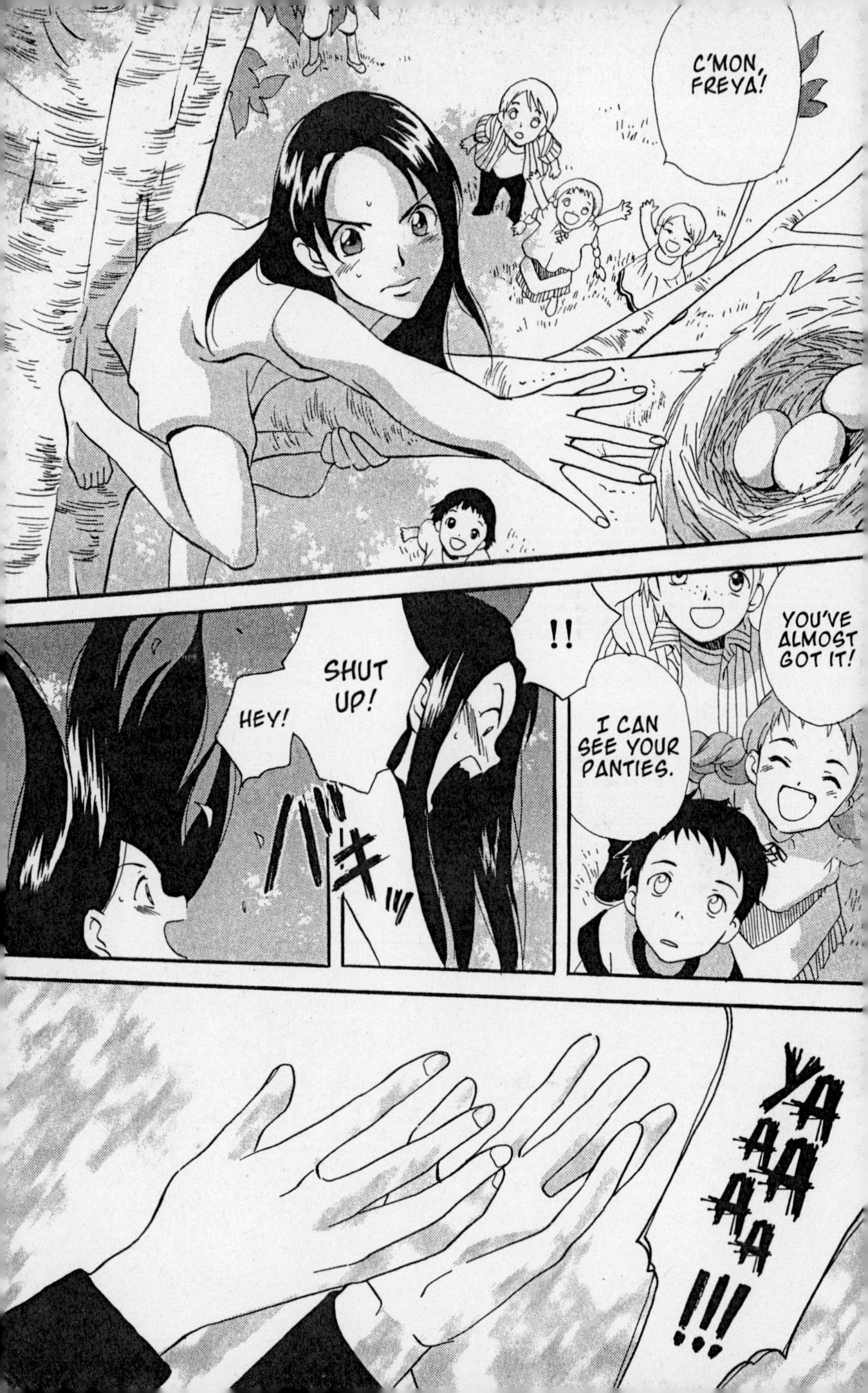
C'MON, FREYA!
YOU'VE ALMOST GOT IT!
I CAN SEE YOUR PANTIES.
!!
SHUT UP!
HEY!
YAAAAA!!!

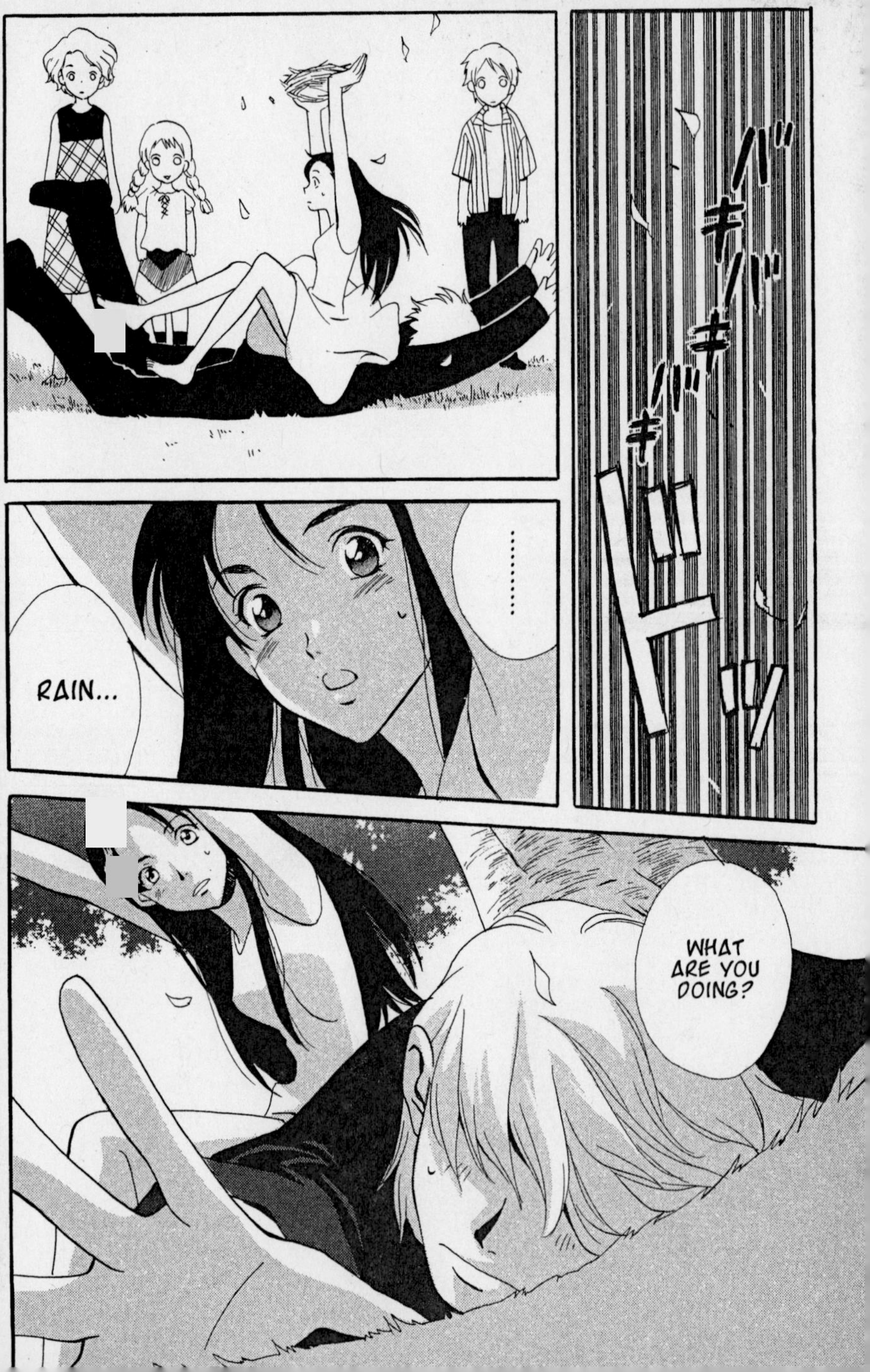
バキバキバキ
ドッ
......
RAIN...
WHAT ARE YOU DOING?

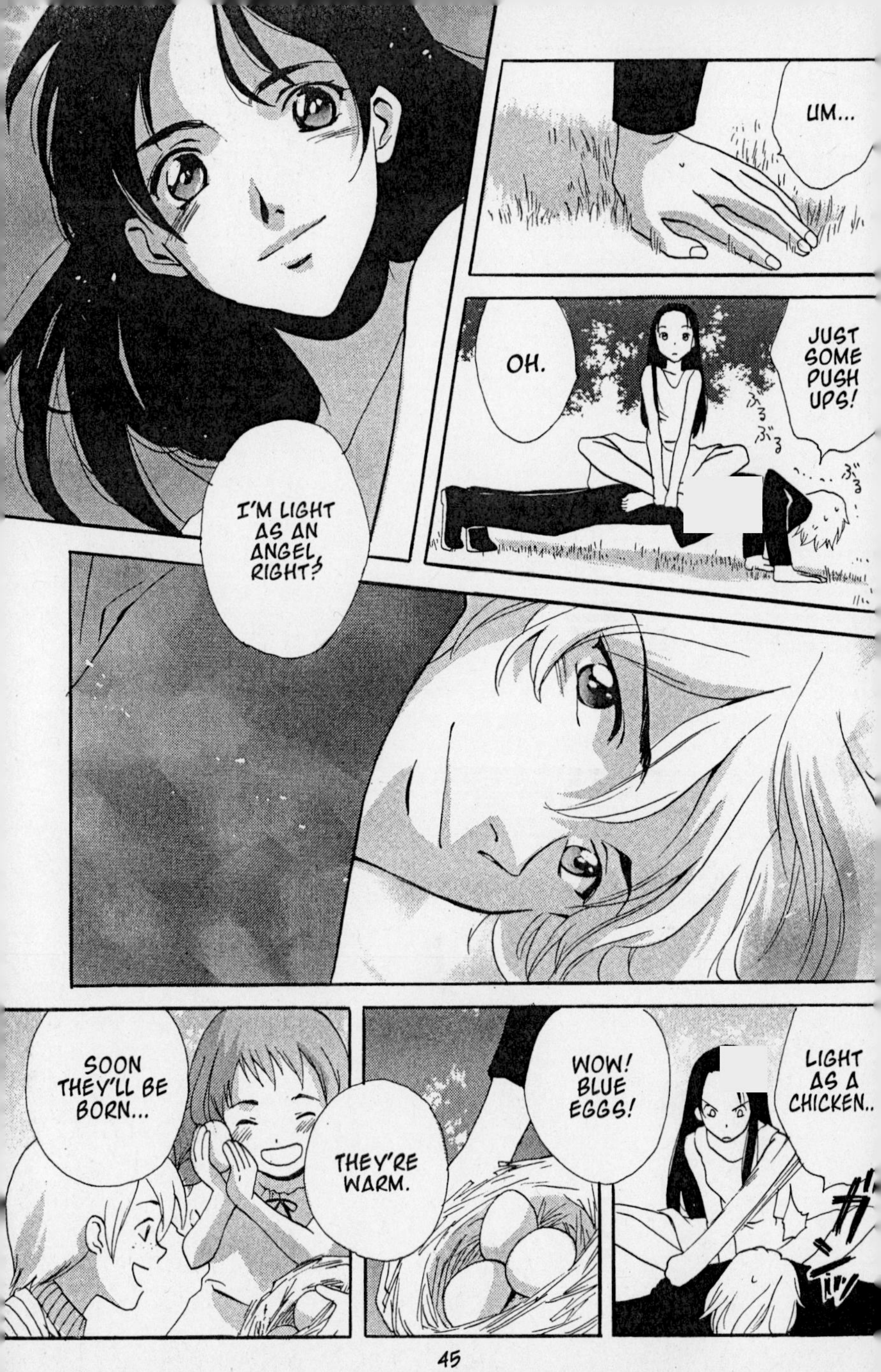
UM...
JUST SOME PUSH UPS!
OH.
I'M LIGHT AS AN ANGEL, RIGHT?
LIGHT AS A CHICKEN..
WOW! BLUE EGGS!
THEY'RE WARM.
SOON THEY'LL BE BORN...

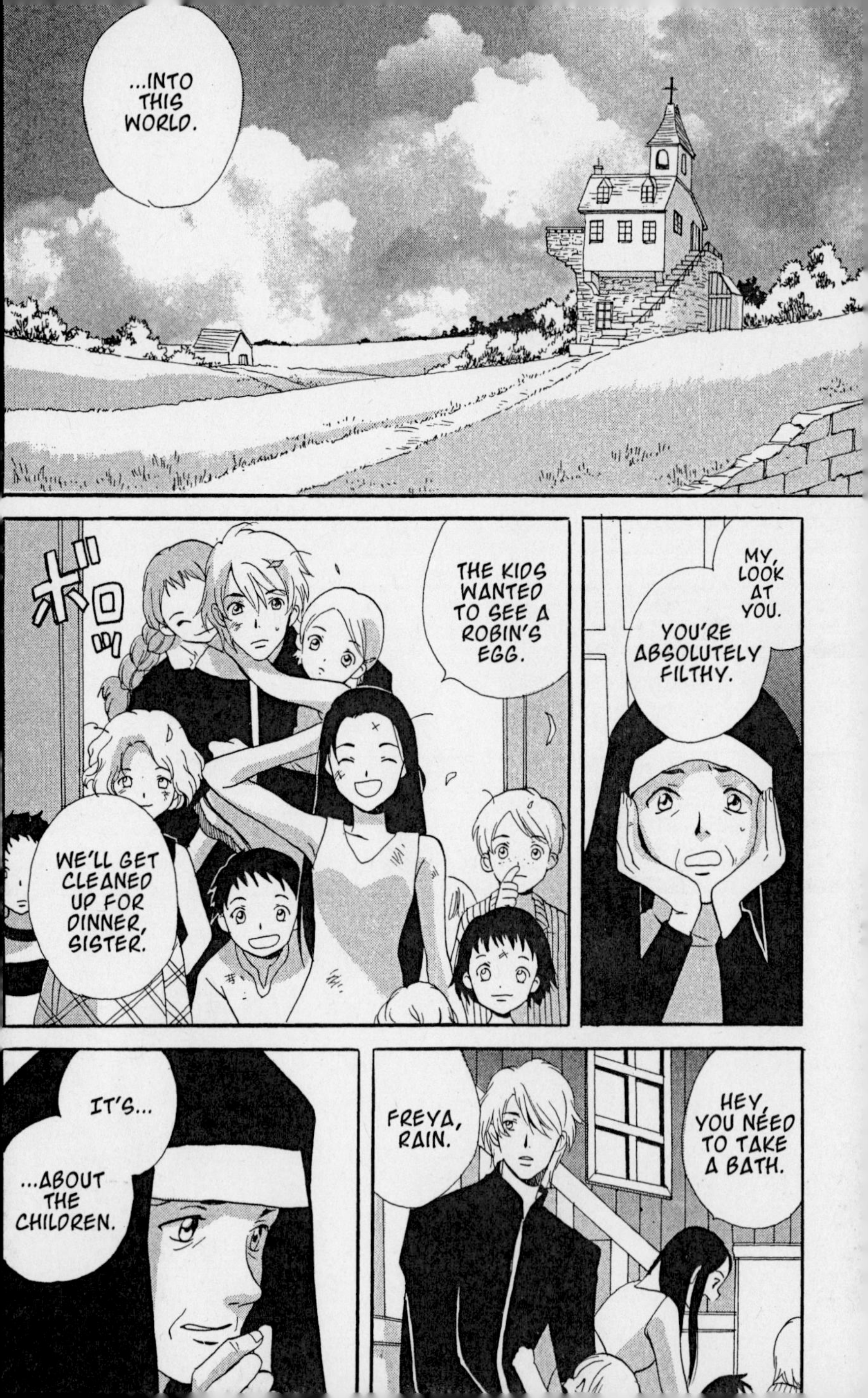
...INTO THIS WORLD.
MY, LOOK AT YOU.
YOU'RE ABSOLUTELY FILTHY.
ボロッ
THE KIDS WANTED TO SEE A ROBIN'S EGG.
WE'LL GET CLEANED UP FOR DINNER, SISTER.
HEY, YOU NEED TO TAKE A BATH.
FREYA, RAIN.
IT'S...
...ABOUT THE CHILDREN.

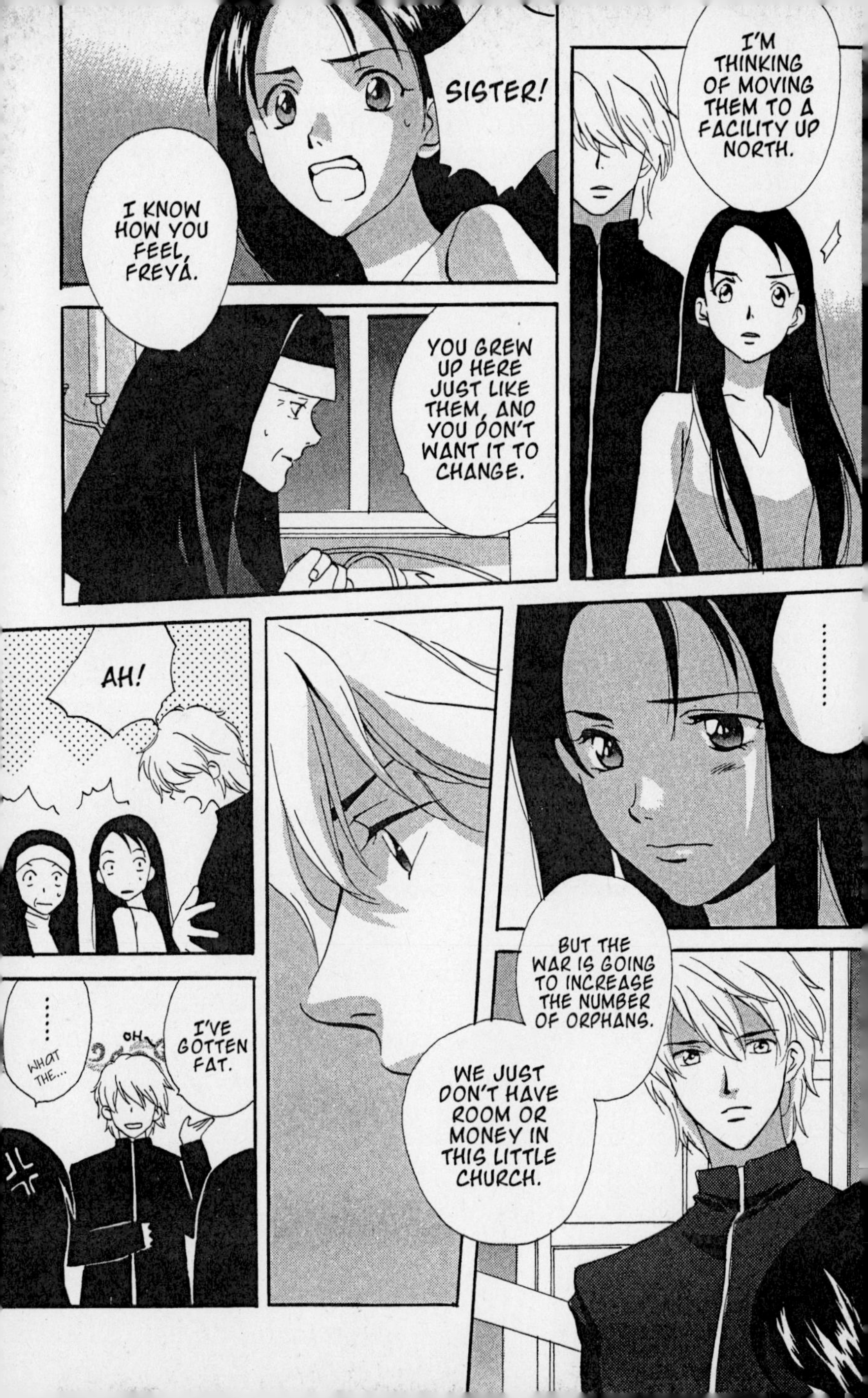
I'M THINKING OF MOVING THEM TO A FACILITY UP NORTH.
SISTER!
I KNOW HOW YOU FEEL, FREYA.
YOU GREW UP HERE JUST LIKE THEM, AND YOU DON'T WANT IT TO CHANGE.
......
BUT THE WAR IS GOING TO INCREASE THE NUMBER OF ORPHANS.
WE JUST DON'T HAVE ROOM OR MONEY IN THIS LITTLE CHURCH.
AH!
I'VE GOTTEN FAT.
OH-
......
WHAT THE...

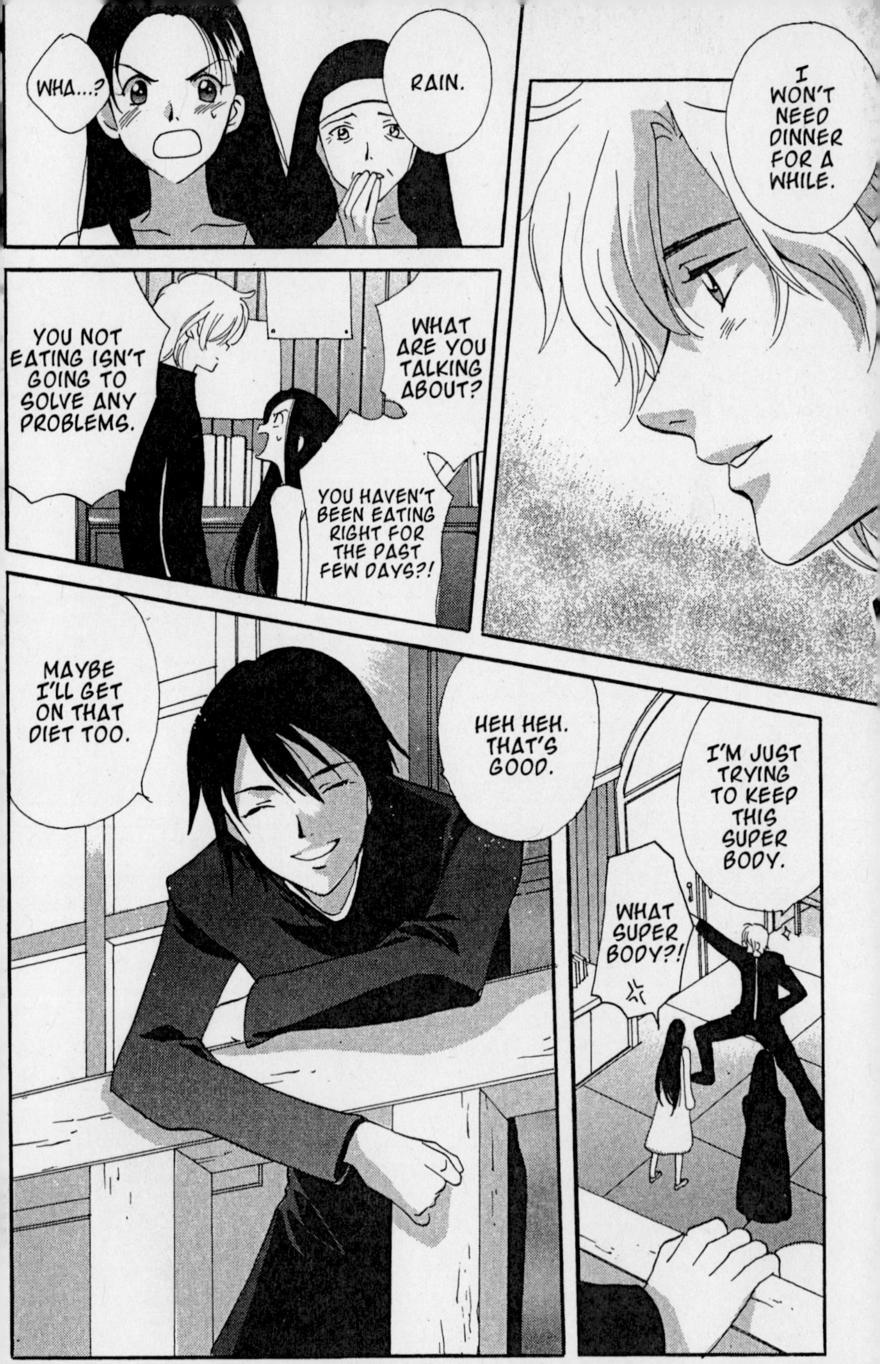
I WON'T NEED DINNER FOR A WHILE.
RAIN.
WHA...?
WHAT ARE YOU TALKING ABOUT?
YOU NOT EATING ISN'T GOING TO SOLVE ANY PROBLEMS.
YOU HAVEN'T BEEN EATING RIGHT FOR THE PAST FEW DAYS?!
I'M JUST TRYING TO KEEP THIS SUPER BODY.
WHAT SUPER BODY?!
HEH HEH. THAT'S GOOD.
MAYBE I'LL GET ON THAT DIET TOO.

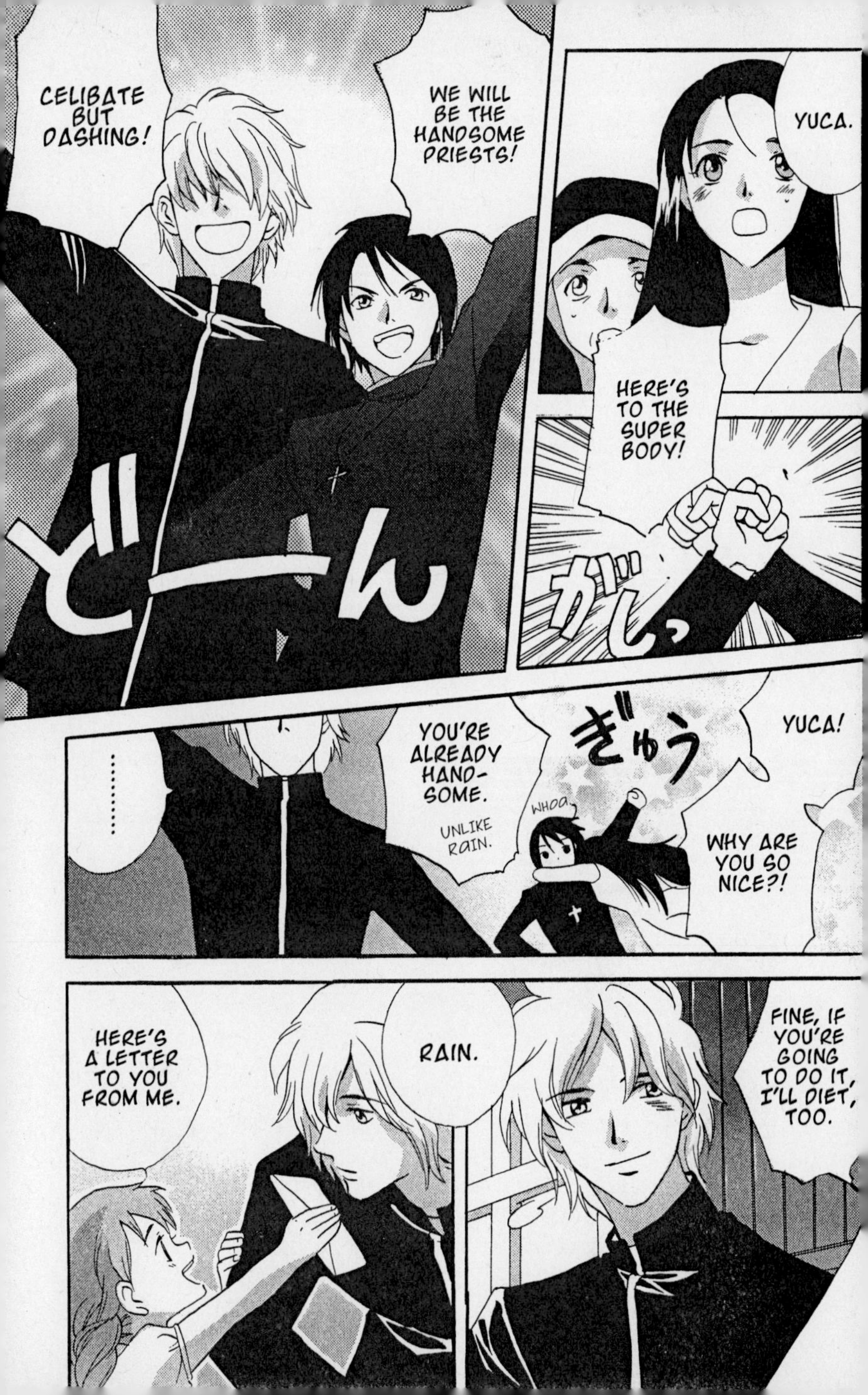
YUCA.
HERE'S TO THE SUPER BODY!
がしっ
WE WILL BE THE HANDSOME PRIESTS!
CELIBATE BUT DASHING!
どーん
YUCA!
WHY ARE YOU SO NICE?!
ぎゅう
WHOA.
YOU'RE ALREADY HANDSOME.
UNLIKE RAIN.
......
FINE, IF YOU'RE GOING TO DO IT, I'LL DIET, TOO.
RAIN.
HERE'S A LETTER TO YOU FROM ME.

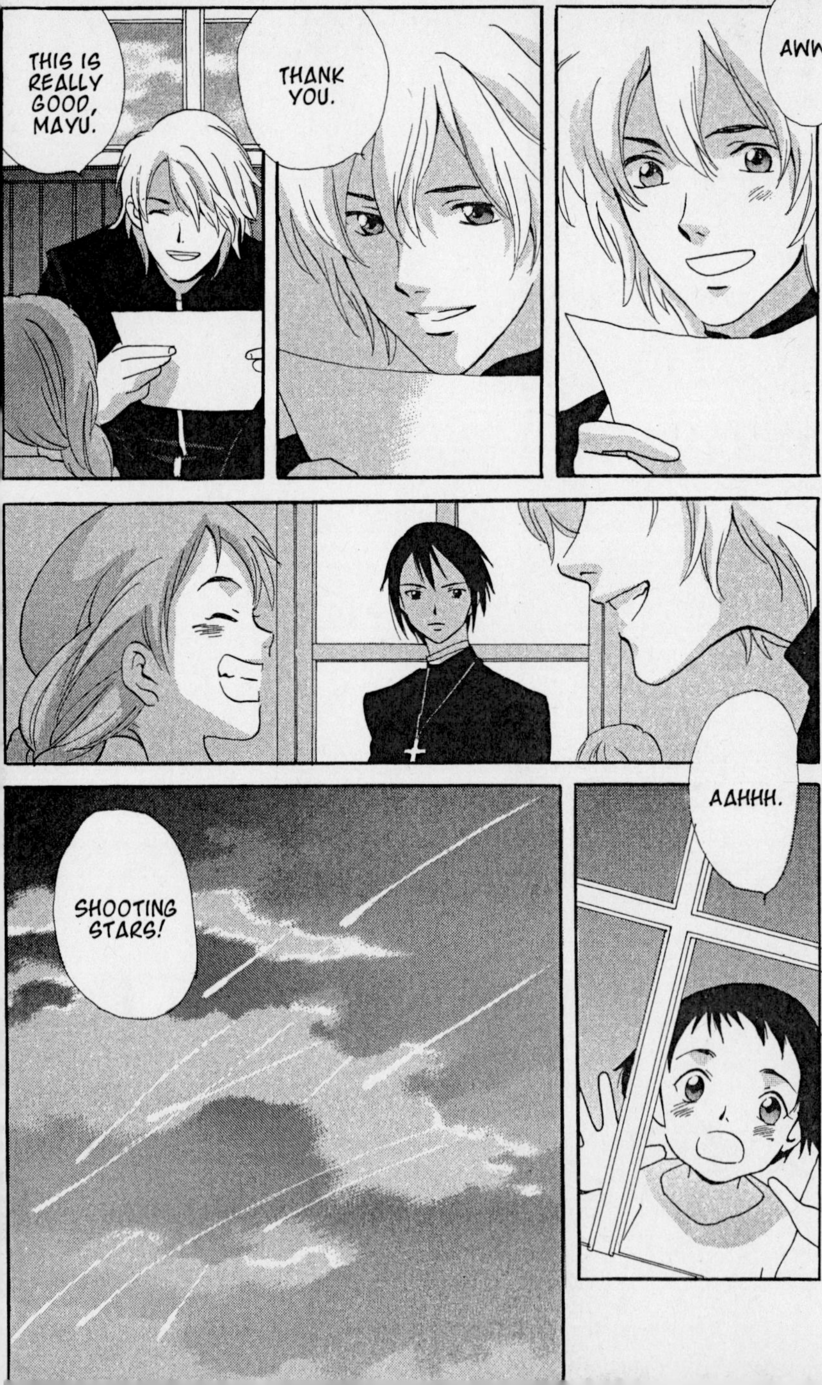
THIS IS REALLY GOOD, MAYU.
THANK YOU.
AWW...
SHOOTING STARS!
AAHHH.

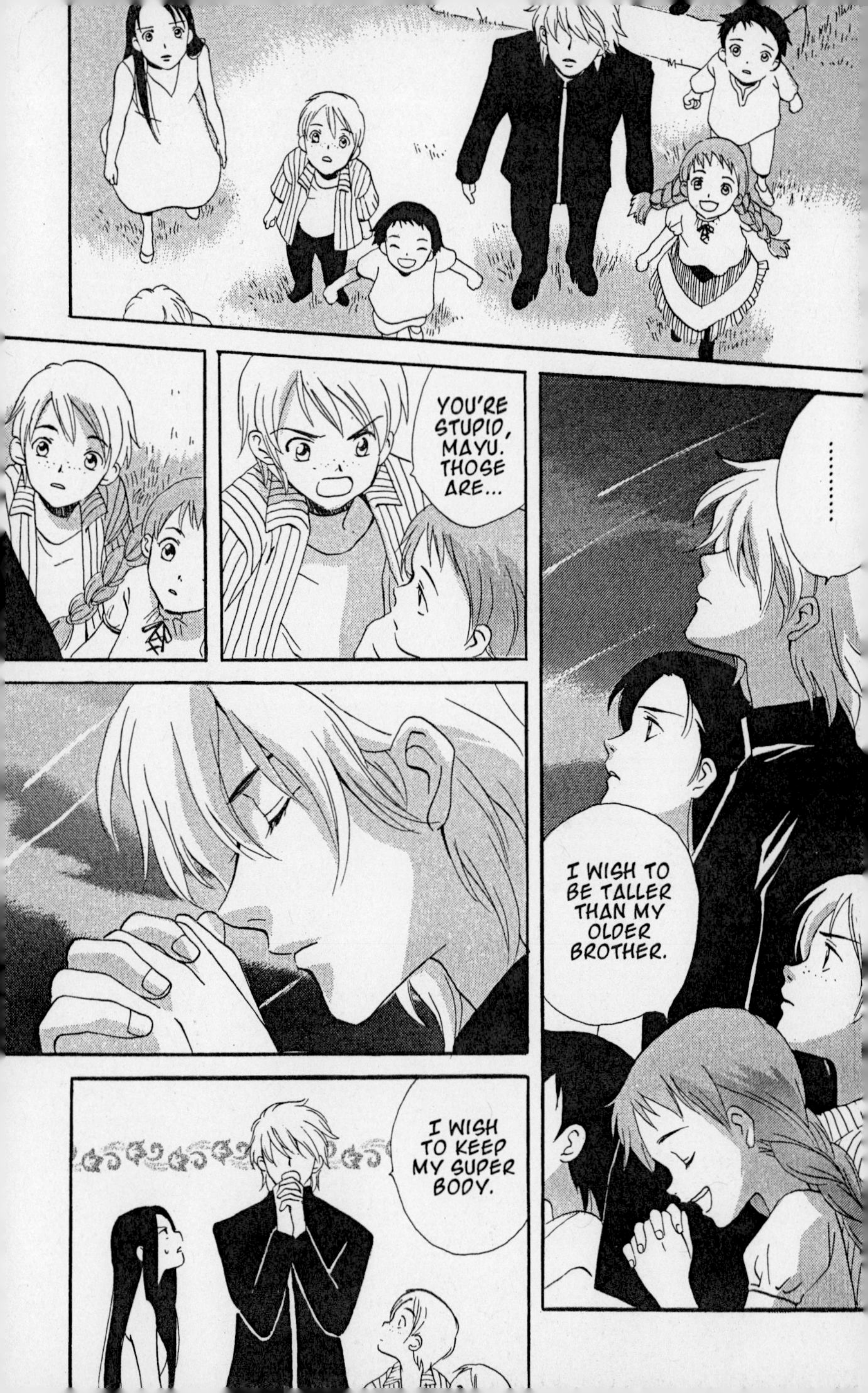
......
I WISH TO BE TALLER THAN MY OLDER BROTHER.
YOU'RE STUPID, MAYU. THOSE ARE...
I WISH TO KEEP MY SUPER BODY.

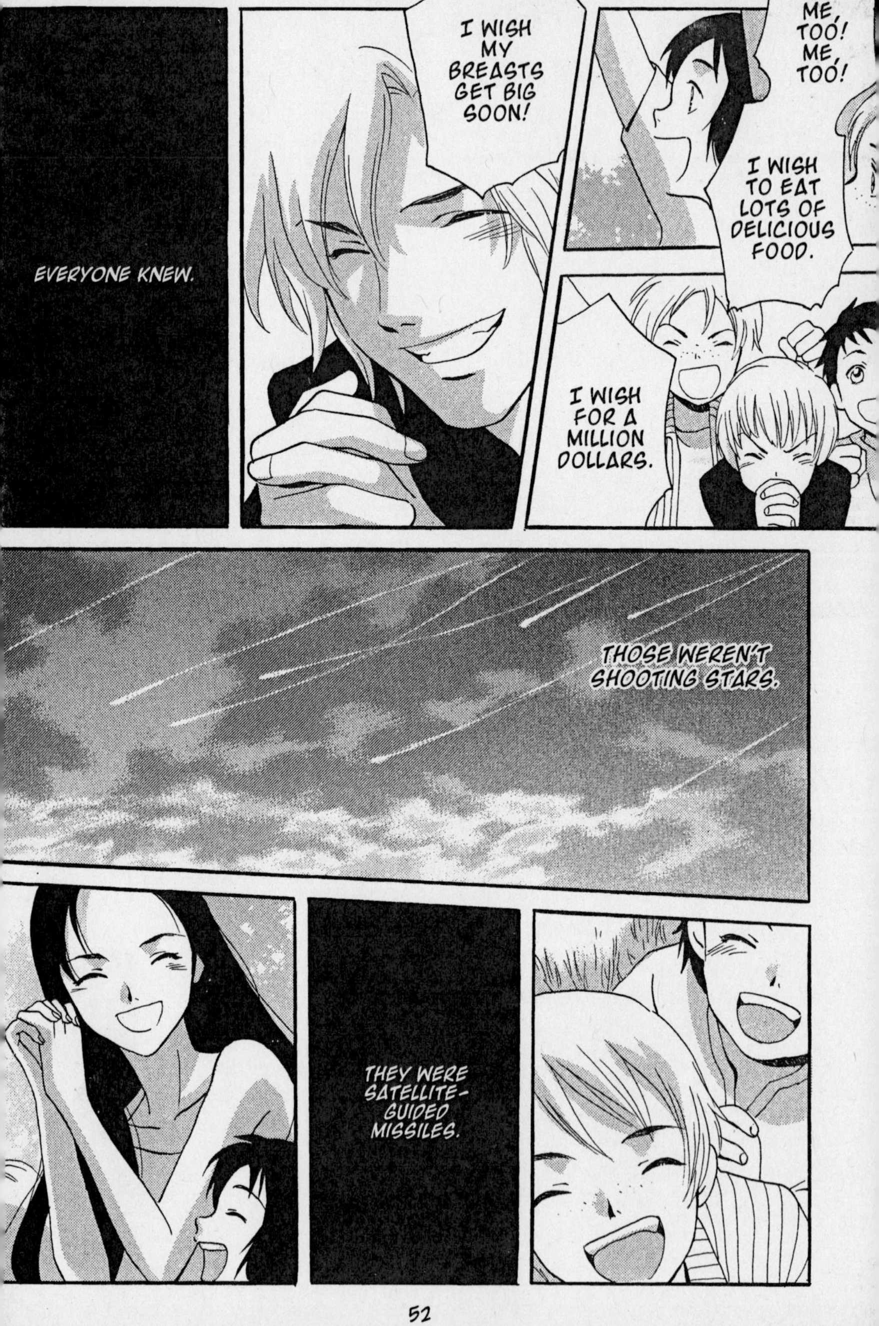
ME, TOO! ME, TOO!
I WISH TO EAT LOTS OF DELICIOUS FOOD.
I WISH FOR A MILLION DOLLARS.
I WISH MY BREASTS GET BIG SOON!
EVERYONE KNEW.
THOSE WEREN'T SHOOTING STARS.
THEY WERE SATELLITE-GUIDED MISSILES.

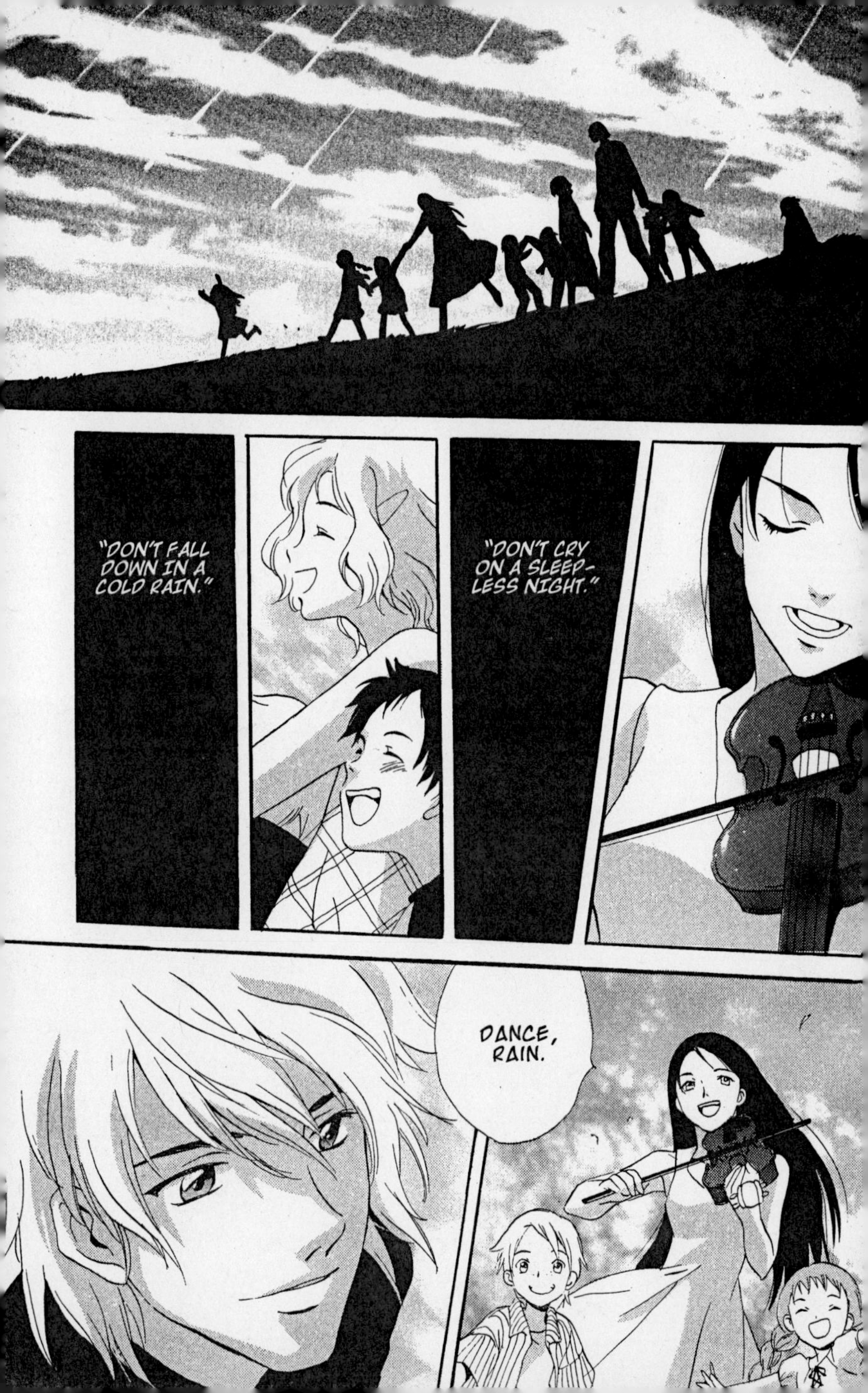
"DON'T CRY ON A SLEEPLESS NIGHT."
"DON'T FALL DOWN IN A COLD RAIN."
DANCE, RAIN.

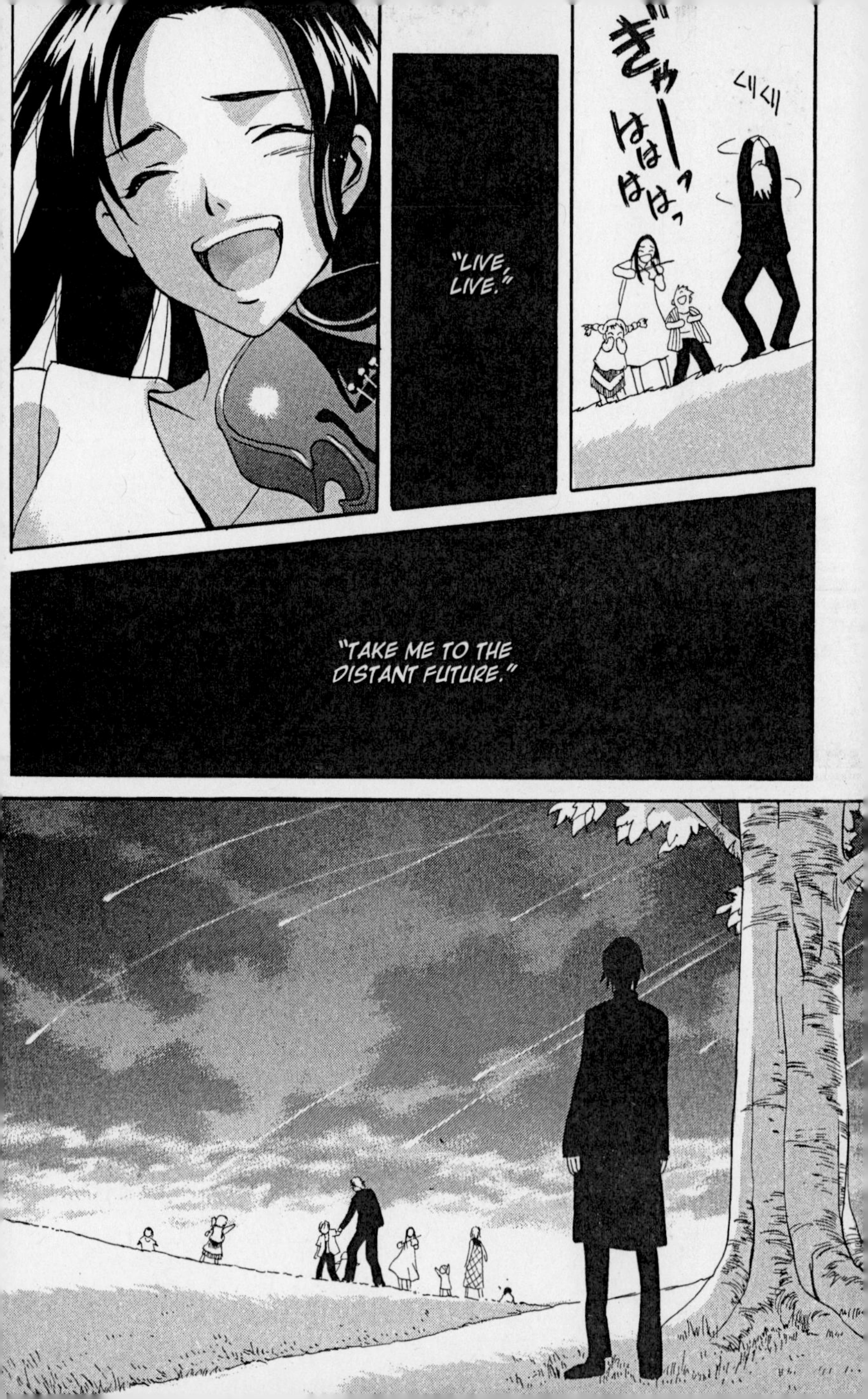
ぎゃーははっははっ
くりくり
"LIVE, LIVE."
"TAKE ME TO THE DISTANT FUTURE."

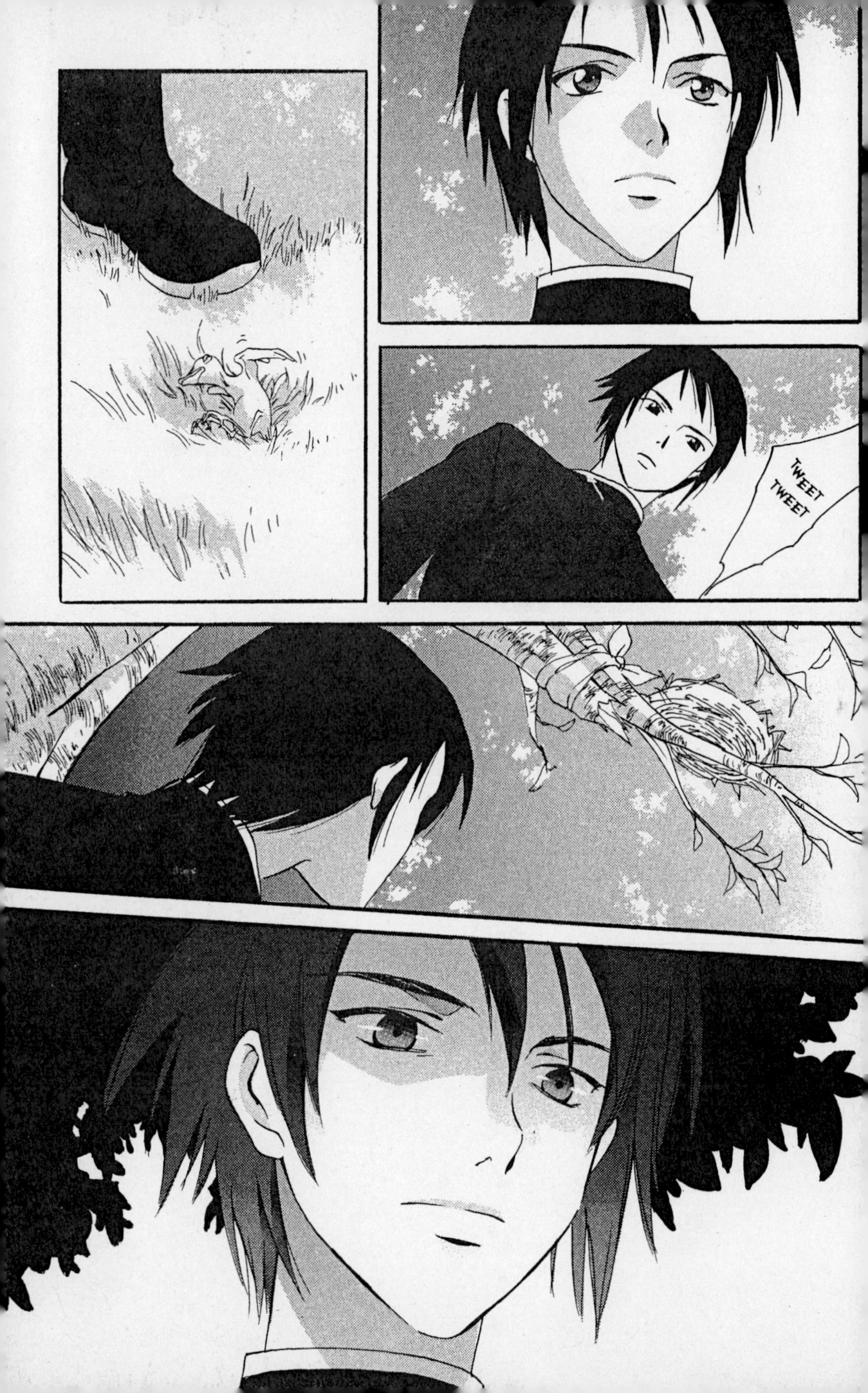
TWEET
TWEET

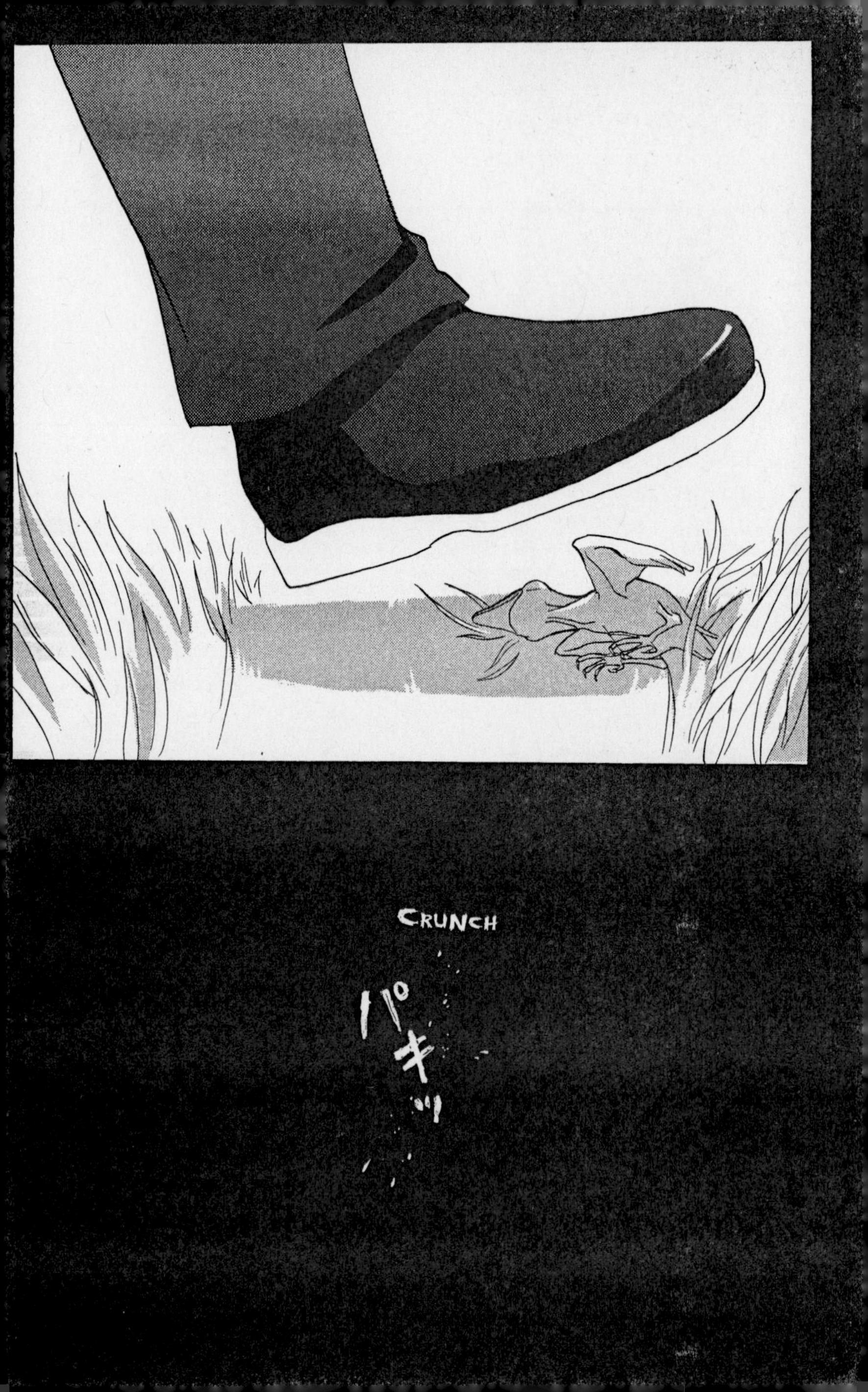
CRUNCH
パキッ

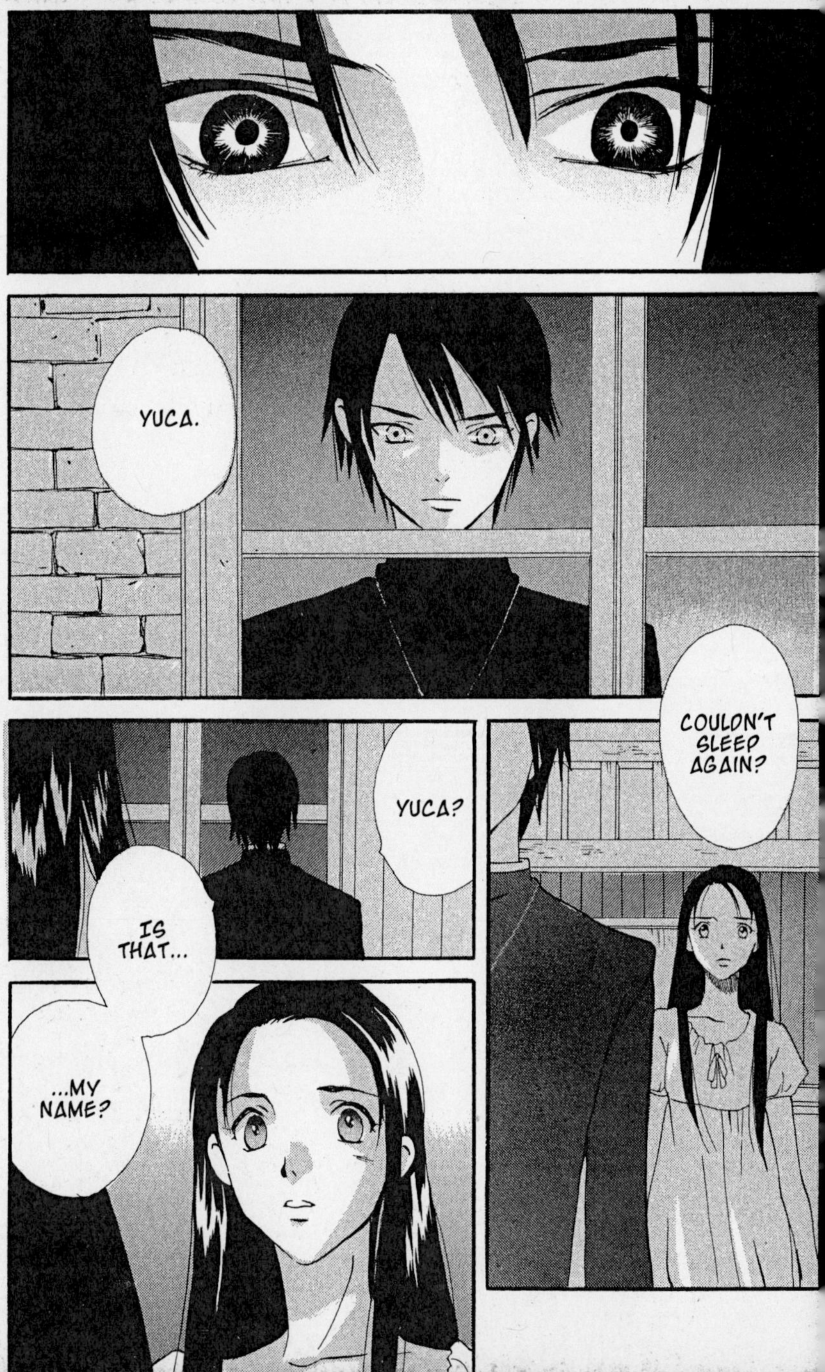
YUCA.
COULDN'T SLEEP AGAIN?
YUCA?
IS THAT...
...MY NAME?

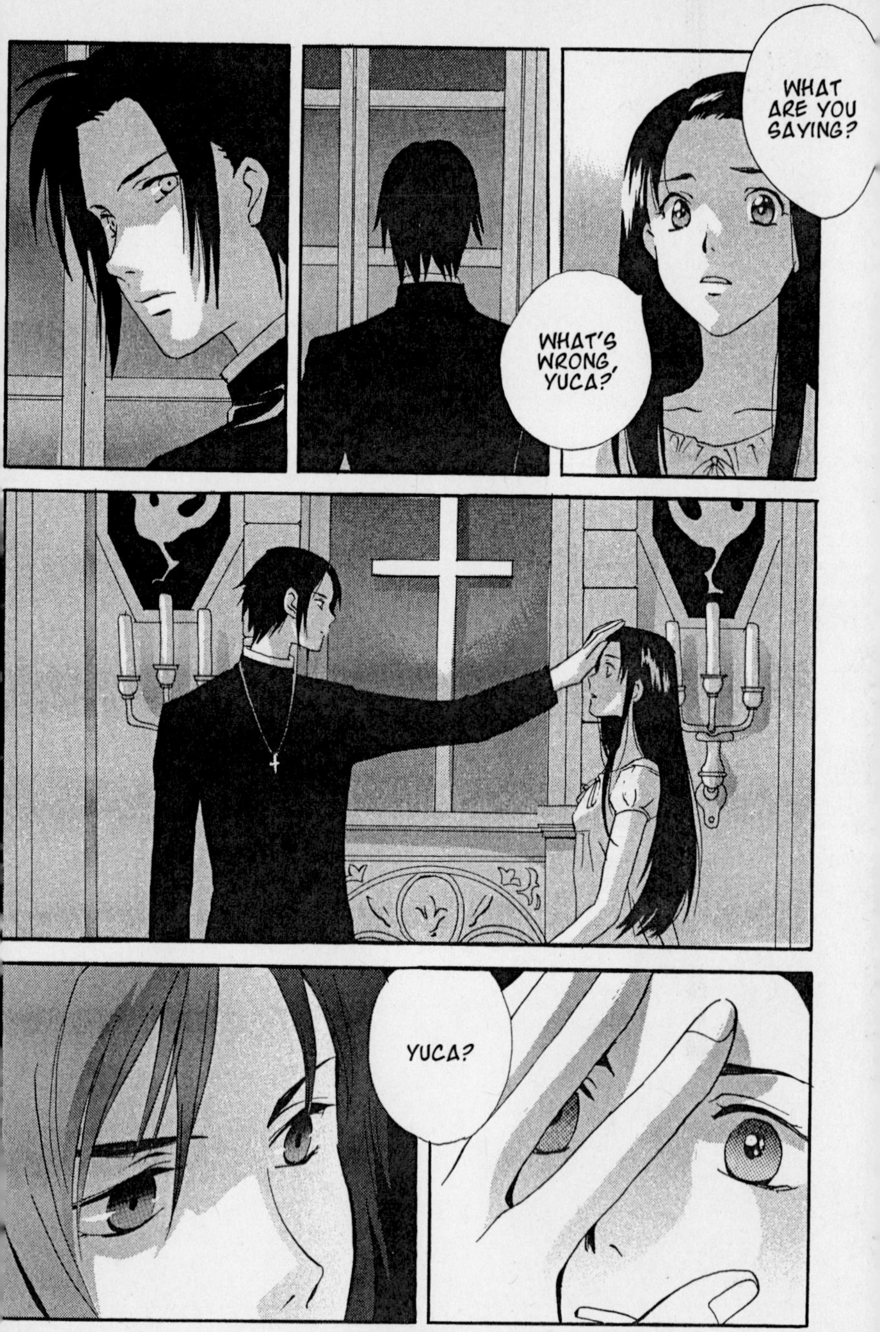
WHAT ARE YOU SAYING?
WHAT'S WRONG, YUCA?
YUCA?

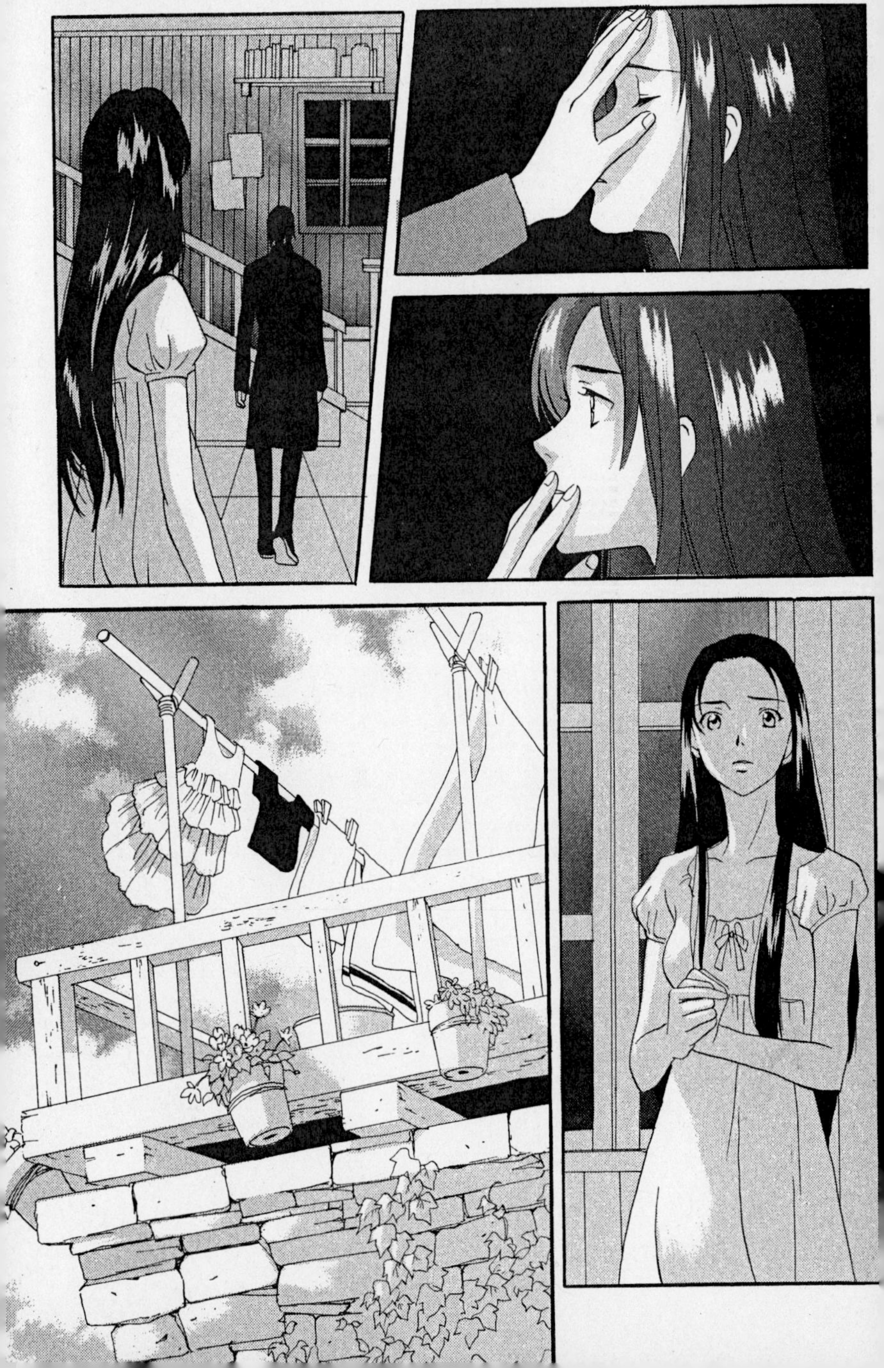

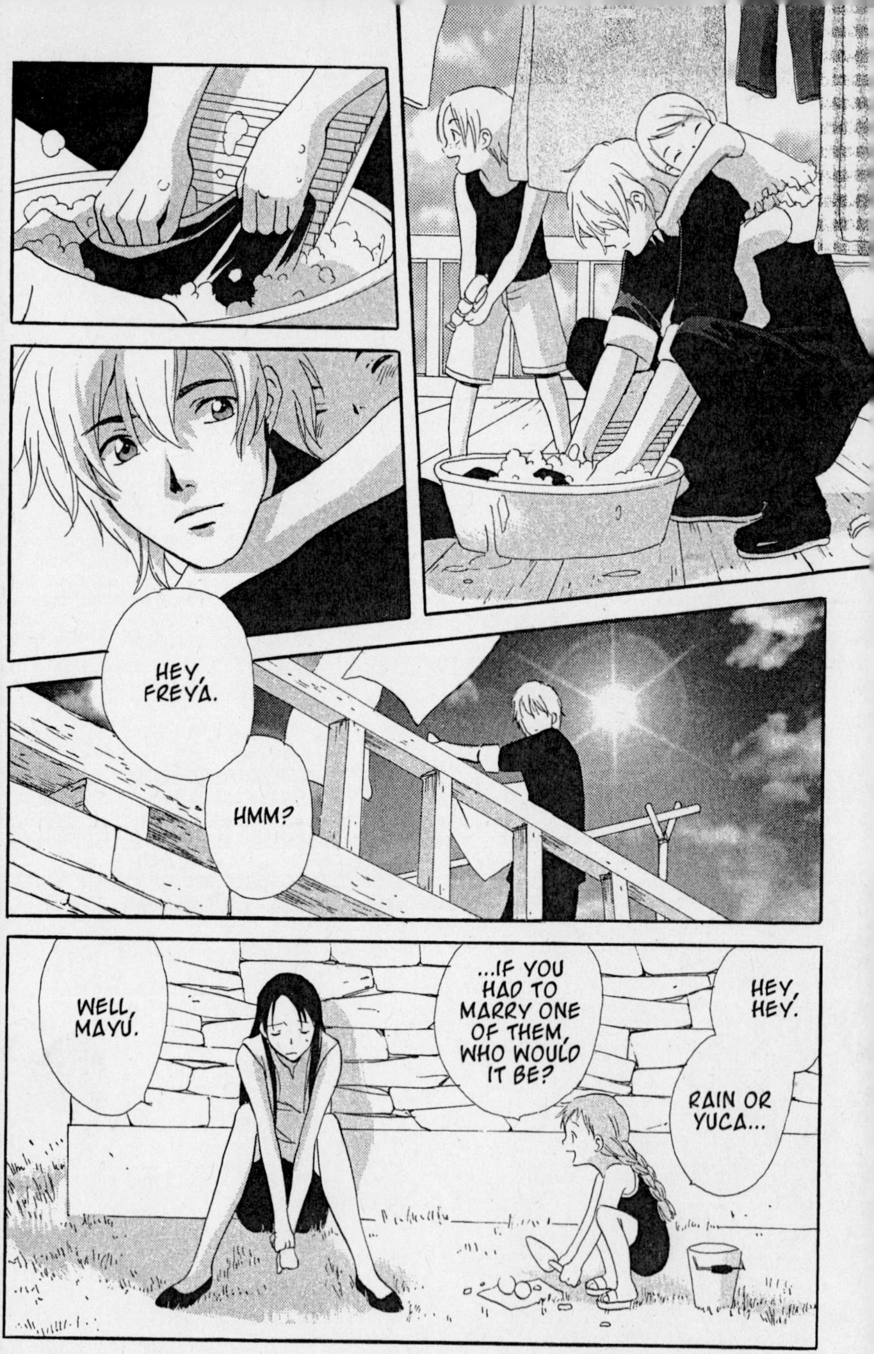
HEY, FREYA.
HMM?
HEY, HEY.
RAIN OR YUCA...
...IF YOU HAD TO MARRY ONE OF THEM, WHO WOULD IT BE?
WELL, MAYU.

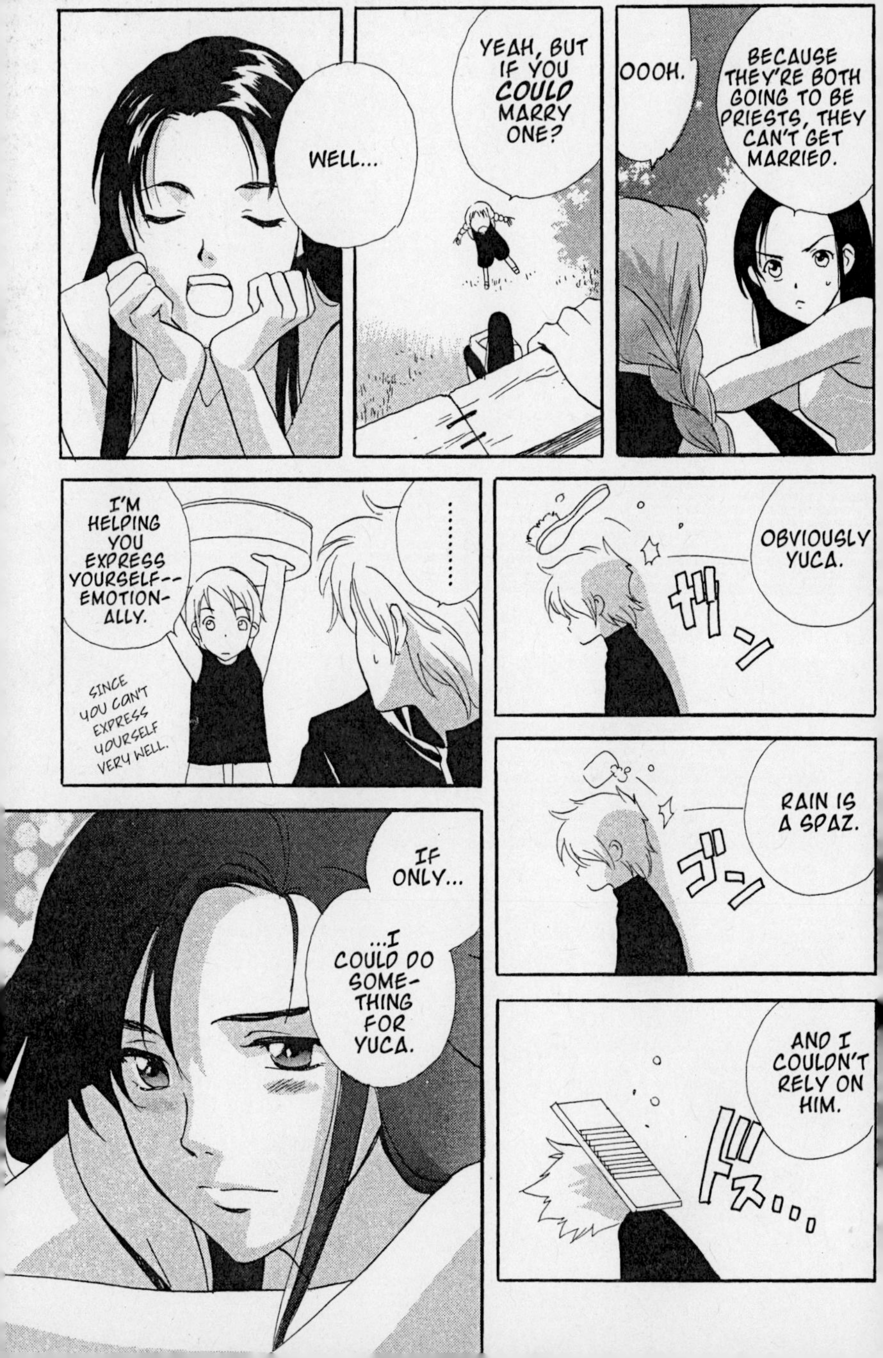
BECAUSE THEY'RE BOTH GOING TO BE PRIESTS, THEY CAN'T GET MARRIED.
OOOH.
YEAH, BUT IF YOU **COULD** MARRY ONE?
WELL...
OBVIOUSLY YUCA.
ガン
RAIN IS A SPAZ.
ゴン
AND I COULDN'T RELY ON HIM.
ドス...
......
I'M HELPING YOU EXPRESS YOURSELF--EMOTIONALLY.
SINCE YOU CAN'T EXPRESS YOURSELF VERY WELL.
IF ONLY...
...I COULD DO SOMETHING FOR YUCA.

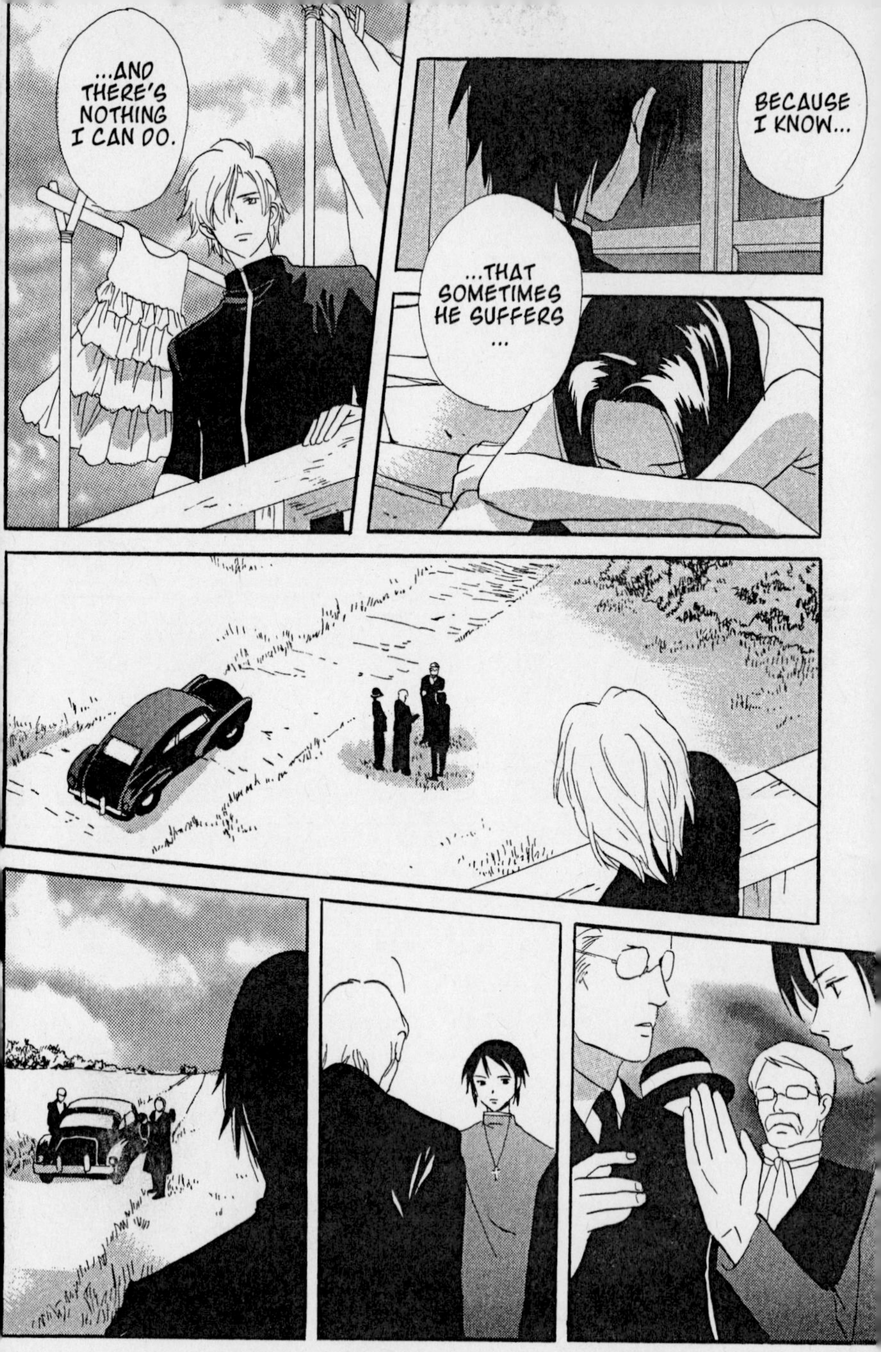
BECAUSE I KNOW...
...THAT SOMETIMES HE SUFFERS ...
...AND THERE'S NOTHING I CAN DO.

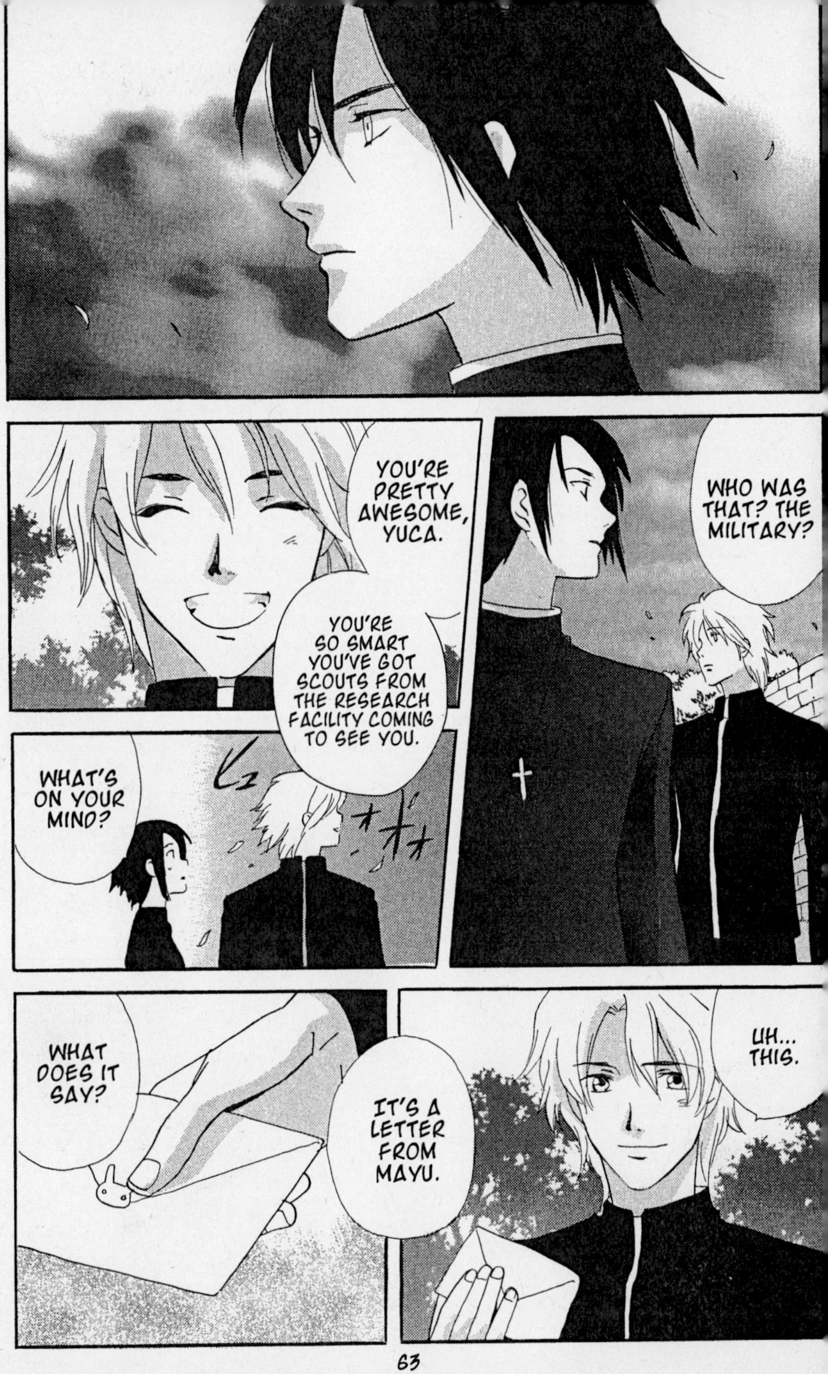
WHO WAS THAT? THE MILITARY?
YOU'RE PRETTY AWESOME, YUCA.
YOU'RE SO SMART YOU'VE GOT SCOUTS FROM THE RESEARCH FACILITY COMING TO SEE YOU.
WHAT'S ON YOUR MIND?
UH... THIS.
IT'S A LETTER FROM MAYU.
WHAT DOES IT SAY?

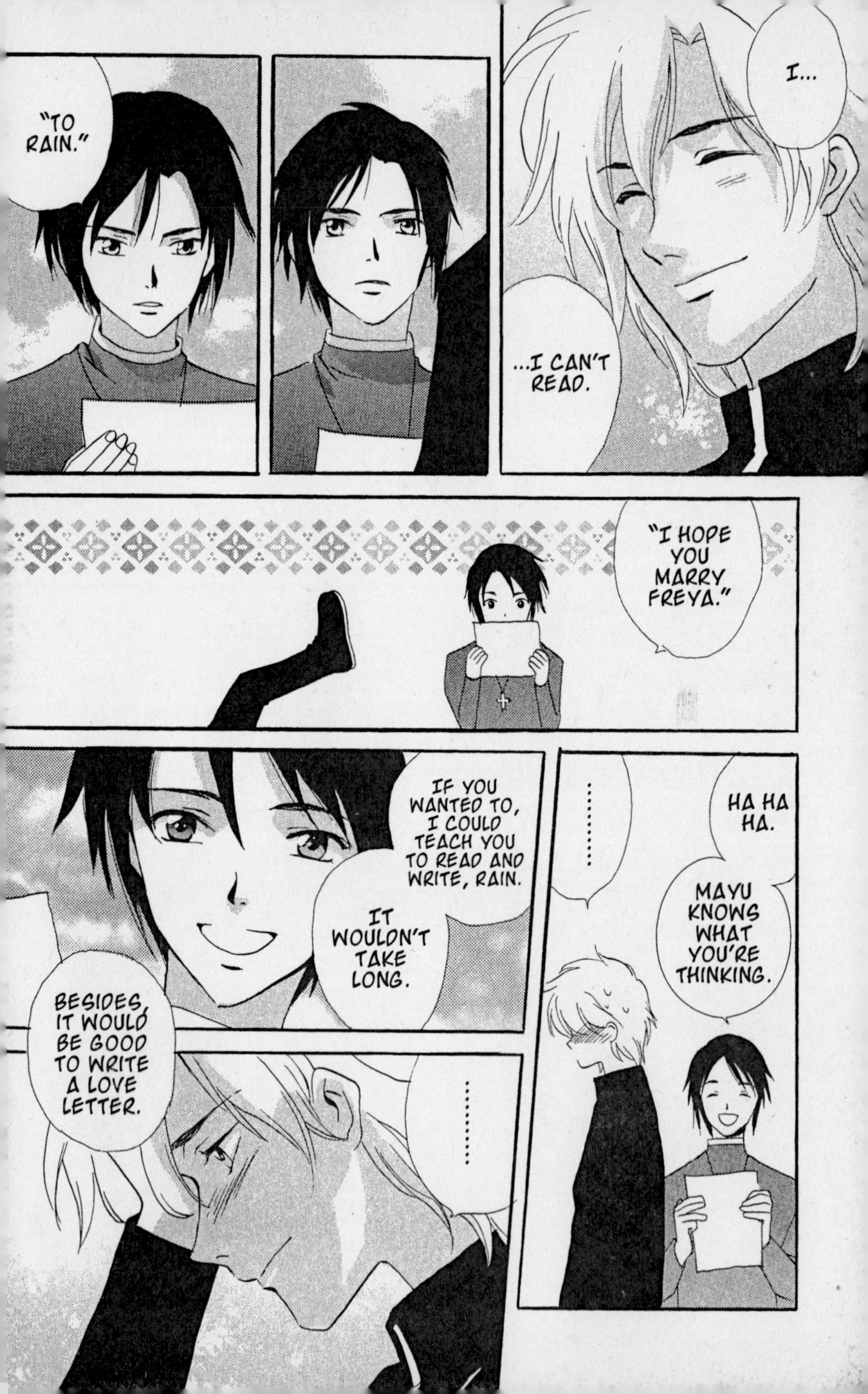
I...
...I CAN'T READ.
"TO RAIN."
"I HOPE YOU MARRY FREYA."
HA HA HA.
......
MAYU KNOWS WHAT YOU'RE THINKING.
IF YOU WANTED TO, I COULD TEACH YOU TO READ AND WRITE, RAIN.
IT WOULDN'T TAKE LONG.
BESIDES, IT WOULD BE GOOD TO WRITE A LOVE LETTER.
......

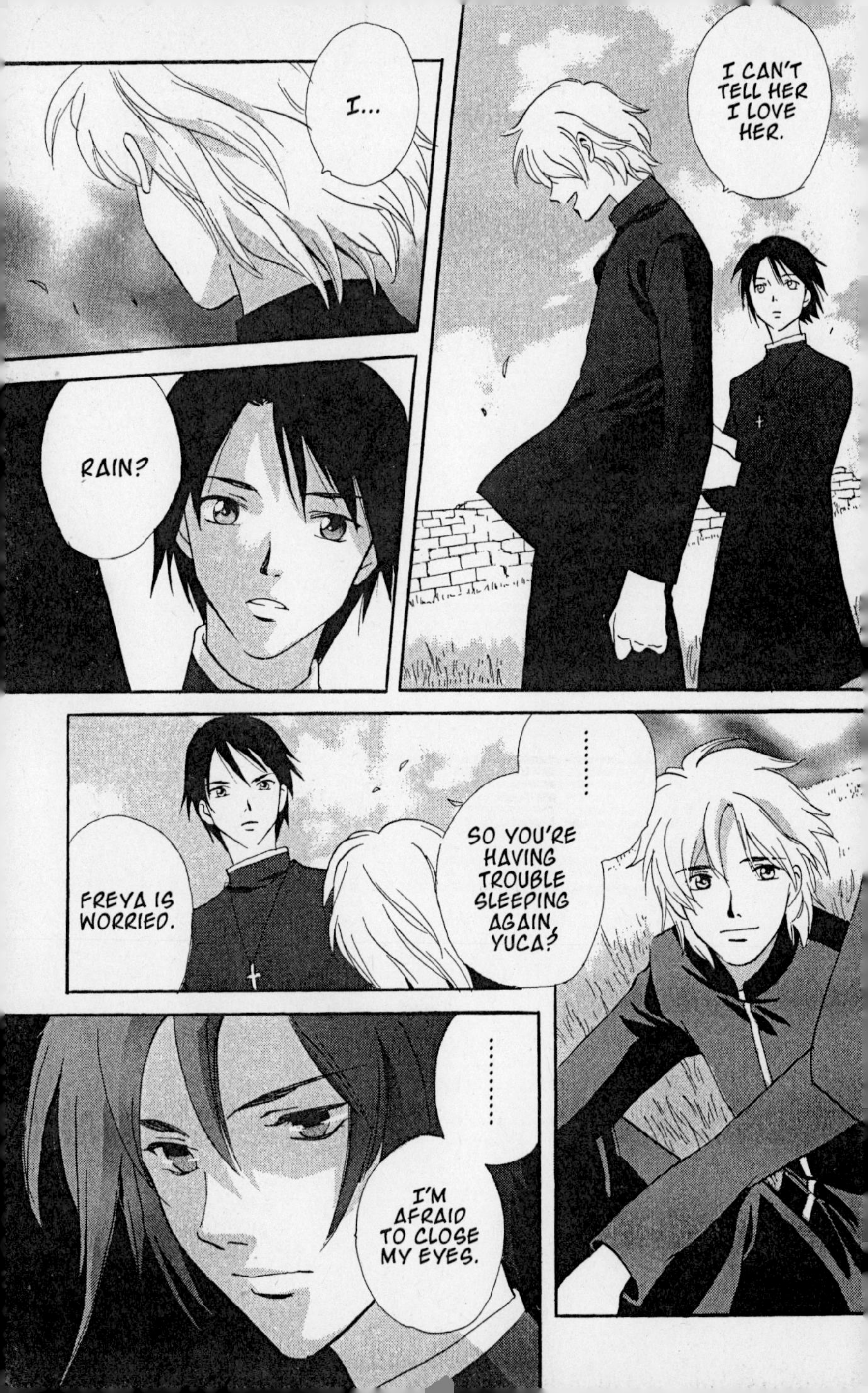
I CAN'T TELL HER I LOVE HER.
I...
RAIN?
......
SO YOU'RE HAVING TROUBLE SLEEPING AGAIN, YUCA?
FREYA IS WORRIED.
......
I'M AFRAID TO CLOSE MY EYES.

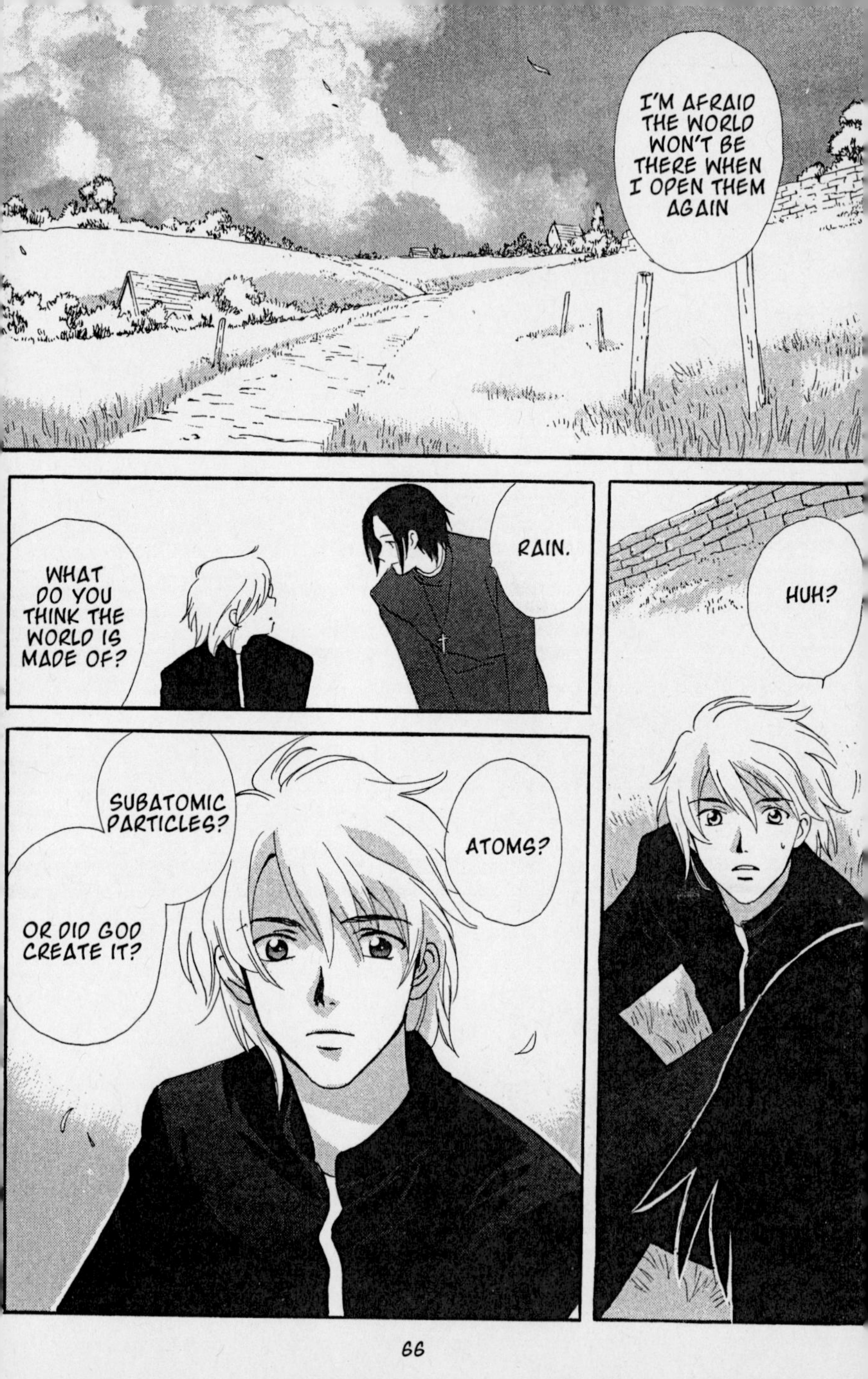
I'M AFRAID THE WORLD WON'T BE THERE WHEN I OPEN THEM AGAIN
HUH?
RAIN.
WHAT DO YOU THINK THE WORLD IS MADE OF?
ATOMS?
SUBATOMIC PARTICLES?
OR DID GOD CREATE IT?

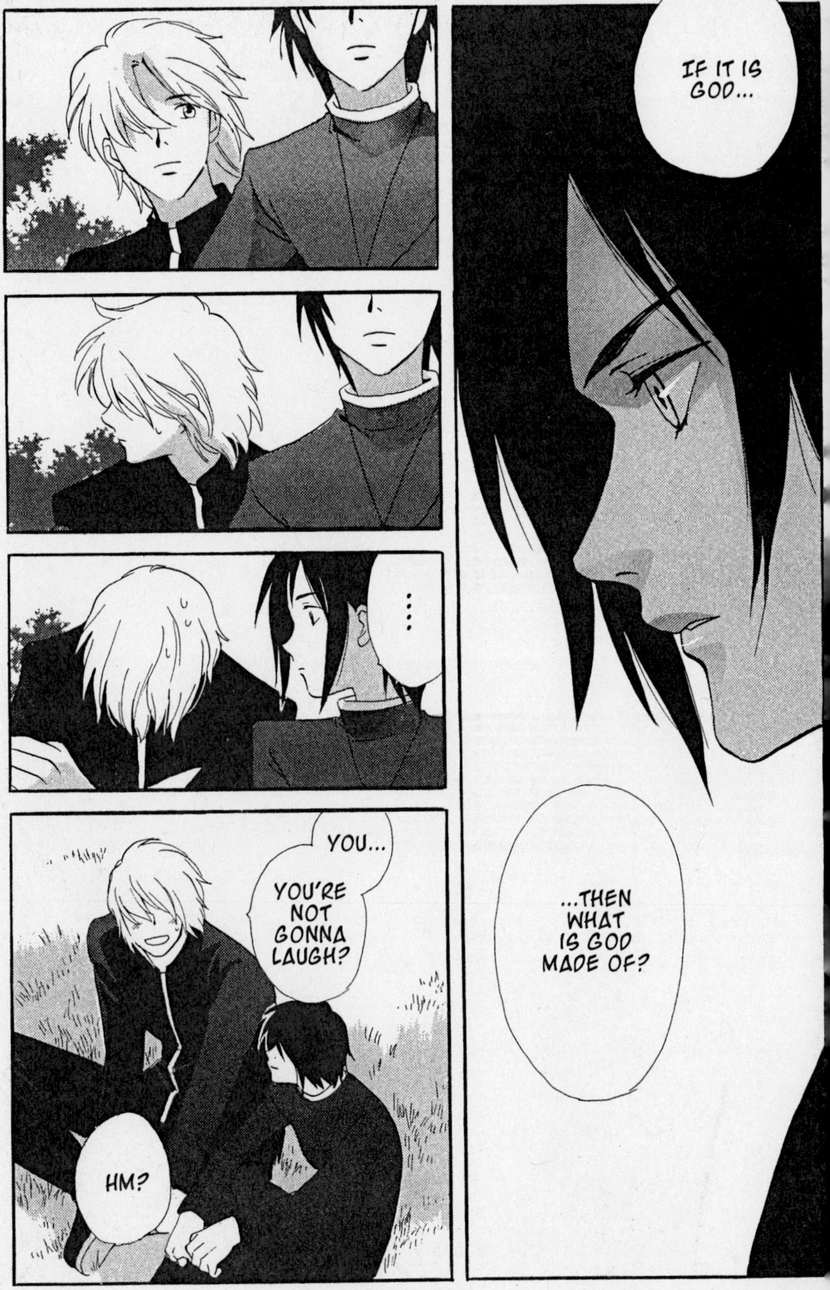
IF IT IS GOD...
...THEN WHAT IS GOD MADE OF?
....
YOU...
YOU'RE NOT GONNA LAUGH?
HM?

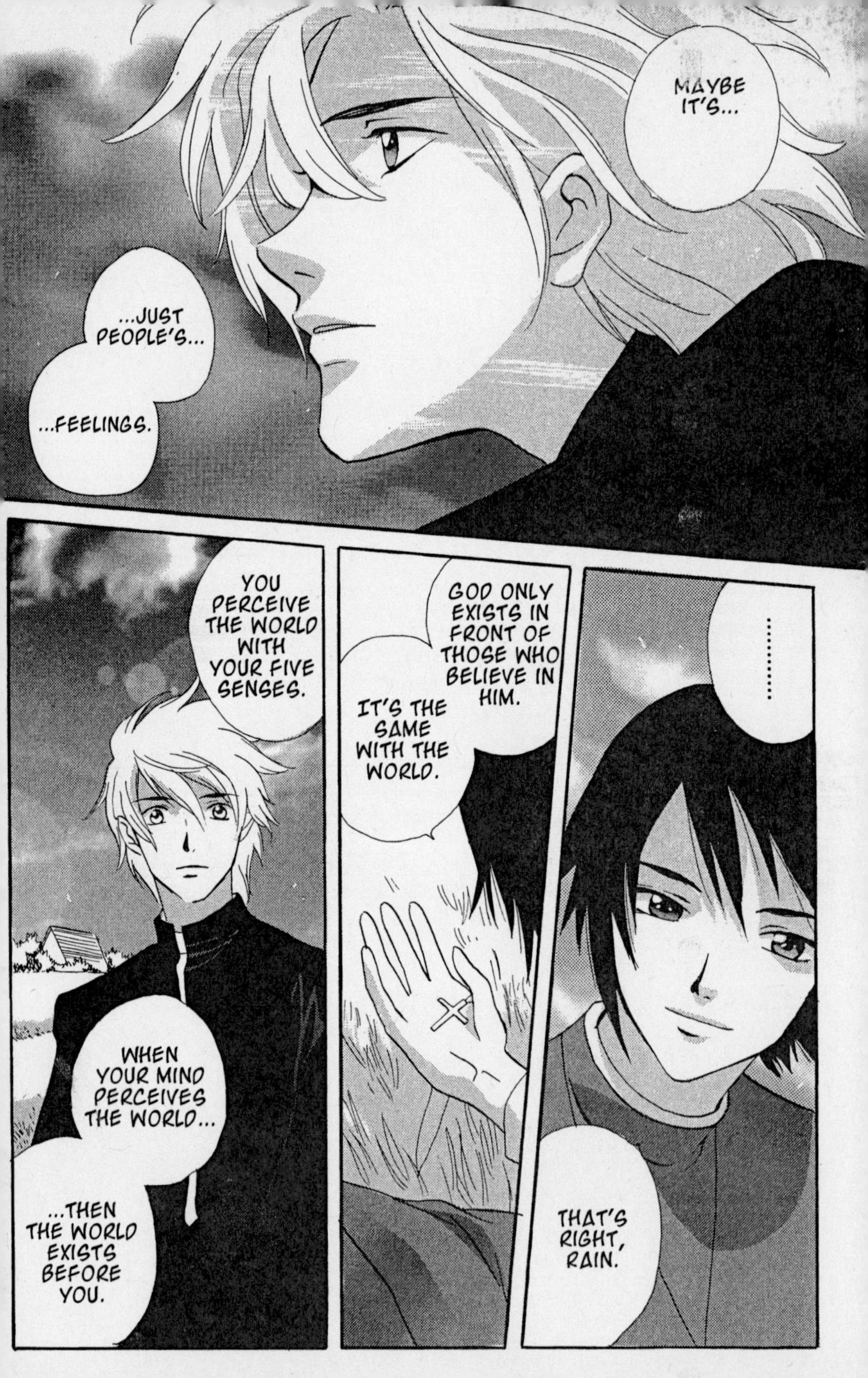
MAYBE IT'S...
...JUST PEOPLE'S...
...FEELINGS.
......
THAT'S RIGHT, RAIN.
GOD ONLY EXISTS IN FRONT OF THOSE WHO BELIEVE IN HIM.
IT'S THE SAME WITH THE WORLD.
YOU PERCEIVE THE WORLD WITH YOUR FIVE SENSES.
WHEN YOUR MIND PERCEIVES THE WORLD...
...THEN THE WORLD EXISTS BEFORE YOU.

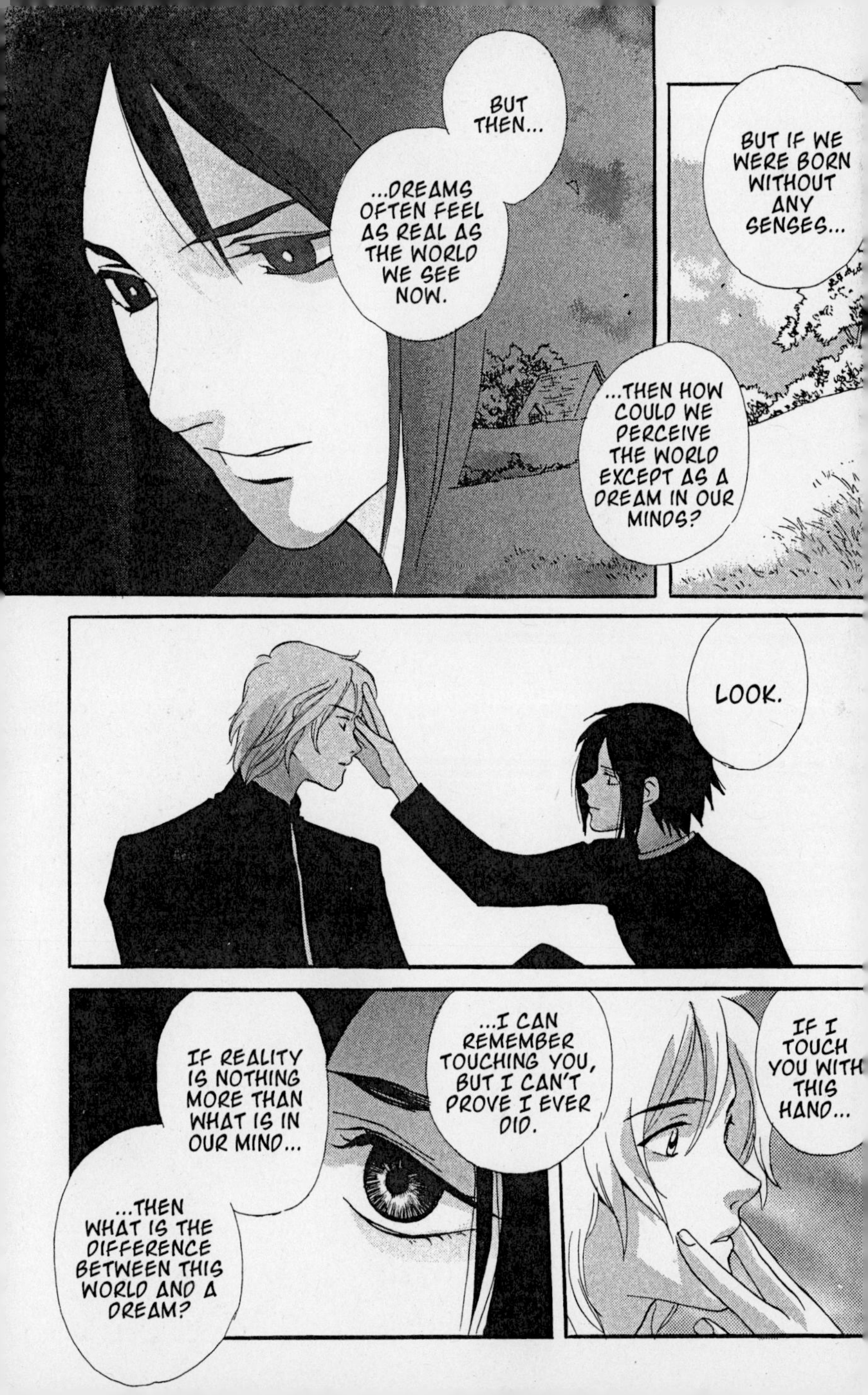
BUT IF WE WERE BORN WITHOUT ANY SENSES...
...THEN HOW COULD WE PERCEIVE THE WORLD EXCEPT AS A DREAM IN OUR MINDS?
BUT THEN...
...DREAMS OFTEN FEEL AS REAL AS THE WORLD WE SEE NOW.
LOOK.
IF I TOUCH YOU WITH THIS HAND...
...I CAN REMEMBER TOUCHING YOU, BUT I CAN'T PROVE I EVER DID.
IF REALITY IS NOTHING MORE THAN WHAT IS IN OUR MIND...
...THEN WHAT IS THE DIFFERENCE BETWEEN THIS WORLD AND A DREAM?

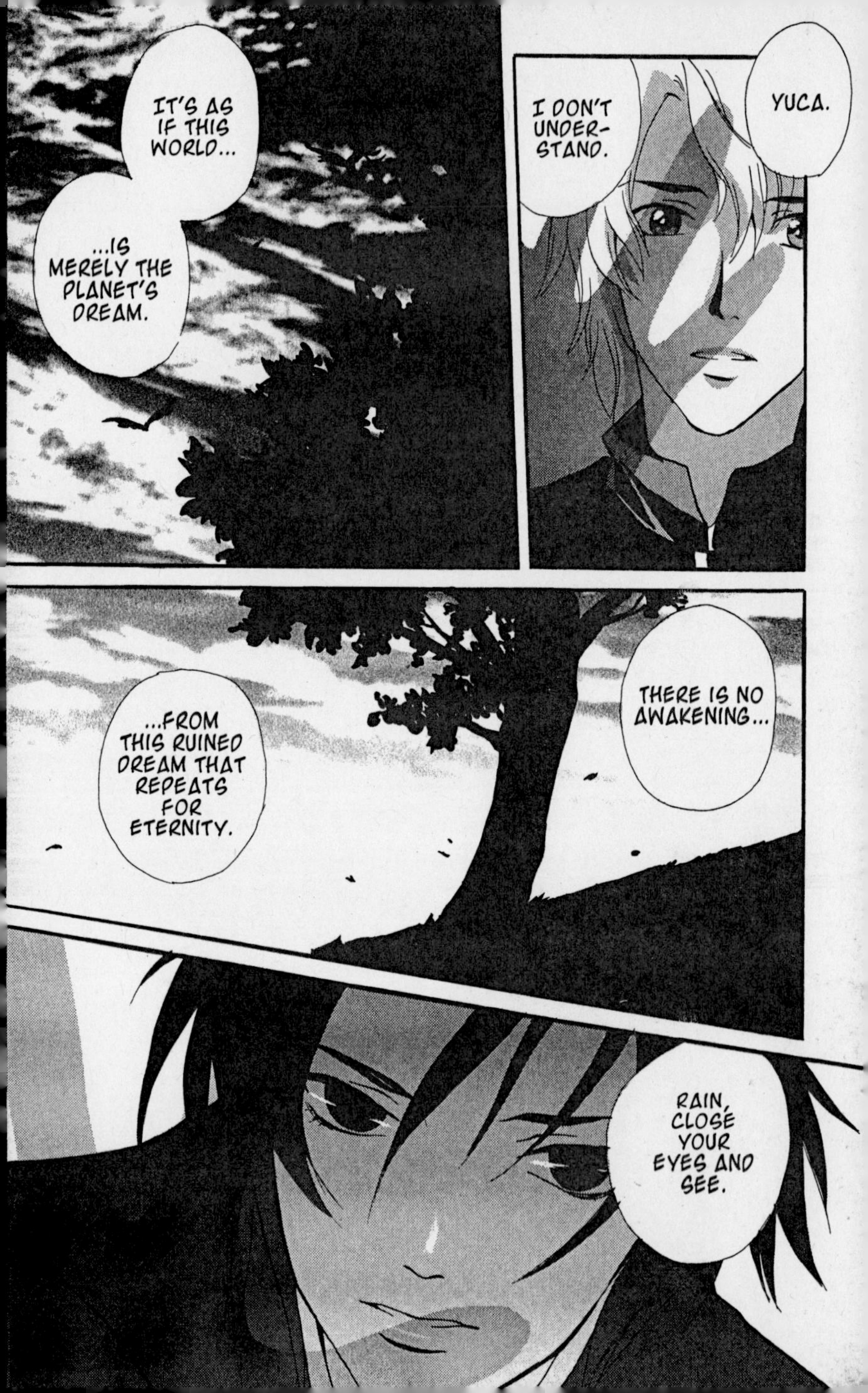
YUCA.
I DON'T UNDER-STAND.
IT'S AS IF THIS WORLD...
...IS MERELY THE PLANET'S DREAM.
THERE IS NO AWAKENING...
...FROM THIS RUINED DREAM THAT REPEATS FOR ETERNITY.
RAIN, CLOSE YOUR EYES AND SEE.

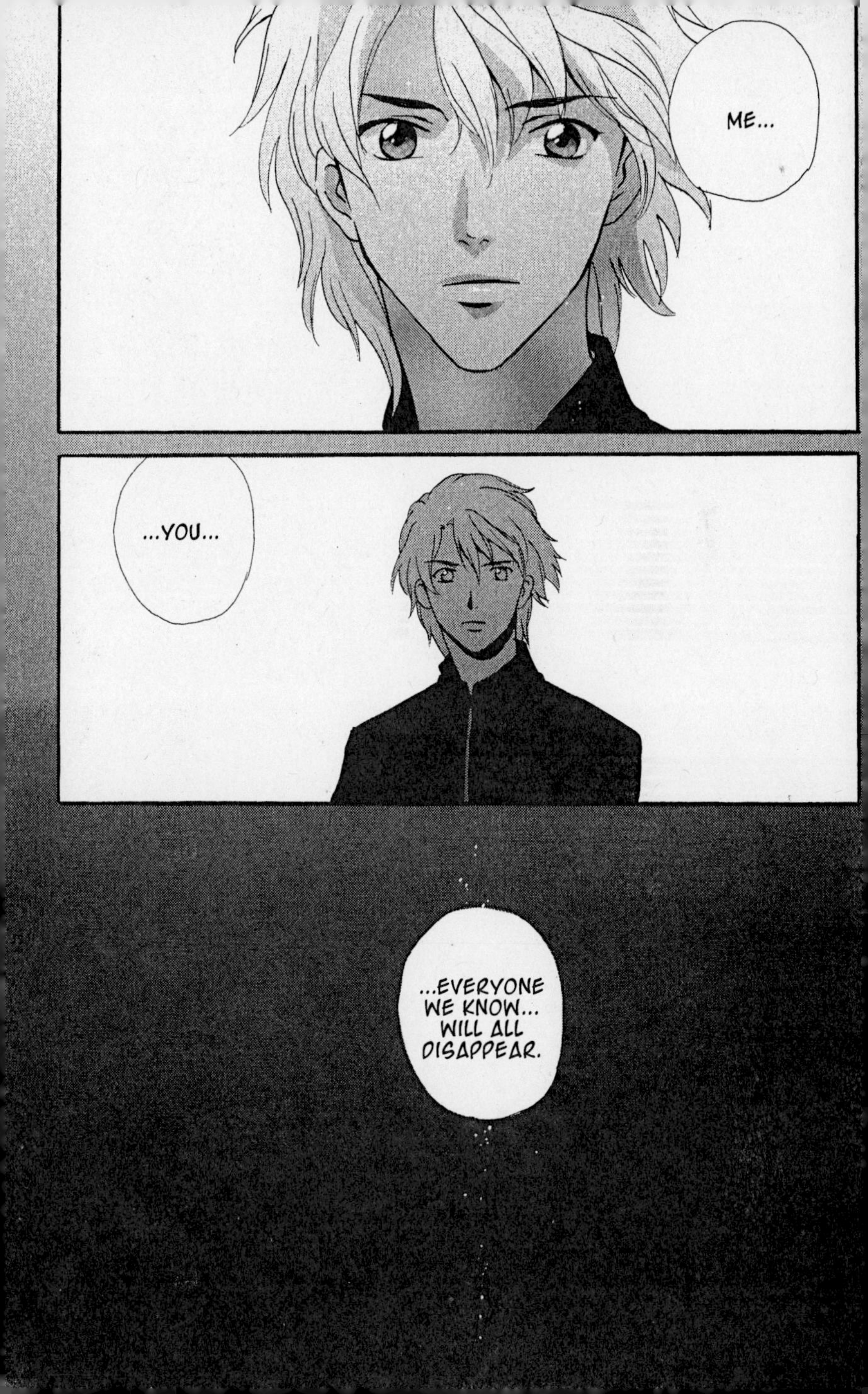
ME...
...YOU...
...EVERYONE WE KNOW... WILL ALL DISAPPEAR.

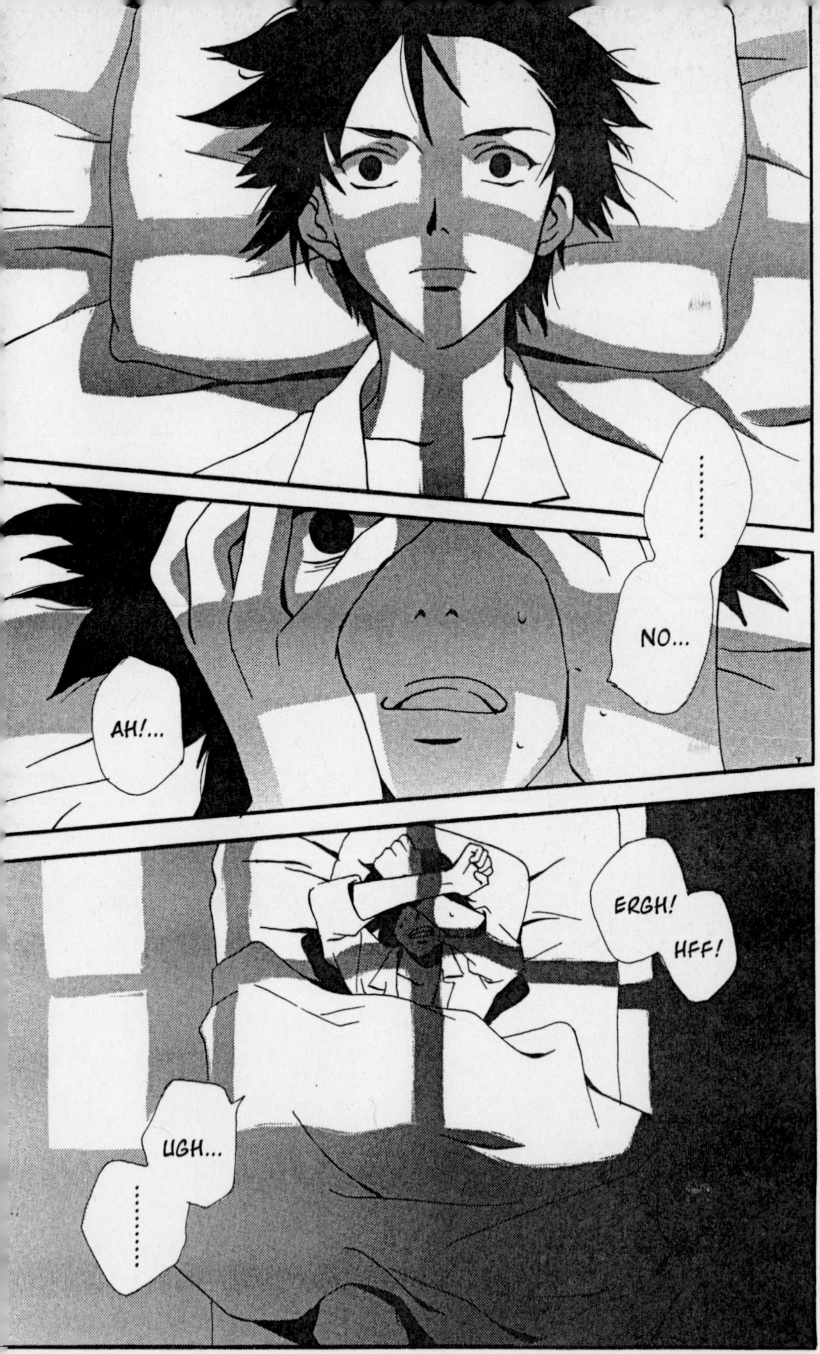
......
NO...
AH!...
ERGH! HFF!
UGH... ......

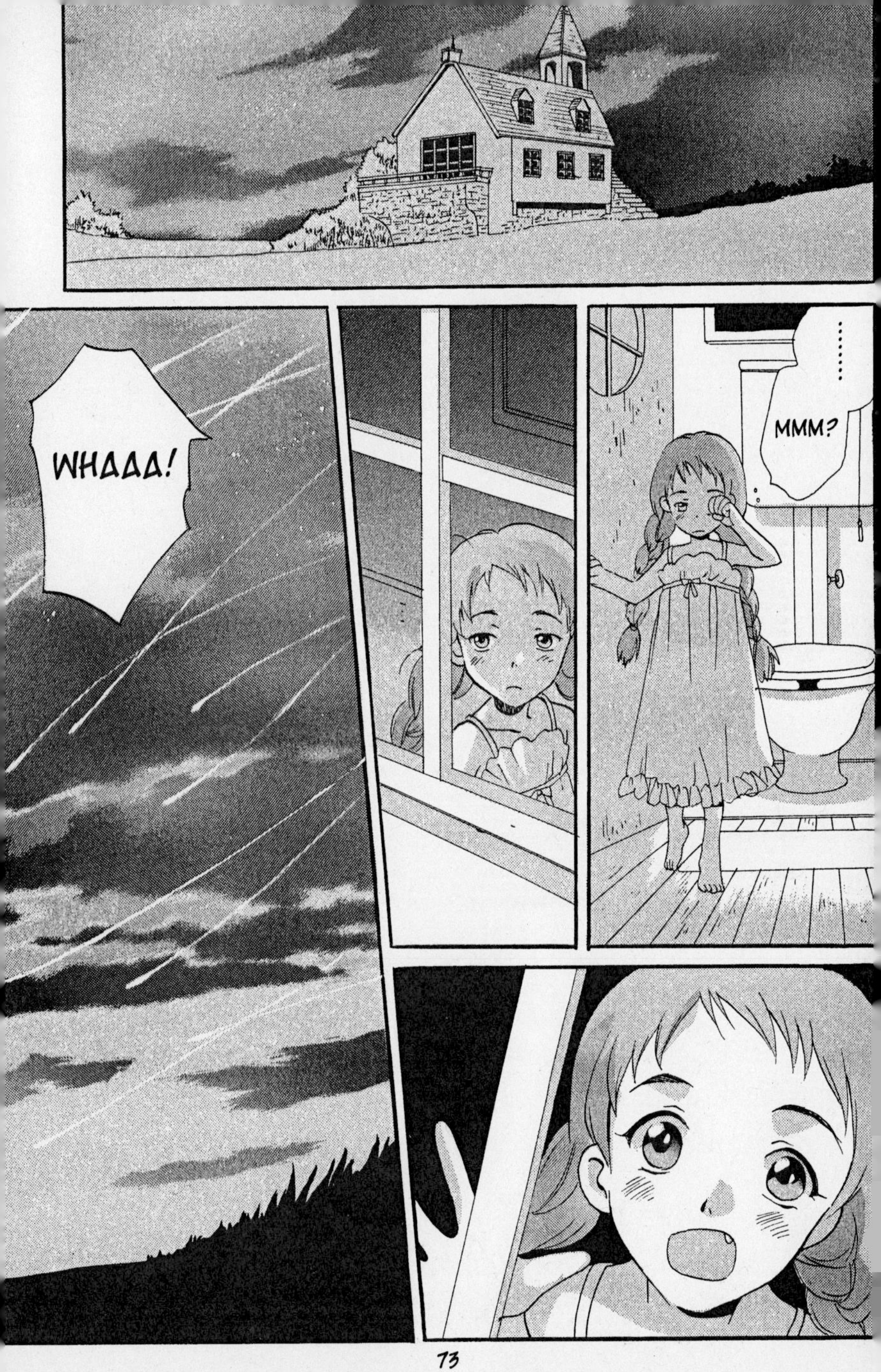

......
MMM?
WHAAA!

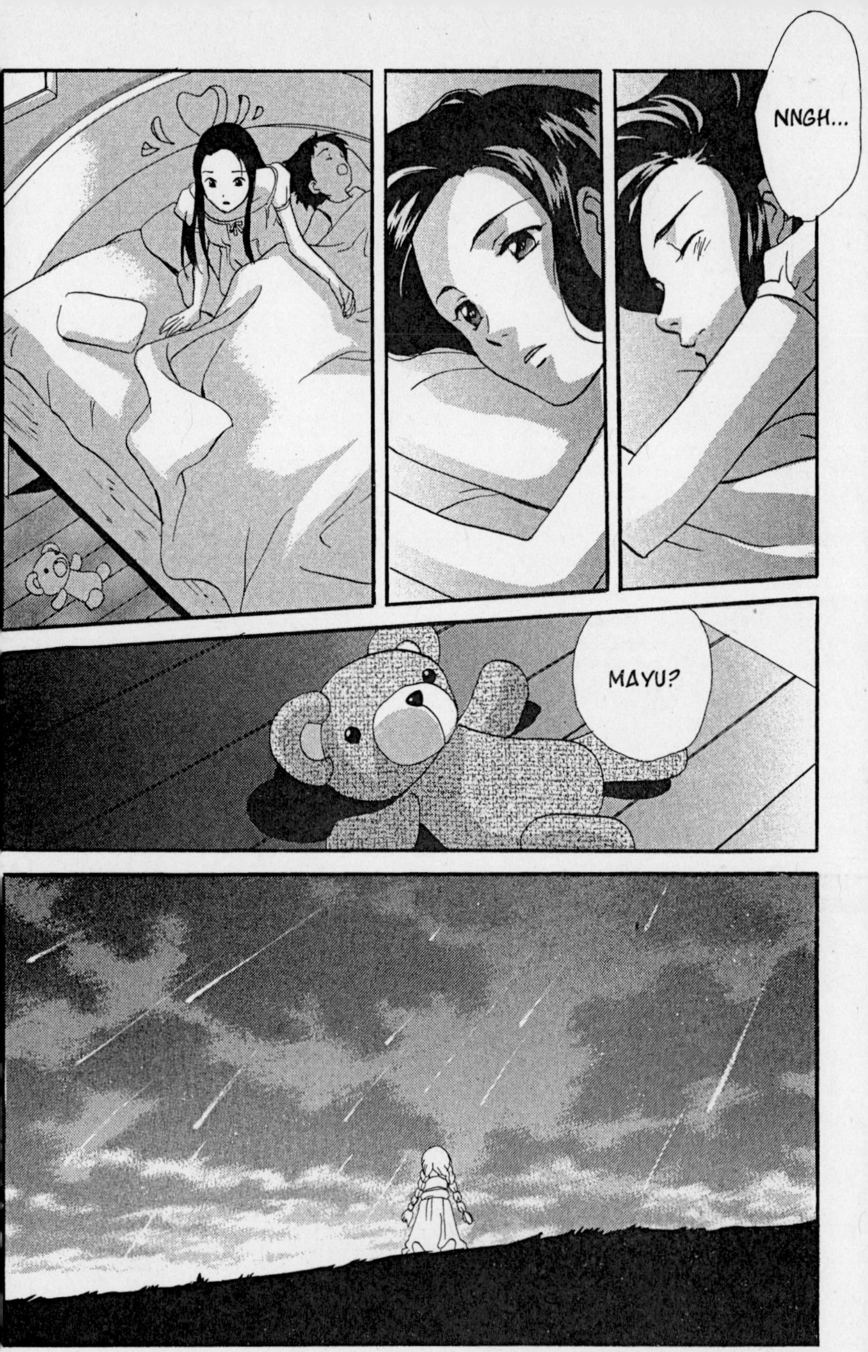
NNGH...
MAYU?

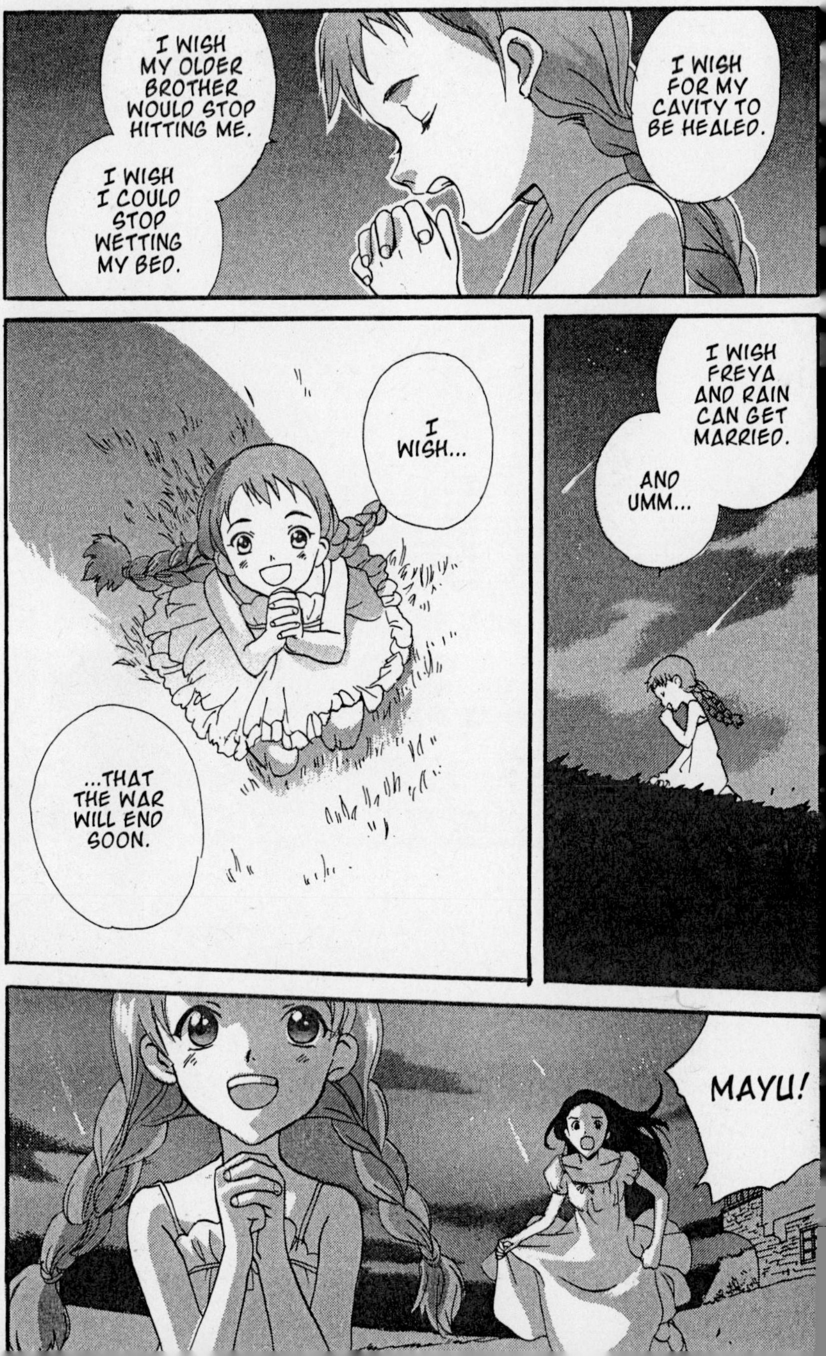
I WISH FOR MY CAVITY TO BE HEALED.
I WISH MY OLDER BROTHER WOULD STOP HITTING ME.
I WISH I COULD STOP WETTING MY BED.
I WISH FREYA AND RAIN CAN GET MARRIED.
AND UMM...
I WISH...
...THAT THE WAR WILL END SOON.
MAYU!

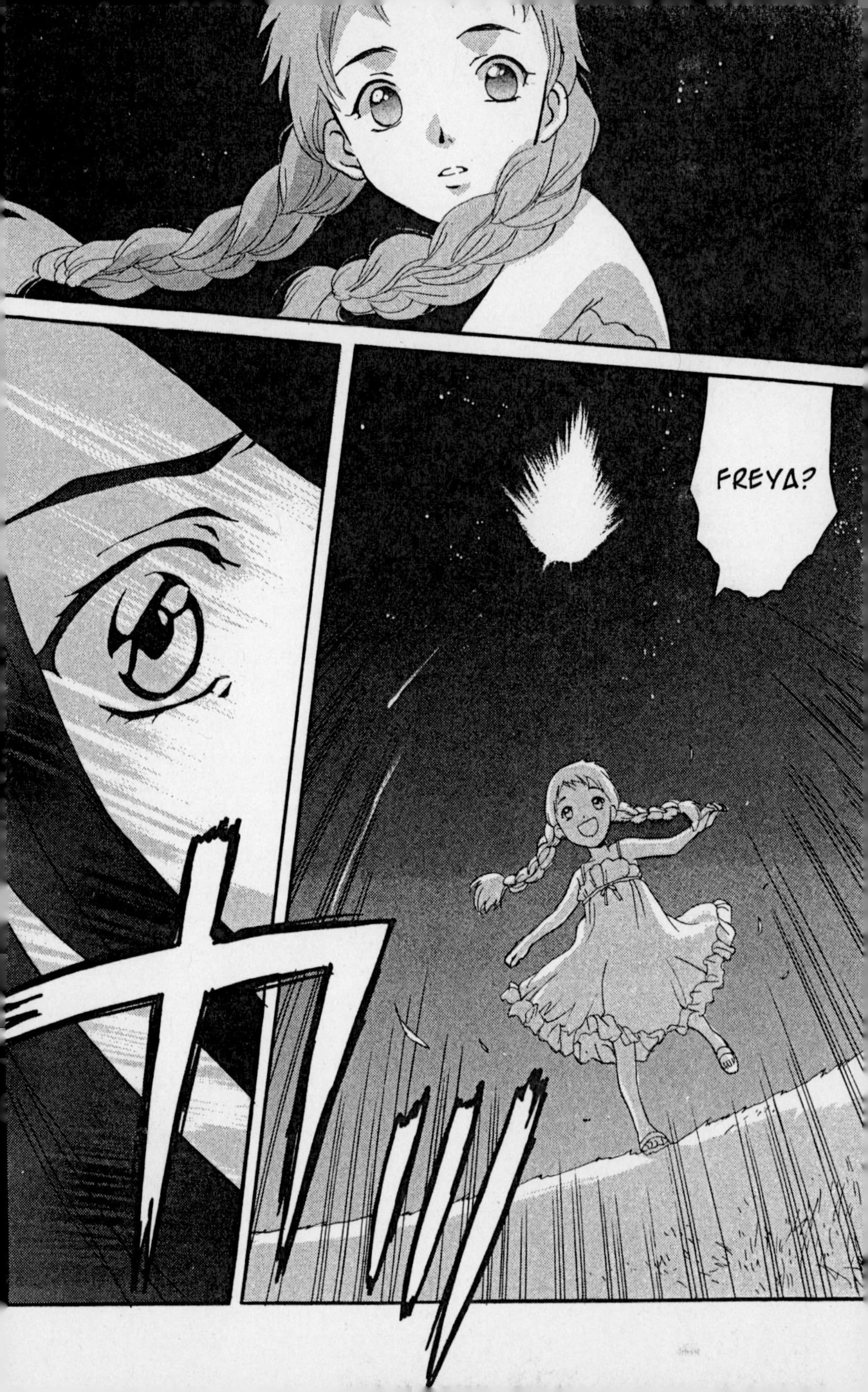
FREYA?

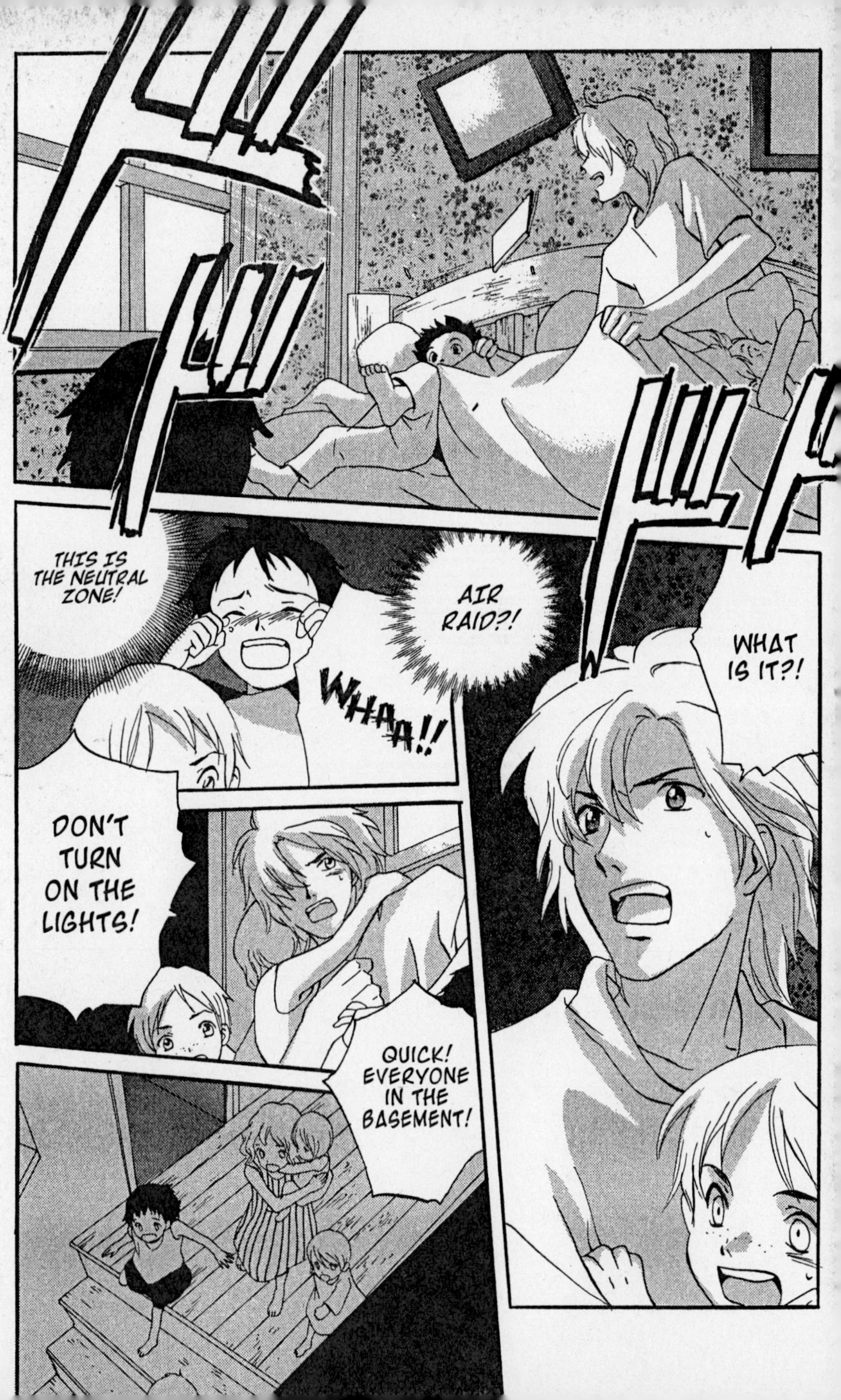
WHAT IS IT?!
AIR RAID?!
WHAA!!
THIS IS THE NEUTRAL ZONE!
DON'T TURN ON THE LIGHTS!
QUICK! EVERYONE IN THE BASEMENT!

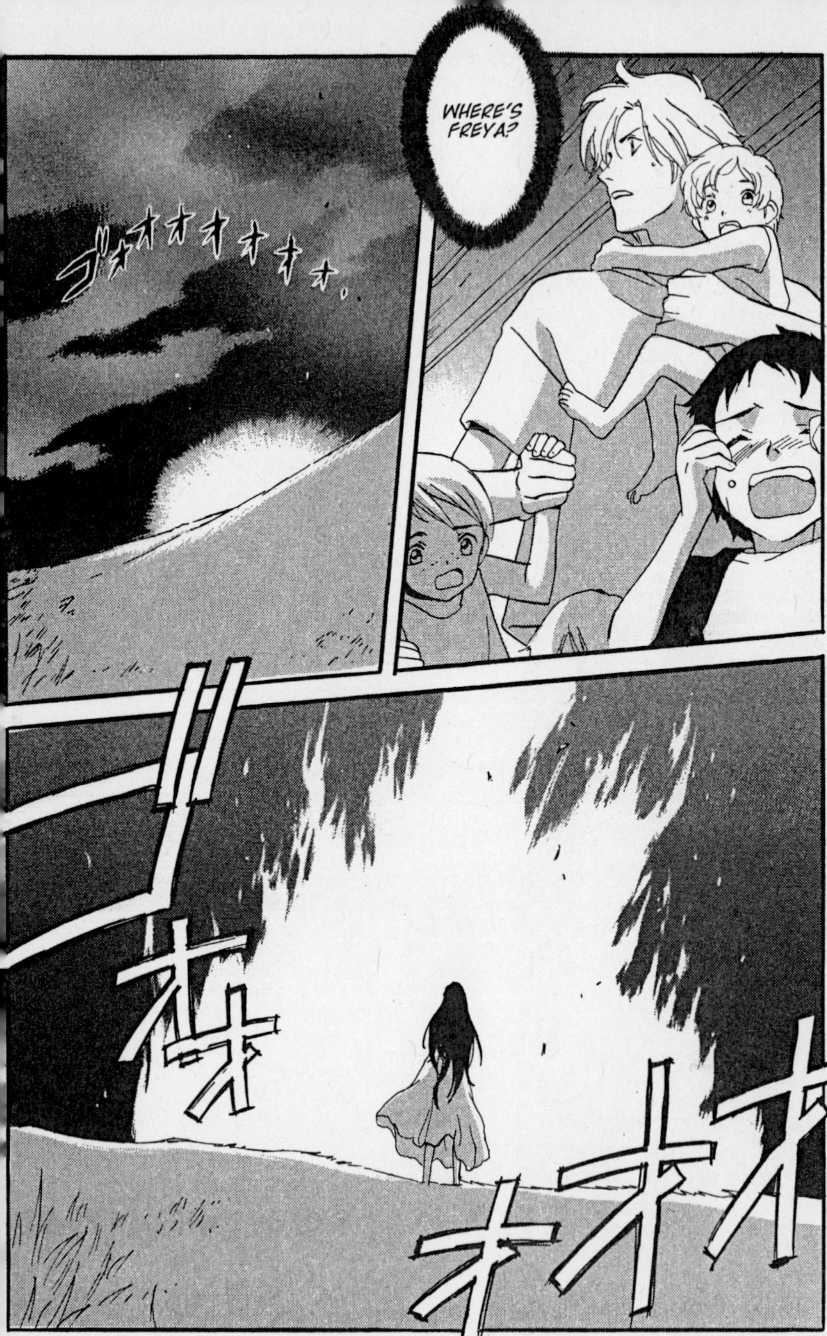
WHERE'S FREYA?
ゴォオオオオオォォ。
ゴオォォオオ

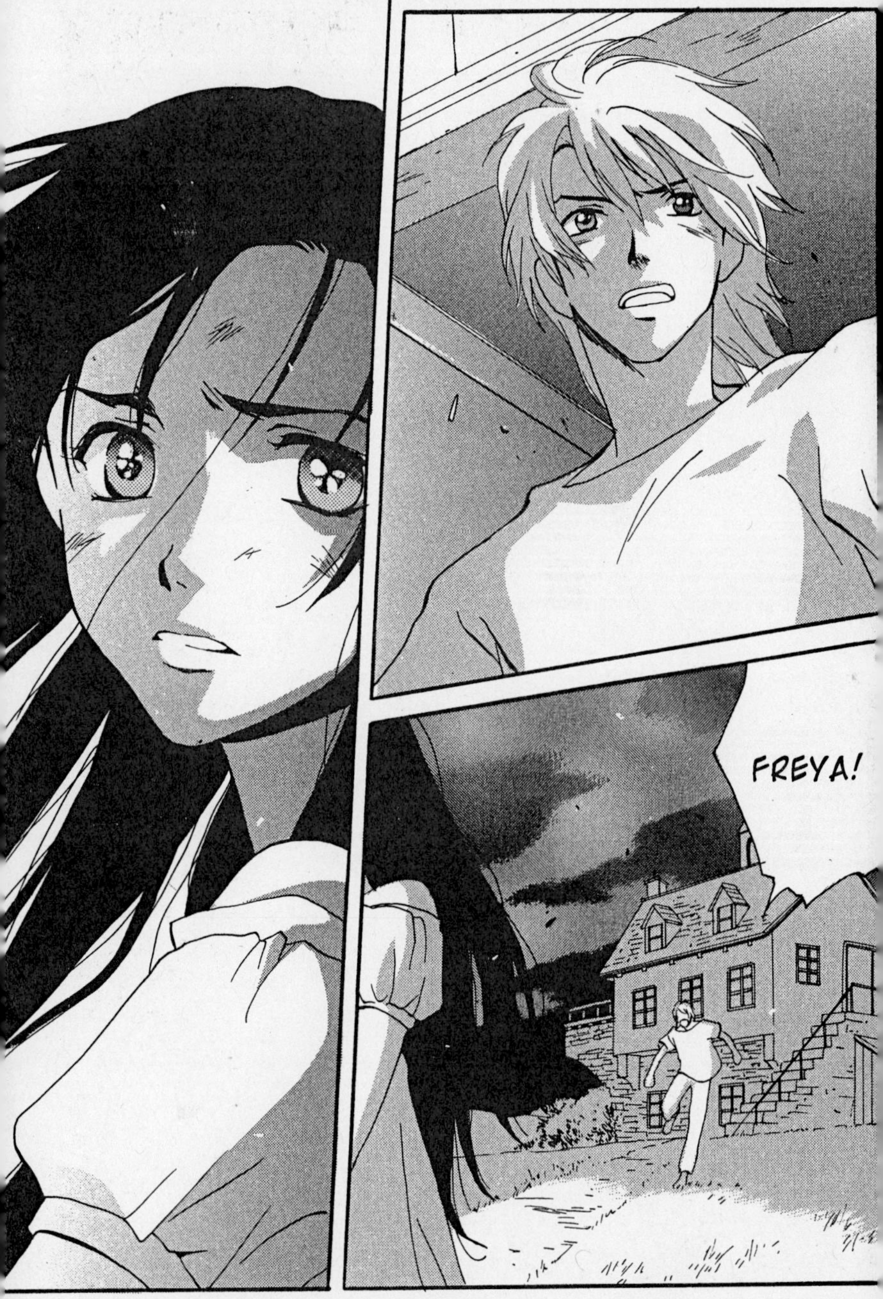
FREYA!

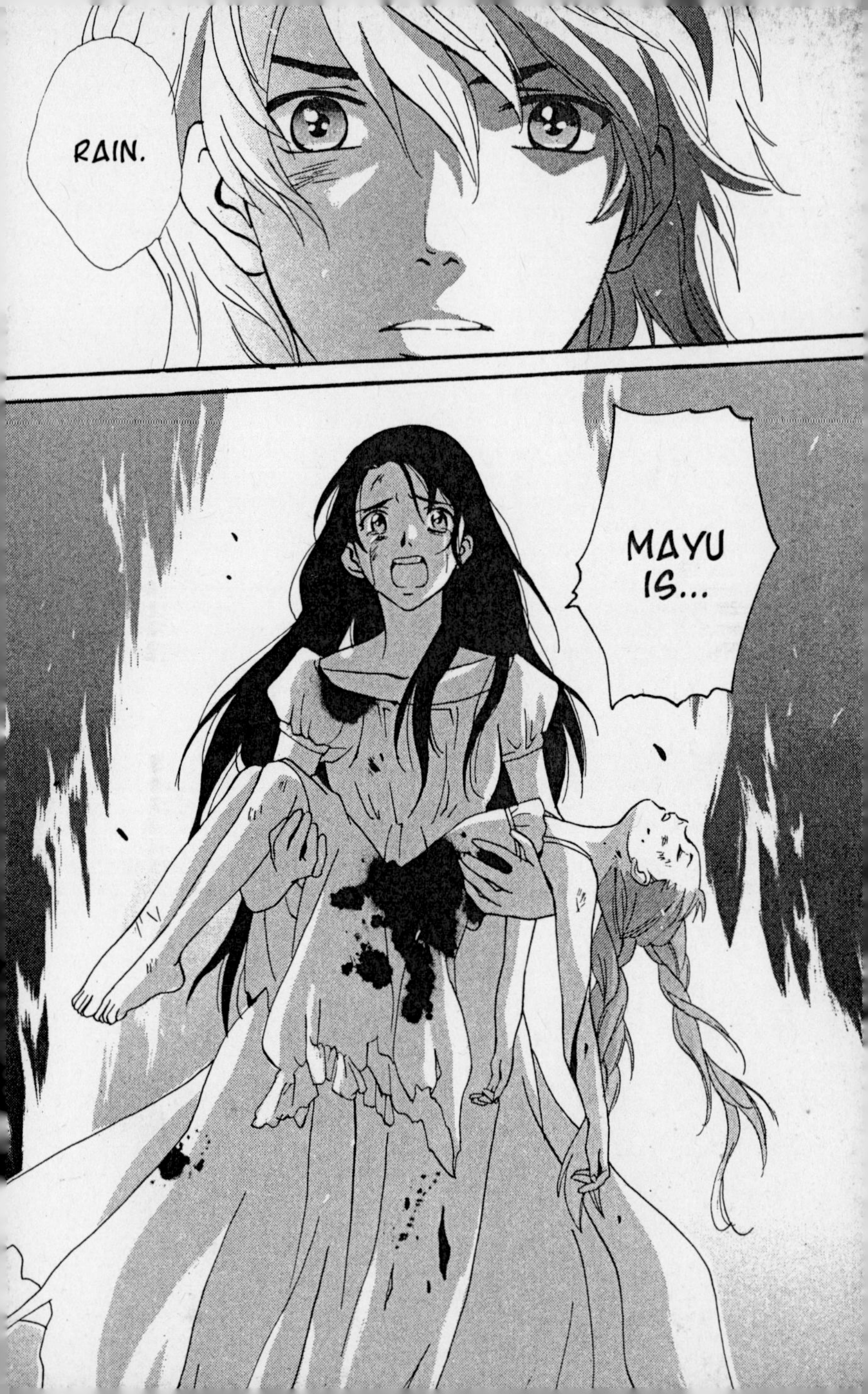
RAIN.
MAYU IS...

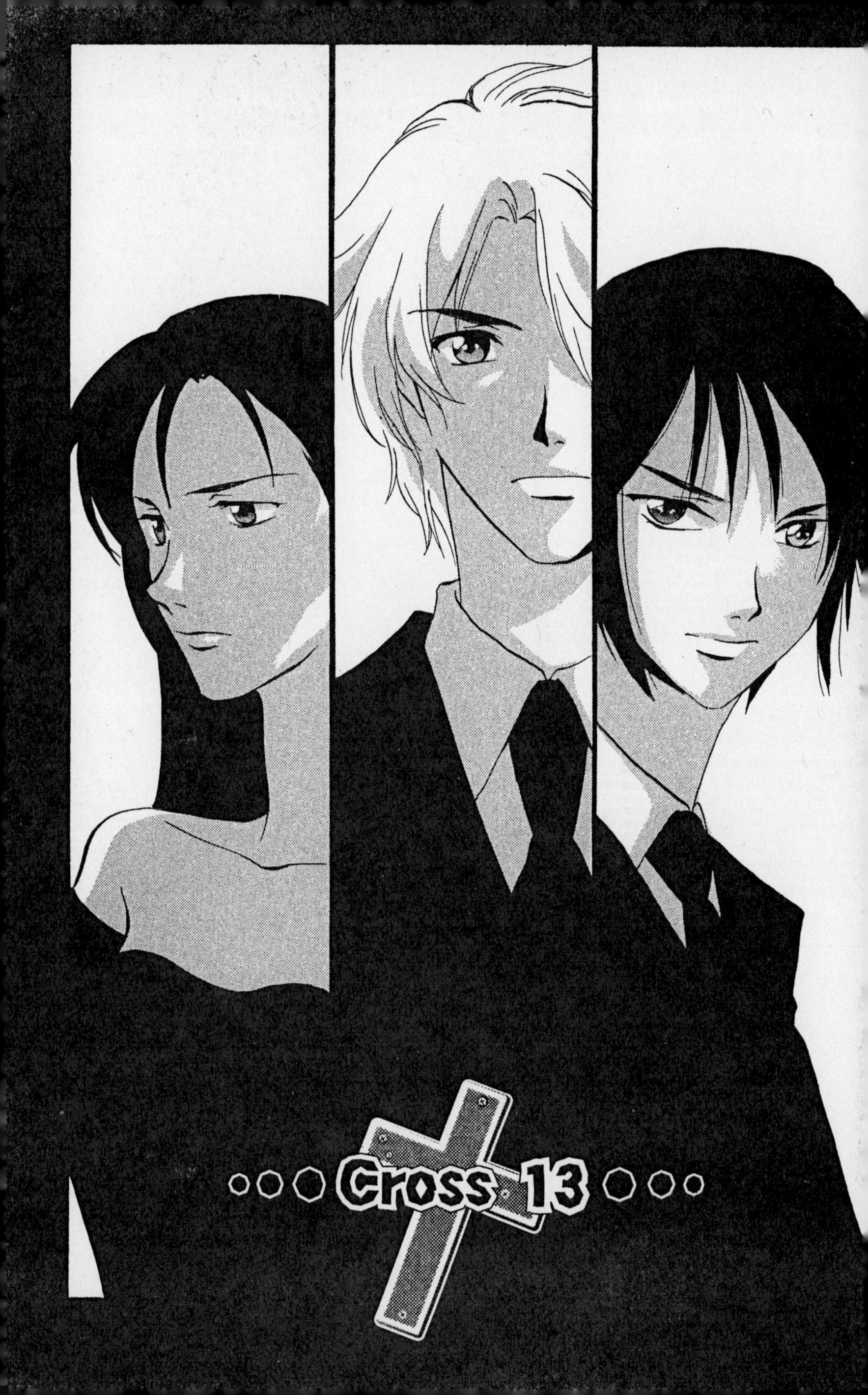
Cross 13

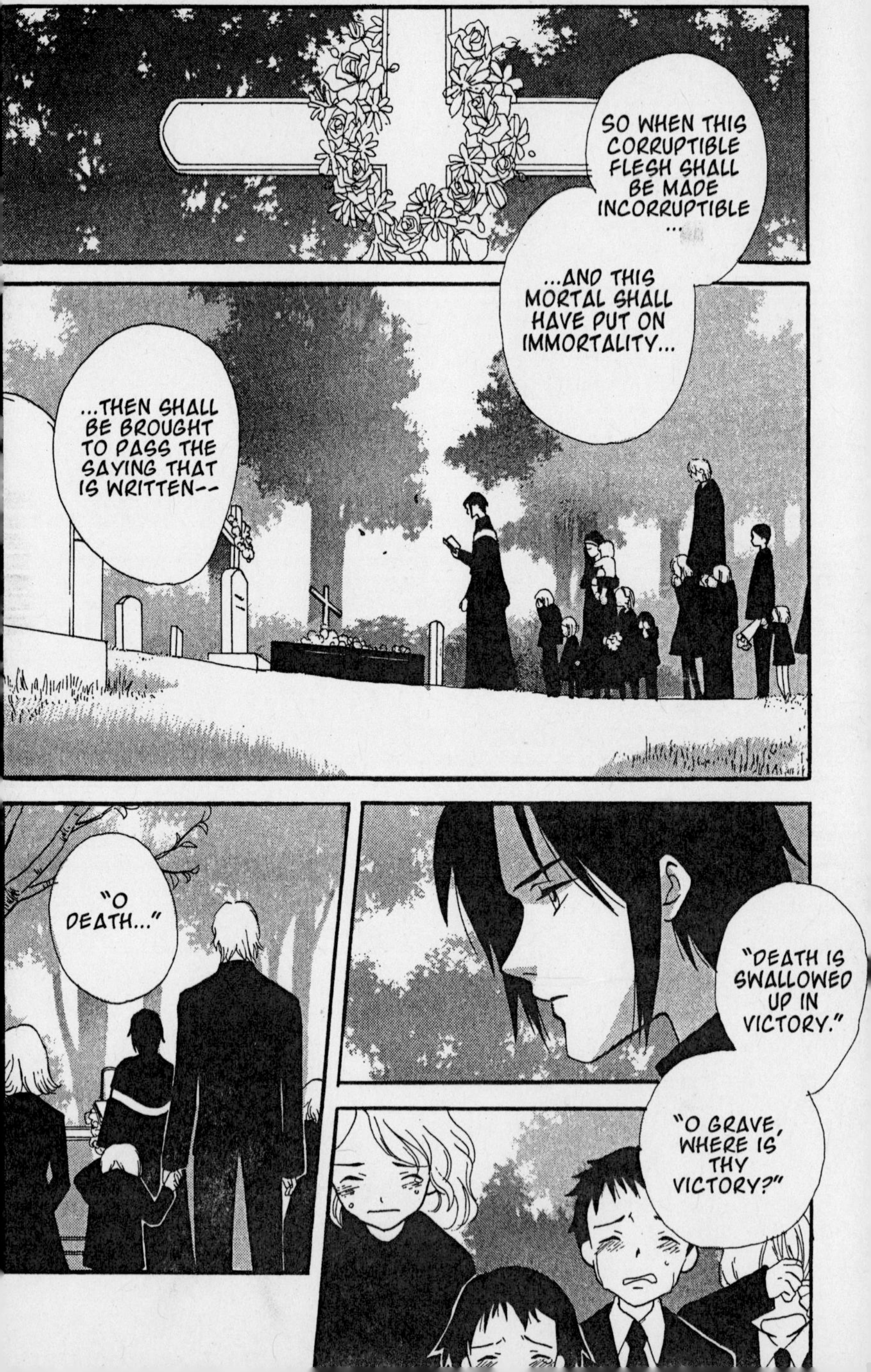
SO WHEN THIS CORRUPTIBLE FLESH SHALL BE MADE INCORRUPTIBLE ...
...AND THIS MORTAL SHALL HAVE PUT ON IMMORTALITY...
...THEN SHALL BE BROUGHT TO PASS THE SAYING THAT IS WRITTEN--
"DEATH IS SWALLOWED UP IN VICTORY."
"O GRAVE, WHERE IS THY VICTORY?"
"O DEATH..."

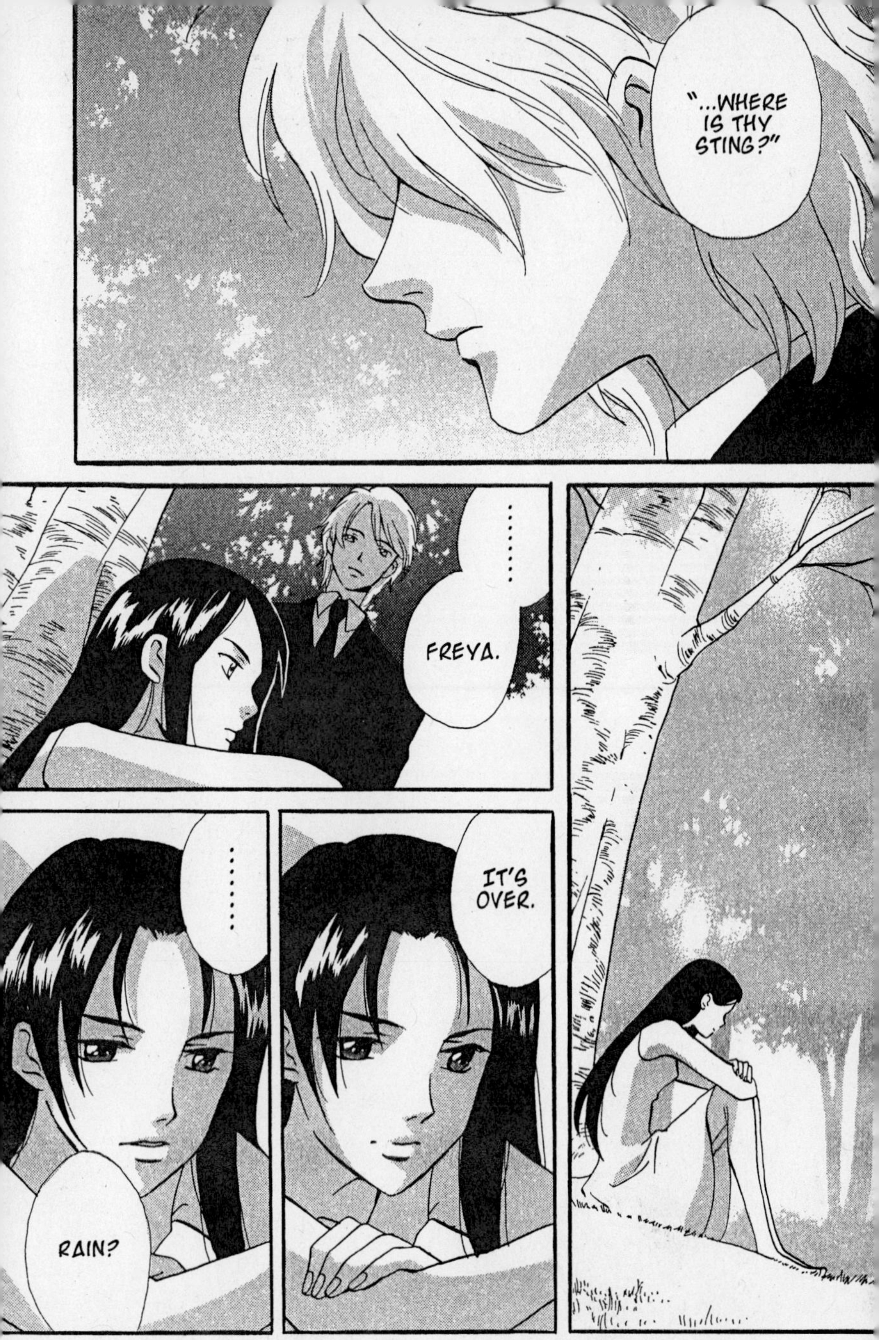
"...WHERE IS THY STING?"
......
FREYA.
IT'S OVER.
......
RAIN?

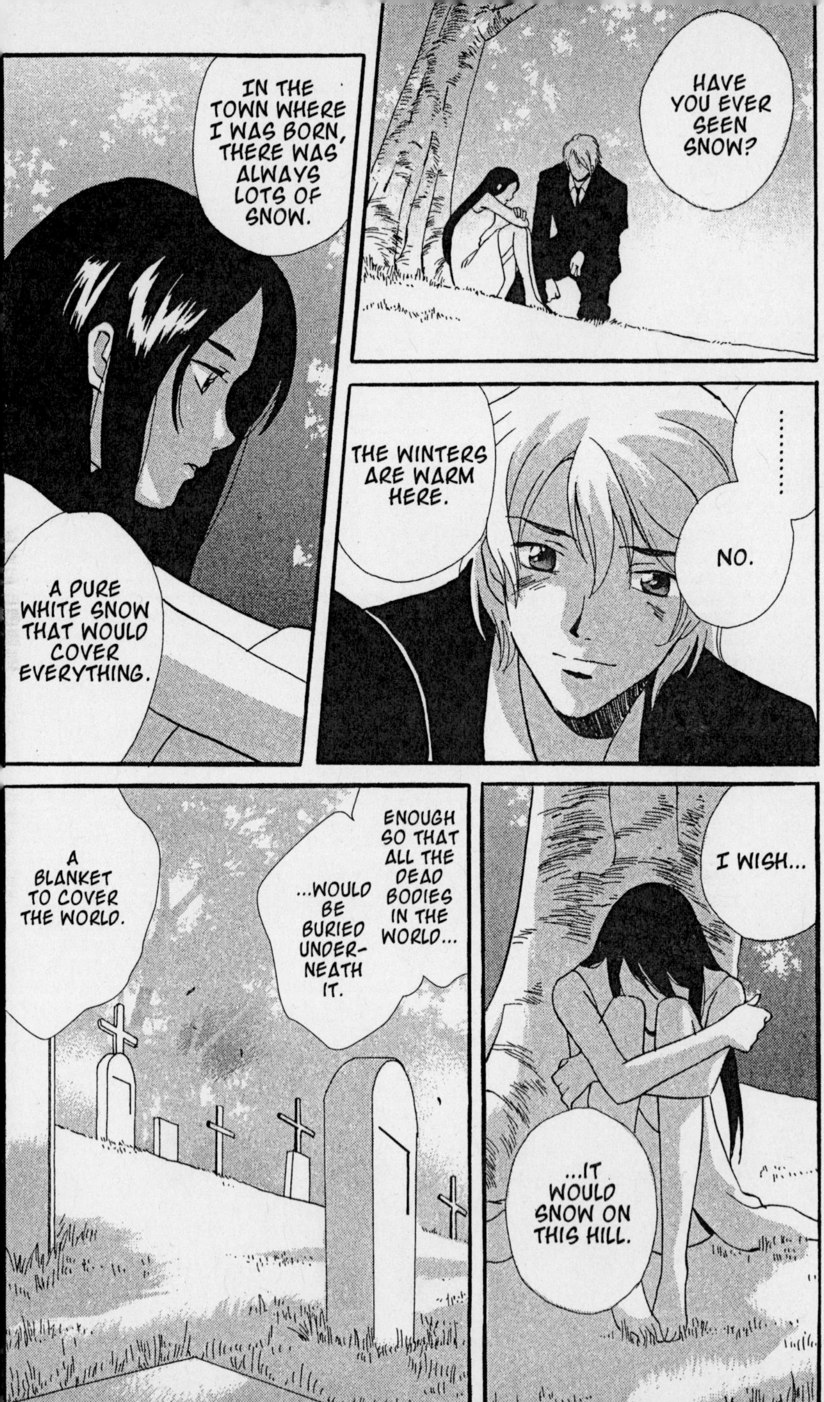
HAVE YOU EVER SEEN SNOW?
......
NO.
THE WINTERS ARE WARM HERE.
IN THE TOWN WHERE I WAS BORN, THERE WAS ALWAYS LOTS OF SNOW.
A PURE WHITE SNOW THAT WOULD COVER EVERYTHING.
I WISH...
...IT WOULD SNOW ON THIS HILL.
ENOUGH SO THAT ALL THE DEAD BODIES IN THE WORLD...
...WOULD BE BURIED UNDER-NEATH IT.
A BLANKET TO COVER THE WORLD.

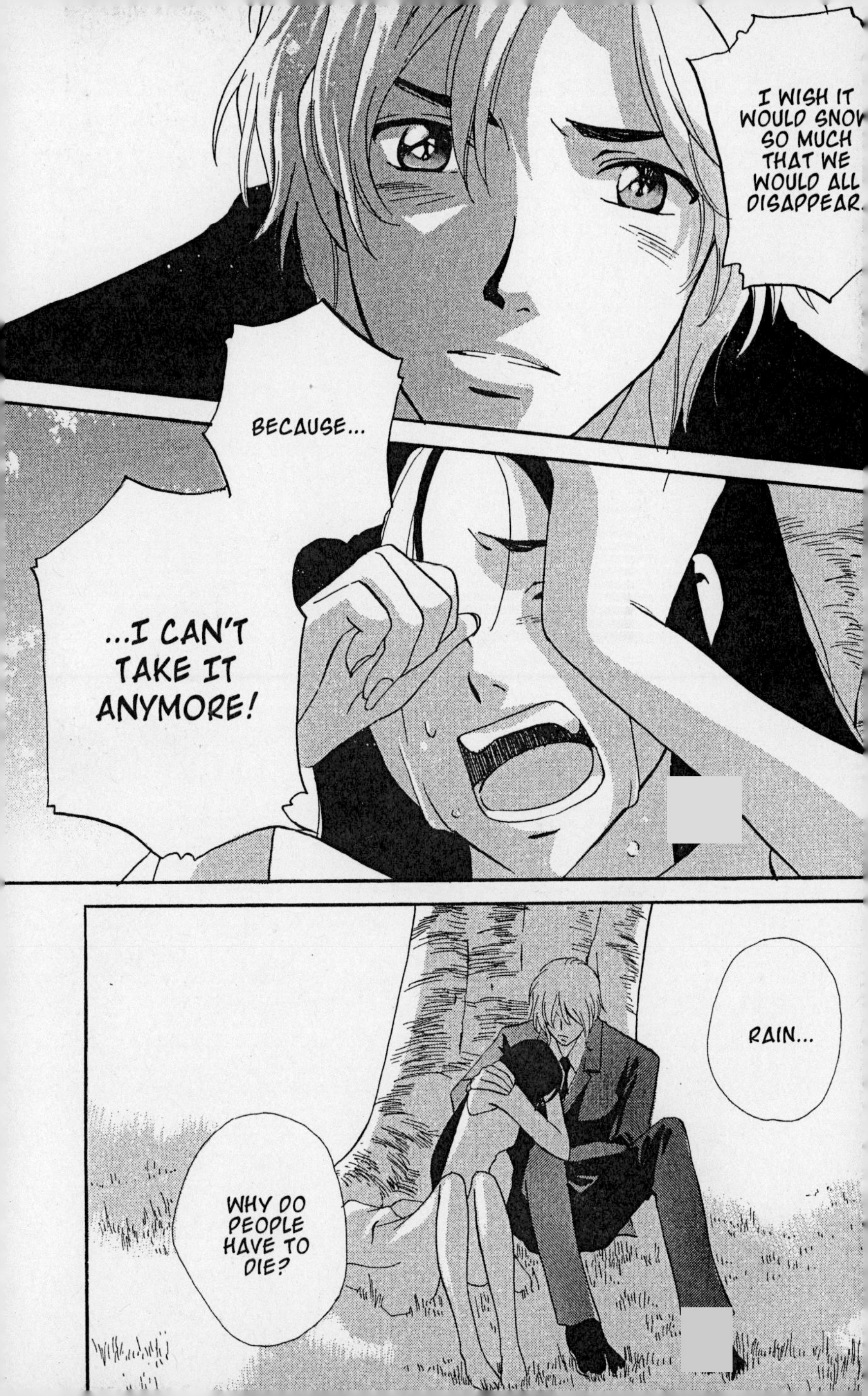
I WISH IT WOULD SNOW SO MUCH THAT WE WOULD ALL DISAPPEAR.
BECAUSE...
...I CAN'T TAKE IT ANYMORE!
RAIN...
WHY DO PEOPLE HAVE TO DIE?

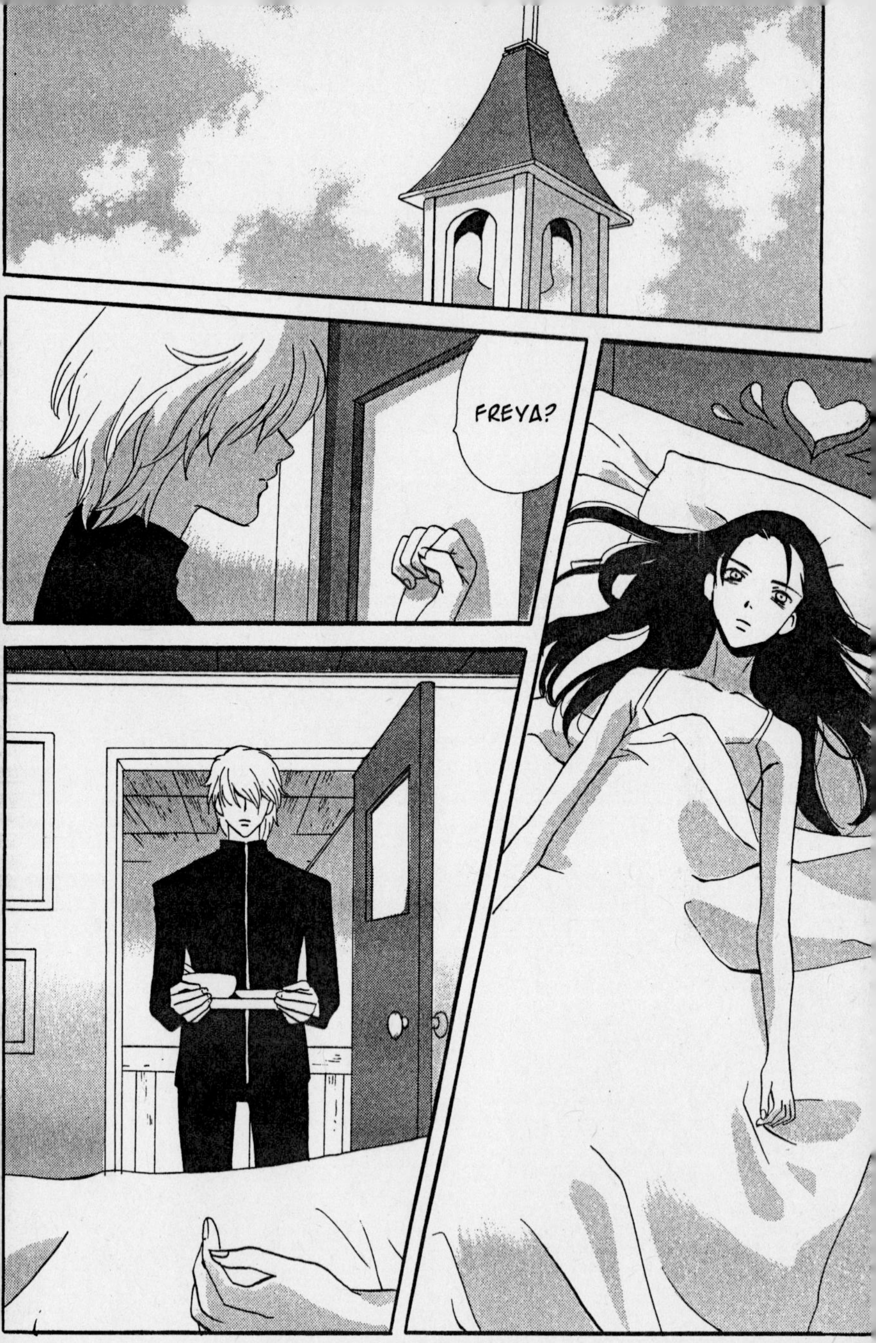
FREYA?

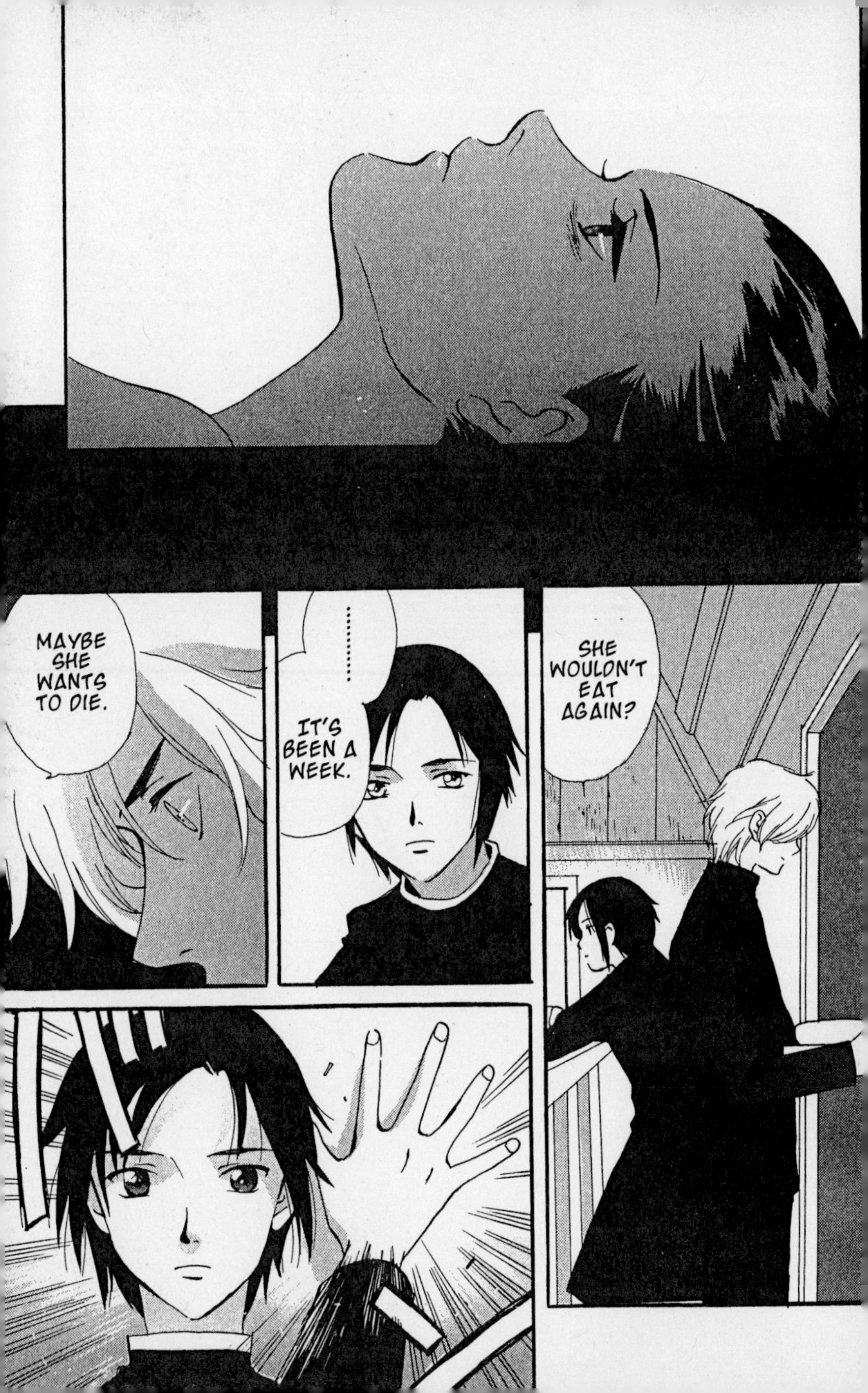
SHE WOULDN'T EAT AGAIN?
......
IT'S BEEN A WEEK.
MAYBE SHE WANTS TO DIE.

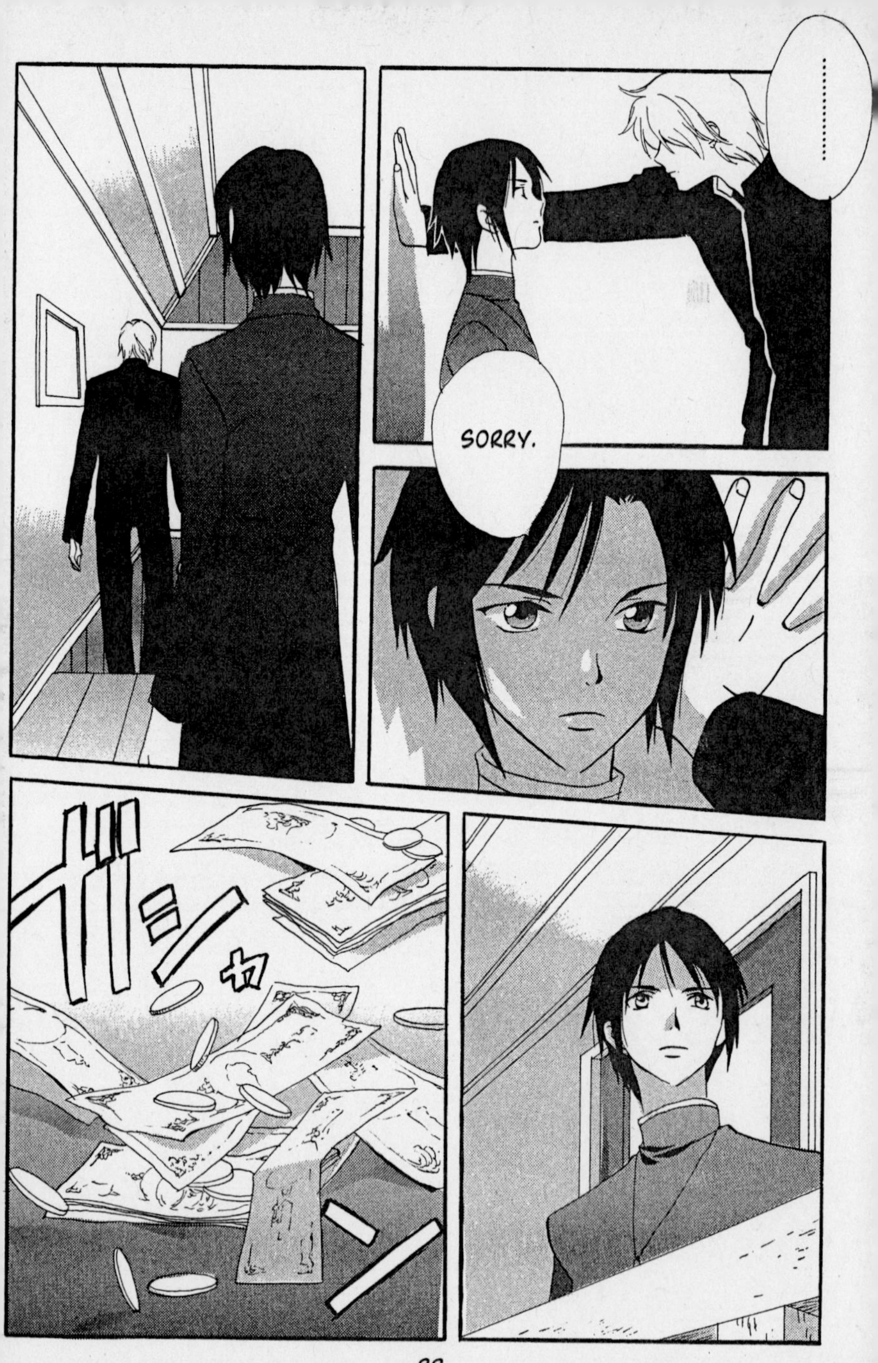
......
SORRY.

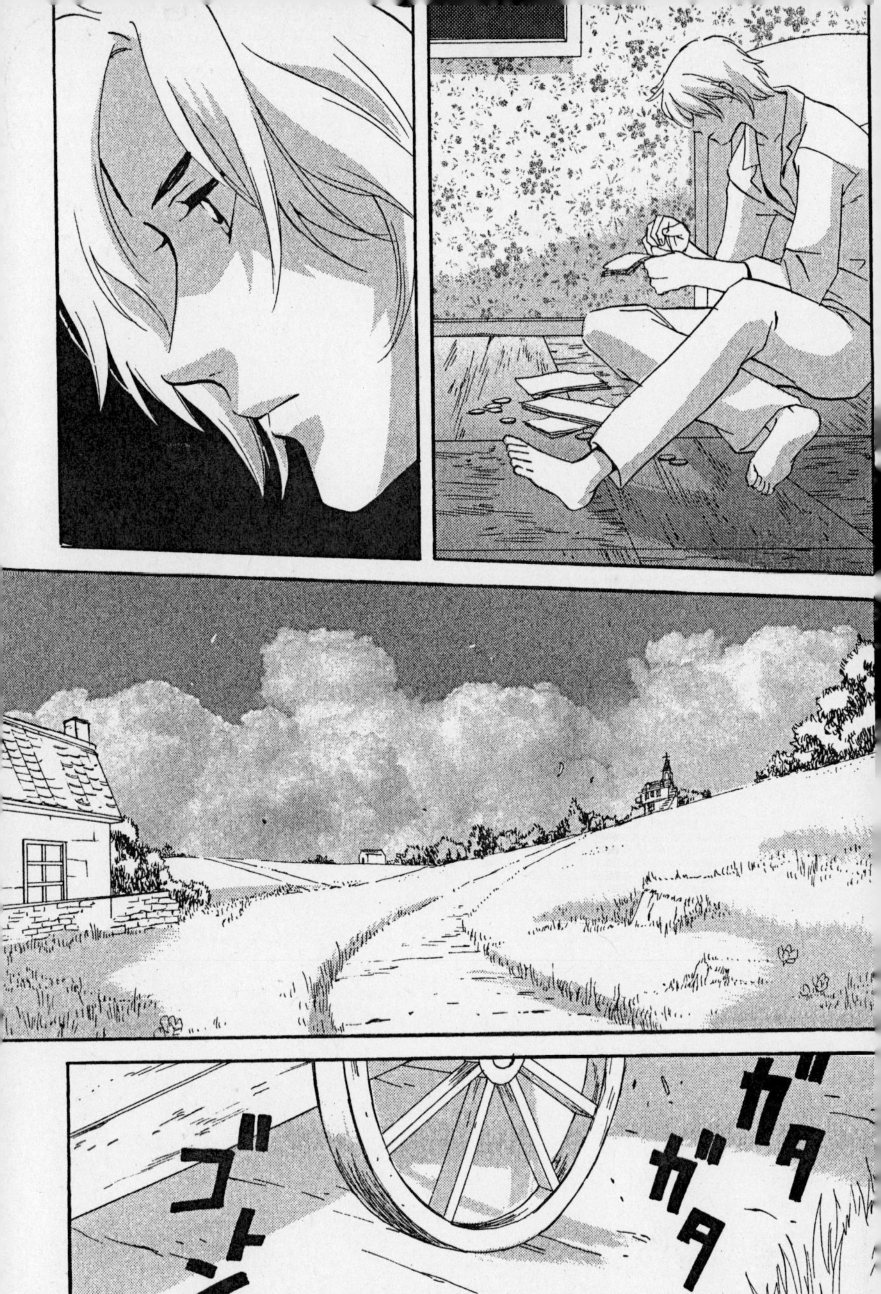
ガタ
ガタ
ゴトン

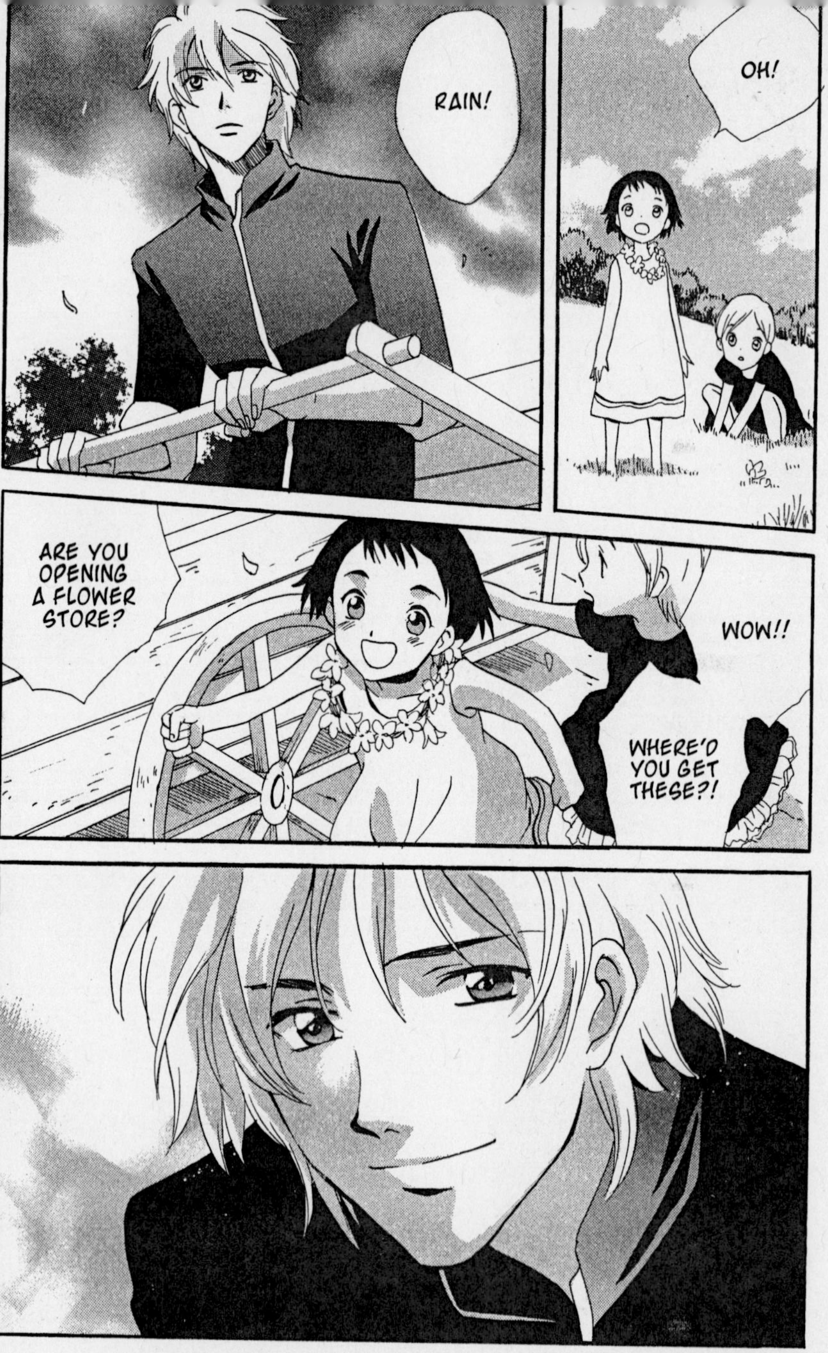
OH!
RAIN!
WOW!!
WHERE'D YOU GET THESE?!
ARE YOU OPENING A FLOWER STORE?

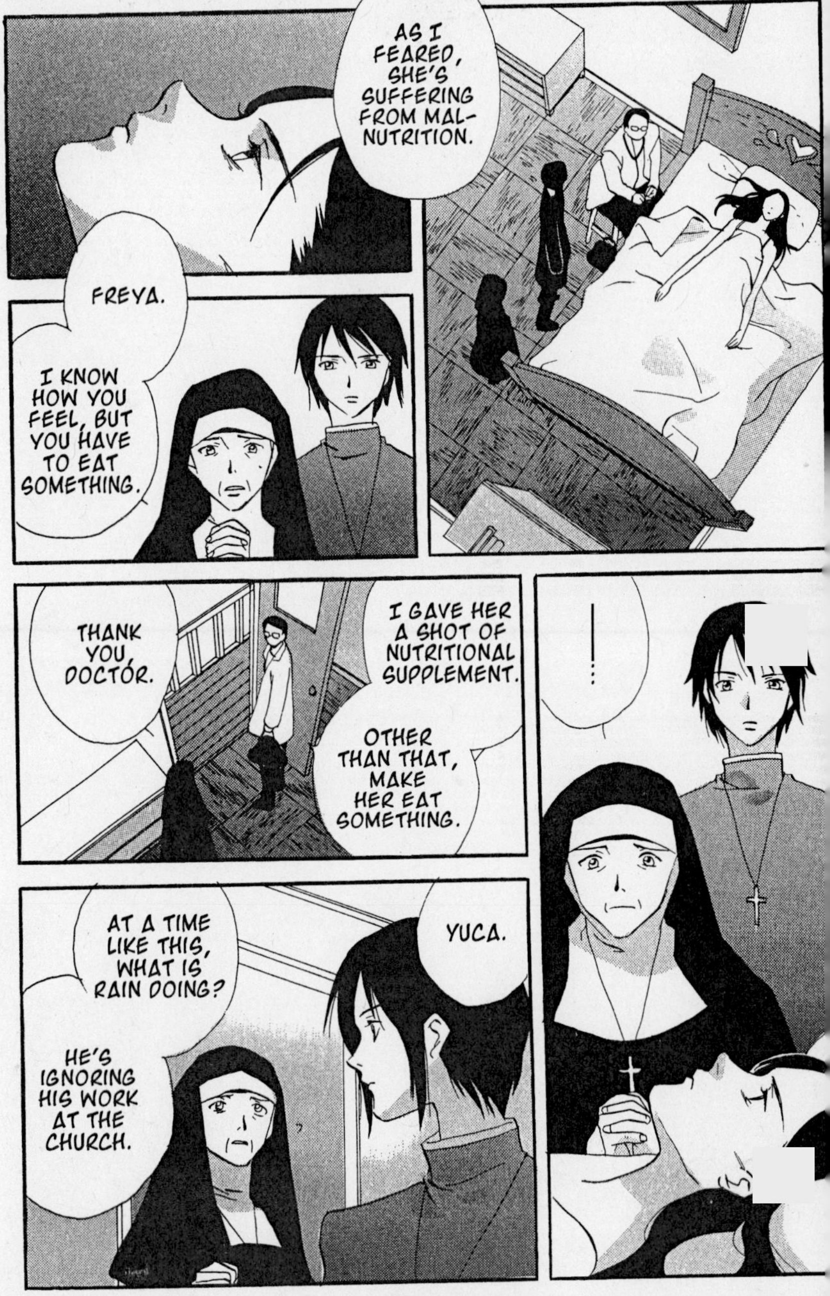
AS I FEARED, SHE'S SUFFERING FROM MAL-NUTRITION.
FREYA.
I KNOW HOW YOU FEEL, BUT YOU HAVE TO EAT SOMETHING.
......
I GAVE HER A SHOT OF NUTRITIONAL SUPPLEMENT.
OTHER THAN THAT, MAKE HER EAT SOMETHING.
THANK YOU, DOCTOR.
YUCA.
AT A TIME LIKE THIS, WHAT IS RAIN DOING?
HE'S IGNORING HIS WORK AT THE CHURCH.

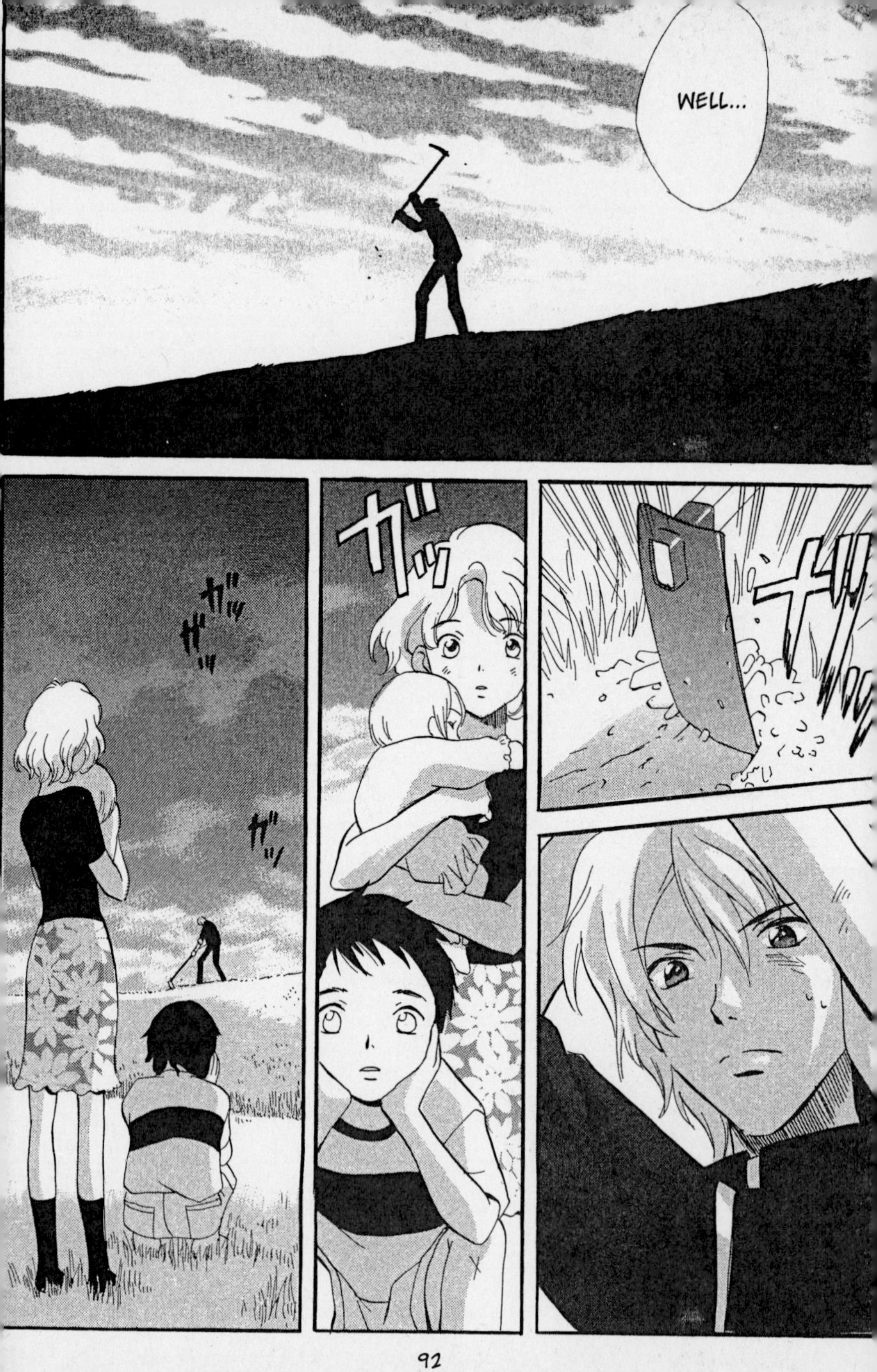
WELL...
ガッ
ザッ

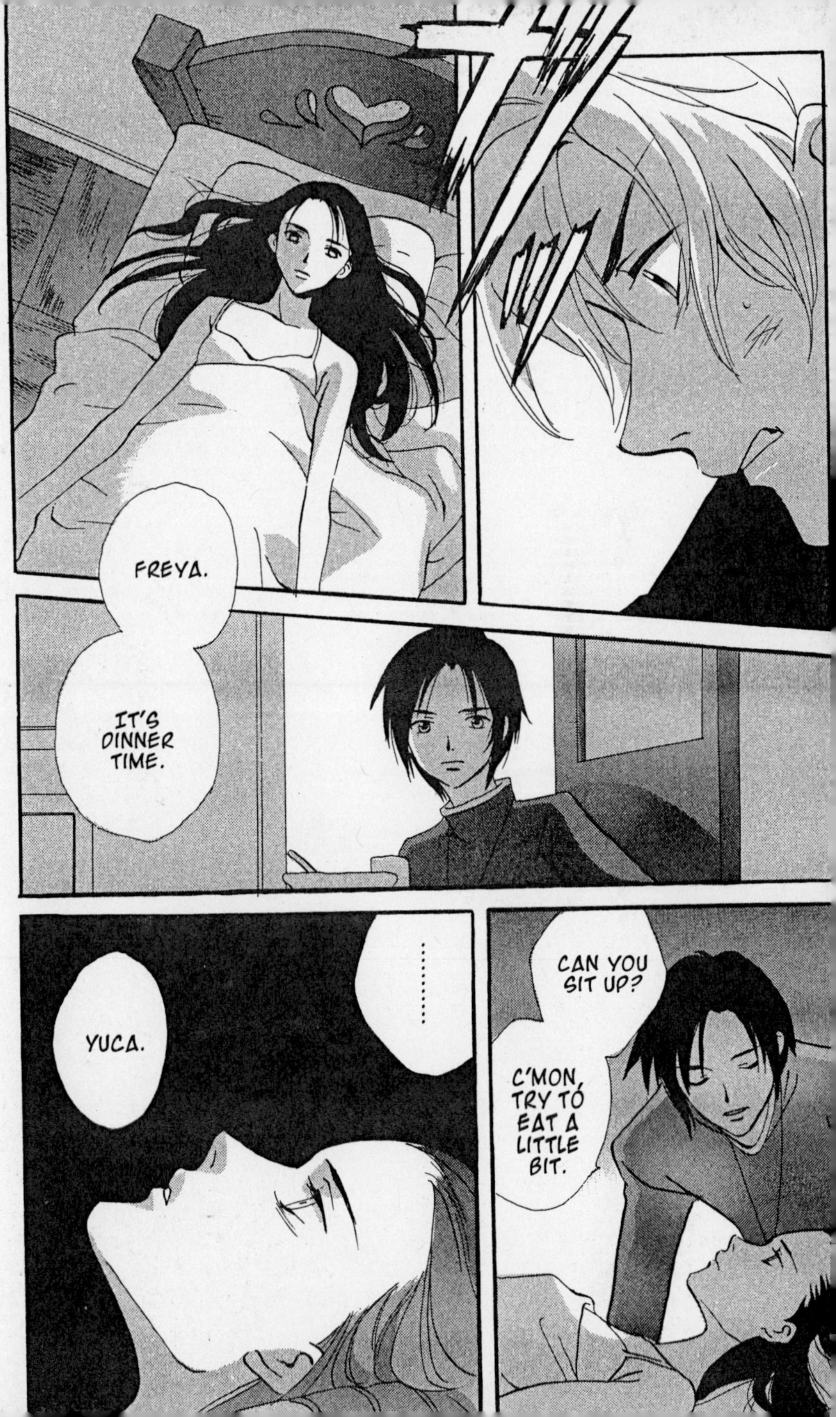
FREYA.
IT'S DINNER TIME.
CAN YOU SIT UP?
C'MON, TRY TO EAT A LITTLE BIT.
......
YUCA.

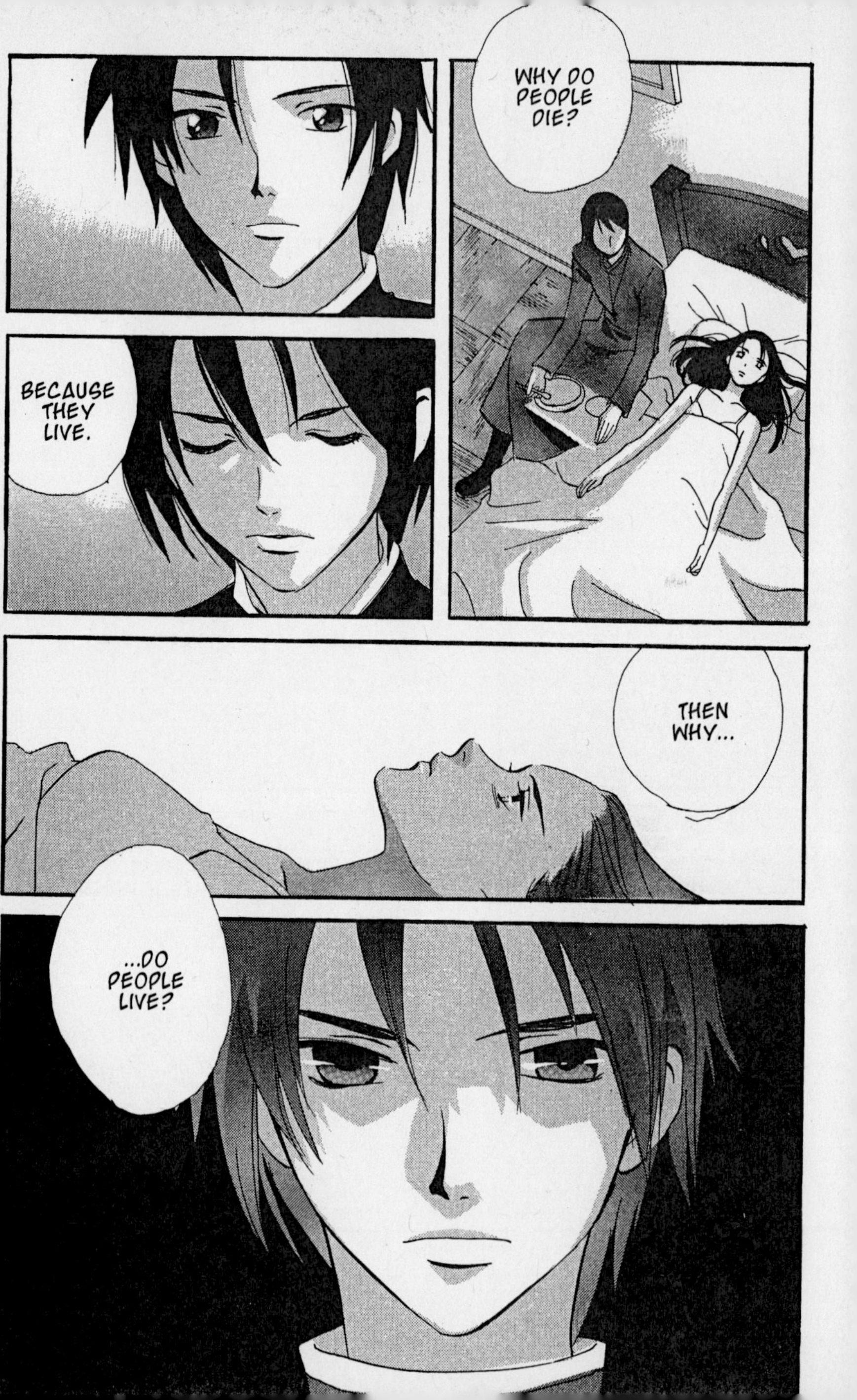
WHY DO PEOPLE DIE?
BECAUSE THEY LIVE.
THEN WHY...
...DO PEOPLE LIVE?

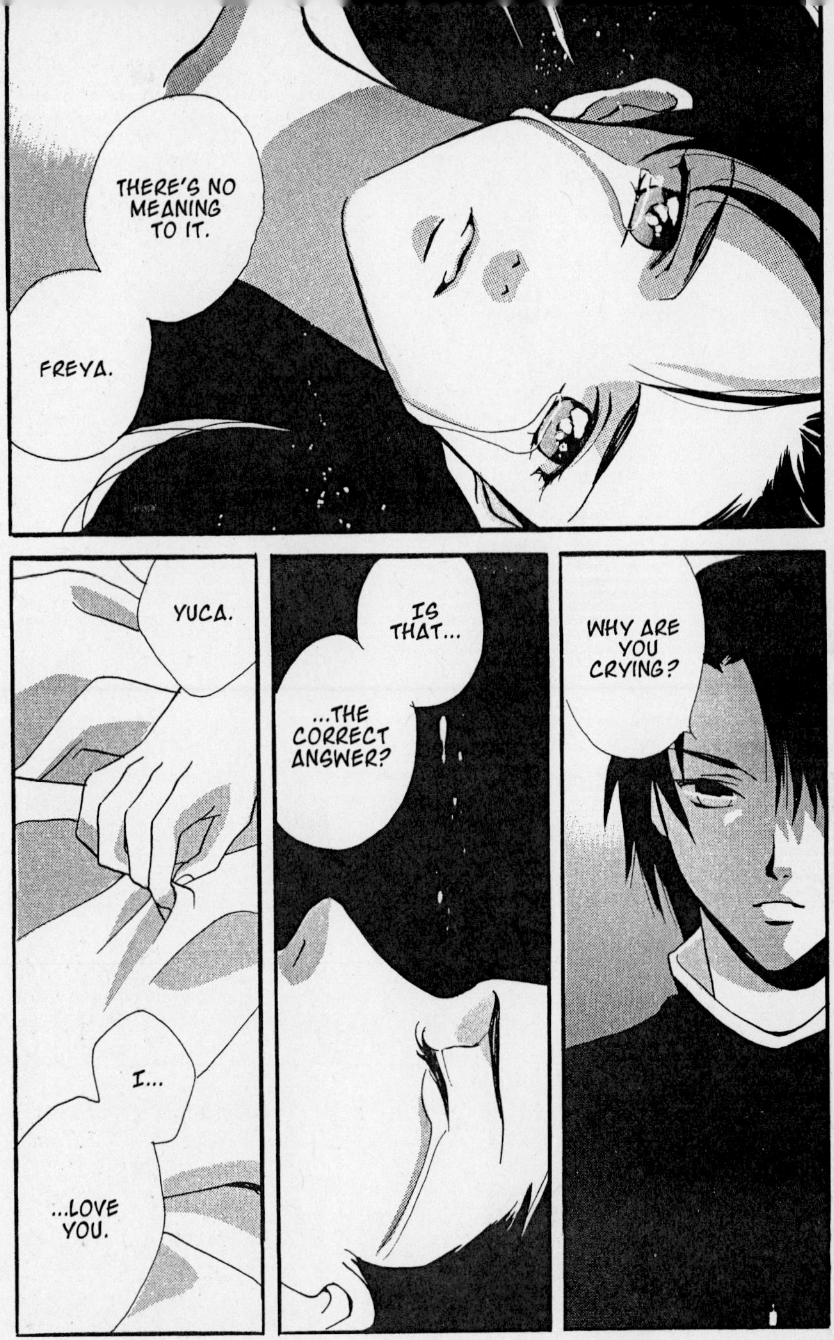
THERE'S NO MEANING TO IT.
FREYA.
WHY ARE YOU CRYING?
IS THAT...
...THE CORRECT ANSWER?
YUCA.
I...
...LOVE YOU.

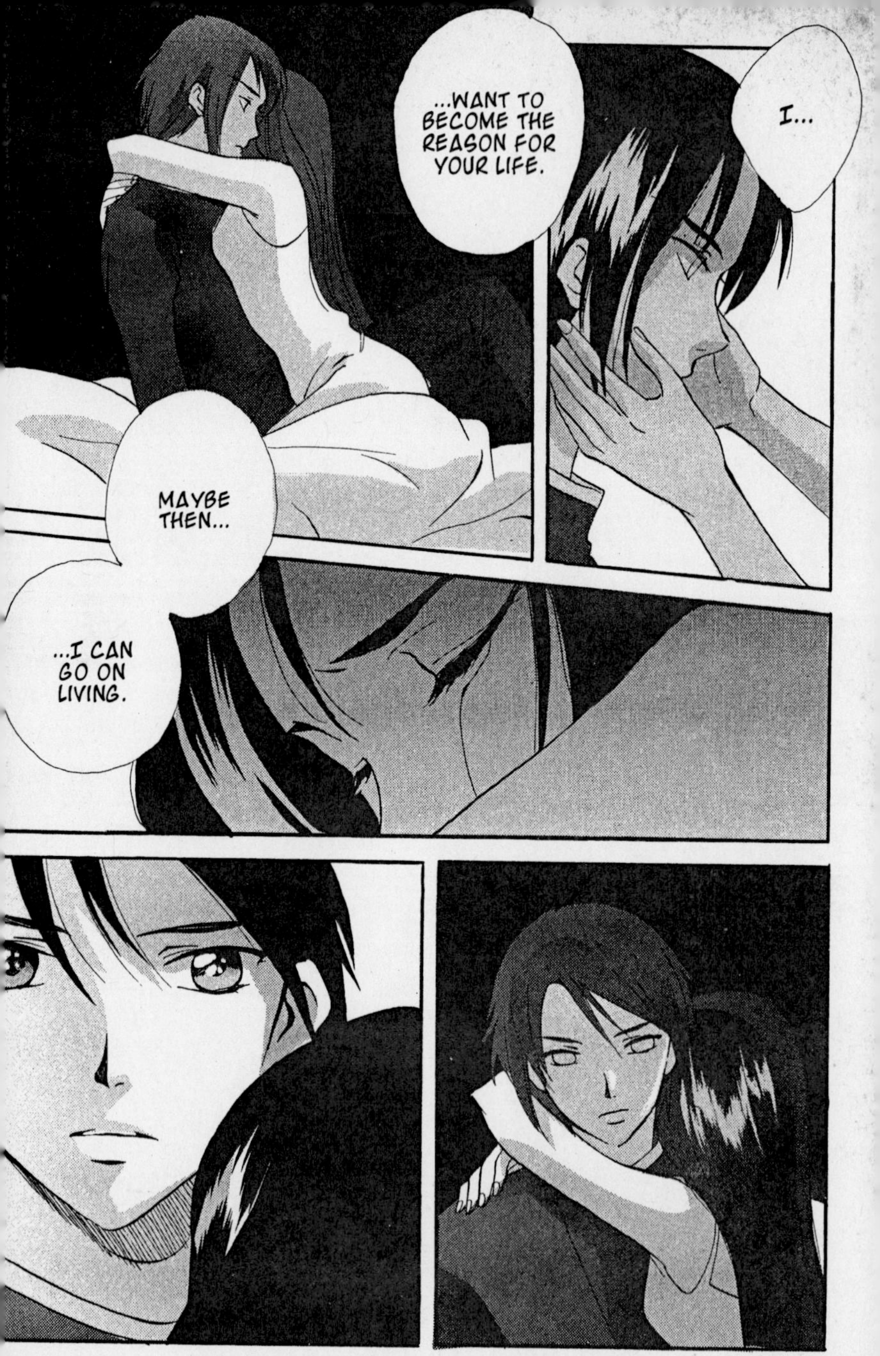
I...
...WANT TO BECOME THE REASON FOR YOUR LIFE.
MAYBE THEN...
...I CAN GO ON LIVING.

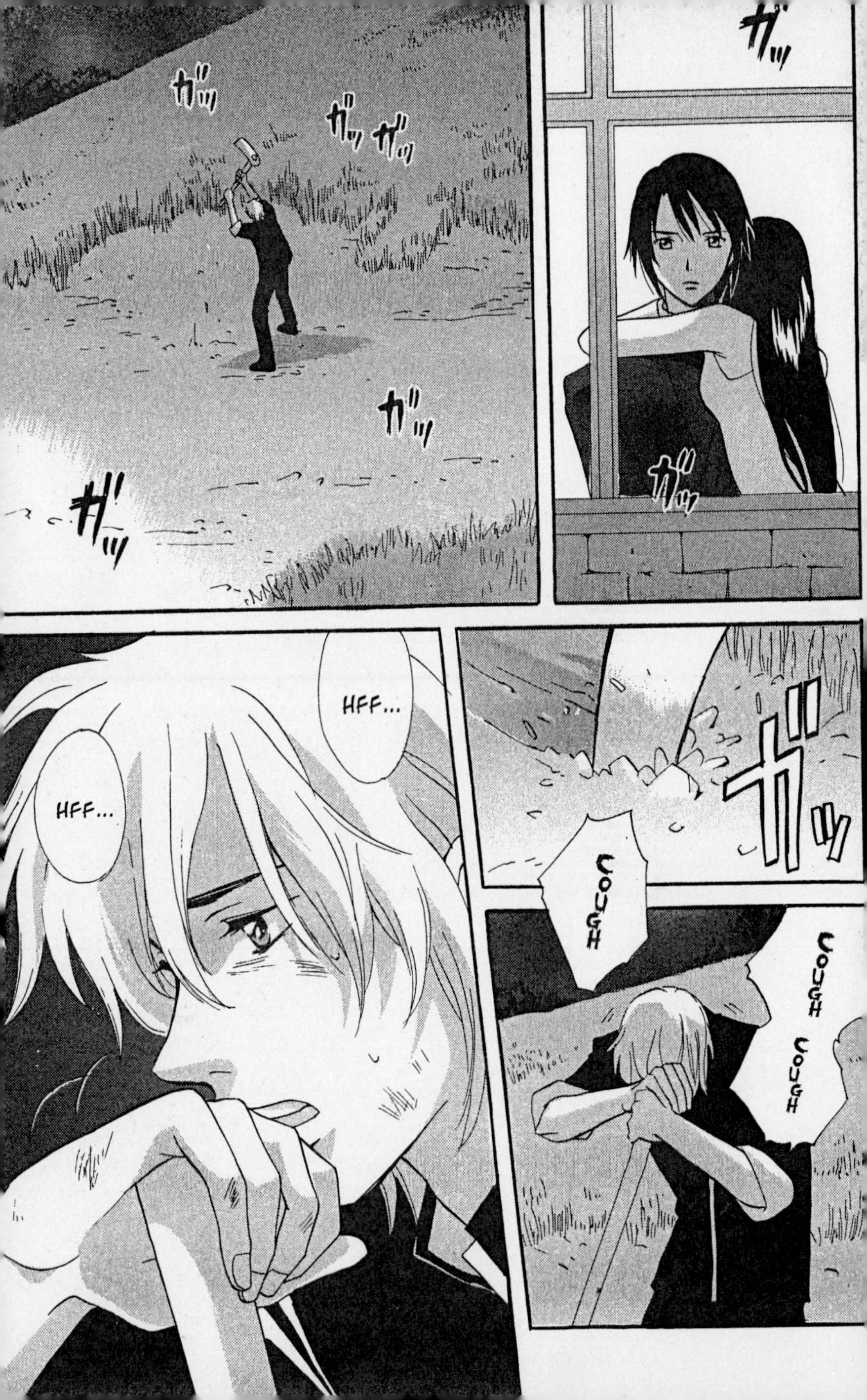
ガッ
ガッ
ガッ
ガッ
ガッ
ガッ
ガッ
ガッ
COUGH
COUGH
COUGH
HFF...
HFF...

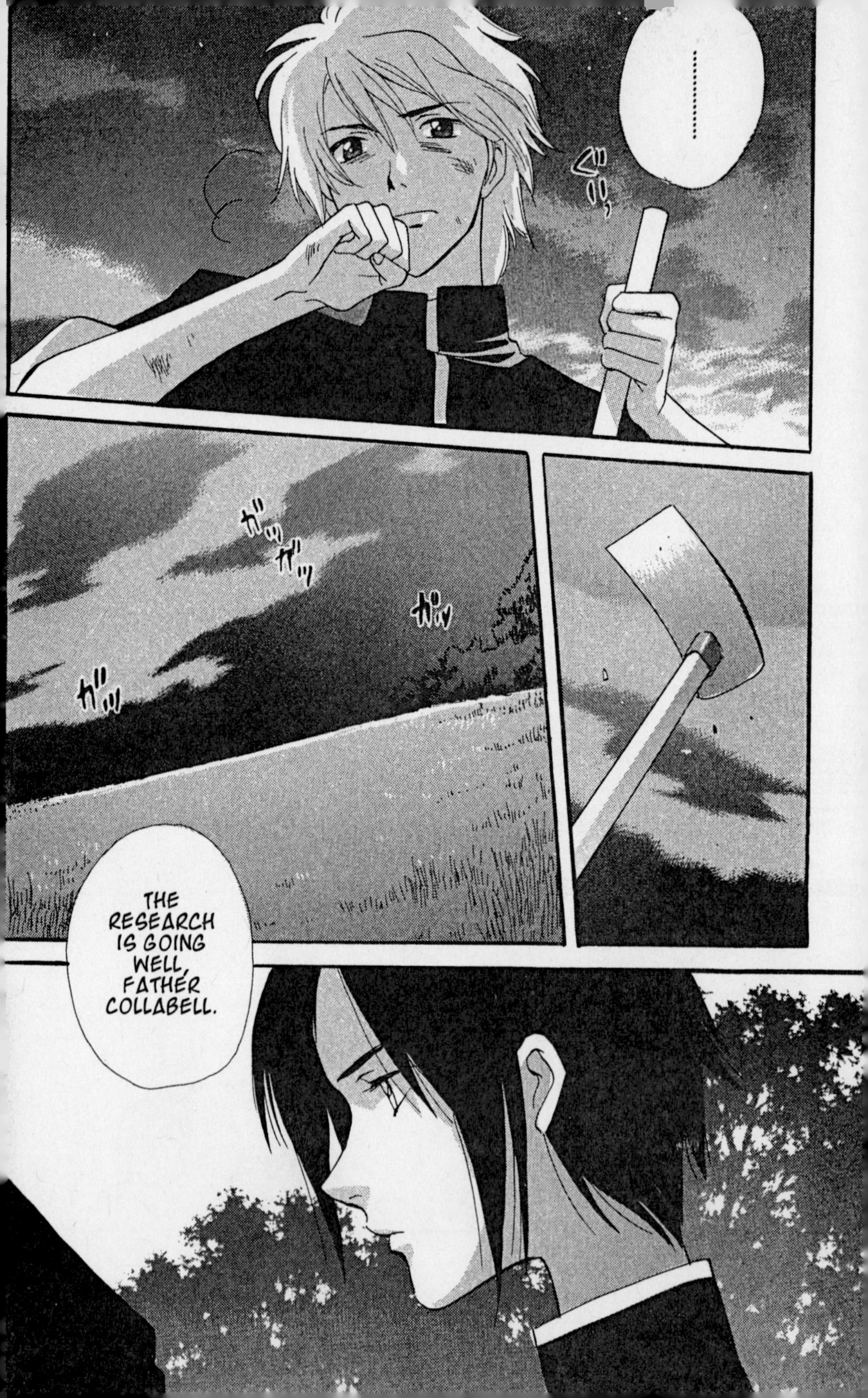
……
ガッ
ガッ
ガッ
ガッ
THE RESEARCH IS GOING WELL, FATHER COLLABELL.

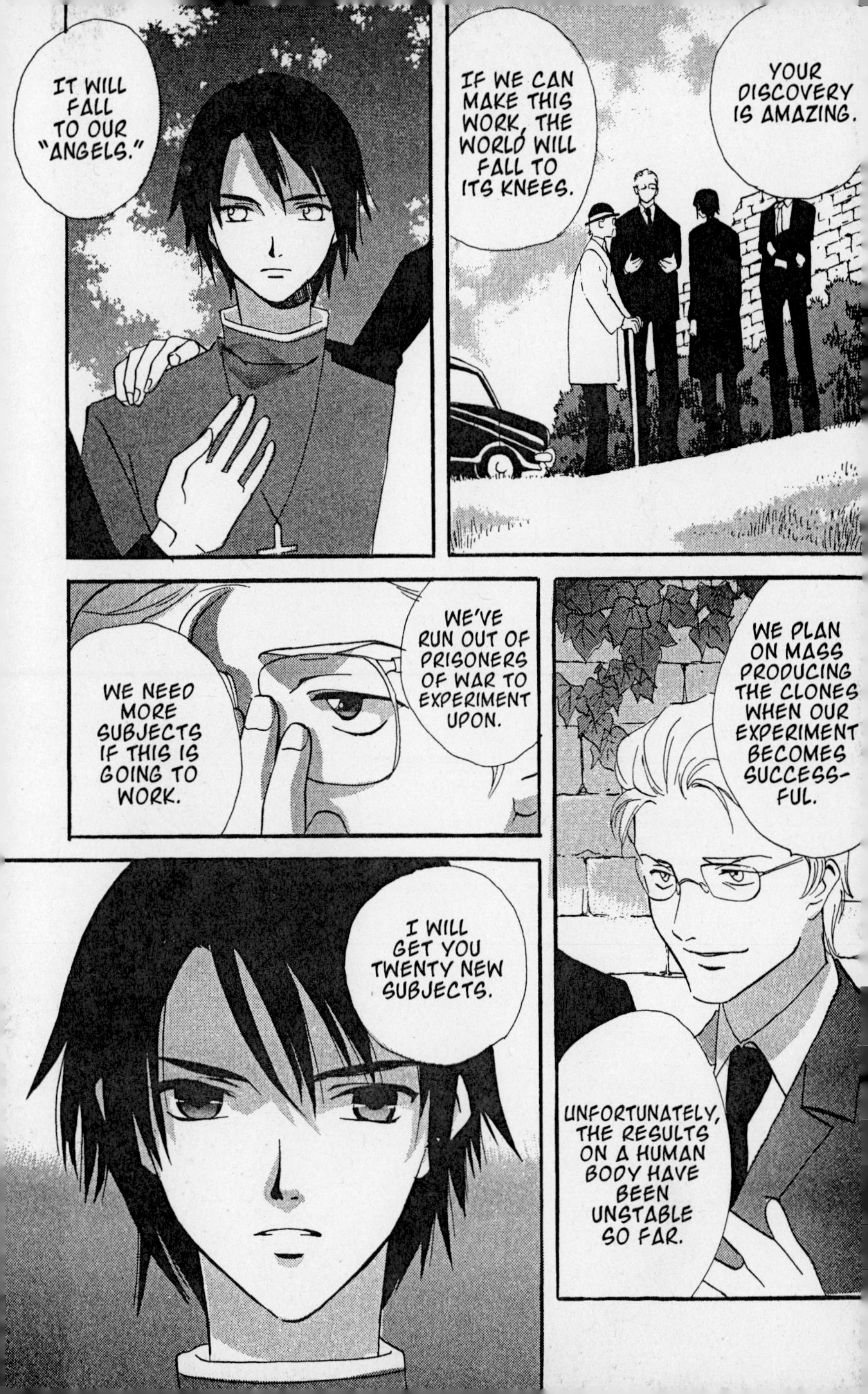
YOUR DISCOVERY IS AMAZING.
IF WE CAN MAKE THIS WORK, THE WORLD WILL FALL TO ITS KNEES.
IT WILL FALL TO OUR "ANGELS."
WE PLAN ON MASS PRODUCING THE CLONES WHEN OUR EXPERIMENT BECOMES SUCCESS-FUL.
UNFORTUNATELY, THE RESULTS ON A HUMAN BODY HAVE BEEN UNSTABLE SO FAR.
WE'VE RUN OUT OF PRISONERS OF WAR TO EXPERIMENT UPON.
WE NEED MORE SUBJECTS IF THIS IS GOING TO WORK.
I WILL GET YOU TWENTY NEW SUBJECTS.

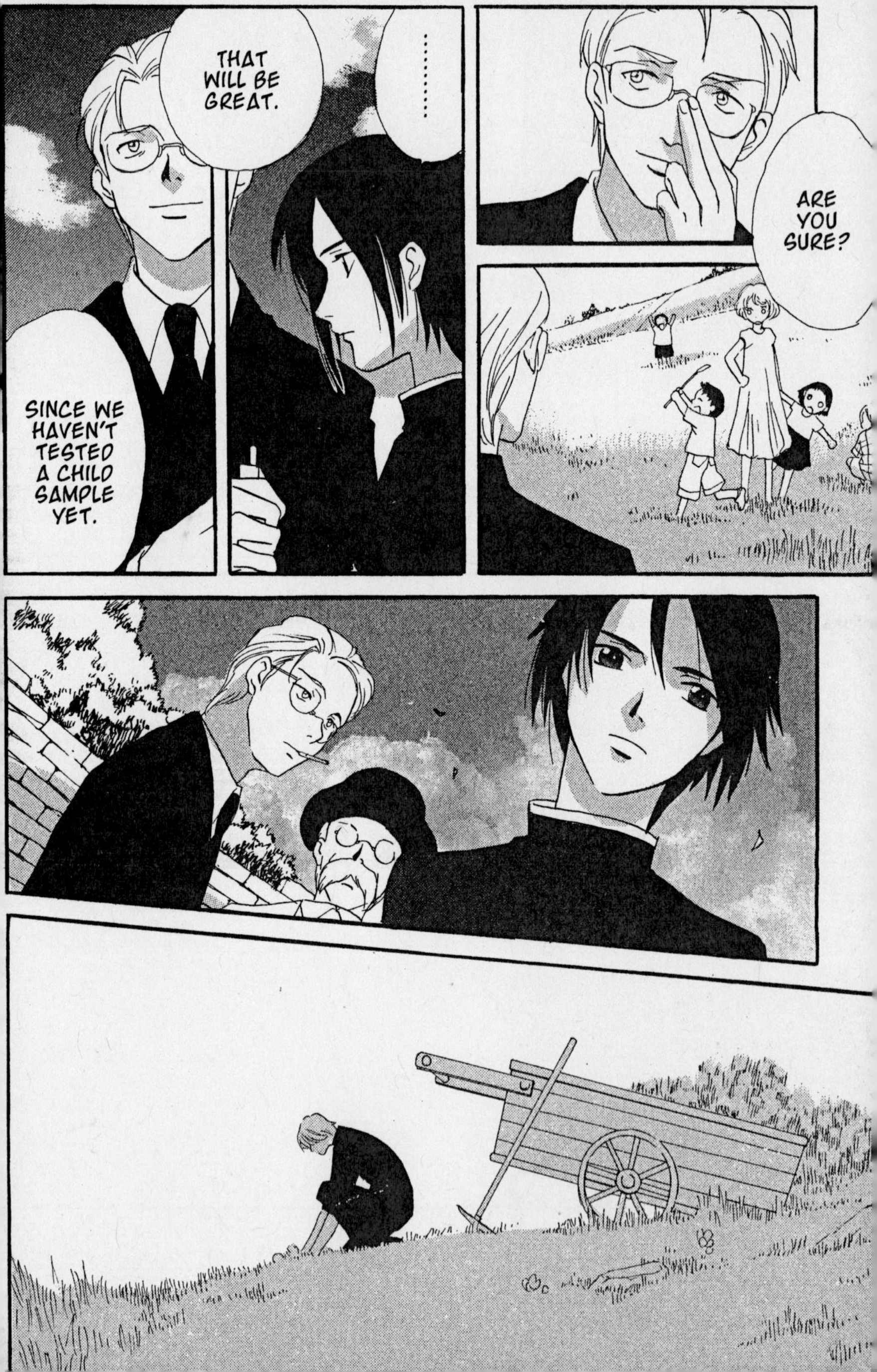
ARE YOU SURE?
......
THAT WILL BE GREAT.
SINCE WE HAVEN'T TESTED A CHILD SAMPLE YET.

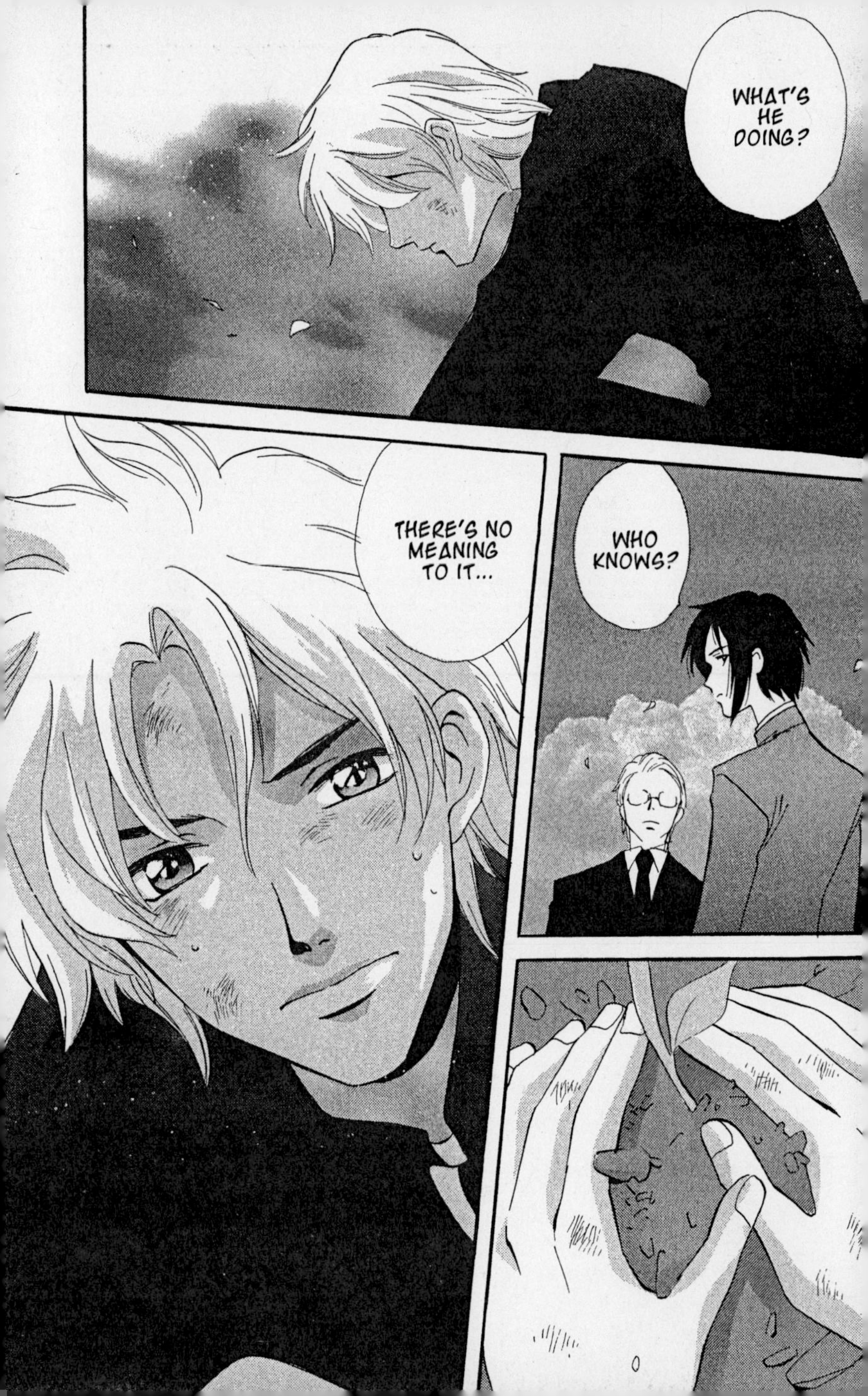
WHAT'S HE DOING?
WHO KNOWS?
THERE'S NO MEANING TO IT...

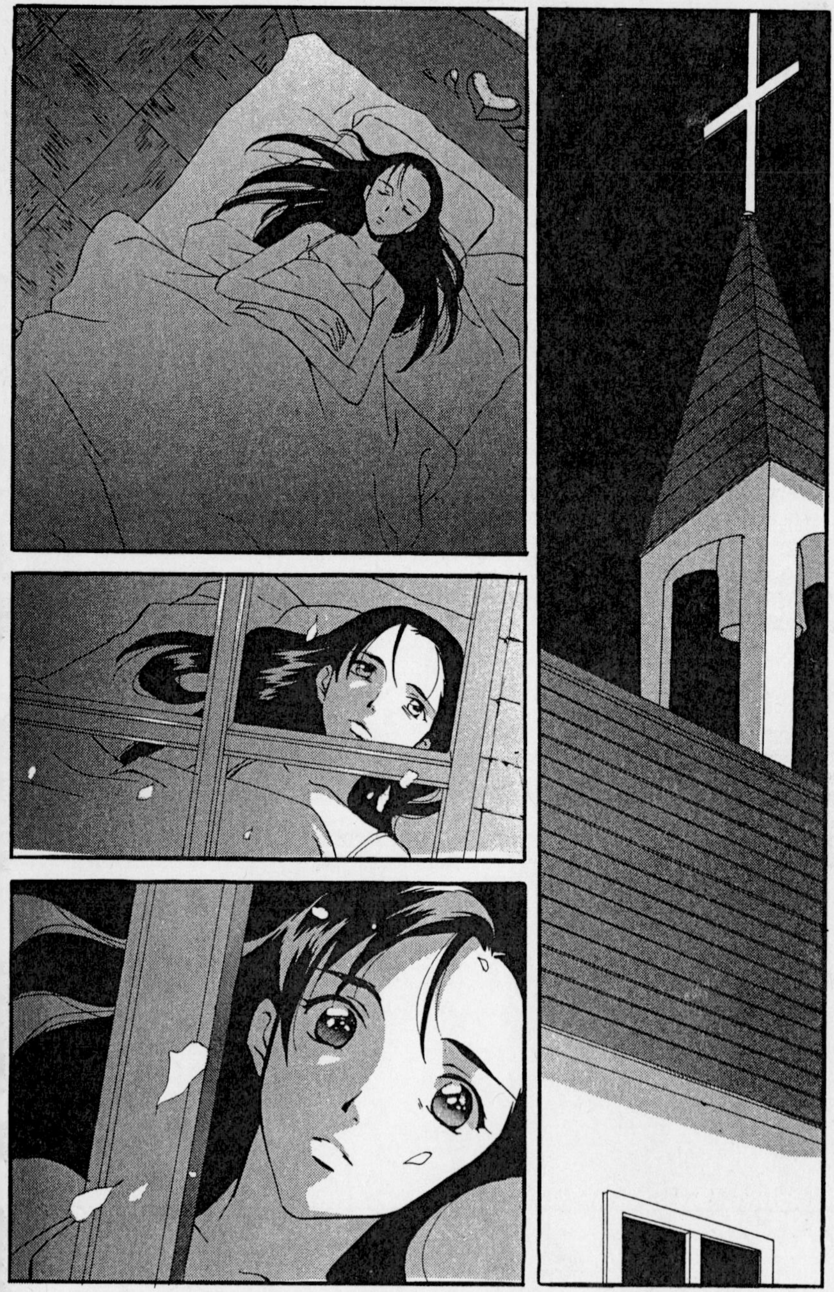

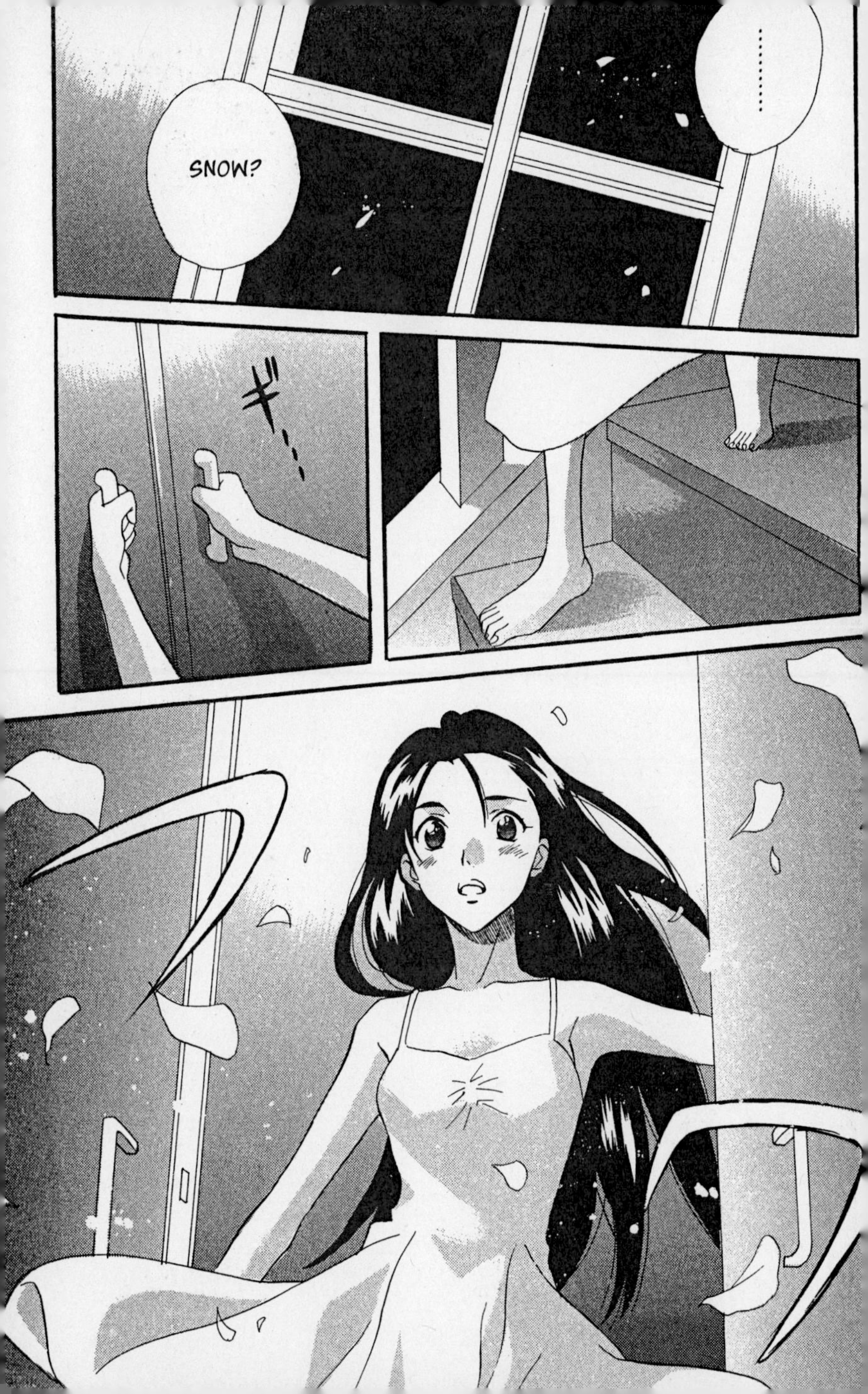
……
SNOW?
ギ…

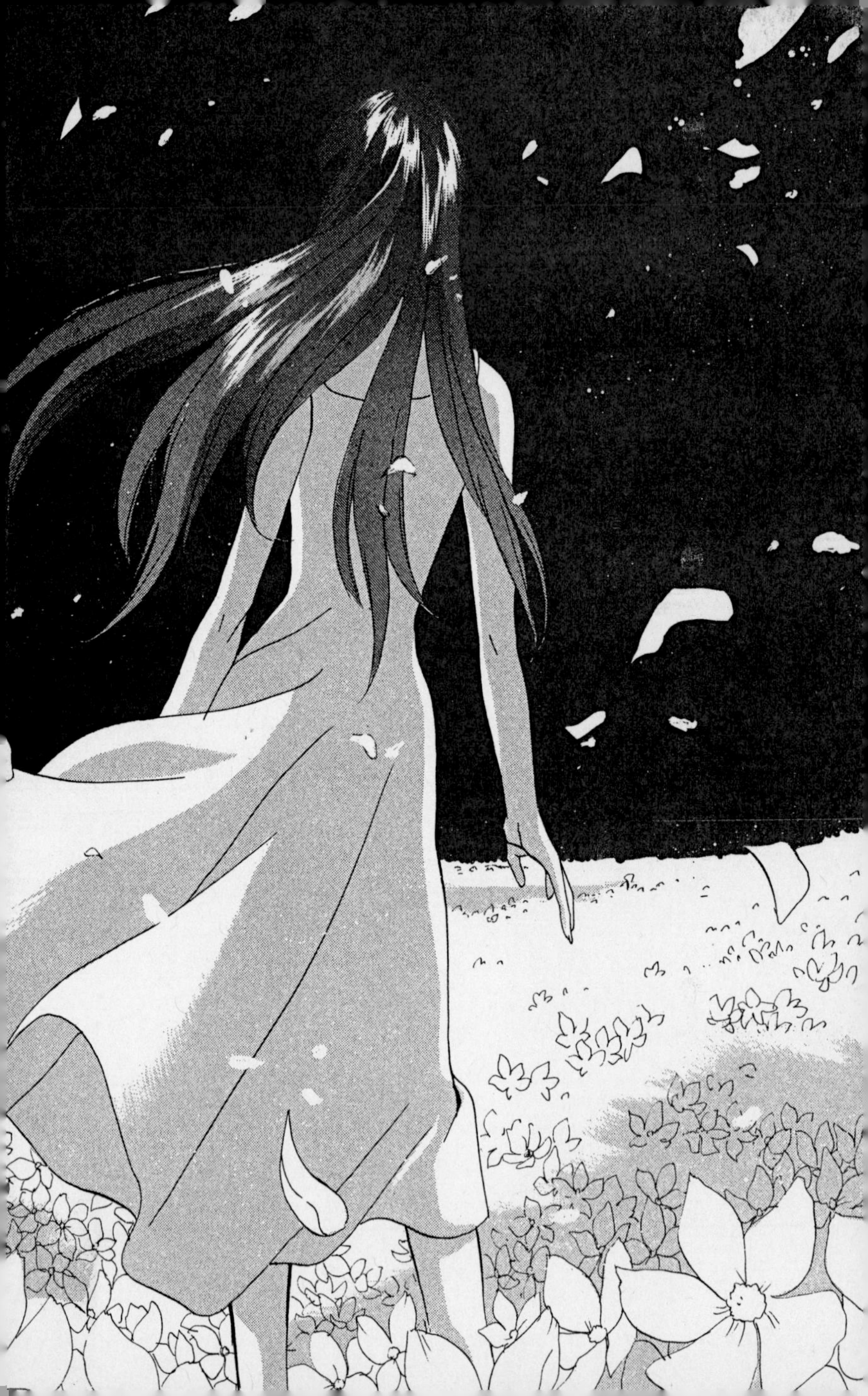

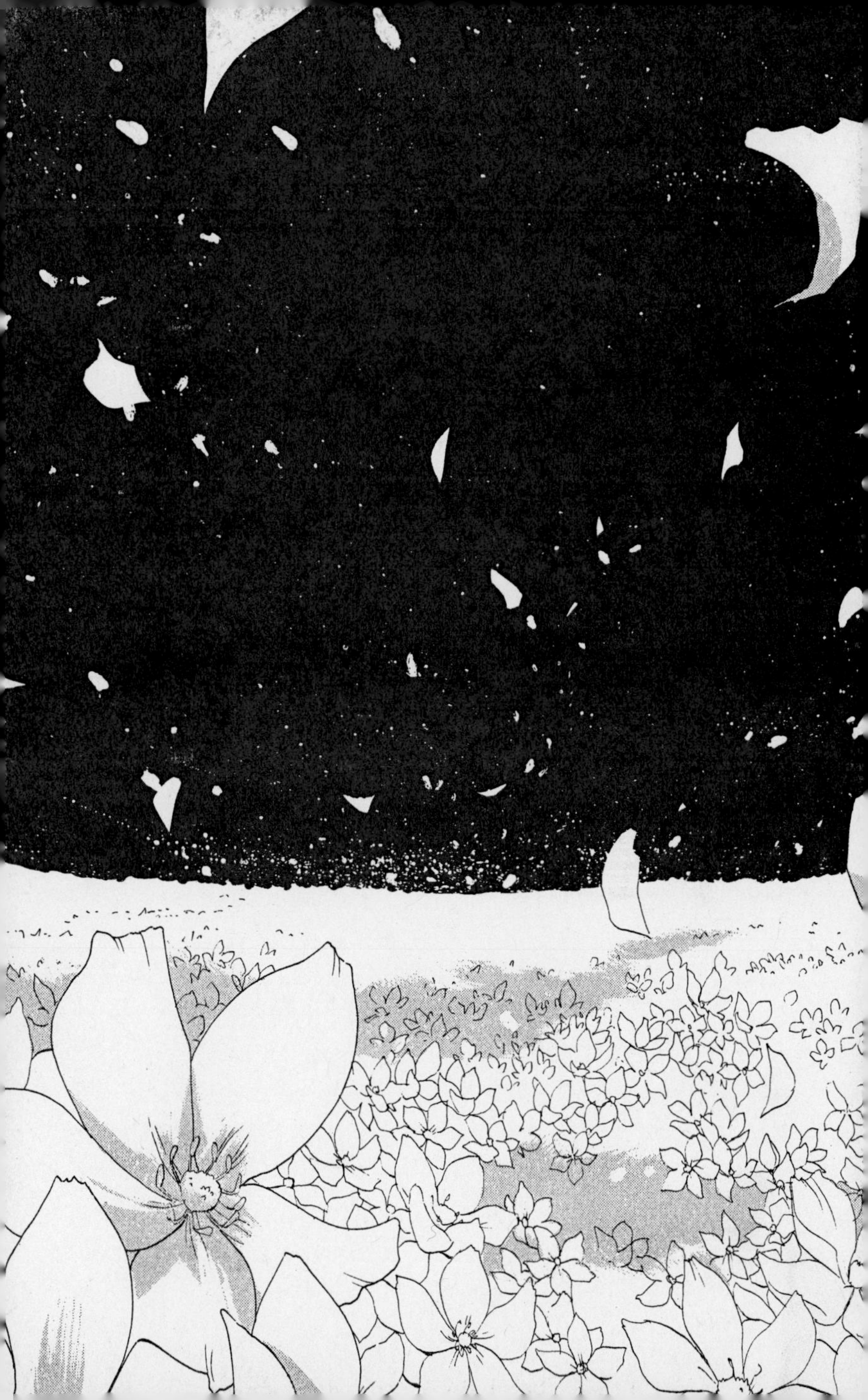

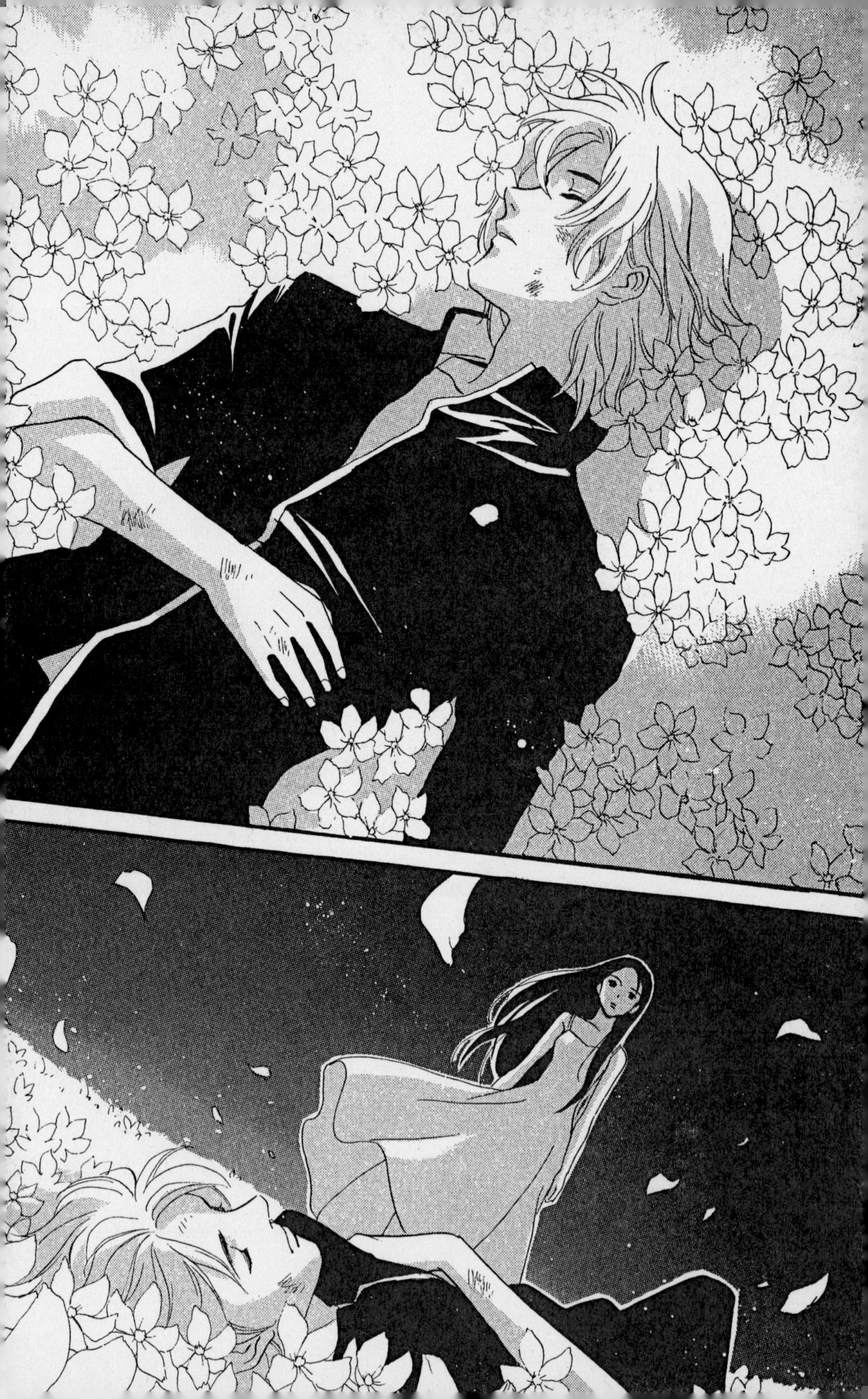

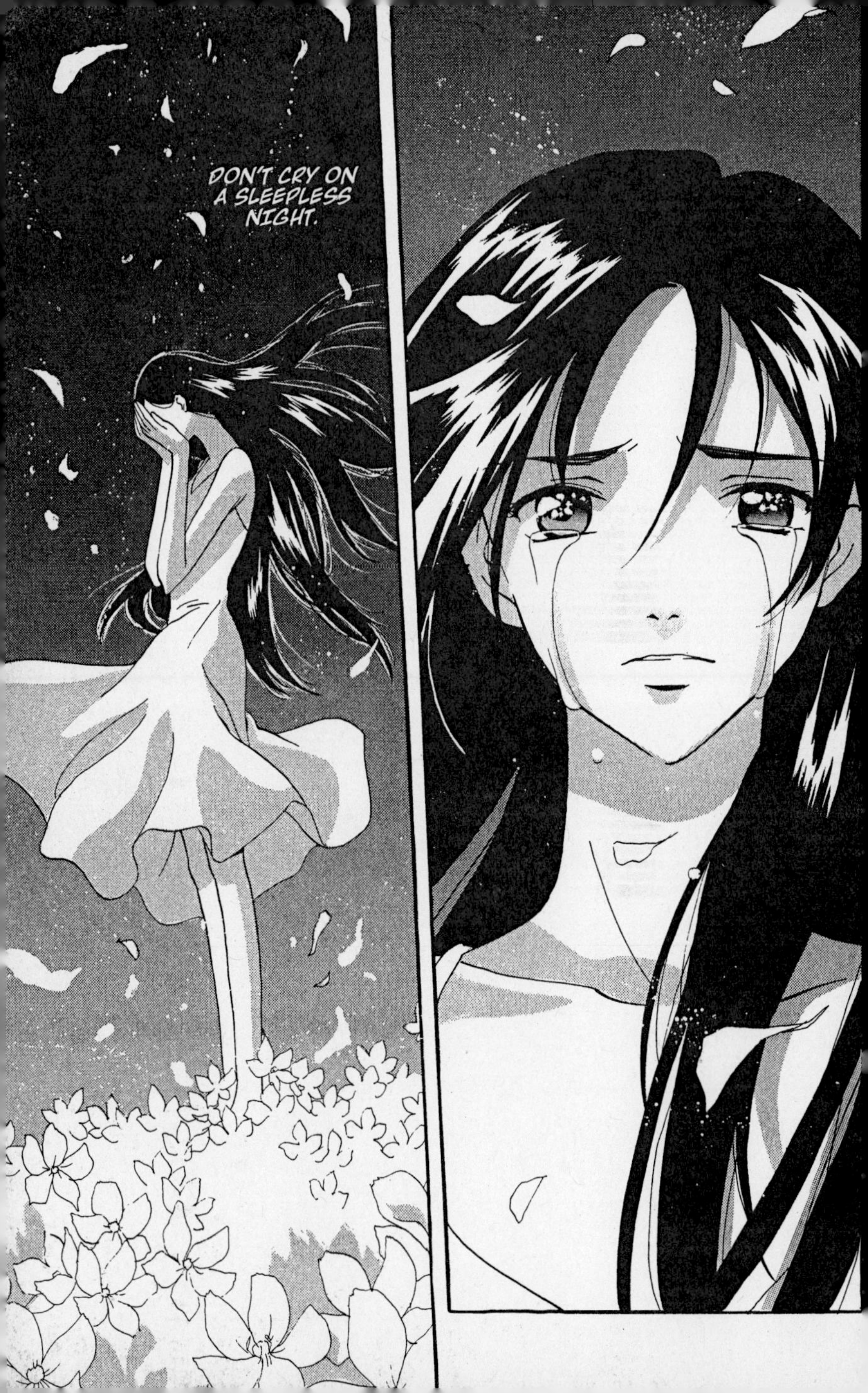
DON'T CRY ON A SLEEPLESS NIGHT.

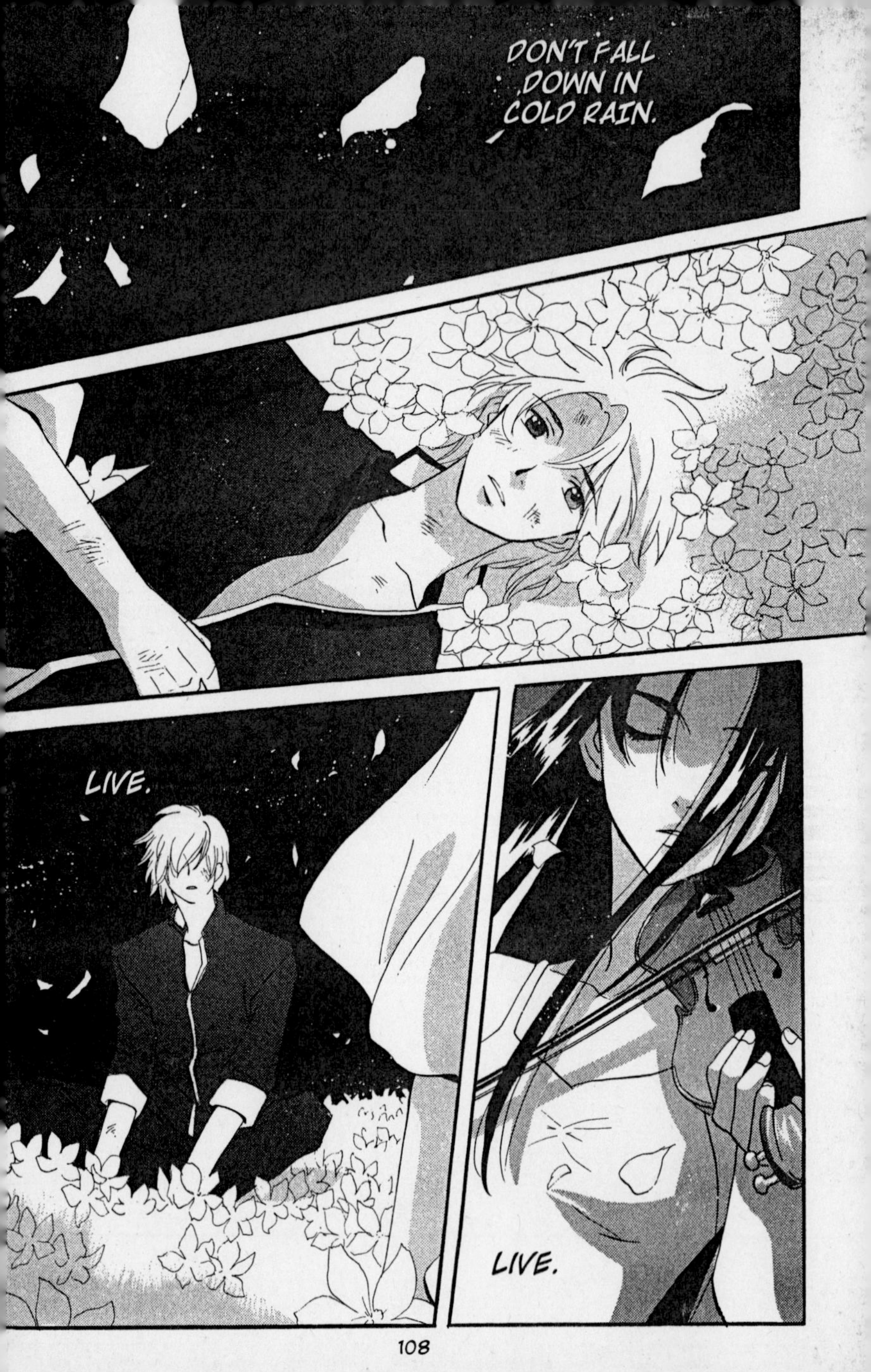
DON'T FALL DOWN IN COLD RAIN.
LIVE.
LIVE.

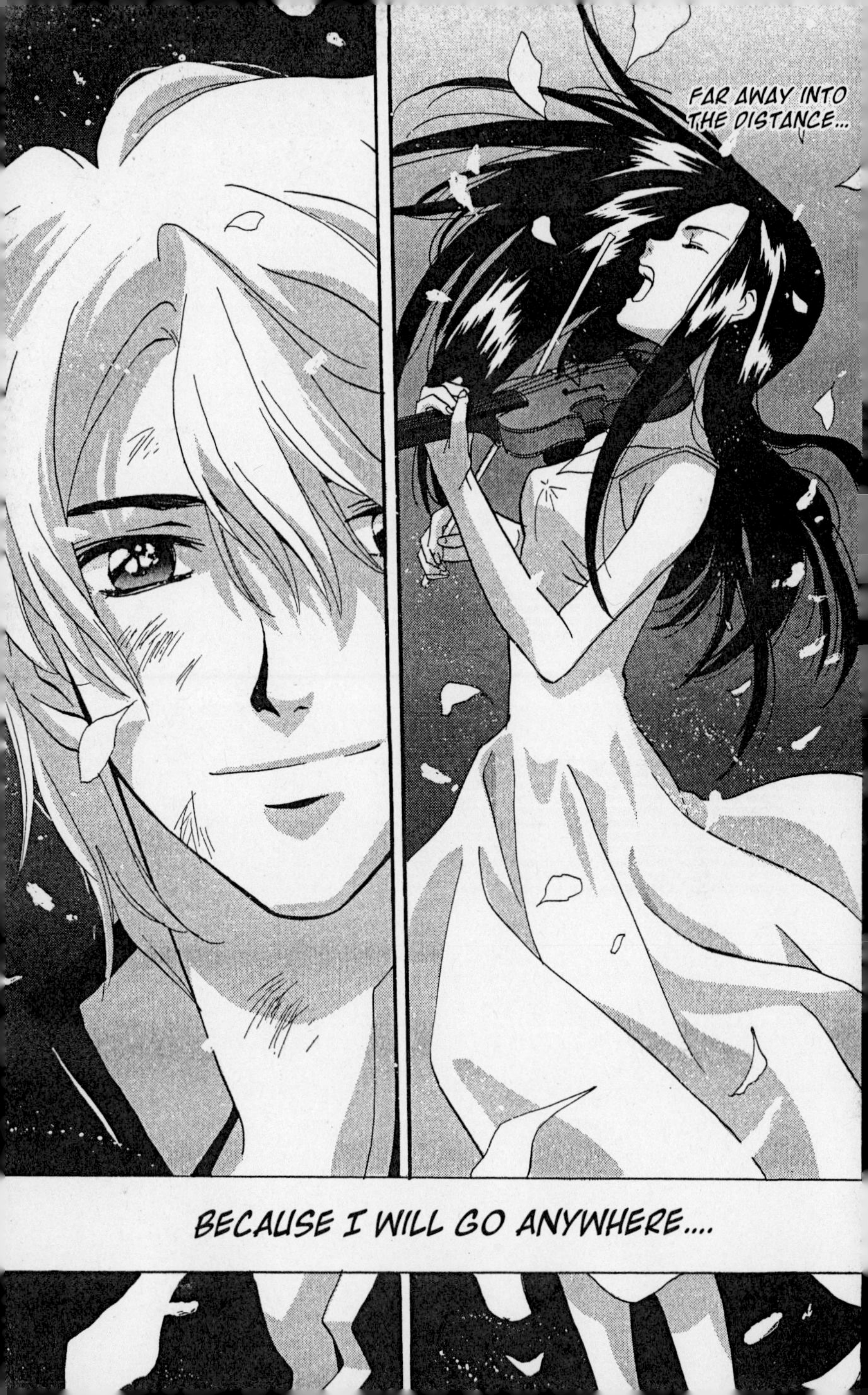
FAR AWAY INTO THE DISTANCE...
BECAUSE I WILL GO ANYWHERE....

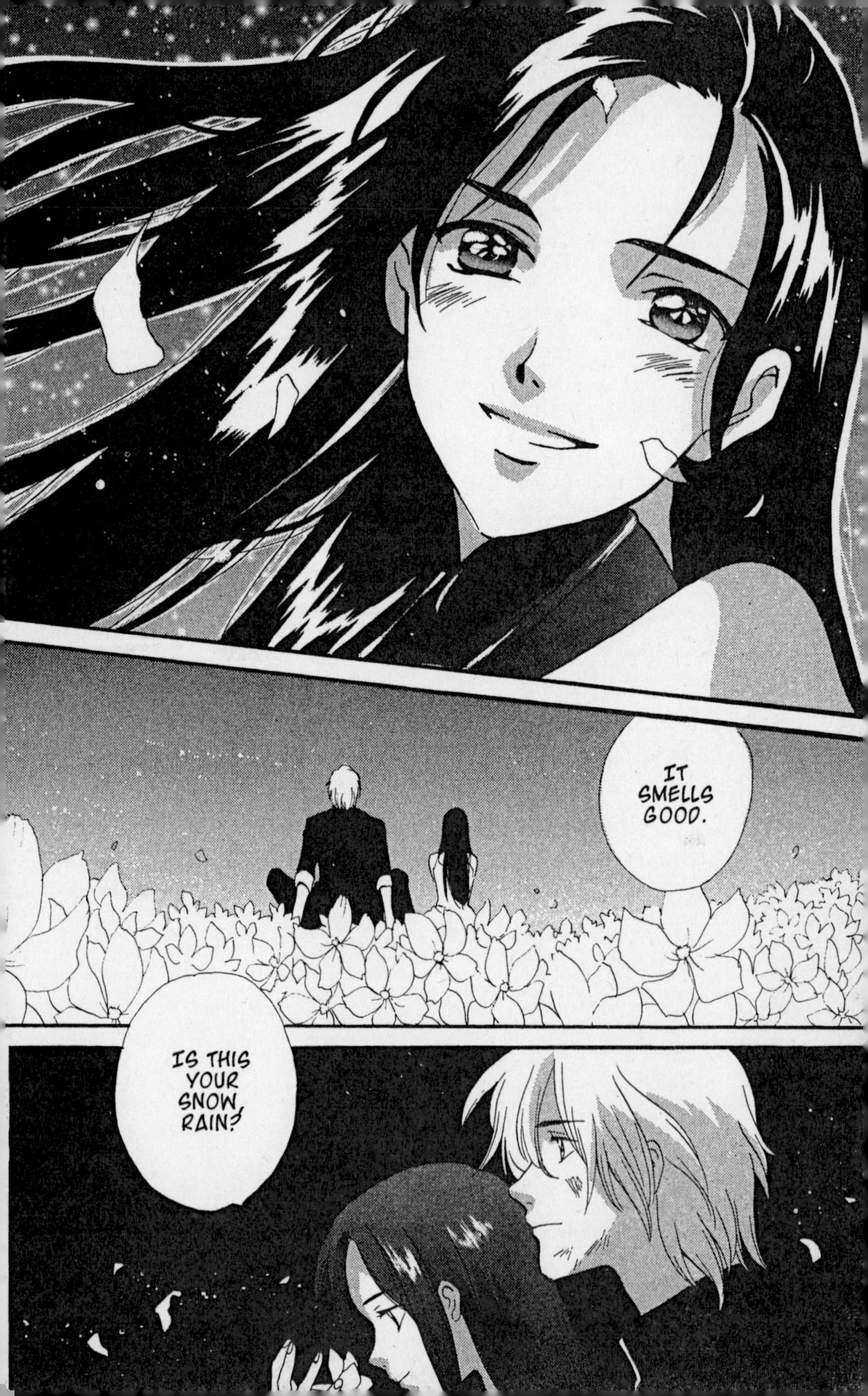
IT SMELLS GOOD.
IS THIS YOUR SNOW, RAIN?

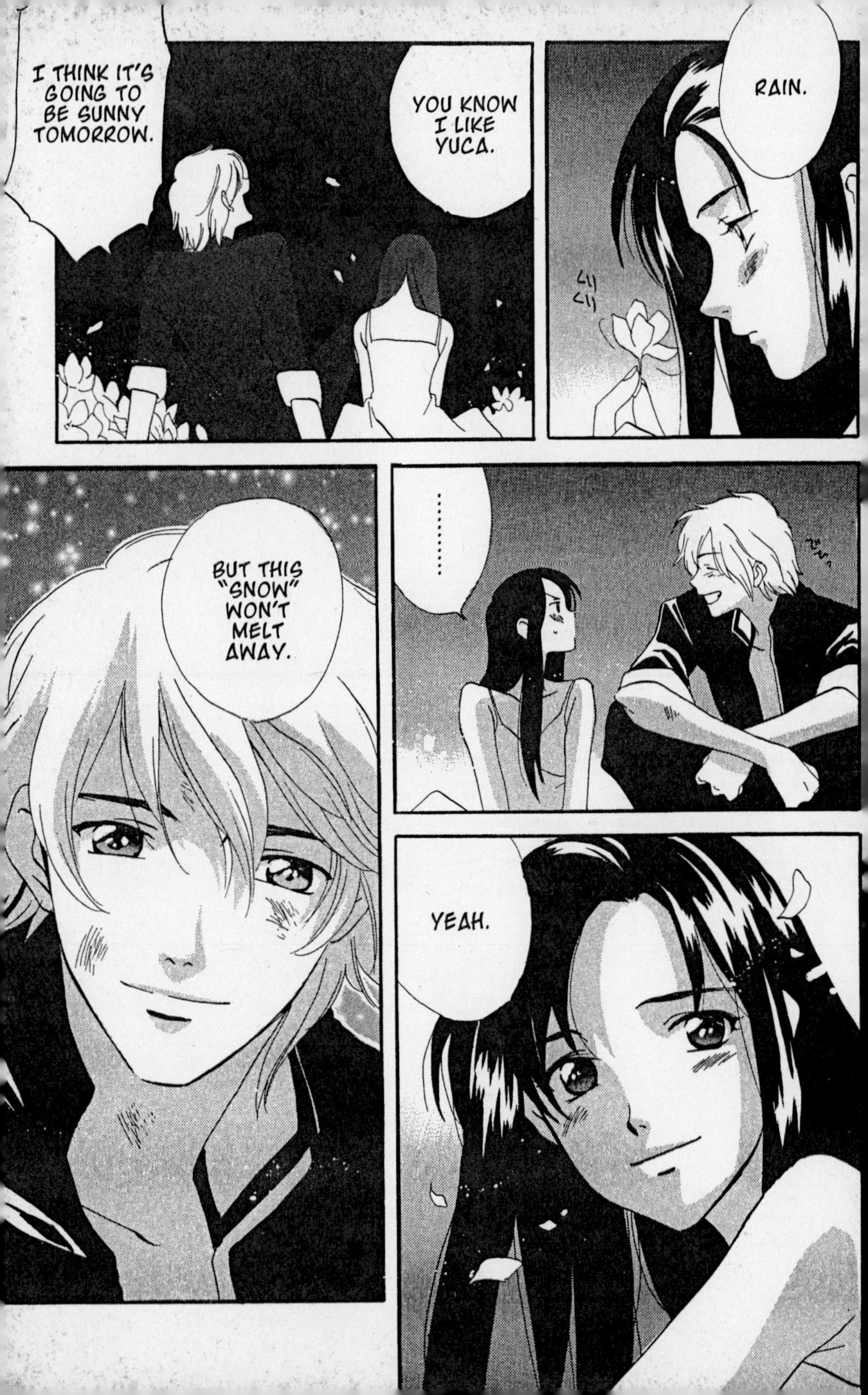
RAIN.
YOU KNOW I LIKE YUCA.
I THINK IT'S GOING TO BE SUNNY TOMORROW.
......
YEAH.
BUT THIS "SNOW" WON'T MELT AWAY.

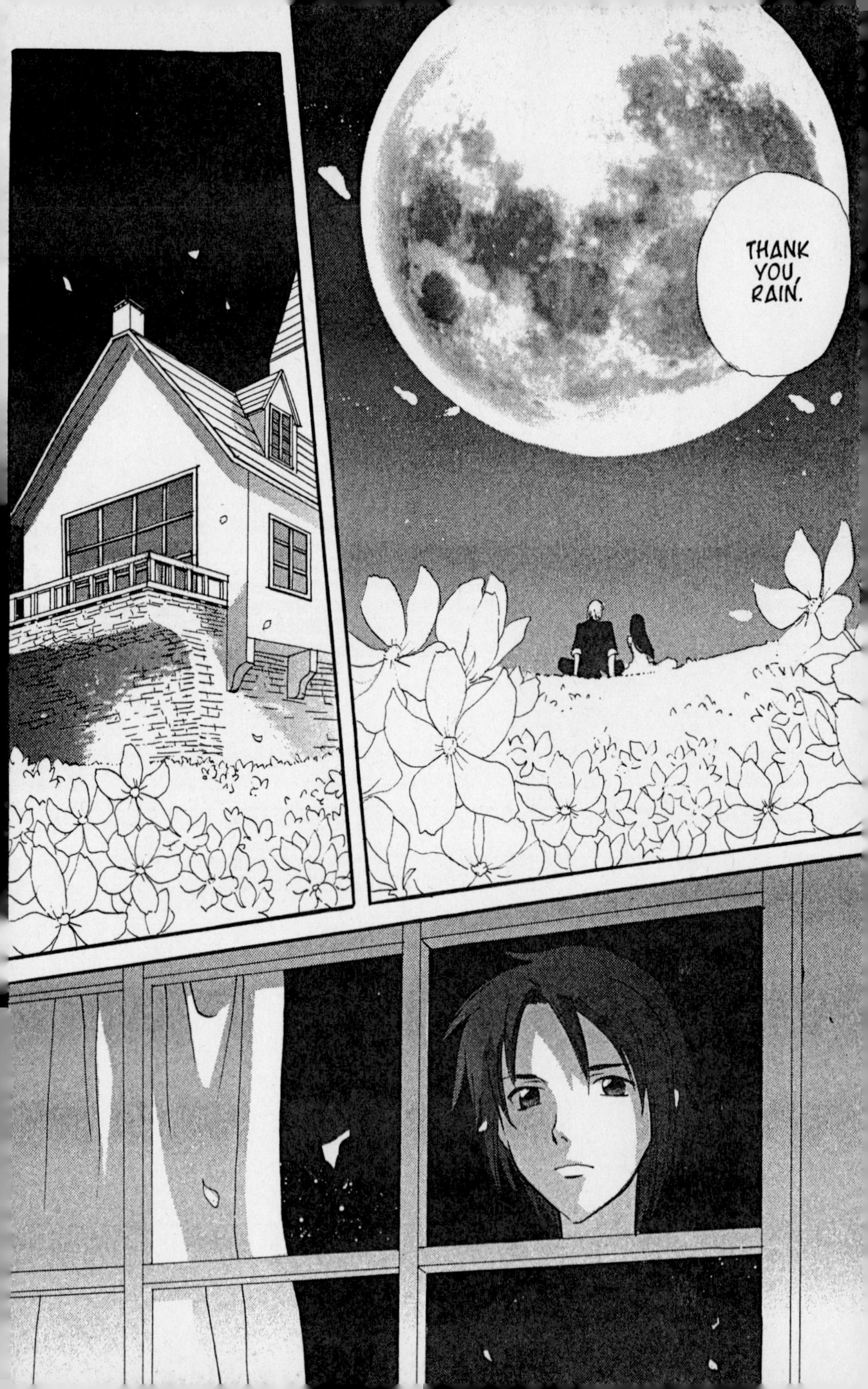
THANK YOU, RAIN.

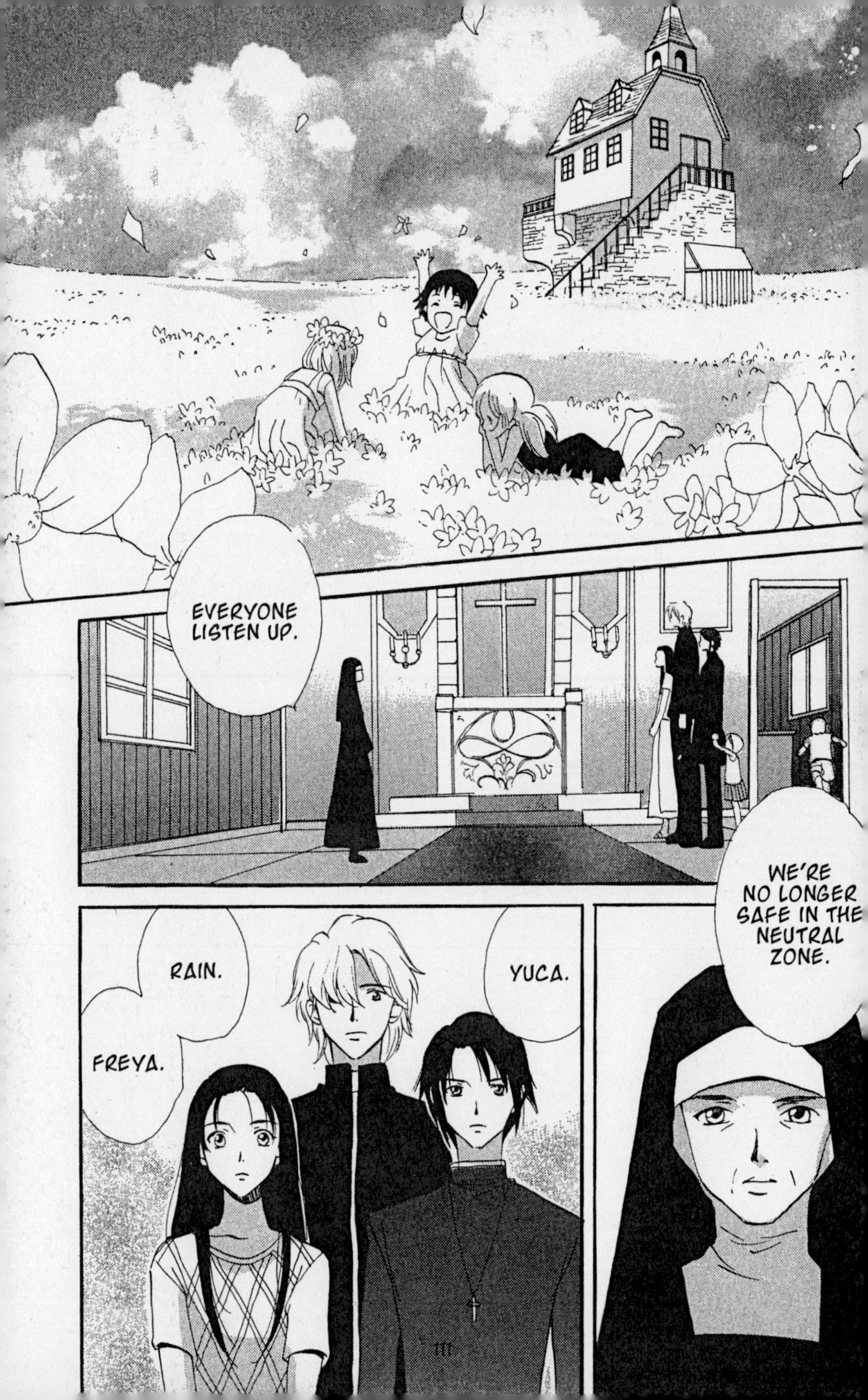
EVERYONE LISTEN UP.
WE'RE NO LONGER SAFE IN THE NEUTRAL ZONE.
YUCA.
RAIN.
FREYA.

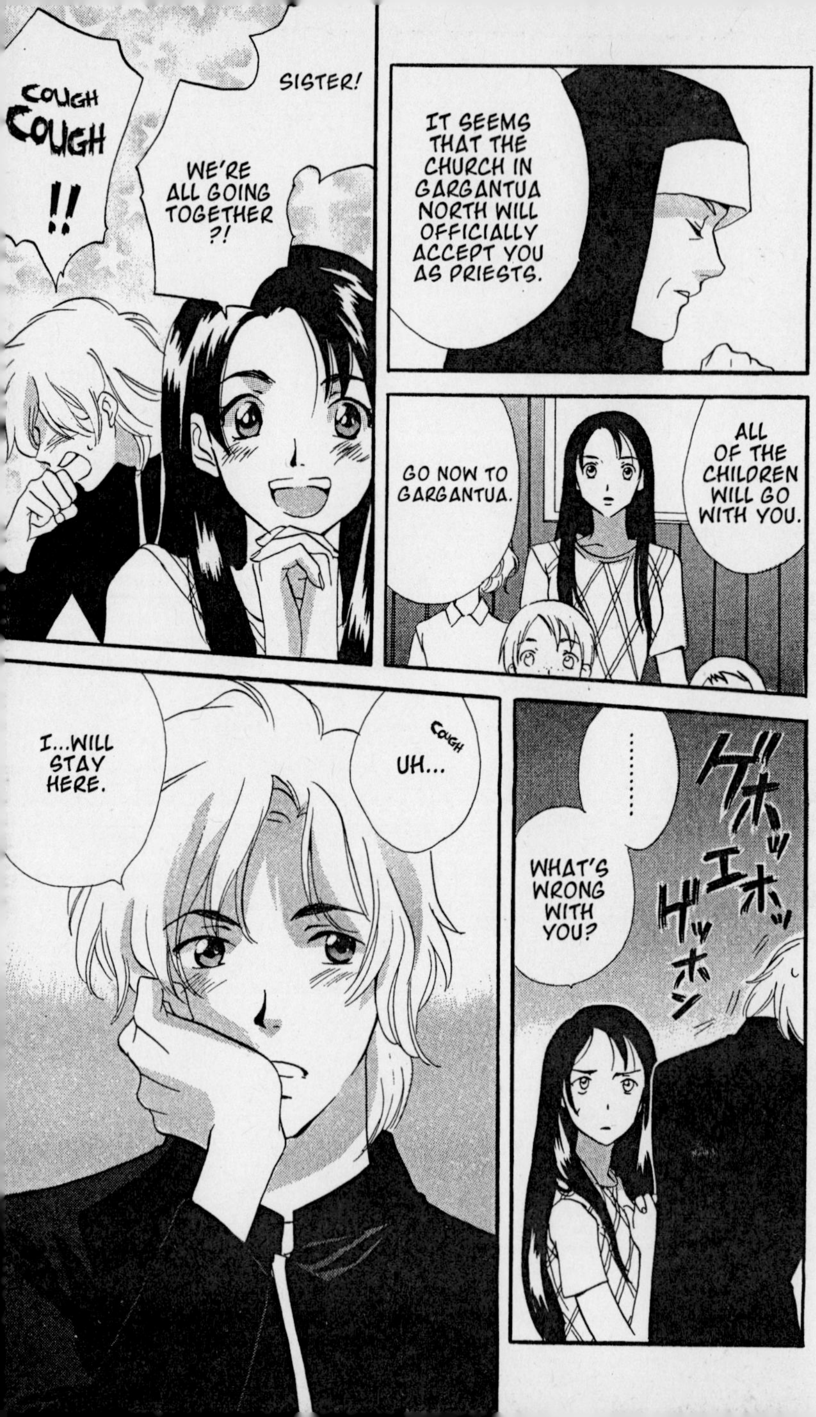
IT SEEMS THAT THE CHURCH IN GARGANTUA NORTH WILL OFFICIALLY ACCEPT YOU AS PRIESTS.
ALL OF THE CHILDREN WILL GO WITH YOU.
GO NOW TO GARGANTUA.
SISTER!
WE'RE ALL GOING TOGETHER ?!
COUGH COUGH !!
......
WHAT'S WRONG WITH YOU?
COUGH
UH...
I...WILL STAY HERE.

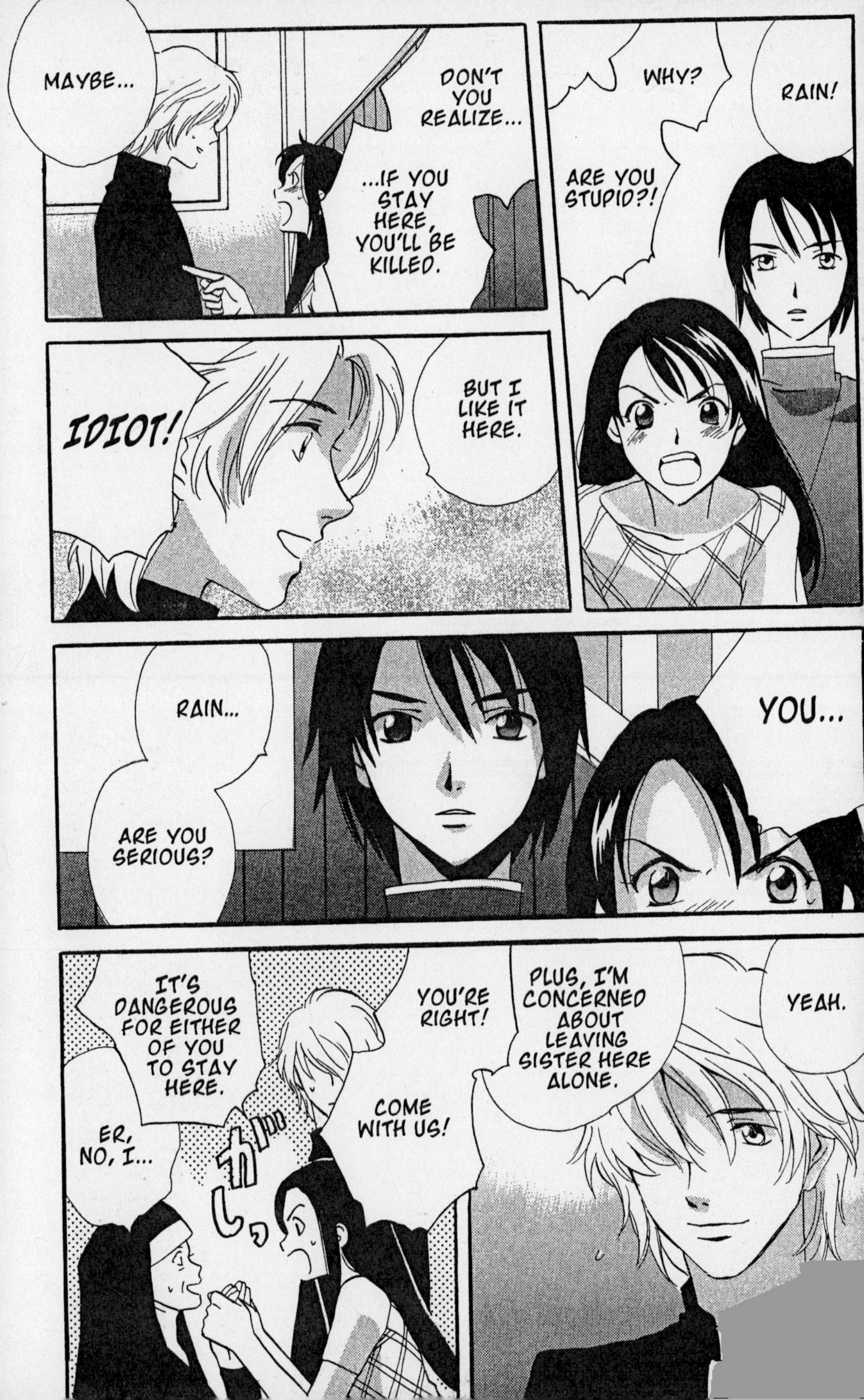

RAIN!
WHY?
ARE YOU STUPID?!
DON'T YOU REALIZE...
...IF YOU STAY HERE, YOU'LL BE KILLED.
MAYBE...
BUT I LIKE IT HERE.
IDIOT!
YOU...
RAIN...
ARE YOU SERIOUS?
YEAH.
PLUS, I'M CONCERNED ABOUT LEAVING SISTER HERE ALONE.
YOU'RE RIGHT!
COME WITH US!
IT'S DANGEROUS FOR EITHER OF YOU TO STAY HERE.
ガしっ
ER, NO, I...

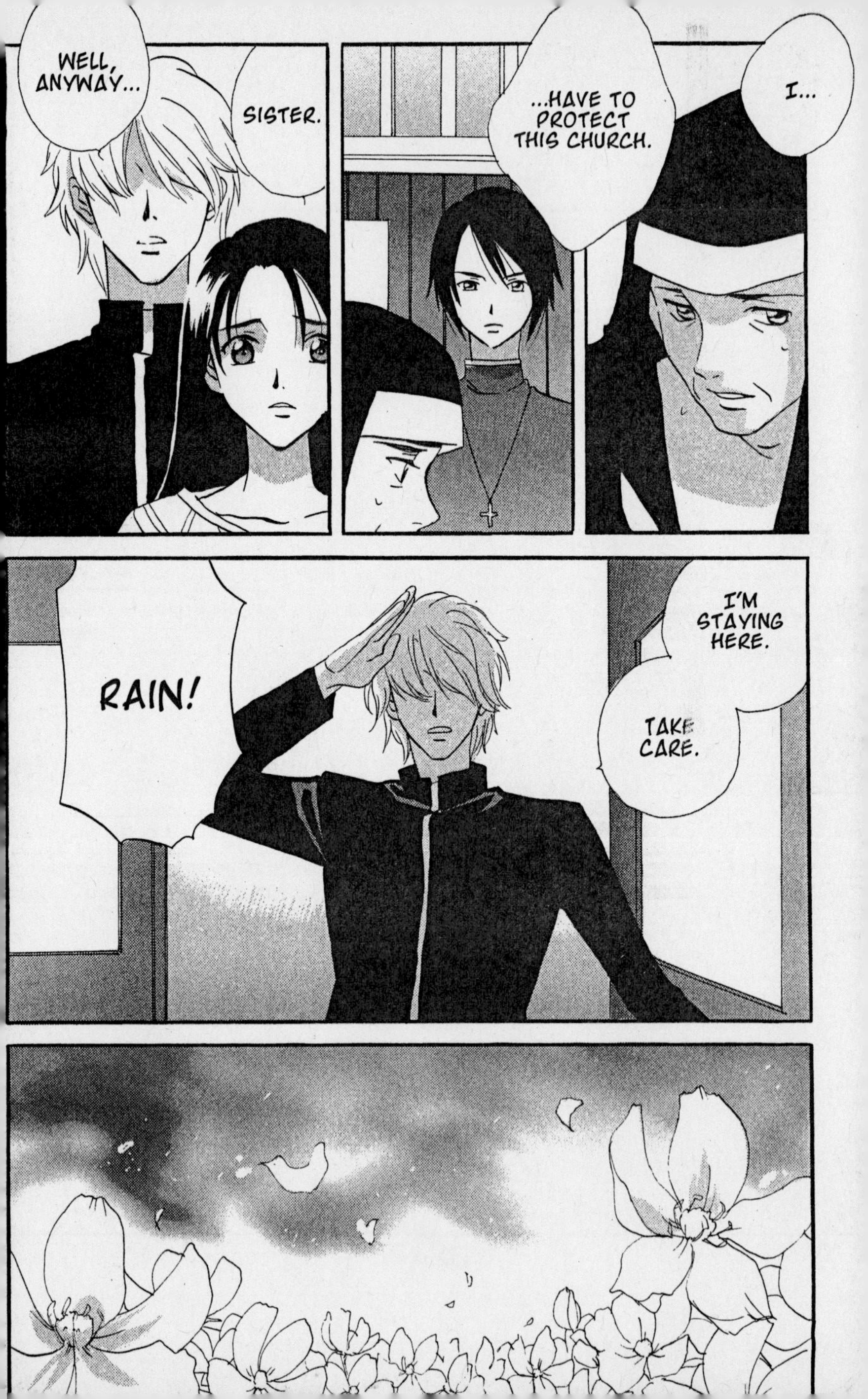
I...
...HAVE TO PROTECT THIS CHURCH.
SISTER.
WELL, ANYWAY...
I'M STAYING HERE.
TAKE CARE.
RAIN!

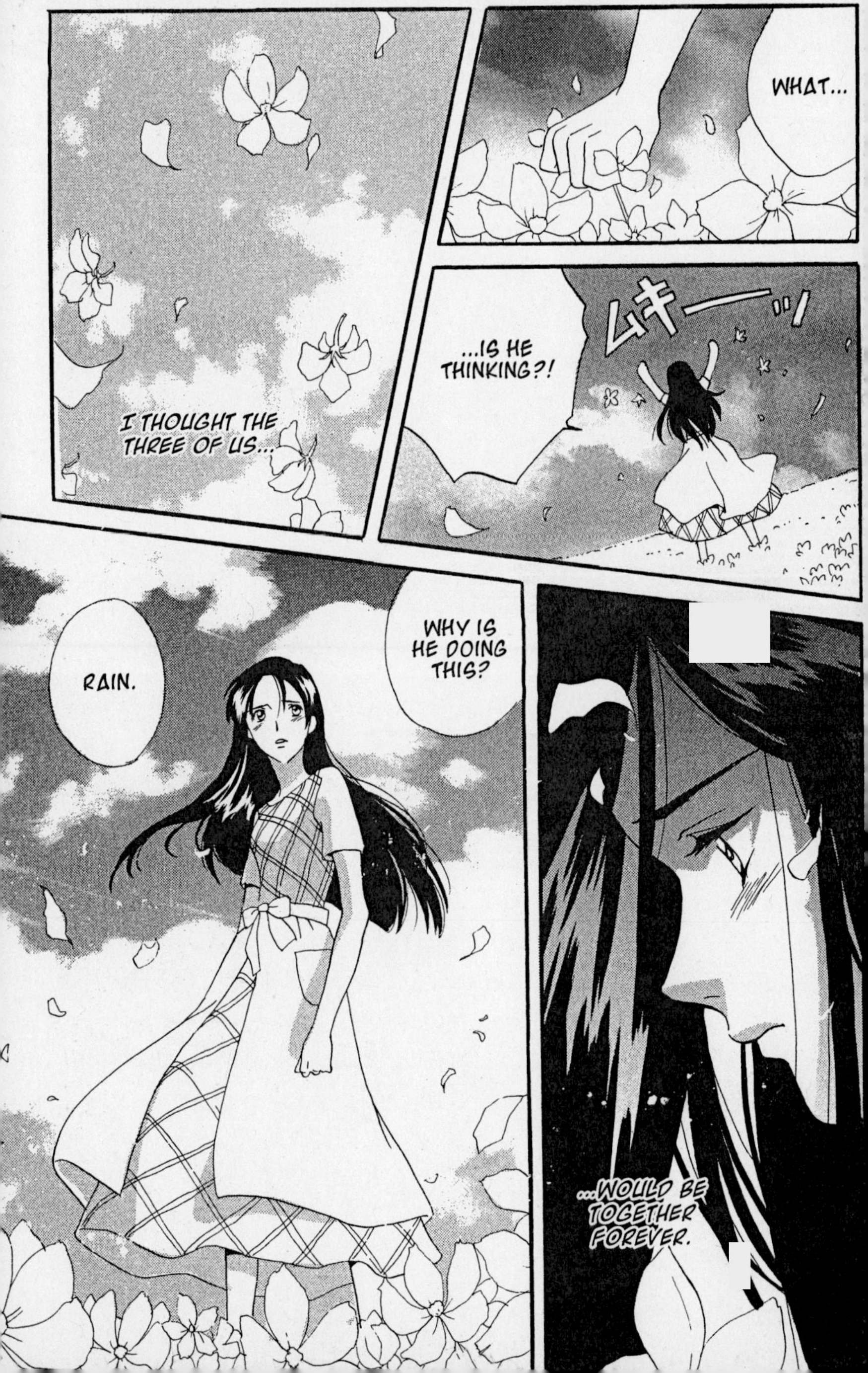
WHAT...
...IS HE THINKING?!
ムキーーッ!
I THOUGHT THE THREE OF US...
...WOULD BE TOGETHER FOREVER.
WHY IS HE DOING THIS?
RAIN.

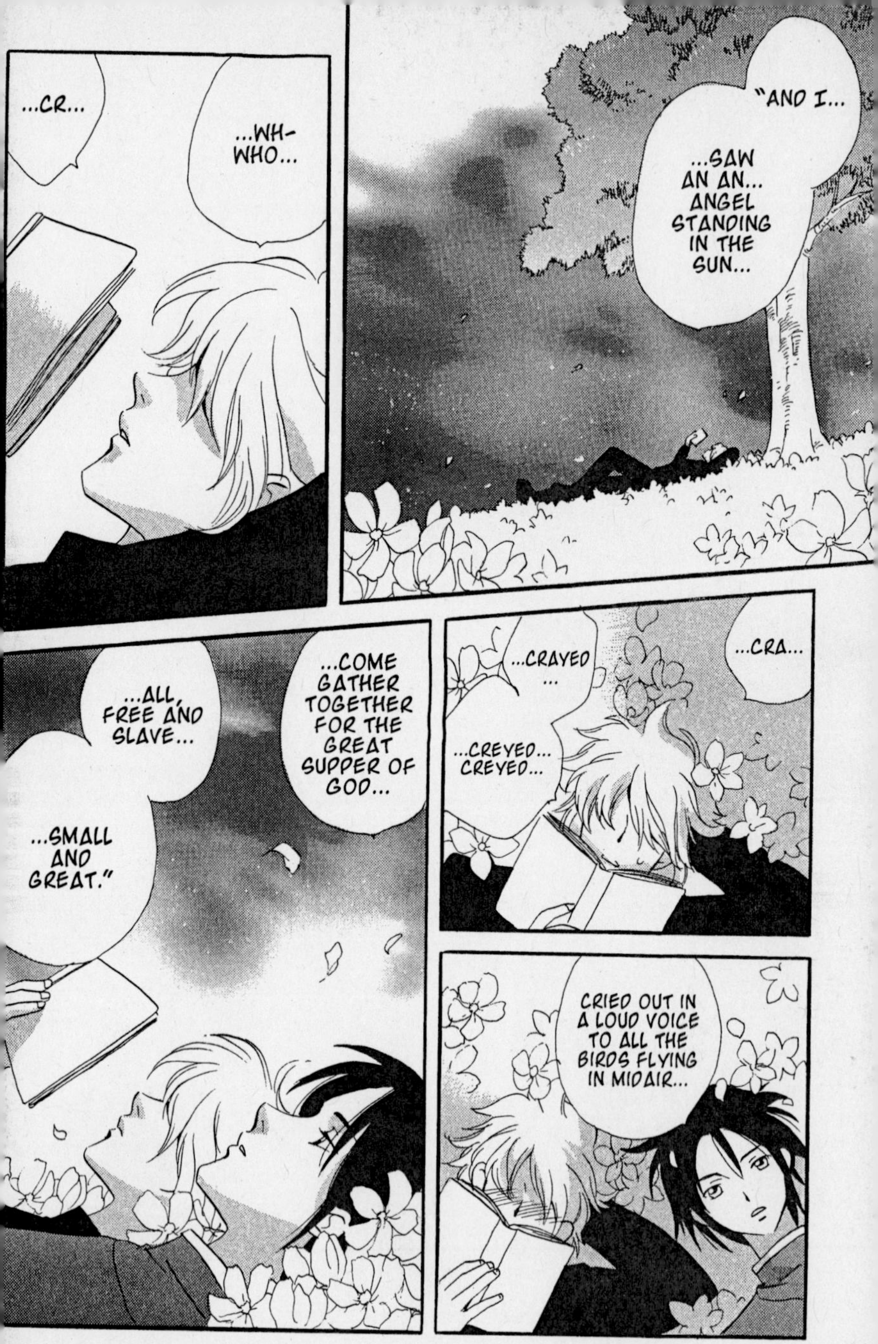
"AND I...
...SAW AN AN... ANGEL STANDING IN THE SUN...
...WH-WHO...
...CR...
...CRA...
...CRAYED ...
...CREYED... CREYED...
CRIED OUT IN A LOUD VOICE TO ALL THE BIRDS FLYING IN MIDAIR...
...COME GATHER TOGETHER FOR THE GREAT SUPPER OF GOD...
...ALL, FREE AND SLAVE...
...SMALL AND GREAT."

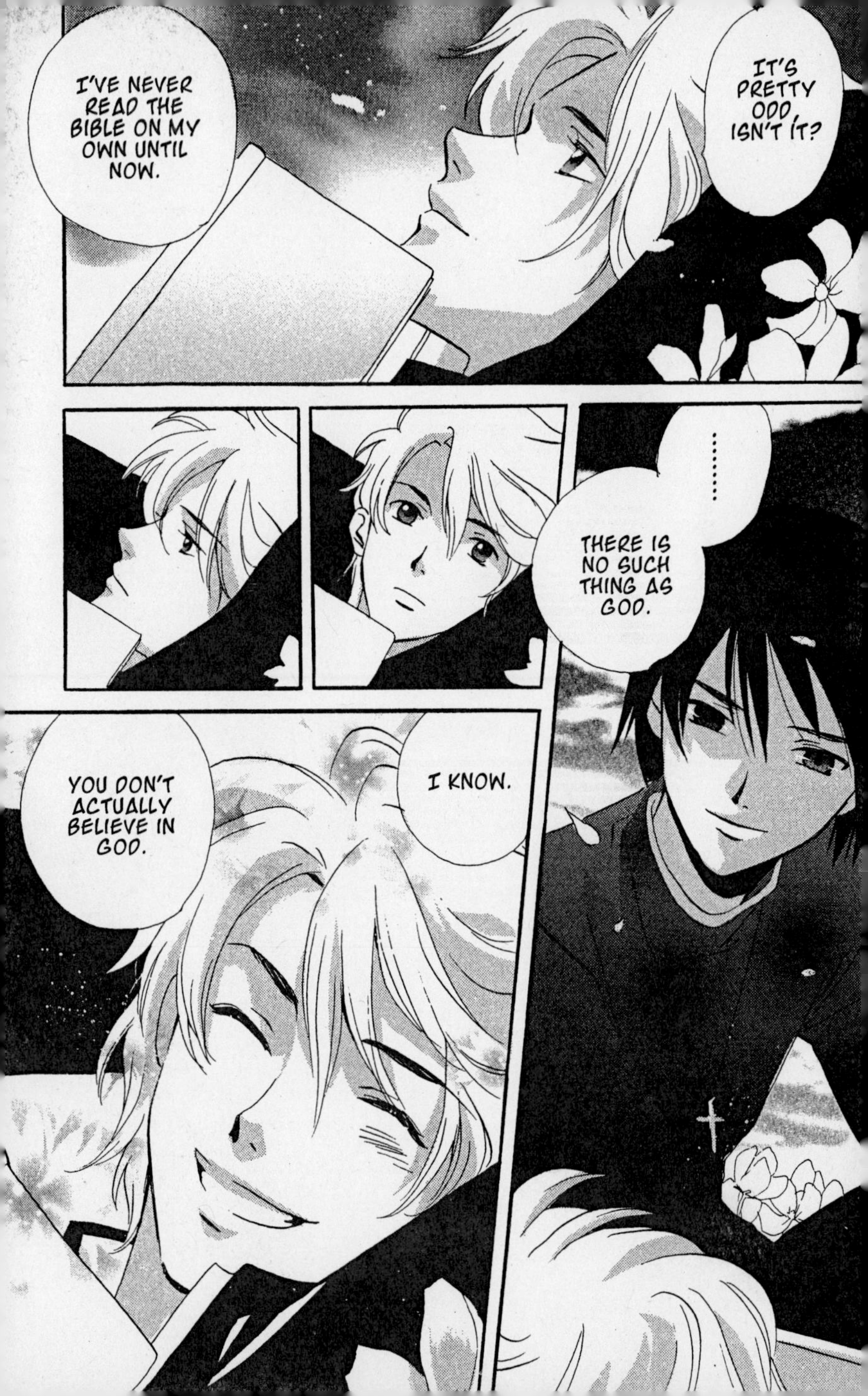
IT'S PRETTY ODD, ISN'T IT?
I'VE NEVER READ THE BIBLE ON MY OWN UNTIL NOW.
......
THERE IS NO SUCH THING AS GOD.
I KNOW.
YOU DON'T ACTUALLY BELIEVE IN GOD.

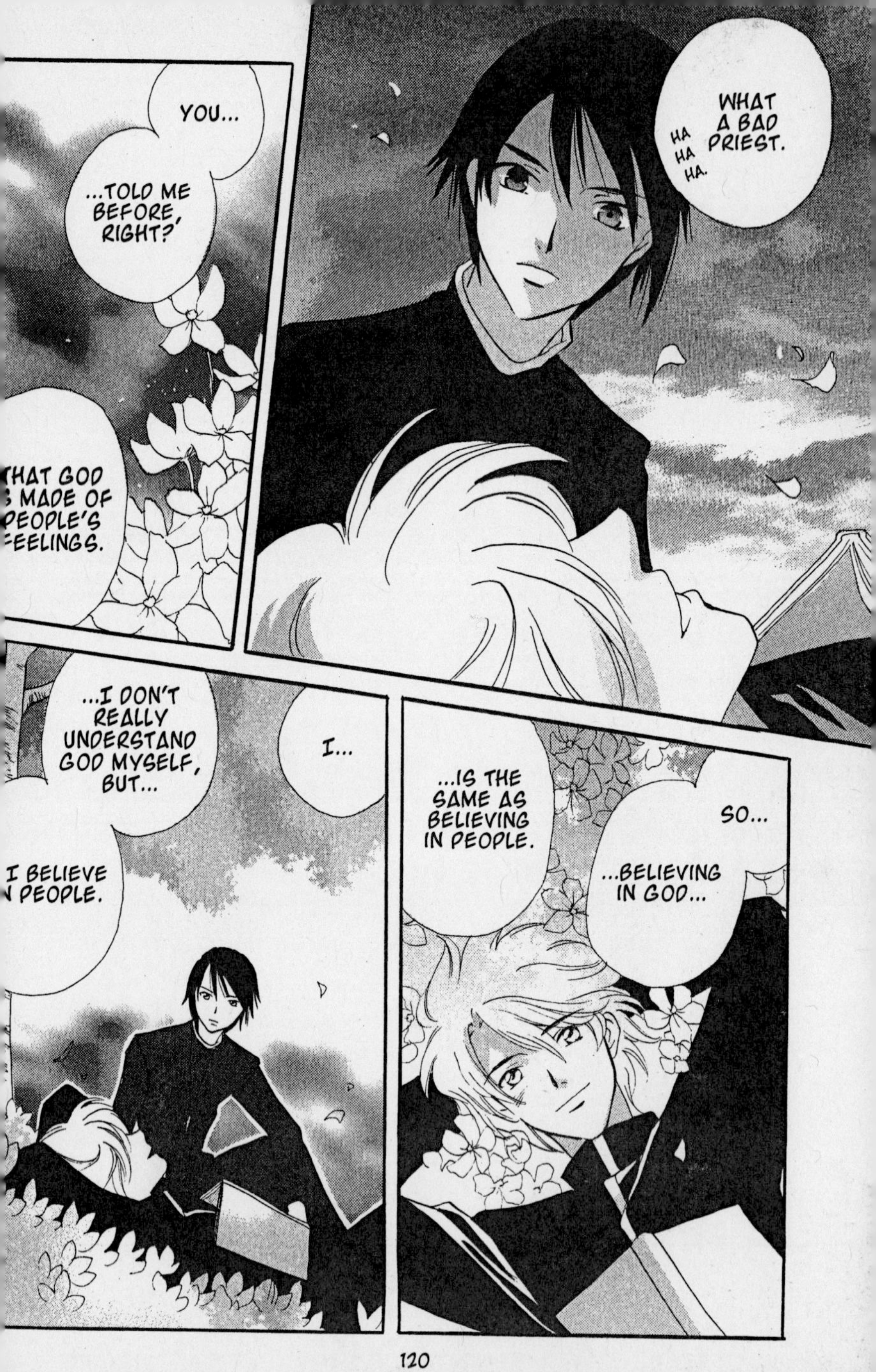
WHAT A BAD PRIEST.
HA HA HA.
YOU...
...TOLD ME BEFORE, RIGHT?'
THAT GOD S MADE OF PEOPLE'S FEELINGS.
SO...
...BELIEVING IN GOD...
...IS THE SAME AS BELIEVING IN PEOPLE.
I...
...I DON'T REALLY UNDERSTAND GOD MYSELF, BUT...
I BELIEVE N PEOPLE.

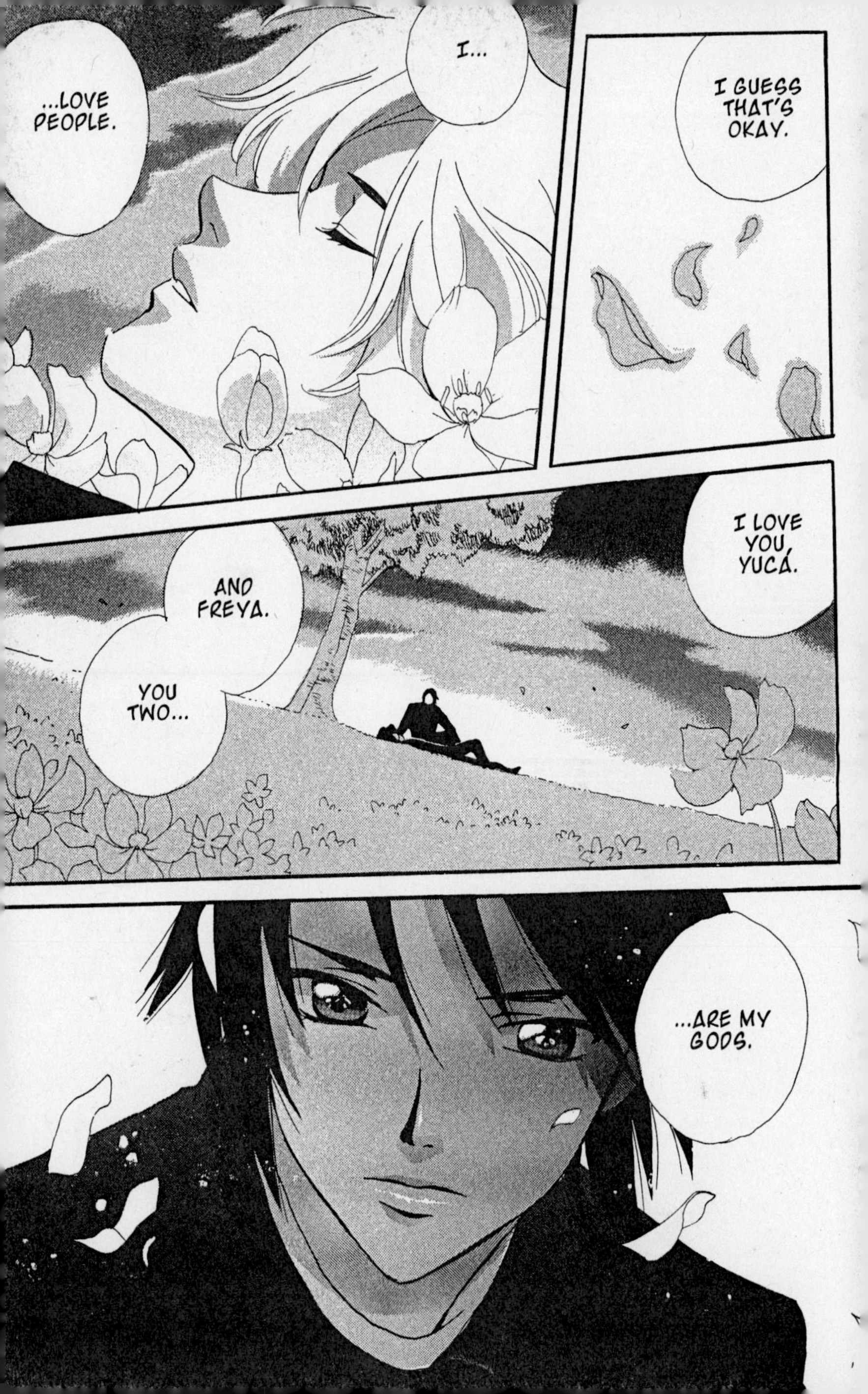
I GUESS THAT'S OKAY.
I...
...LOVE PEOPLE.
I LOVE YOU, YUCA.
AND FREYA.
YOU TWO...
...ARE MY GODS.

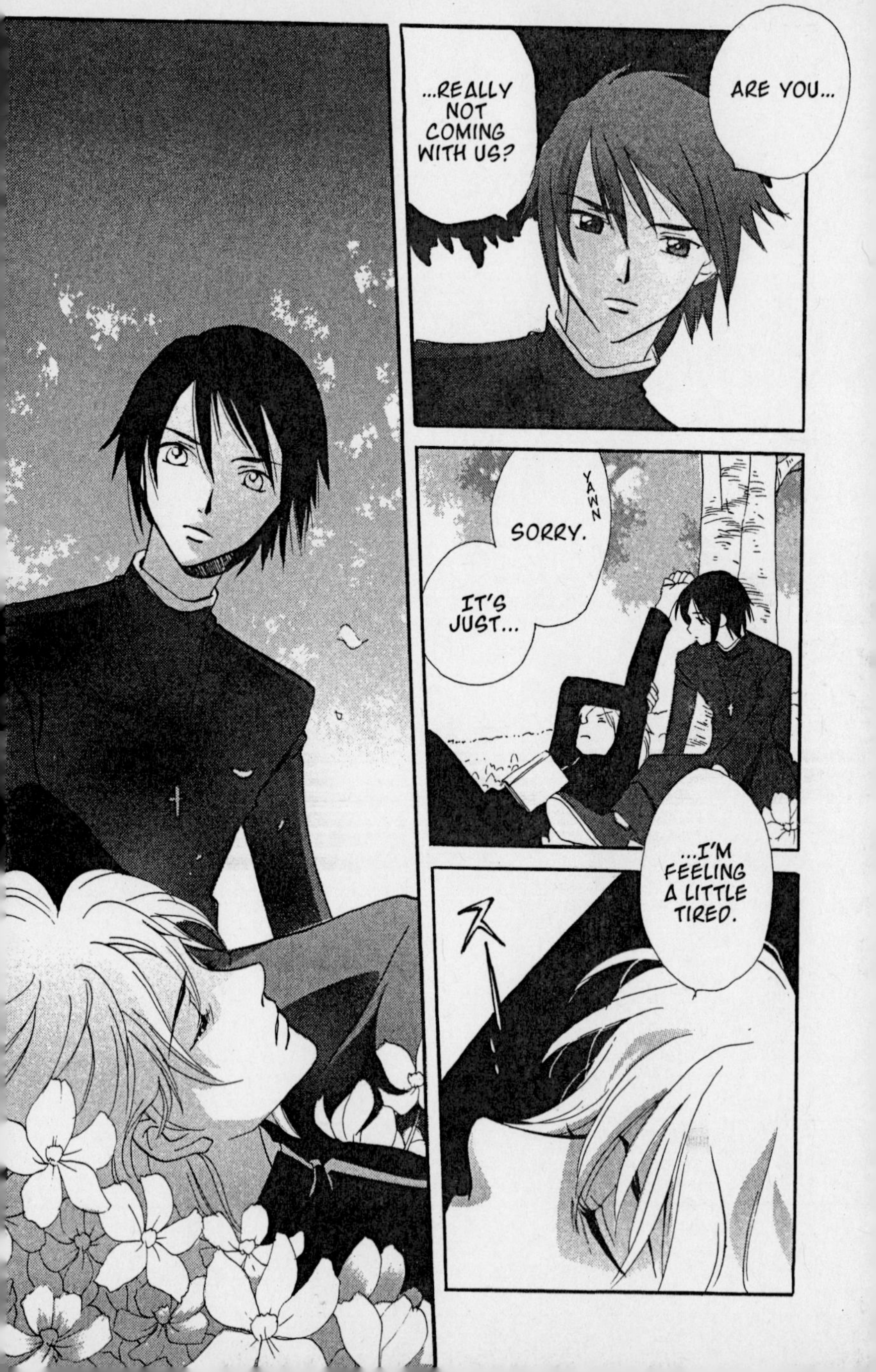
ARE YOU...
...REALLY NOT COMING WITH US?
YAWN
SORRY.
IT'S JUST...
...I'M FEELING A LITTLE TIRED.
ス

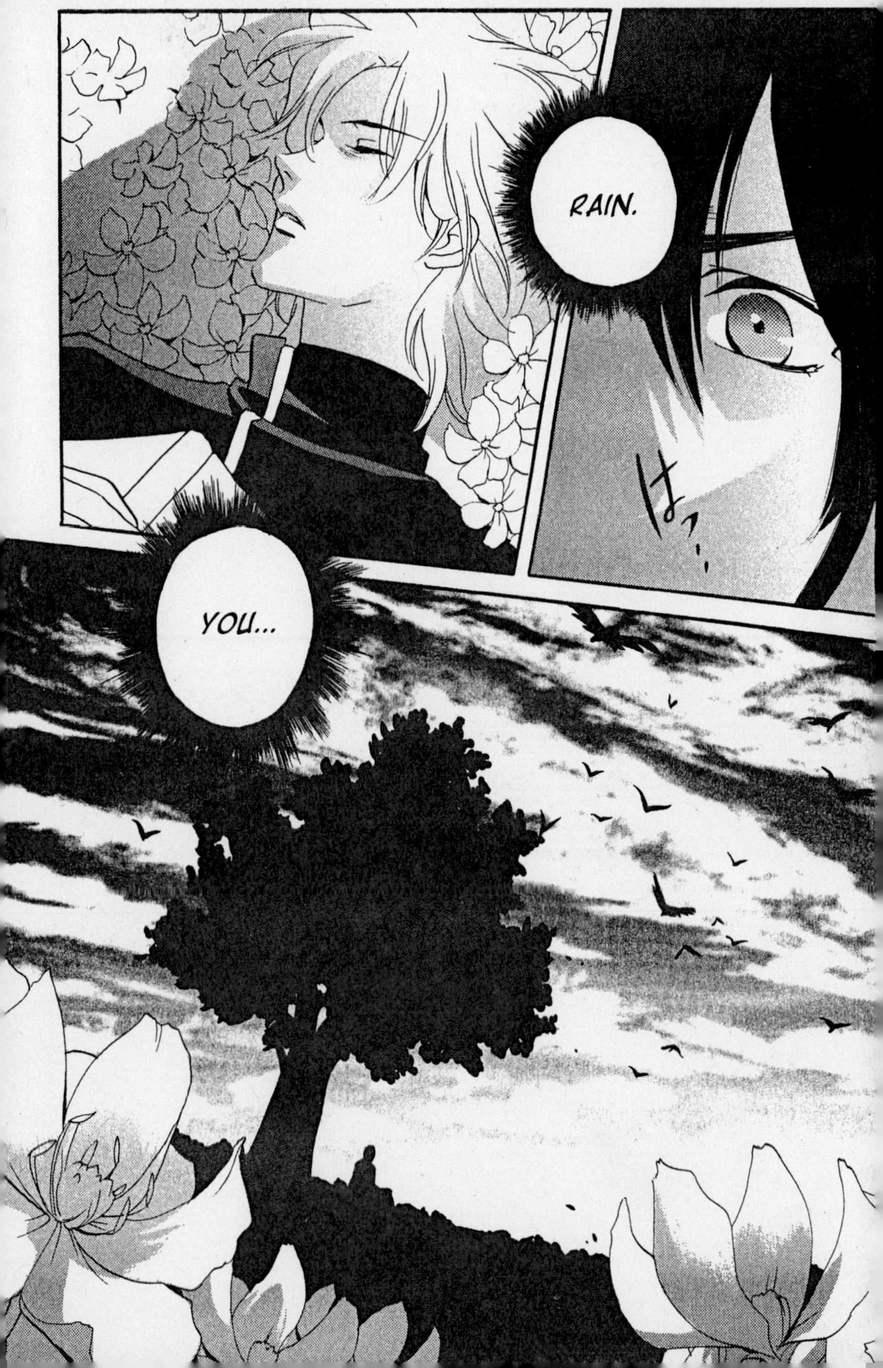
RAIN.
はっ
YOU...

Freya Gaudry

Age:17
Height:164cm
Blood type:B

This character can only be used during Rain's flashback scenes.
When she enters Sudden Fasting Mode, all the men worry about her!

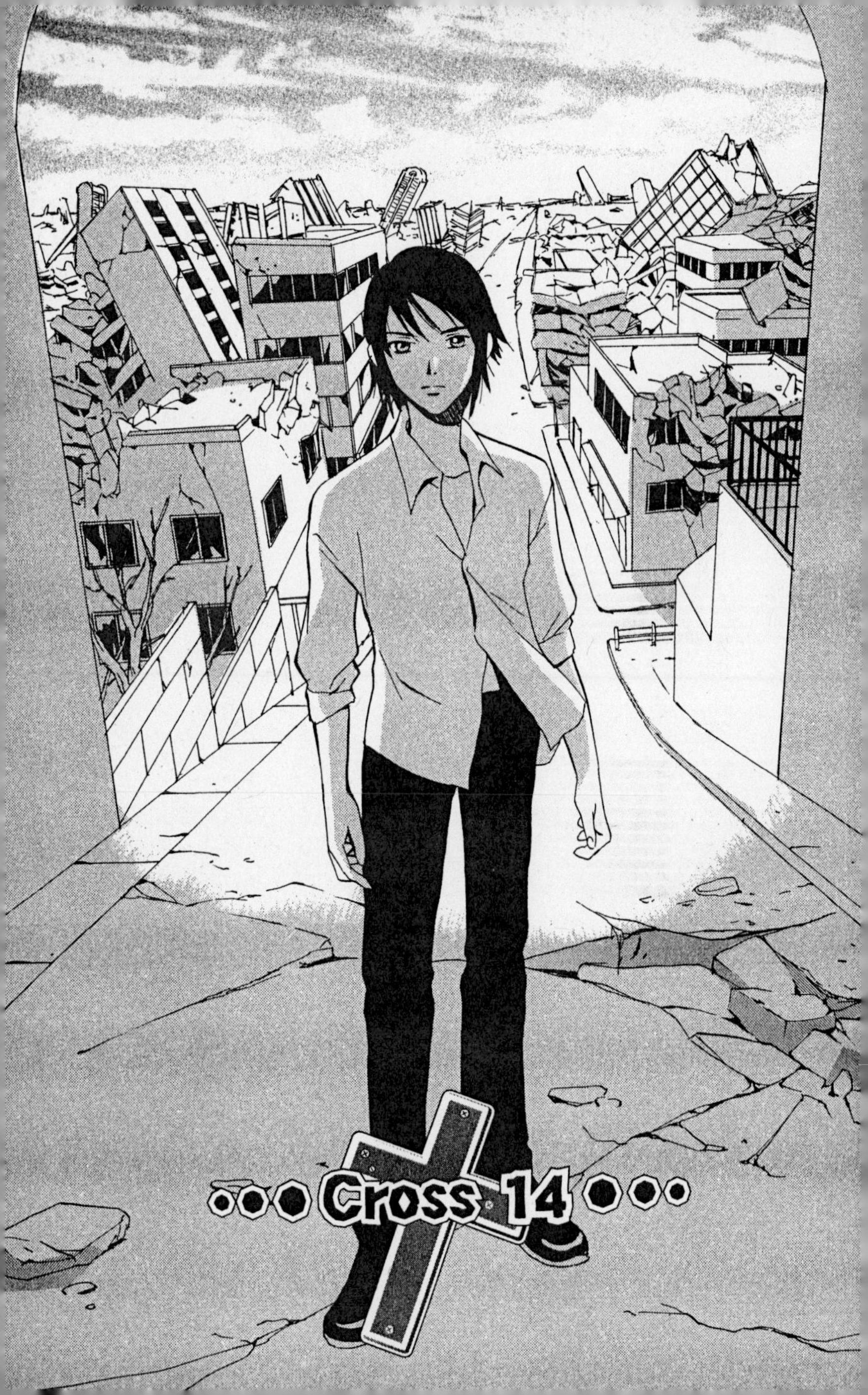
Cross 14

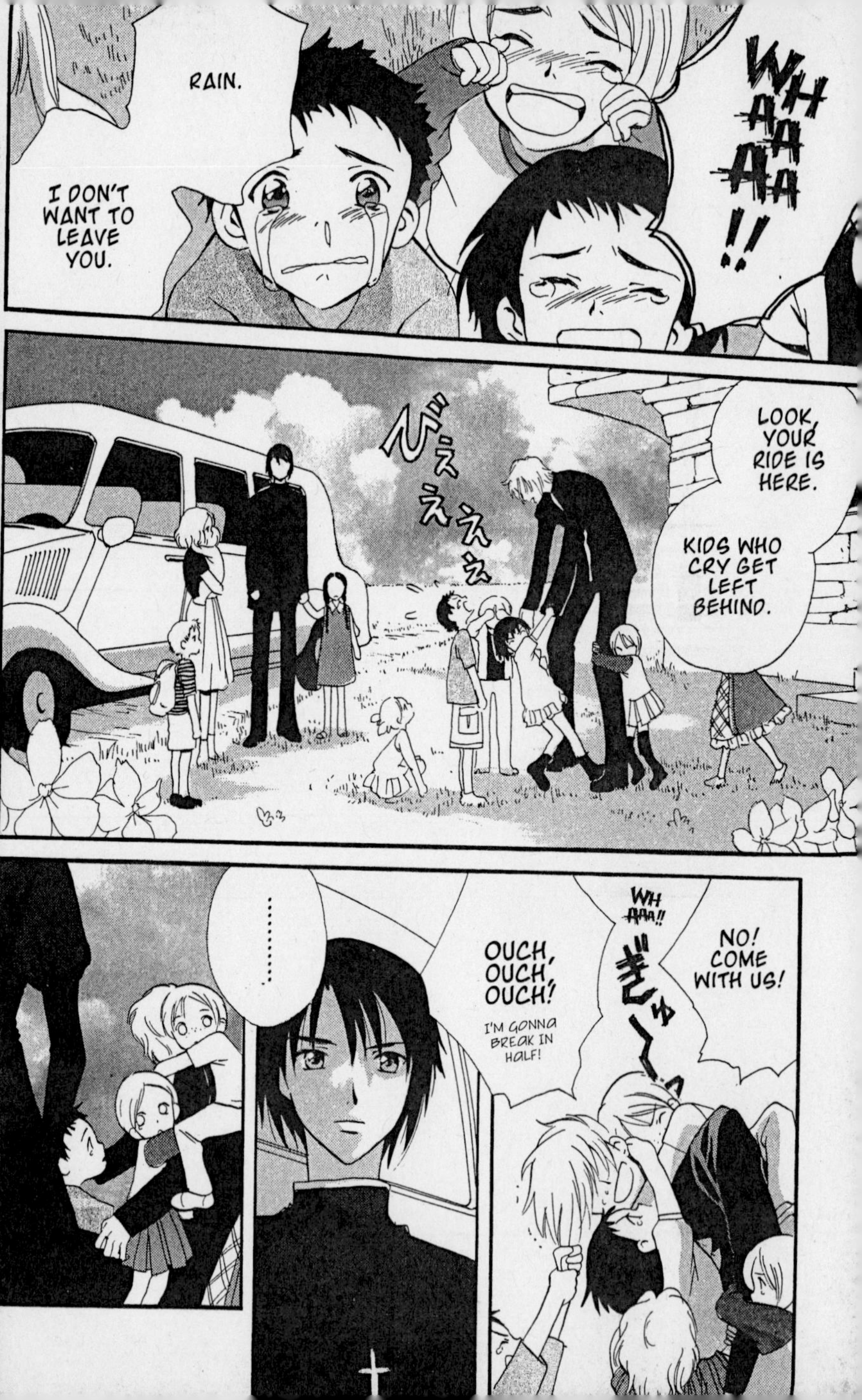
WHAAAAA!!
RAIN.
I DON'T WANT TO LEAVE YOU.
LOOK, YOUR RIDE IS HERE.
KIDS WHO CRY GET LEFT BEHIND.
びええええ
NO! COME WITH US!
WHAAA!!
ぎゅ〜
OUCH, OUCH, OUCH!
I'M GONNA BREAK IN HALF!
......

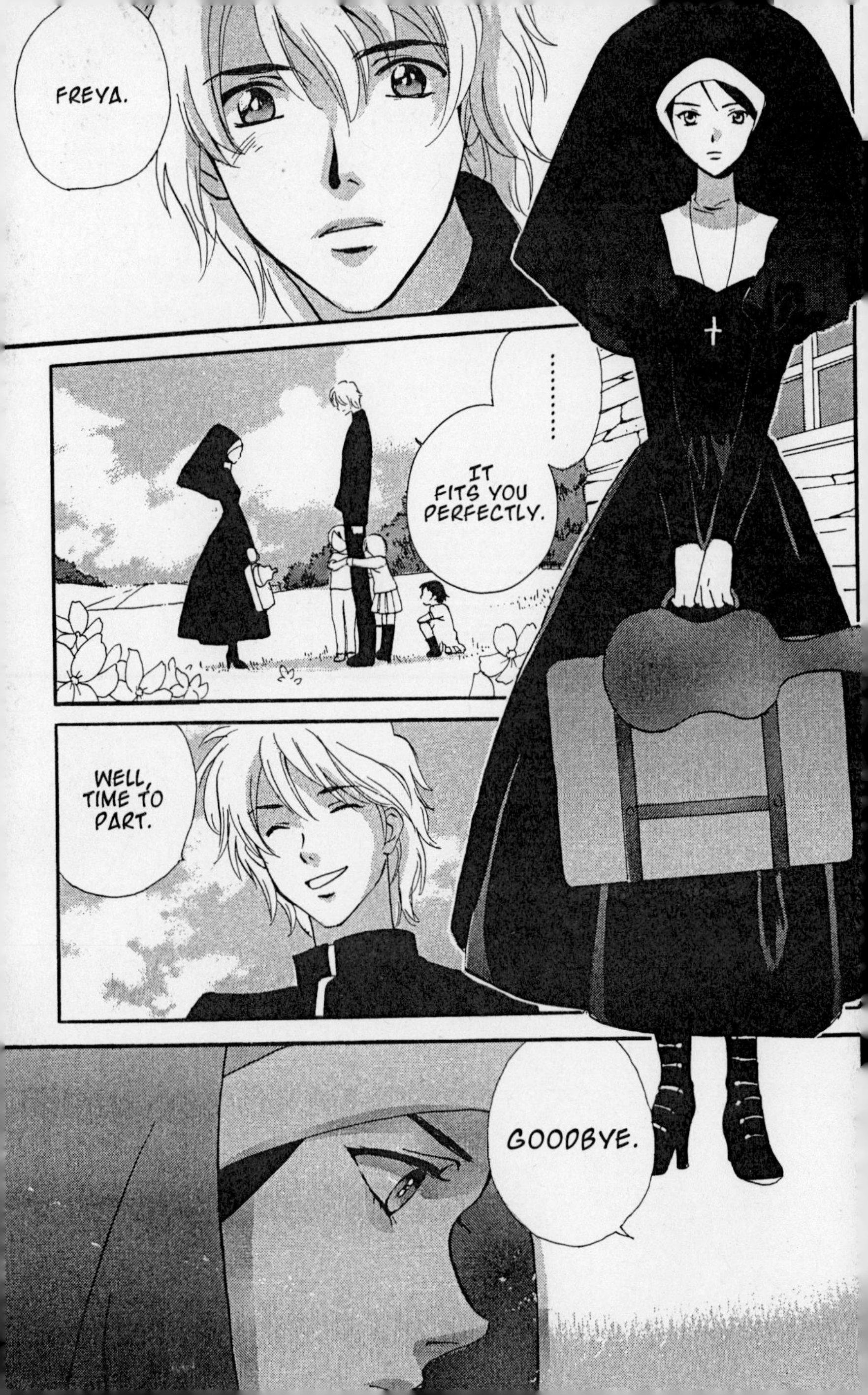
FREYA.
......
IT FITS YOU PERFECTLY.
WELL, TIME TO PART.
GOODBYE.

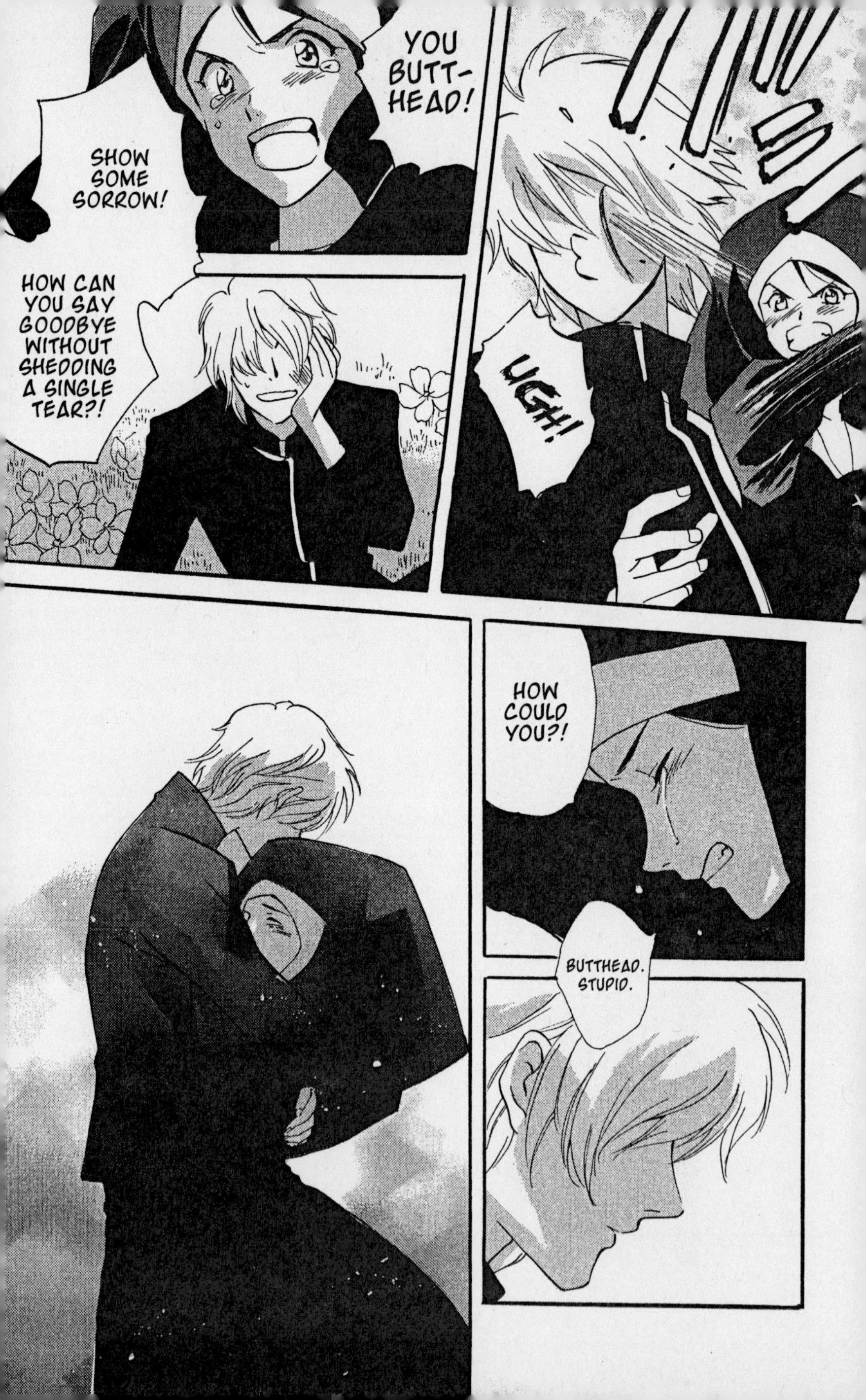
UGH!
YOU BUTT-HEAD!
SHOW SOME SORROW!
HOW CAN YOU SAY GOODBYE WITHOUT SHEDDING A SINGLE TEAR?!
HOW COULD YOU?!
BUTTHEAD. STUPID.

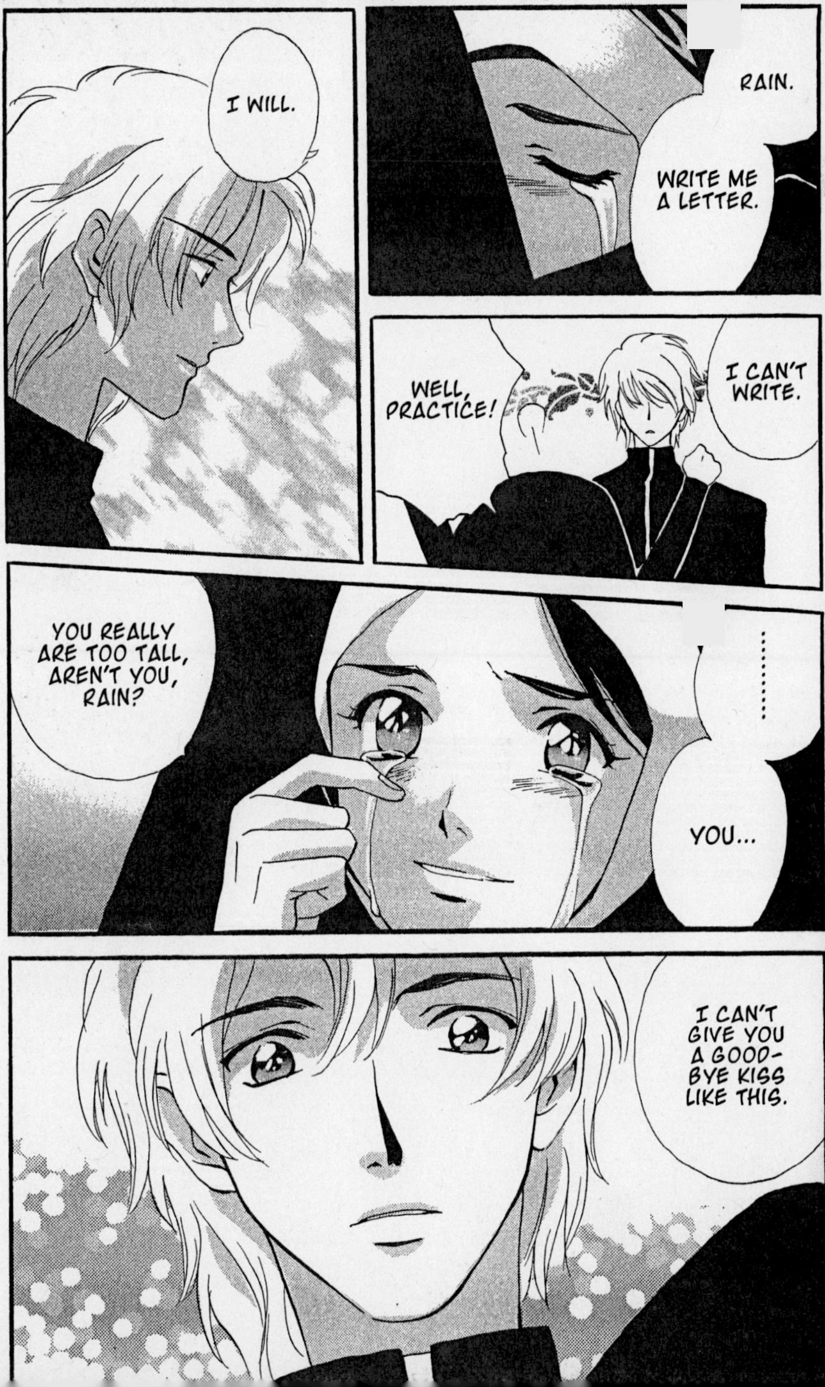
RAIN.
WRITE ME A LETTER.
I CAN'T WRITE.
WELL, PRACTICE!
I WILL.
......
YOU...
YOU REALLY ARE TOO TALL, AREN'T YOU, RAIN?
I CAN'T GIVE YOU A GOOD-BYE KISS LIKE THIS.

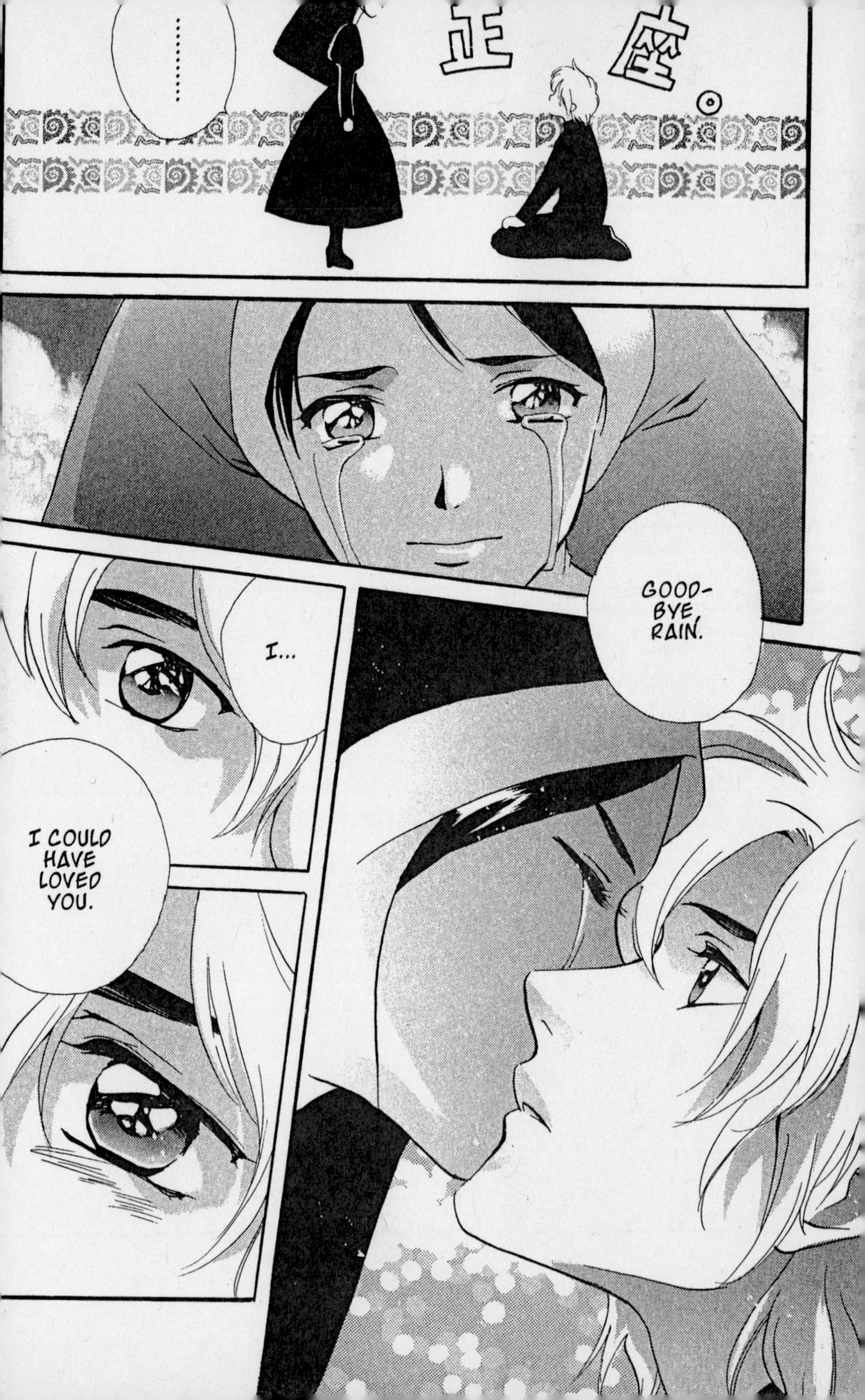
正座。
……
GOOD-BYE RAIN.
I...
I COULD HAVE LOVED YOU.

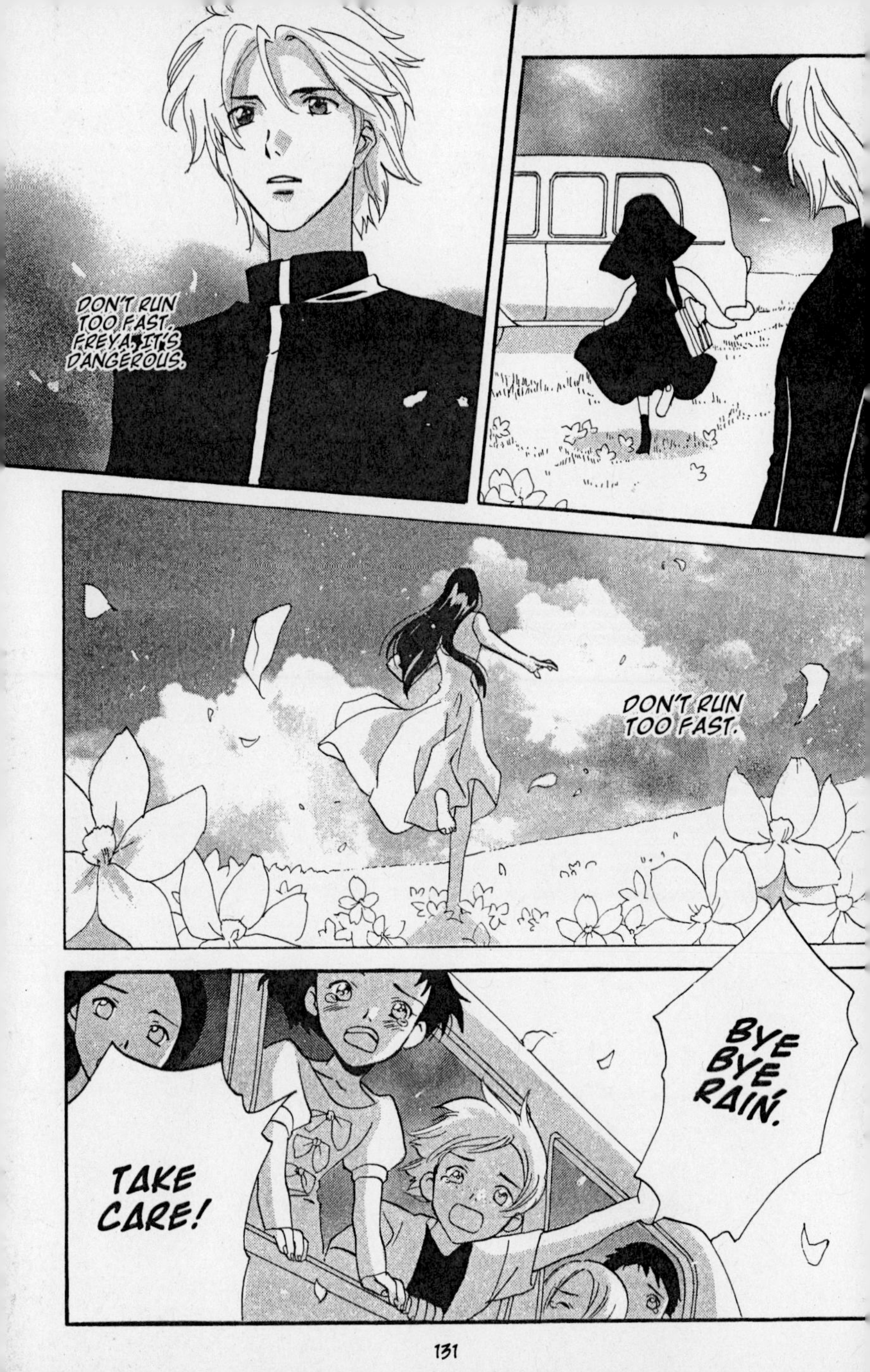
DON'T RUN TOO FAST, FREYA, IT'S DANGEROUS.
DON'T RUN TOO FAST.
BYE BYE RAIN.
TAKE CARE!

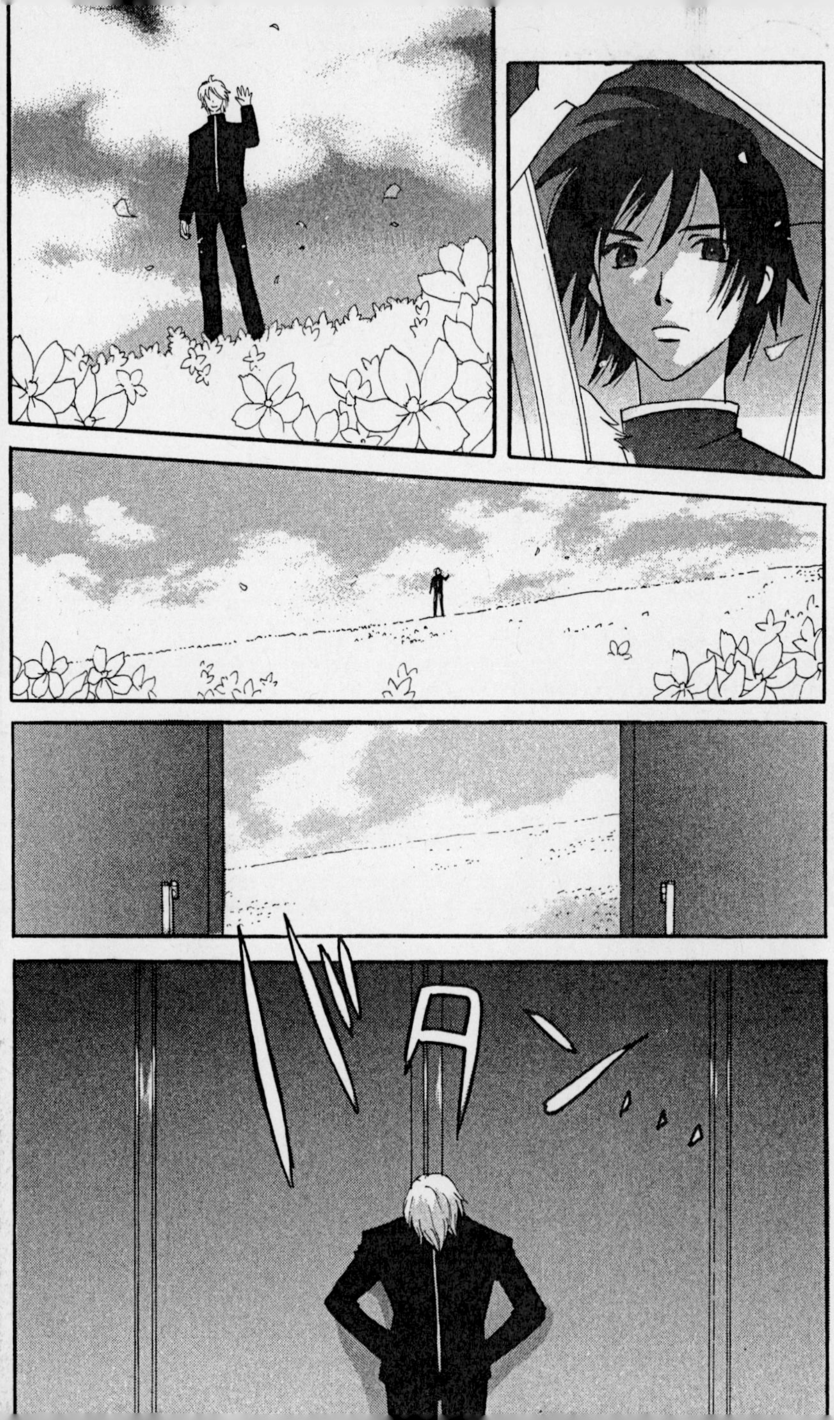
バタン

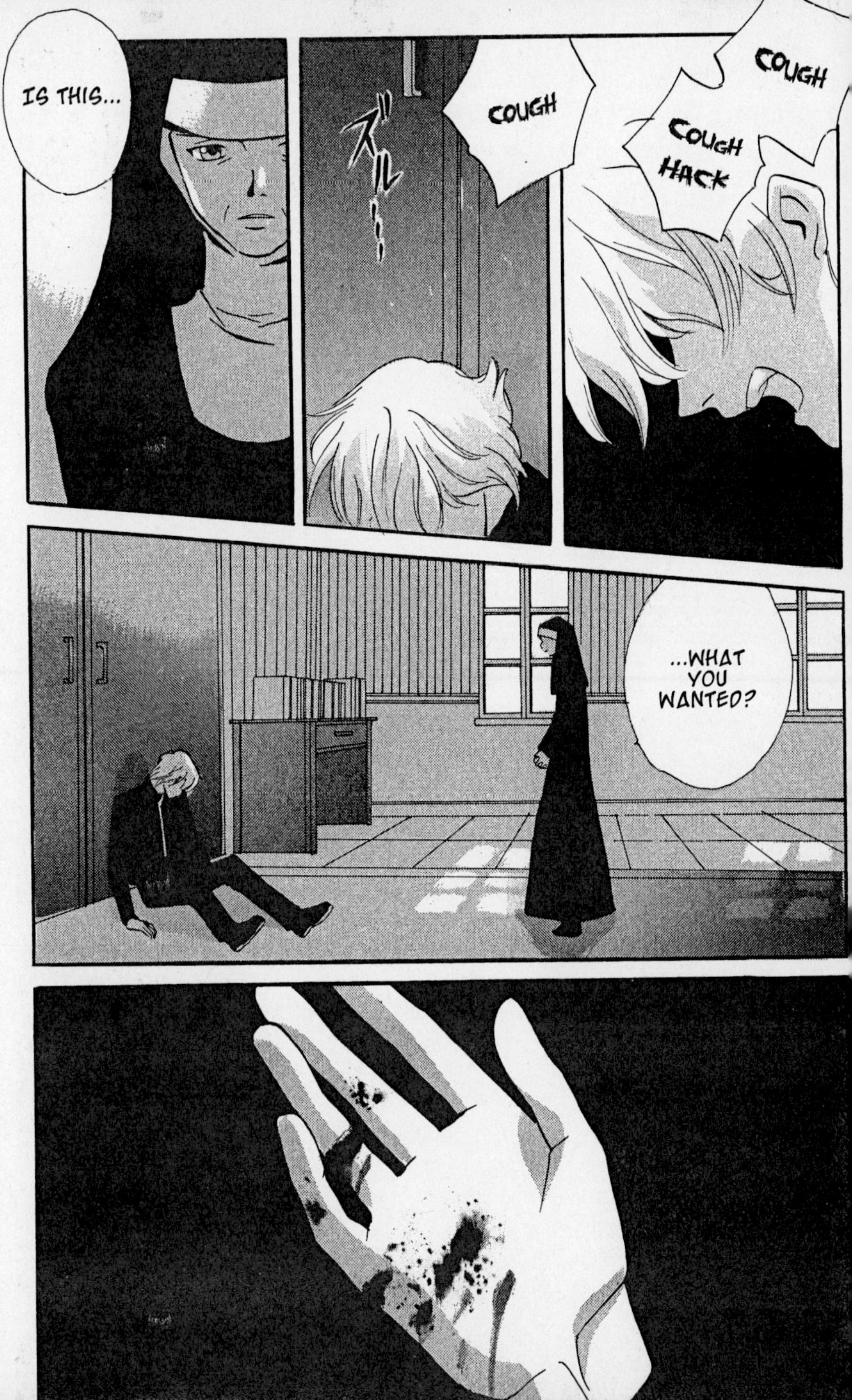
COUGH
COUGH
HACK
COUGH
ズル…
IS THIS...
...WHAT YOU WANTED?

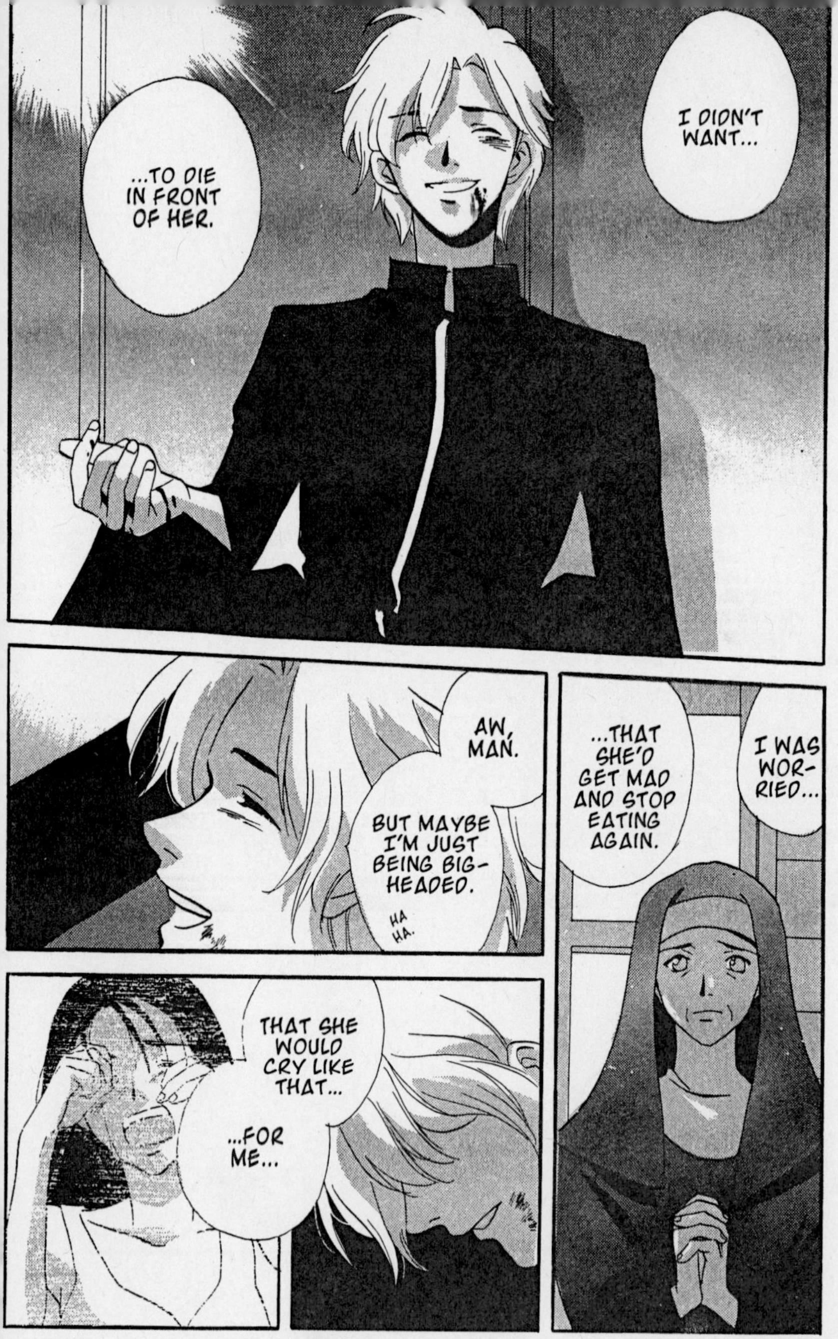
I DIDN'T WANT...
...TO DIE IN FRONT OF HER.
I WAS WOR-RIED...
...THAT SHE'D GET MAD AND STOP EATING AGAIN.
AW, MAN.
BUT MAYBE I'M JUST BEING BIG-HEADED.
HA HA.
THAT SHE WOULD CRY LIKE THAT...
...FOR ME...

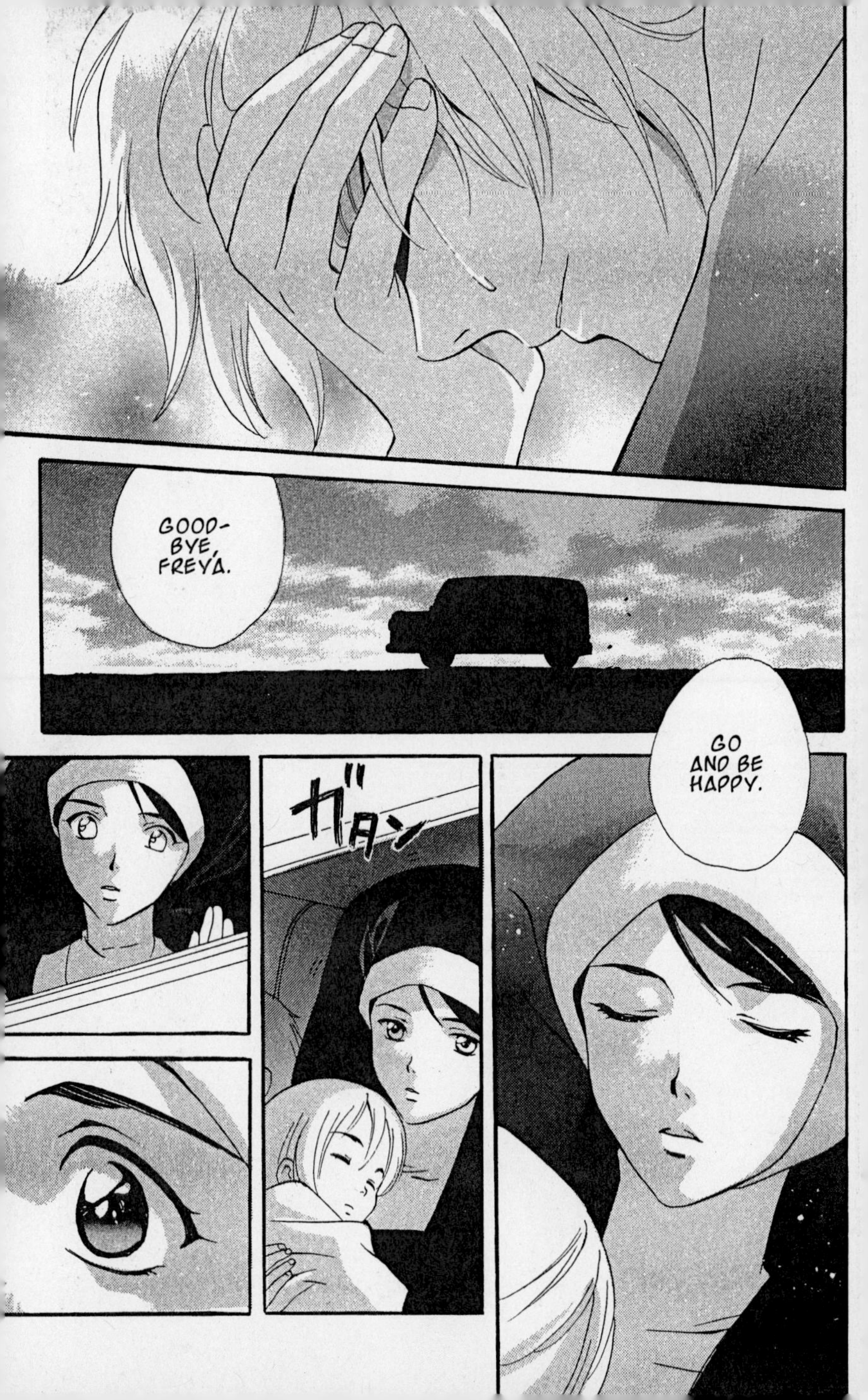
GOOD-BYE, FREYA.
GO AND BE HAPPY.
ガタン

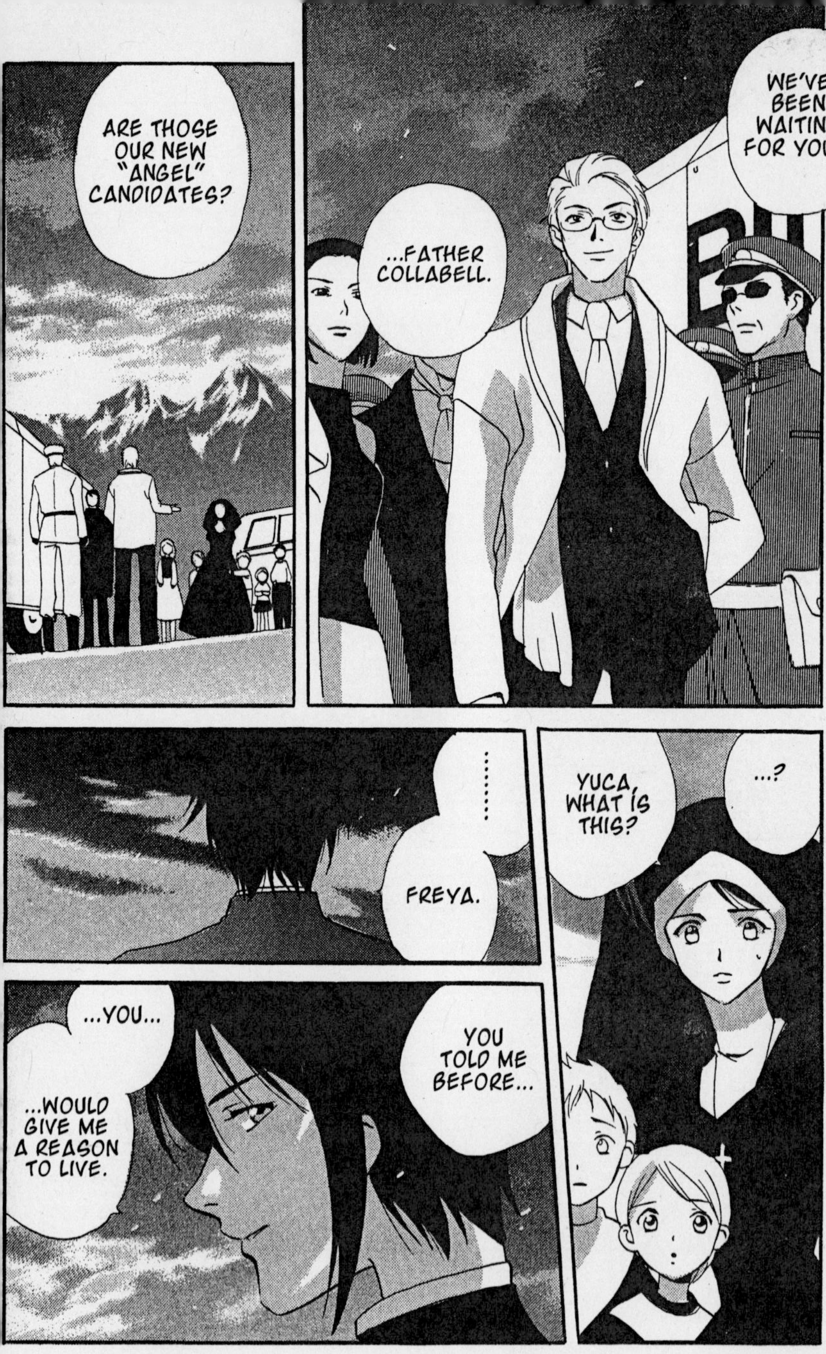
WE'VE BEEN WAITING FOR YOU...
...FATHER COLLABELL.
ARE THOSE OUR NEW "ANGEL" CANDIDATES?
...?
YUCA, WHAT IS THIS?
....
FREYA.
YOU TOLD ME BEFORE...
...YOU...
...WOULD GIVE ME A REASON TO LIVE.

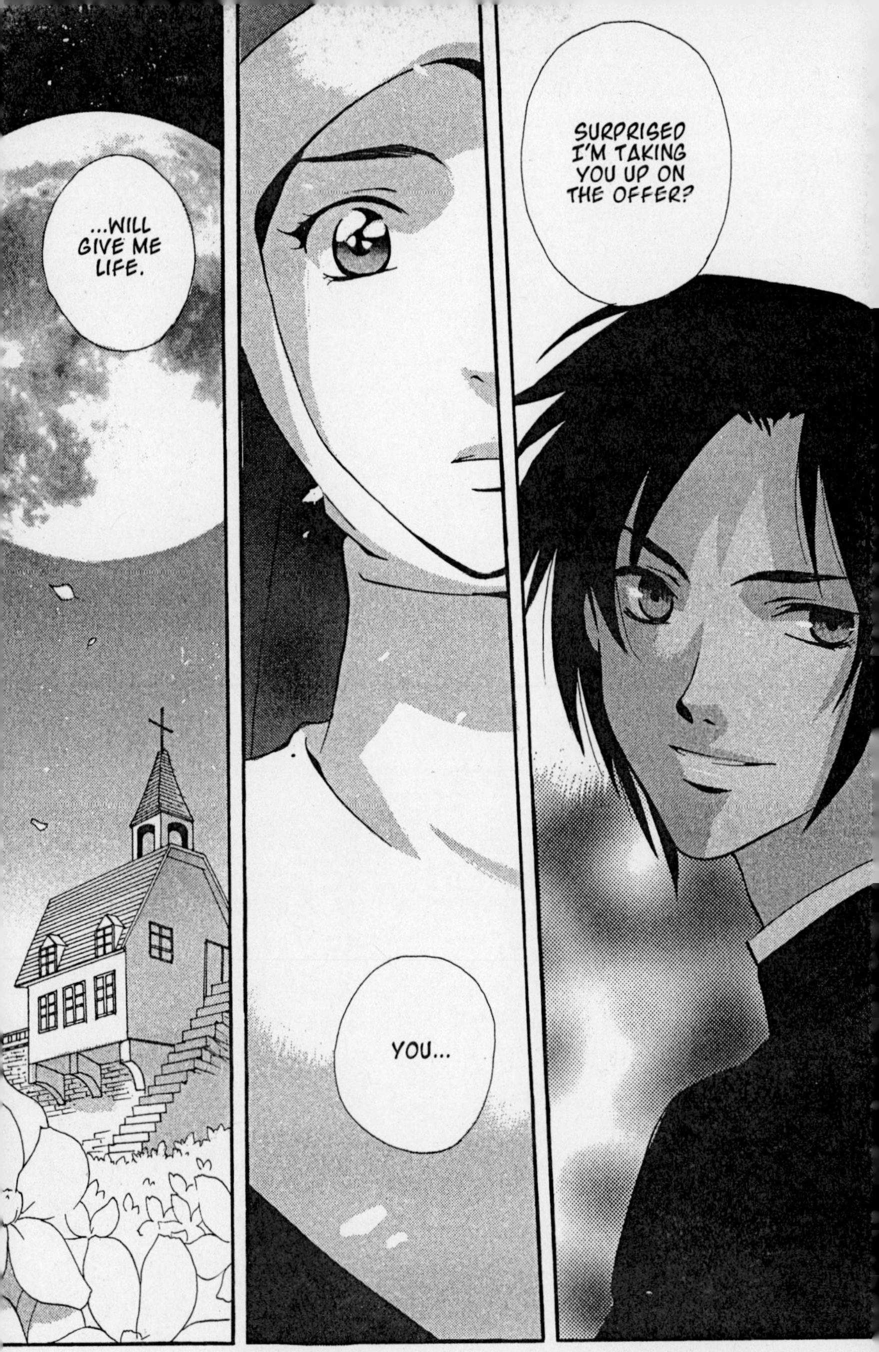
SURPRISED I'M TAKING YOU UP ON THE OFFER?
YOU...
...WILL GIVE ME LIFE.

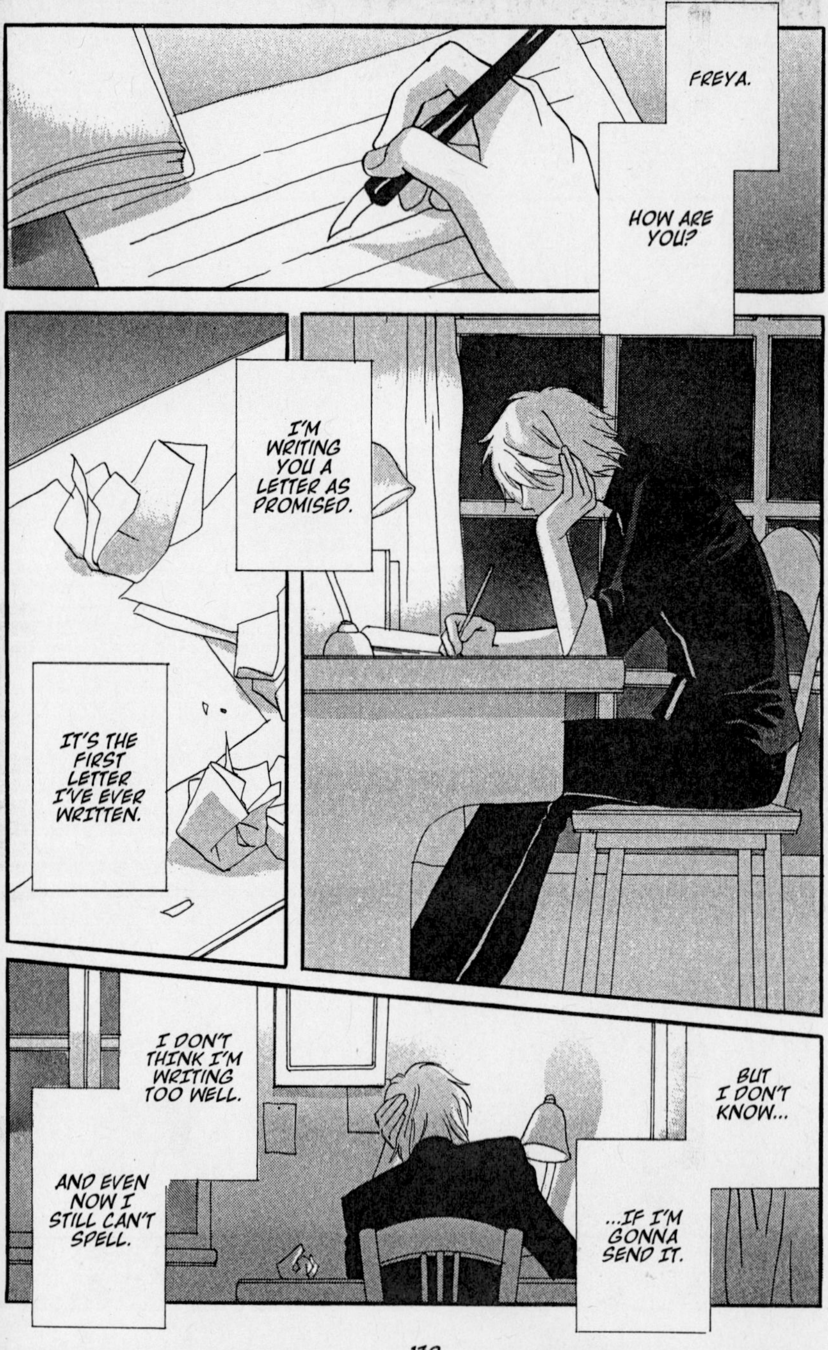
FREYA.
HOW ARE YOU?
I'M WRITING YOU A LETTER AS PROMISED.
IT'S THE FIRST LETTER I'VE EVER WRITTEN.
BUT I DON'T KNOW...
...IF I'M GONNA SEND IT.
I DON'T THINK I'M WRITING TOO WELL.
AND EVEN NOW I STILL CAN'T SPELL.

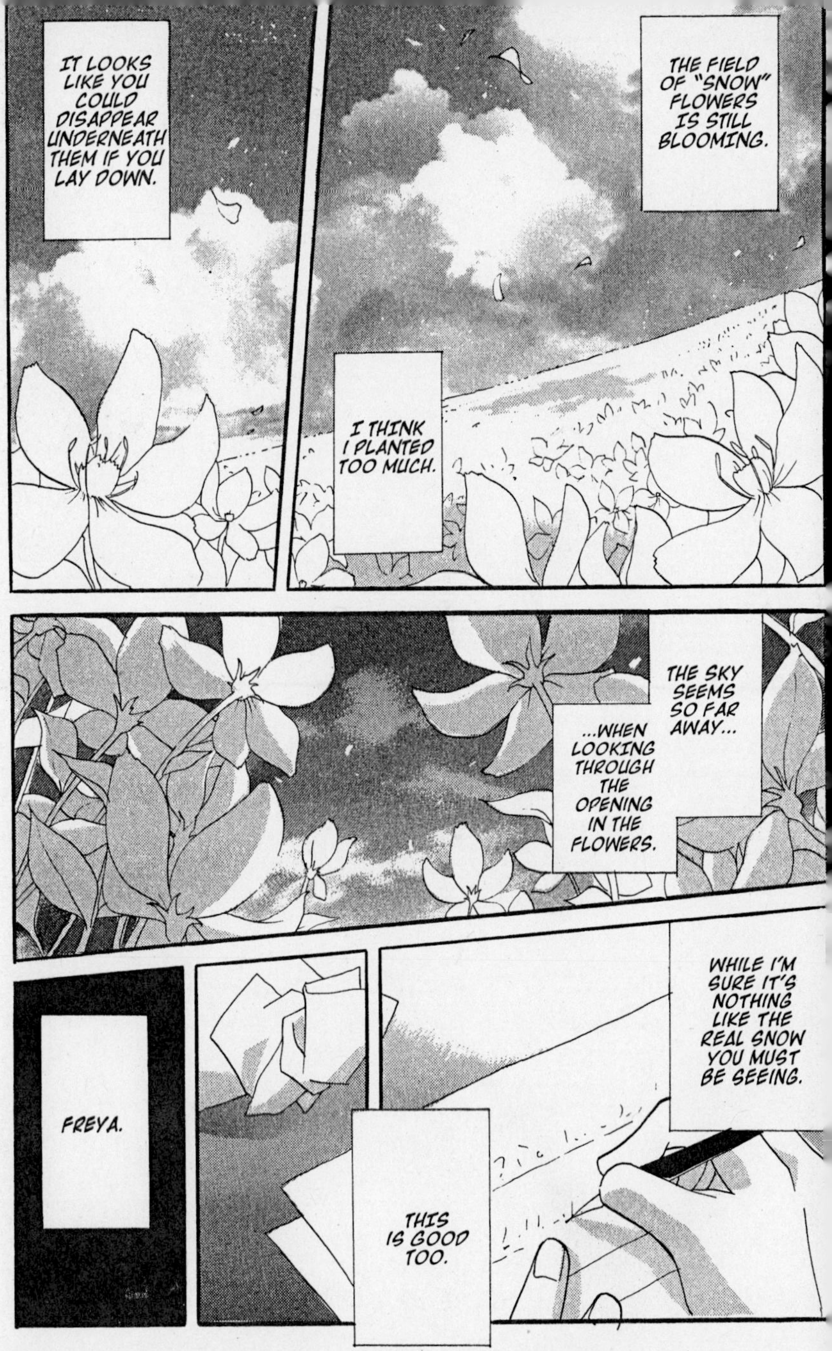
THE FIELD OF "SNOW" FLOWERS IS STILL BLOOMING.
I THINK I PLANTED TOO MUCH.
IT LOOKS LIKE YOU COULD DISAPPEAR UNDERNEATH THEM IF YOU LAY DOWN.
THE SKY SEEMS SO FAR AWAY...
...WHEN LOOKING THROUGH THE OPENING IN THE FLOWERS.
WHILE I'M SURE IT'S NOTHING LIKE THE REAL SNOW YOU MUST BE SEEING.
THIS IS GOOD TOO.
FREYA.

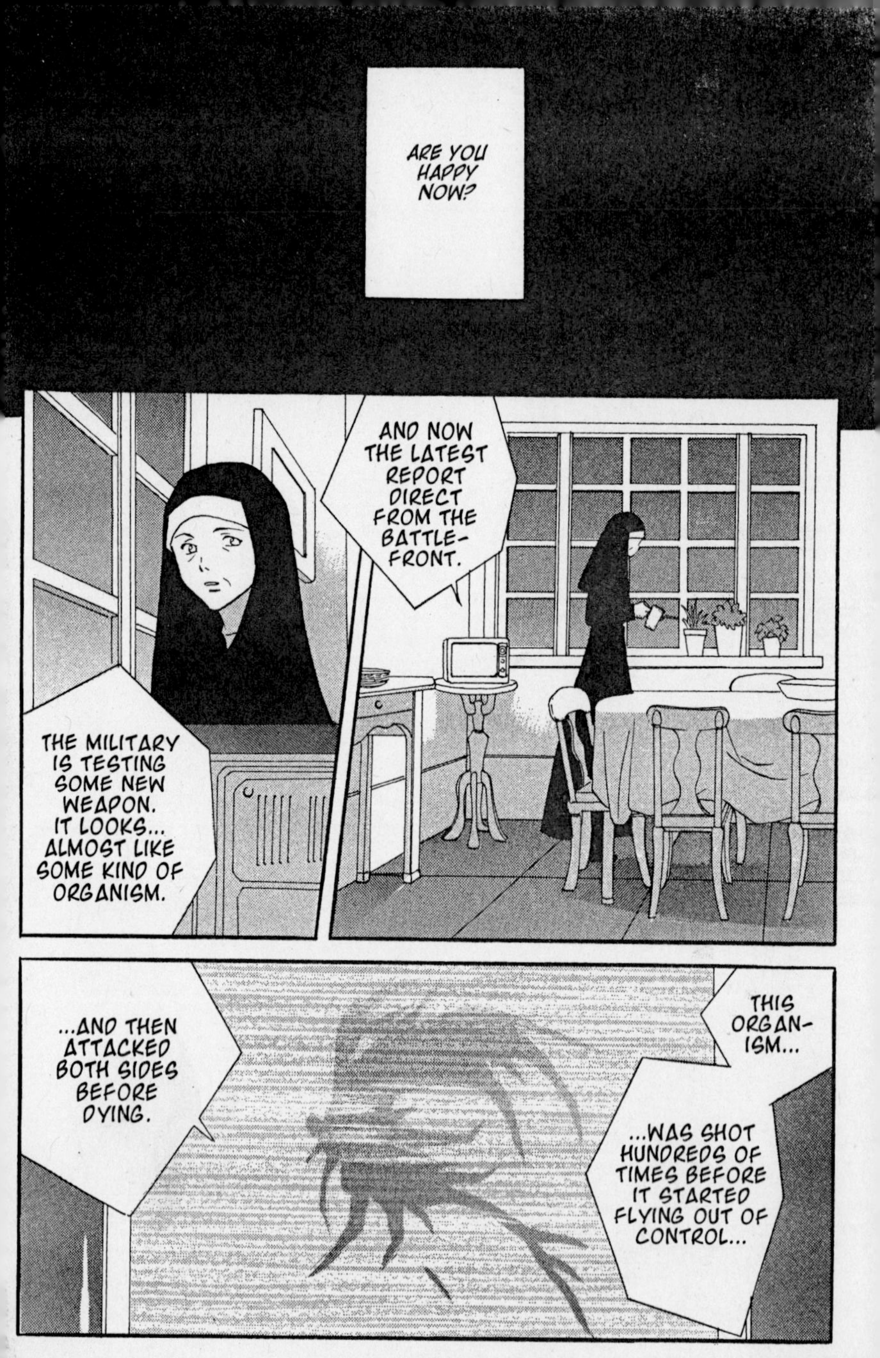
ARE YOU HAPPY NOW?
AND NOW THE LATEST REPORT DIRECT FROM THE BATTLE-FRONT.
THE MILITARY IS TESTING SOME NEW WEAPON. IT LOOKS... ALMOST LIKE SOME KIND OF ORGANISM.
THIS ORGAN-ISM...
...WAS SHOT HUNDREDS OF TIMES BEFORE IT STARTED FLYING OUT OF CONTROL...
...AND THEN ATTACKED BOTH SIDES BEFORE DYING.

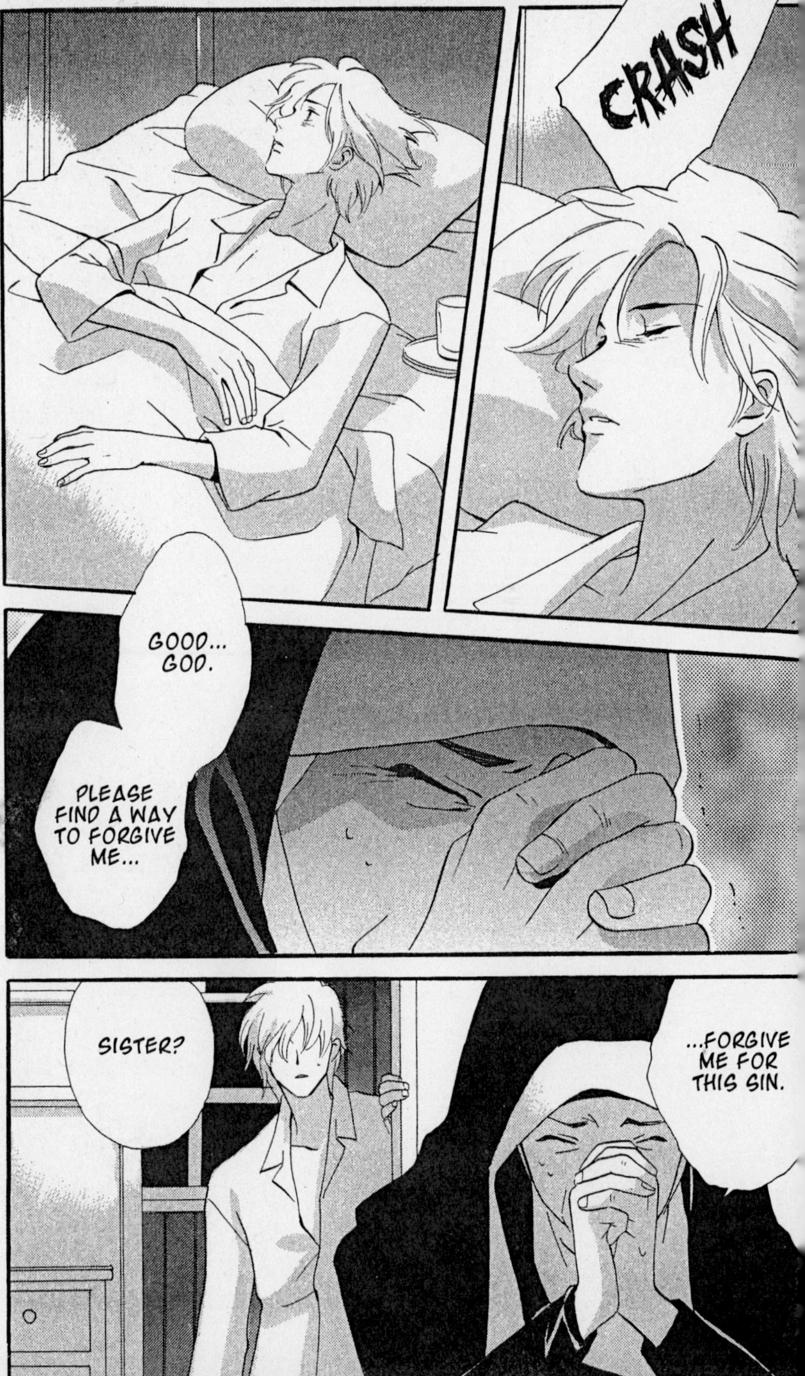
CRASH
GOOD... GOD.
PLEASE FIND A WAY TO FORGIVE ME...
...FORGIVE ME FOR THIS SIN.
SISTER?

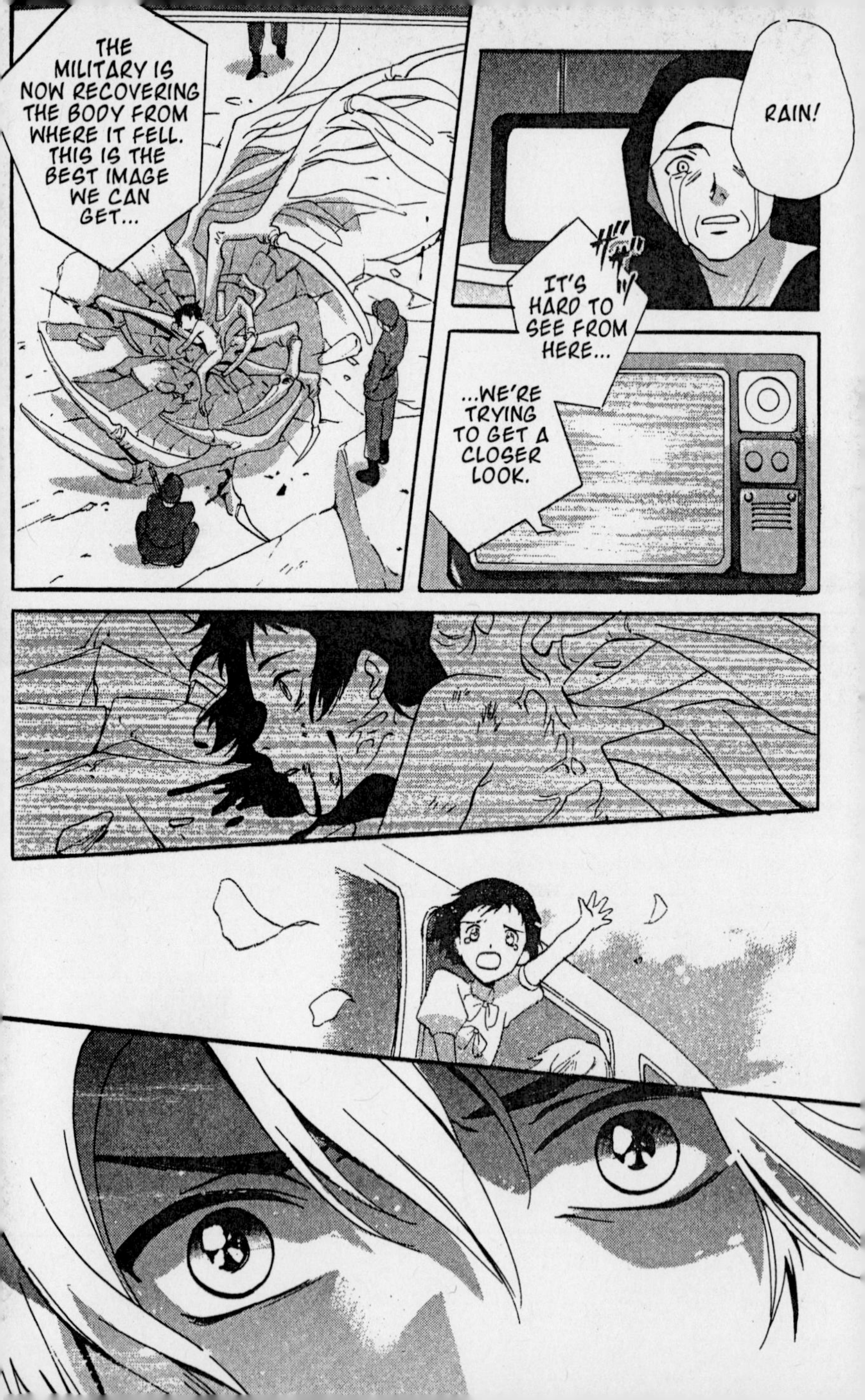
RAIN!
IT'S HARD TO SEE FROM HERE...
...WE'RE TRYING TO GET A CLOSER LOOK.
THE MILITARY IS NOW RECOVERING THE BODY FROM WHERE IT FELL. THIS IS THE BEST IMAGE WE CAN GET...

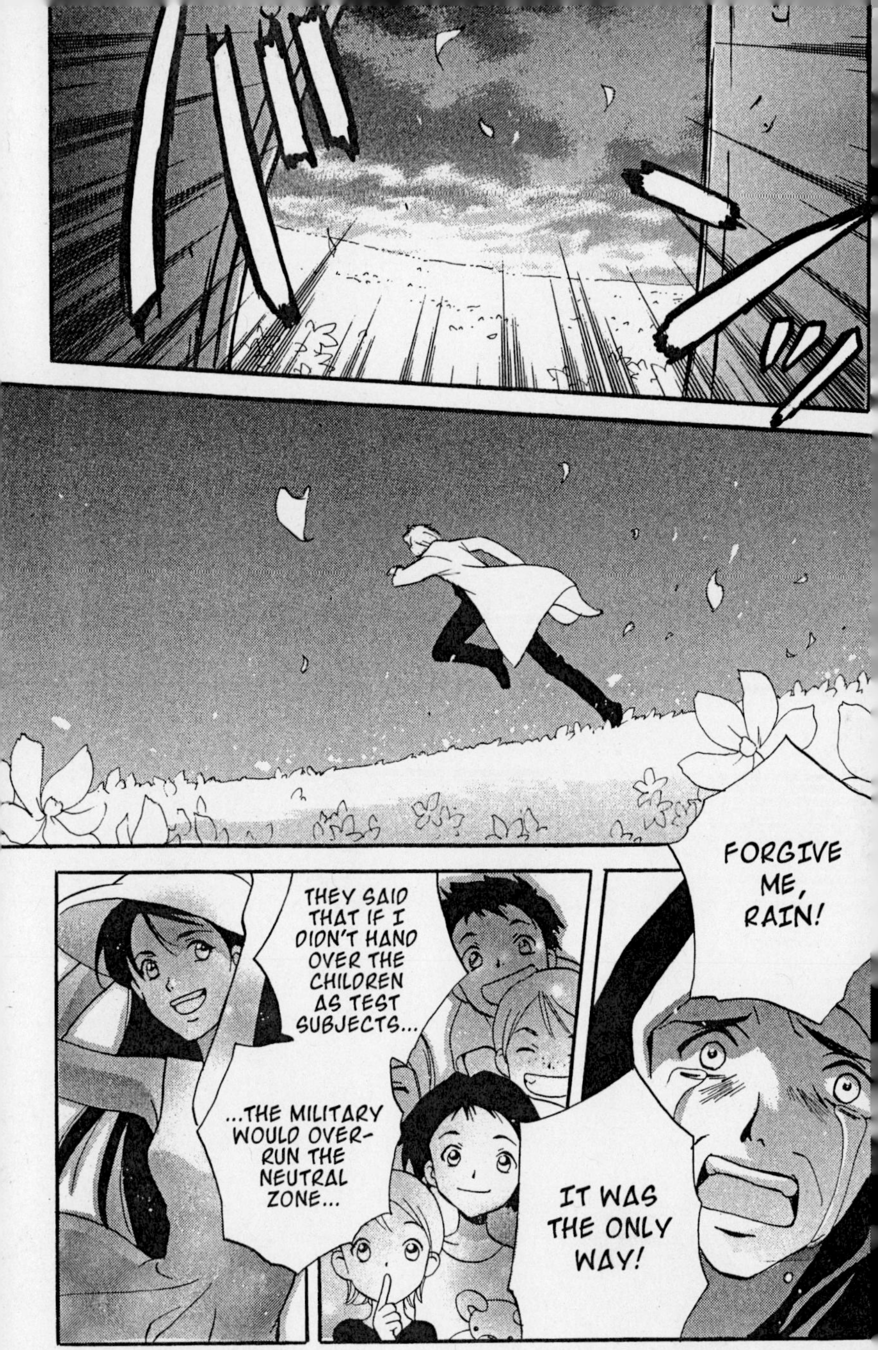
FORGIVE ME, RAIN!
IT WAS THE ONLY WAY!
THEY SAID THAT IF I DIDN'T HAND OVER THE CHILDREN AS TEST SUBJECTS...
...THE MILITARY WOULD OVER-RUN THE NEUTRAL ZONE...

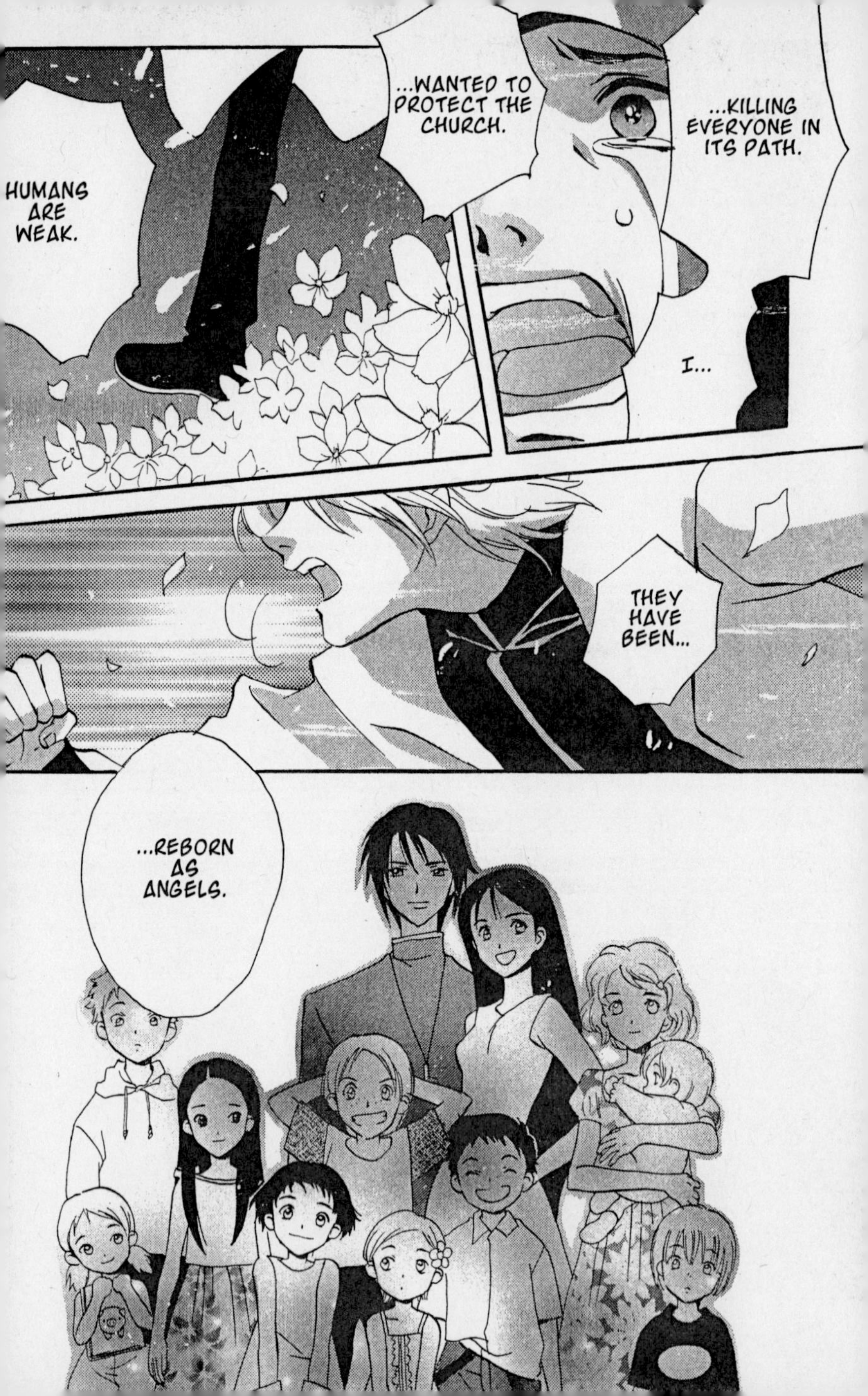
...KILLING EVERYONE IN ITS PATH.
I...
...WANTED TO PROTECT THE CHURCH.
HUMANS ARE WEAK.
THEY HAVE BEEN...
...REBORN AS ANGELS.

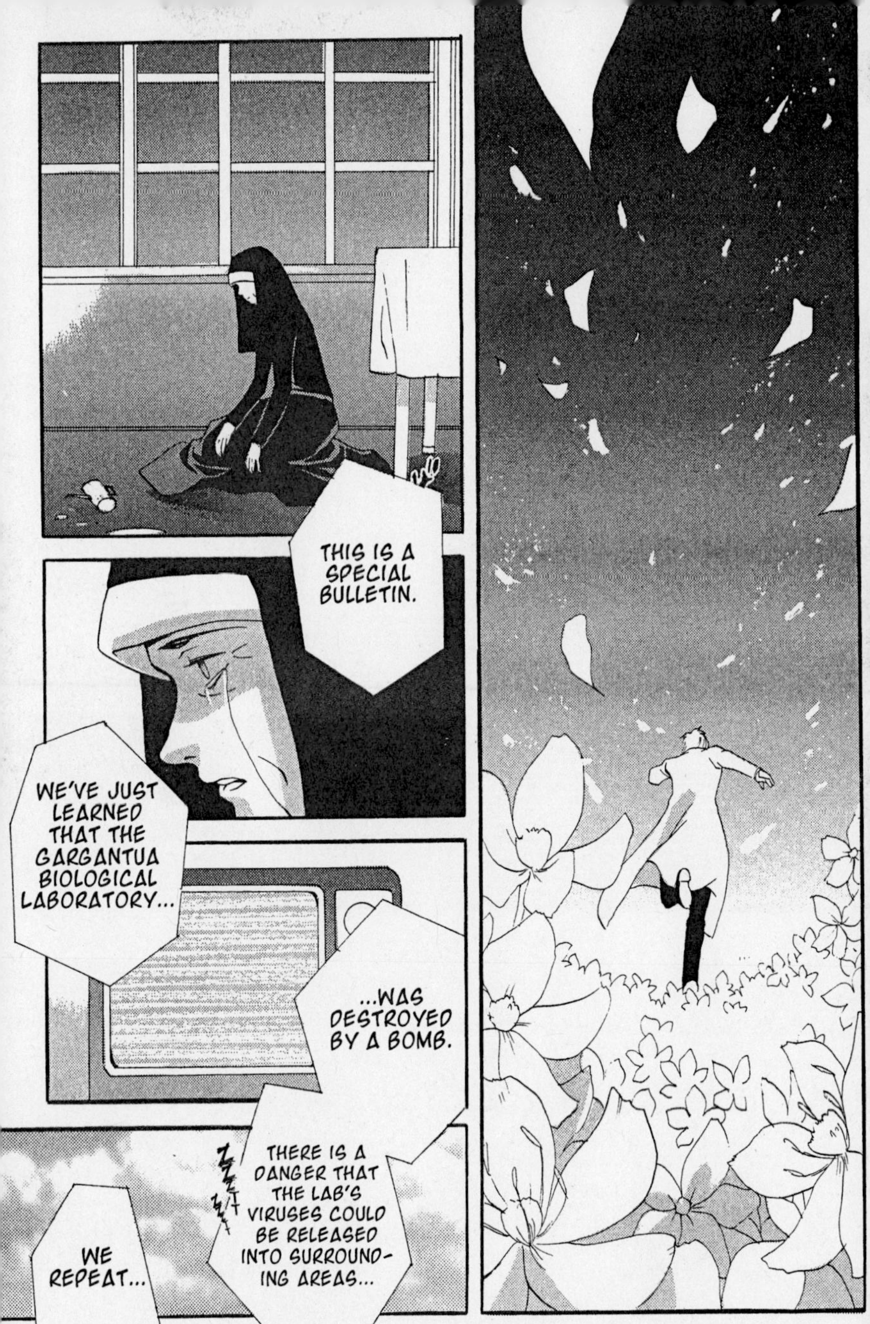

THIS IS A SPECIAL BULLETIN.
WE'VE JUST LEARNED THAT THE GARGANTUA BIOLOGICAL LABORATORY...
...WAS DESTROYED BY A BOMB.
THERE IS A DANGER THAT THE LAB'S VIRUSES COULD BE RELEASED INTO SURROUND-ING AREAS...
WE REPEAT...

THE BIOLOGICAL LABORATORY...

...HAS BEEN DESTROYED.

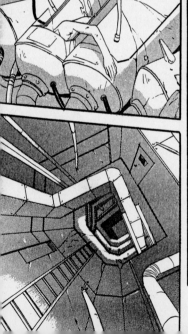

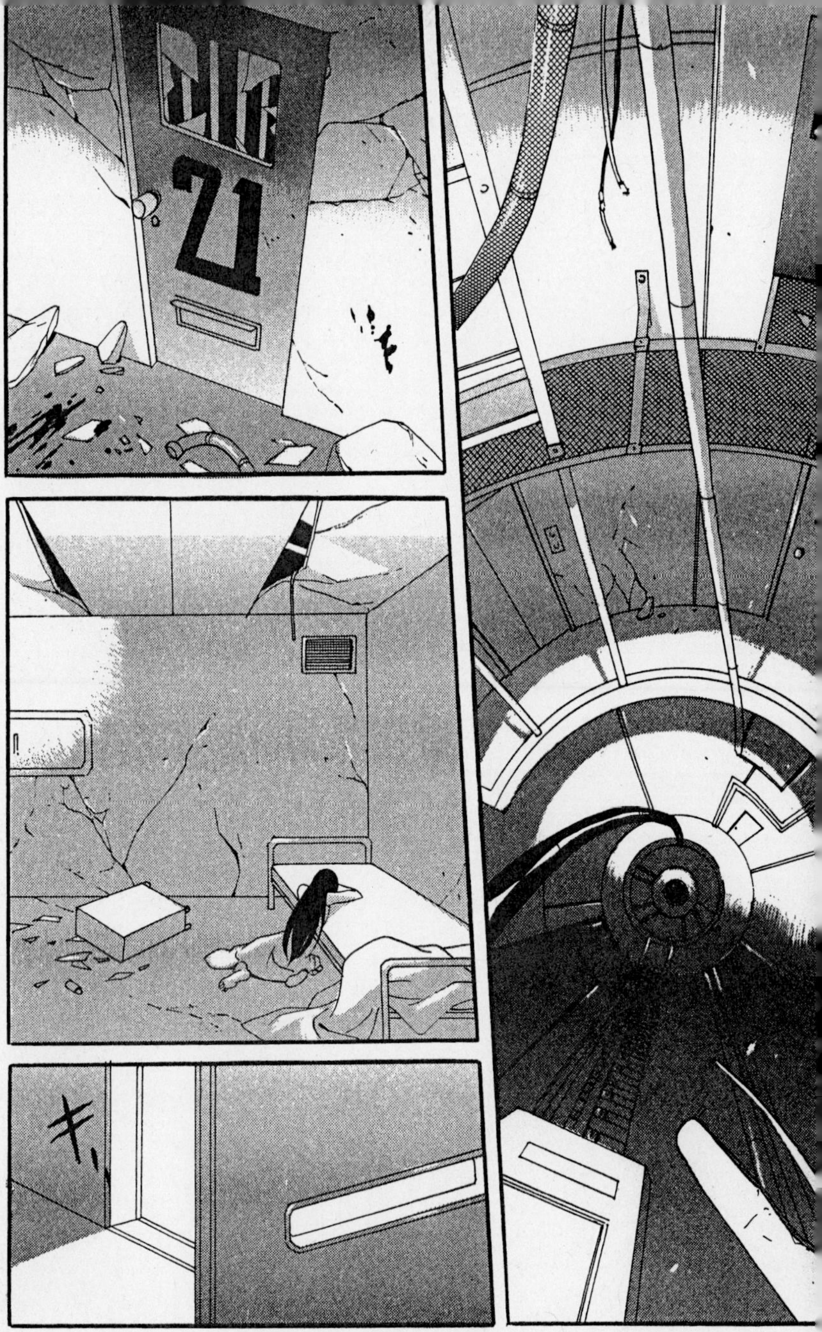
21
キ

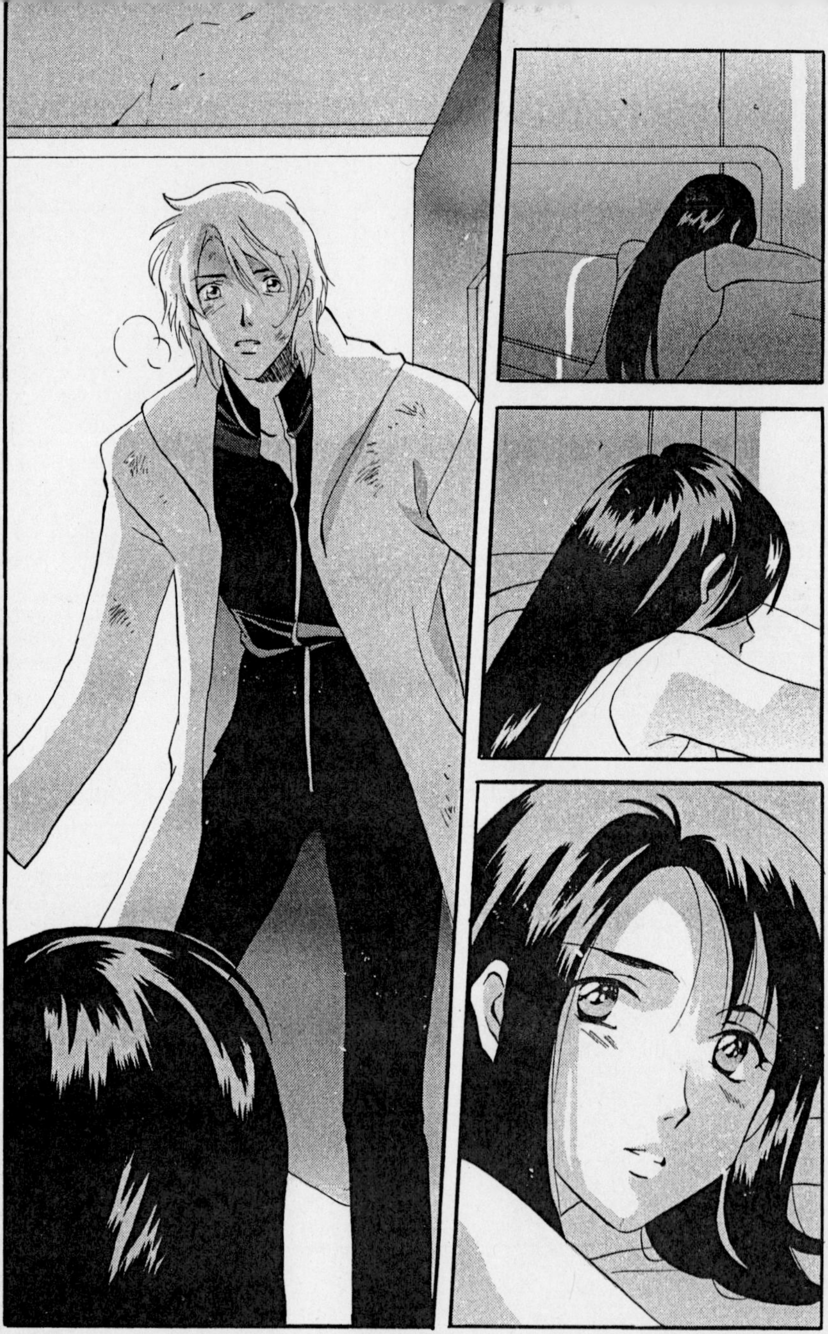

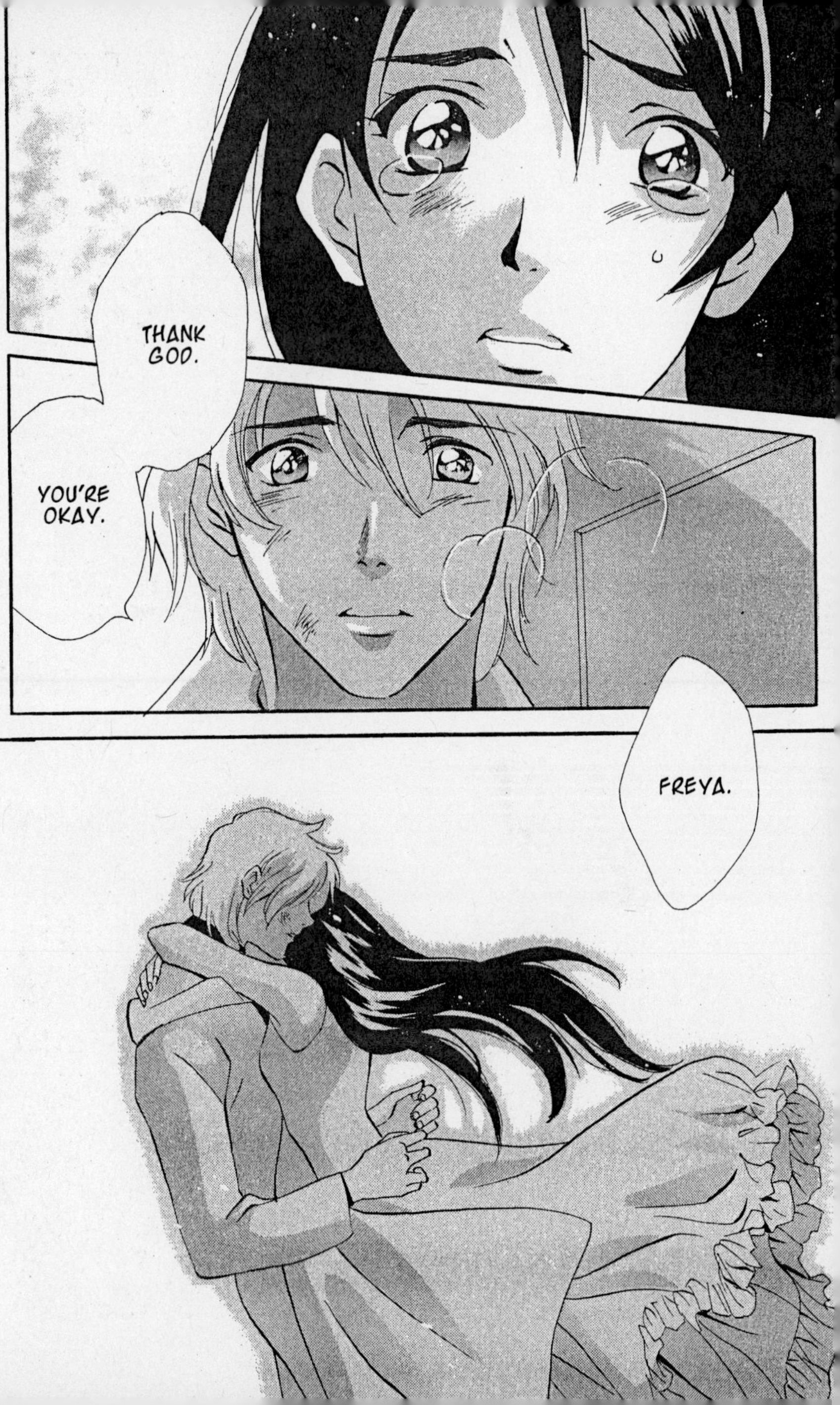
THANK GOD.
YOU'RE OKAY.
FREYA.

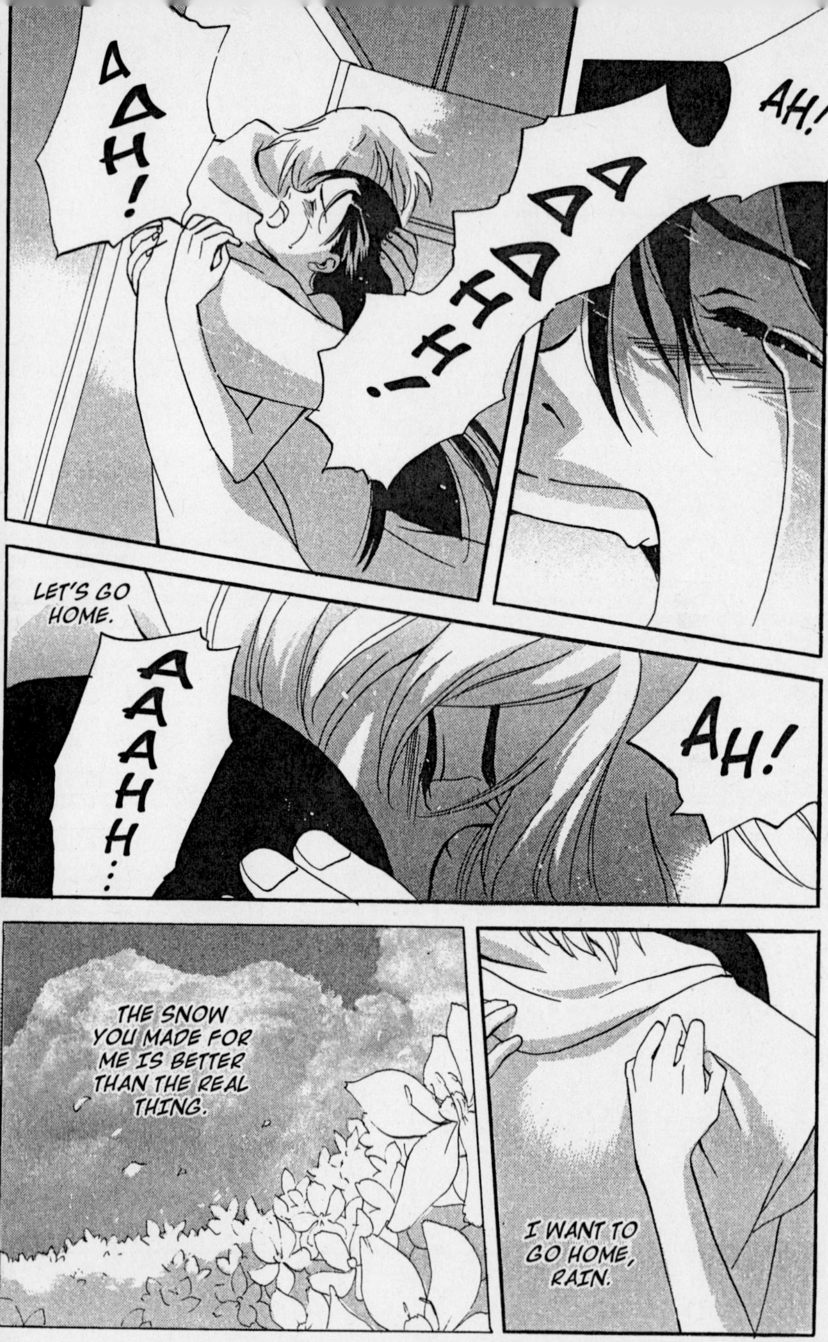
AH!
AAAAH!
AAH!
AH!
AAAAH...
LET'S GO HOME.
I WANT TO GO HOME, RAIN.
THE SNOW YOU MADE FOR ME IS BETTER THAN THE REAL THING.

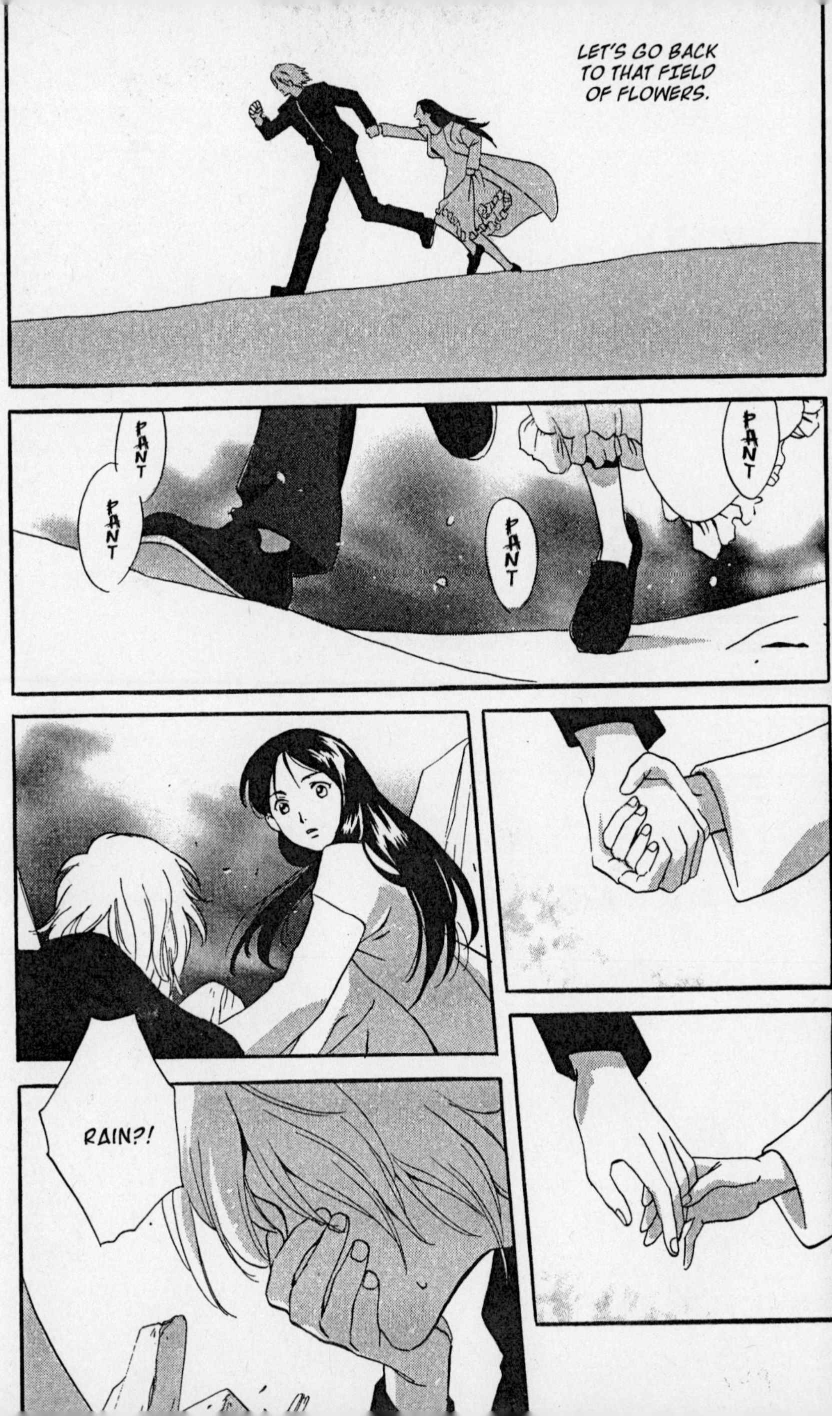
LET'S GO BACK TO THAT FIELD OF FLOWERS.
PANT
PANT
PANT
PANT
RAIN?!

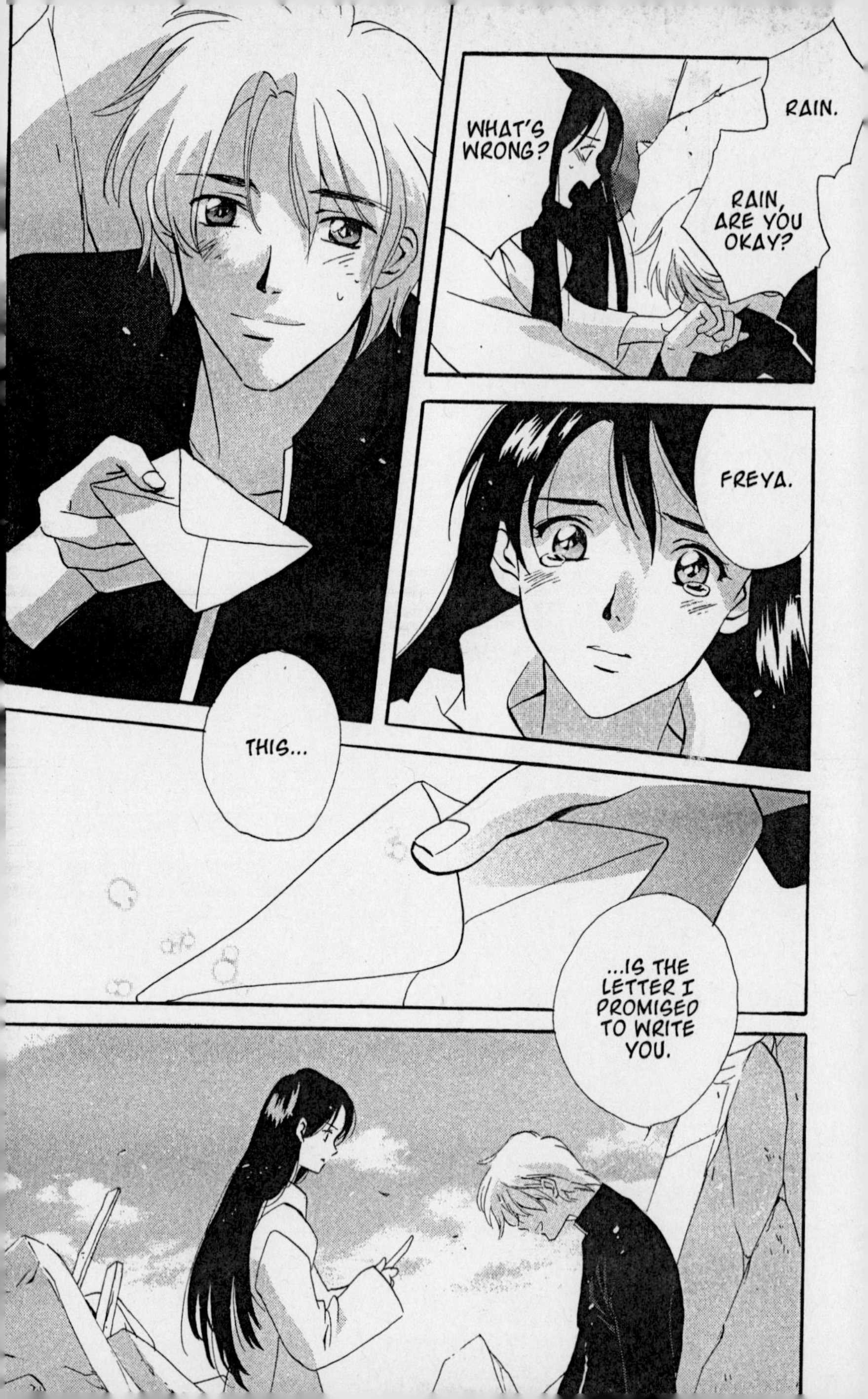
RAIN.
RAIN, ARE YOU OKAY?
WHAT'S WRONG?
FREYA.
THIS...
...IS THE LETTER I PROMISED TO WRITE YOU.

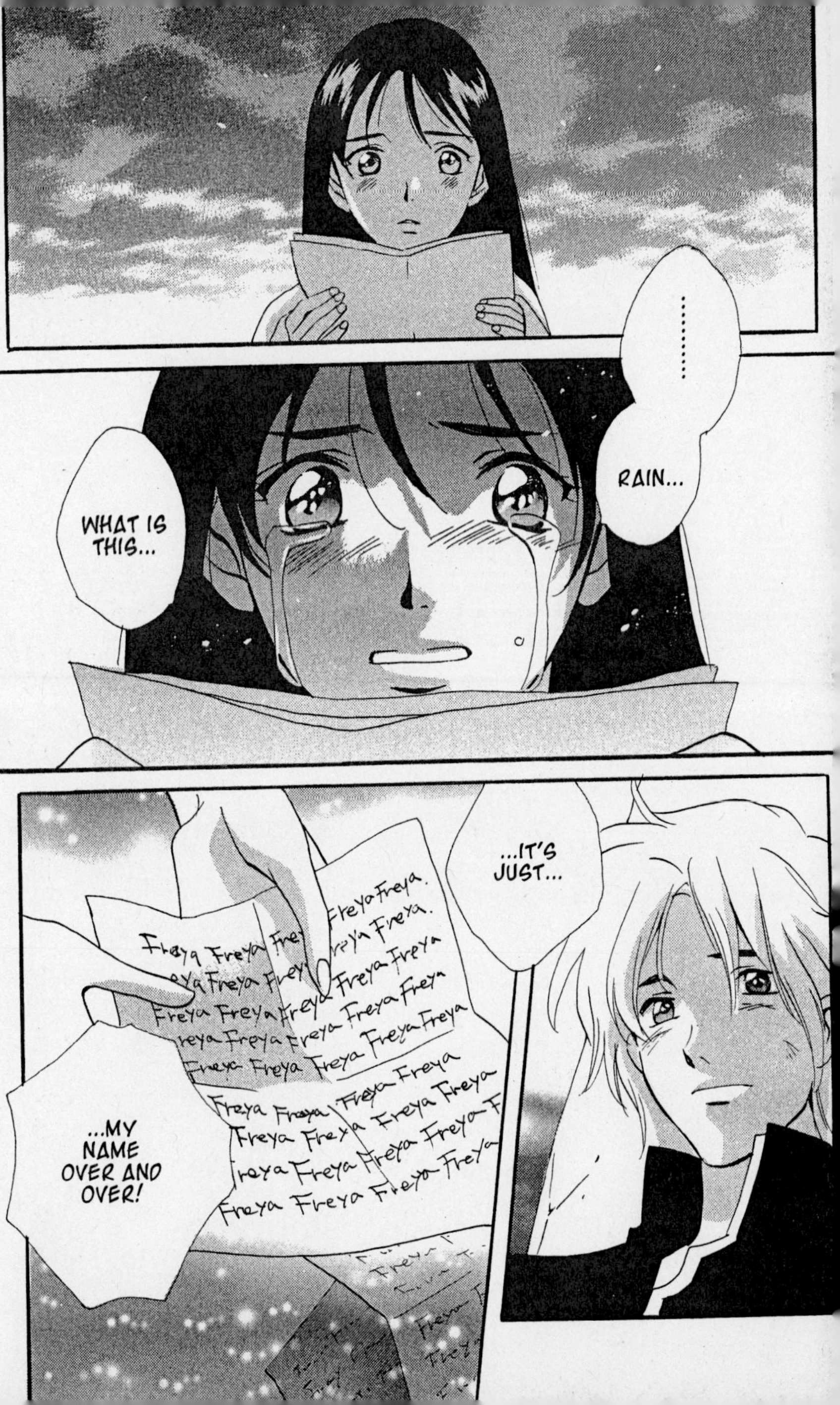
......
RAIN...
WHAT IS THIS...
...IT'S JUST...
...MY NAME OVER AND OVER!

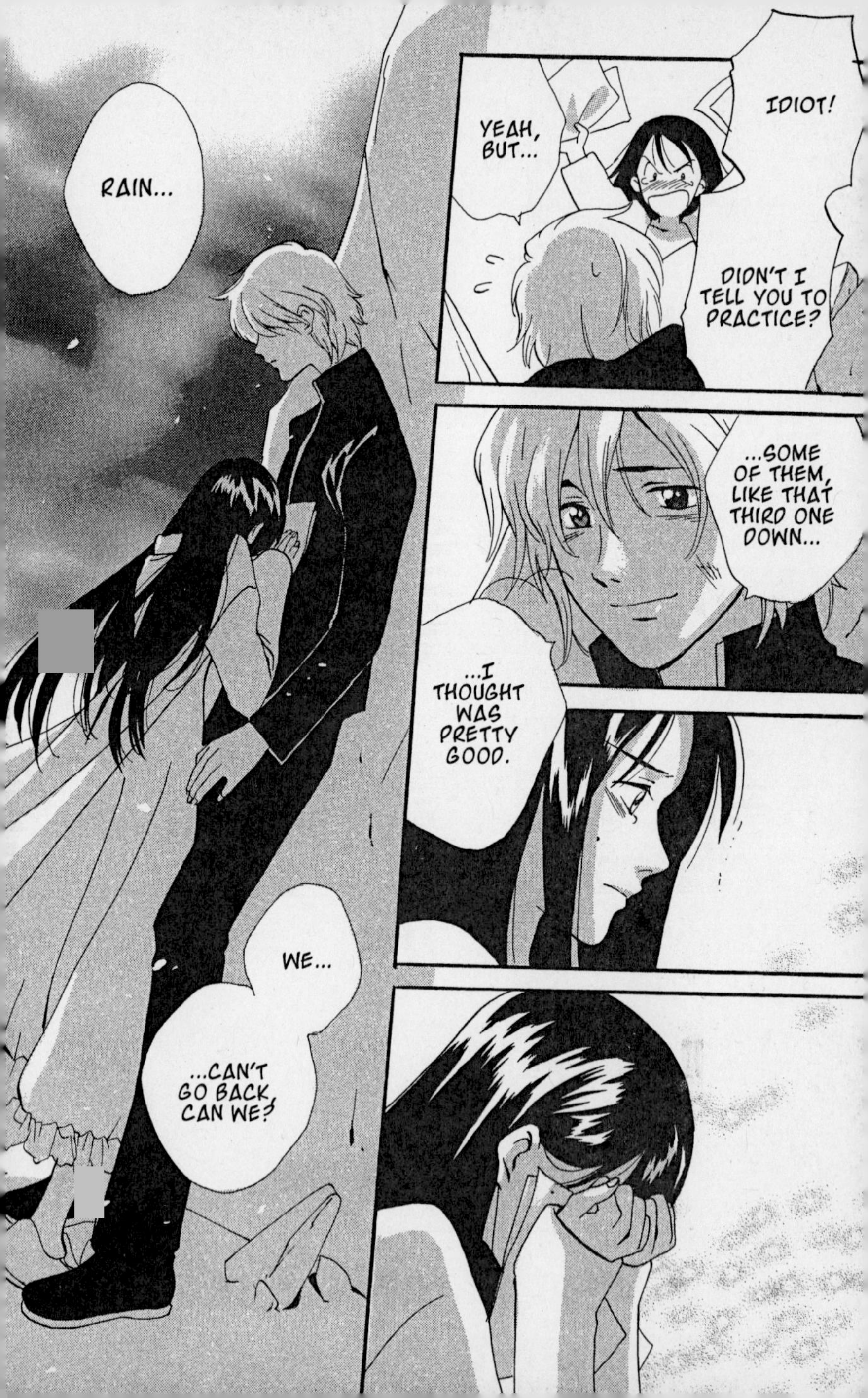
IDIOT!
YEAH, BUT...
DIDN'T I TELL YOU TO PRACTICE?
...SOME OF THEM, LIKE THAT THIRD ONE DOWN...
...I THOUGHT WAS PRETTY GOOD.
RAIN...
WE...
...CAN'T GO BACK, CAN WE?

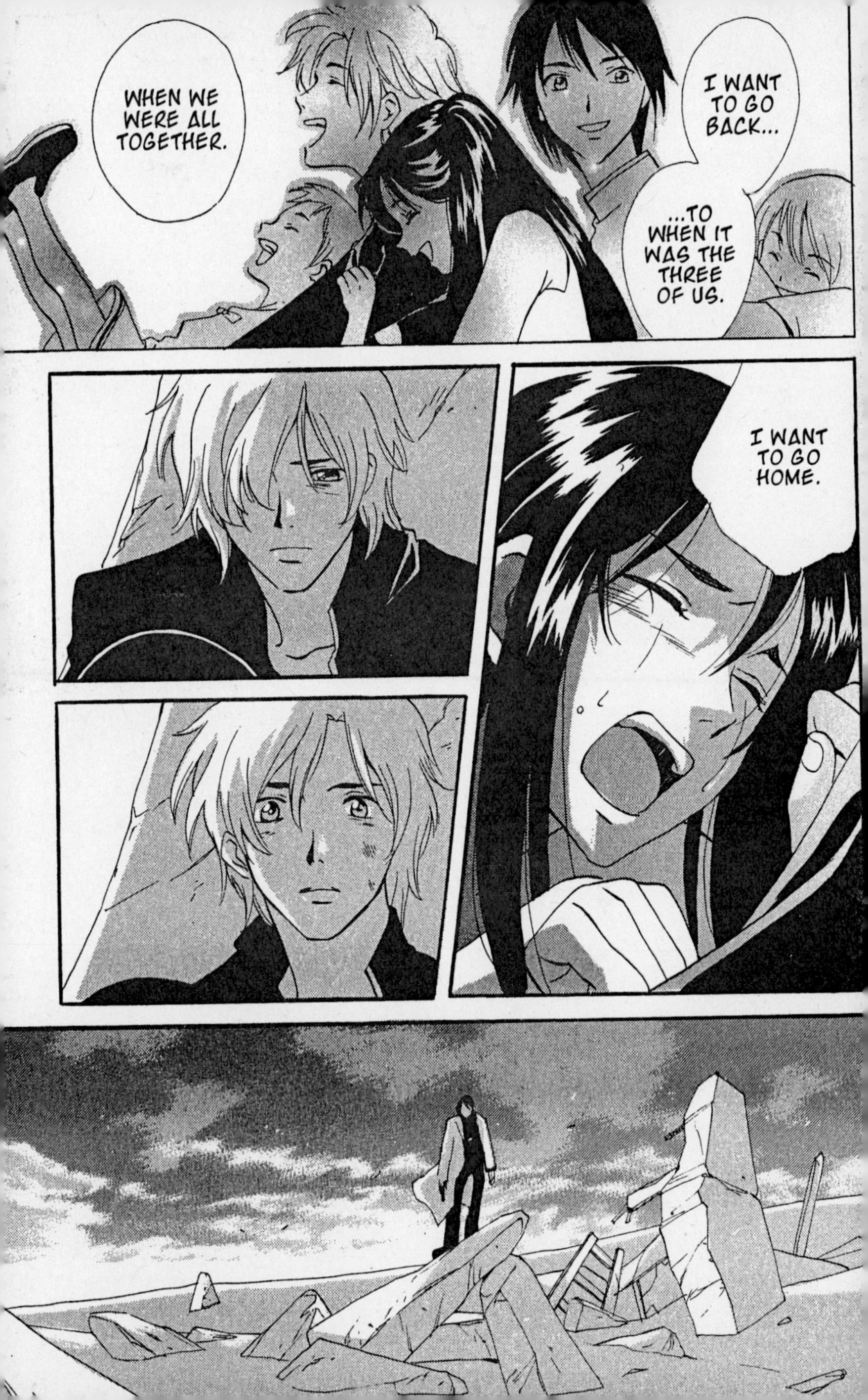
I WANT TO GO BACK...
...TO WHEN IT WAS THE THREE OF US.
WHEN WE WERE ALL TOGETHER.
I WANT TO GO HOME.

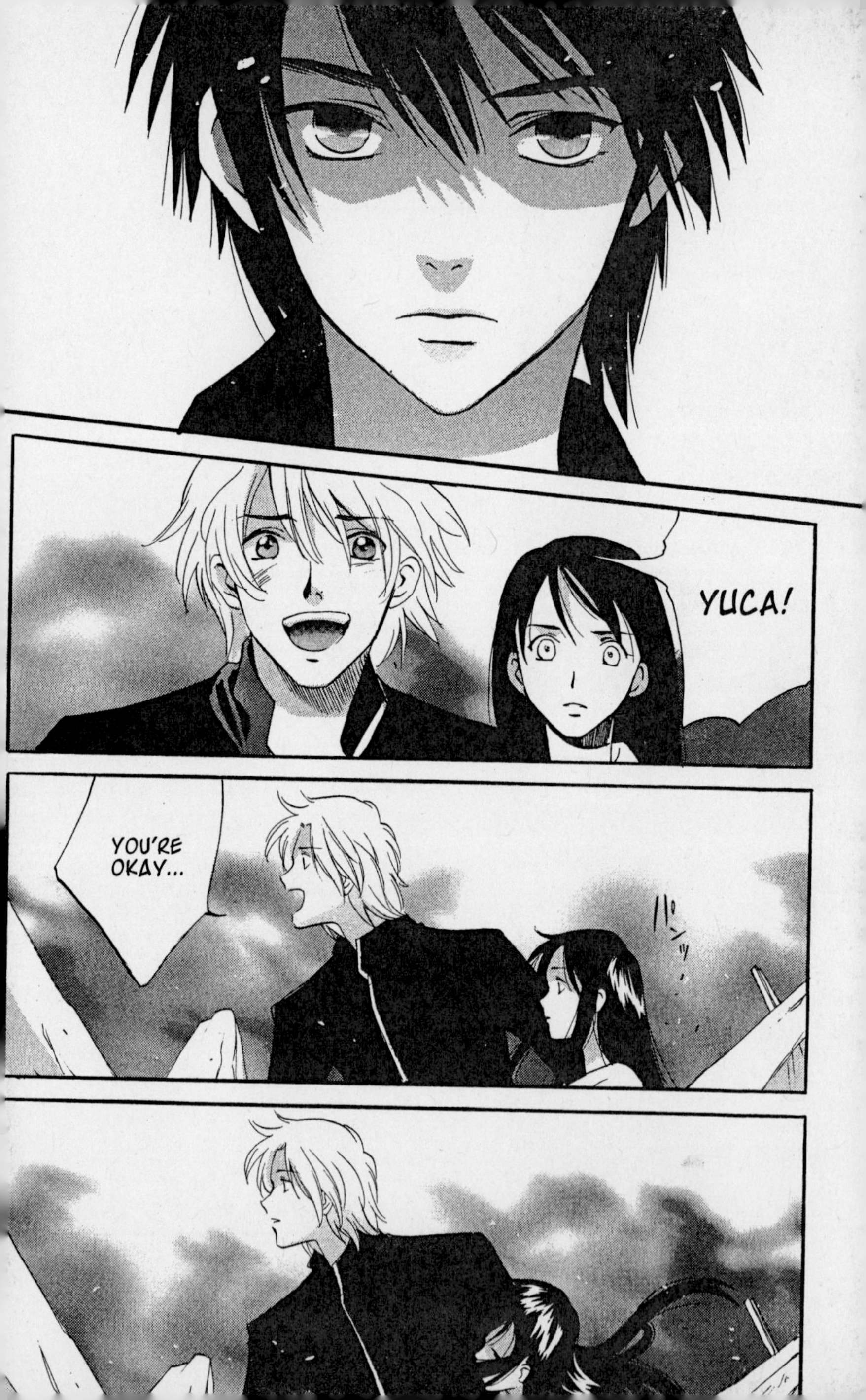
YUCA!
YOU'RE OKAY...

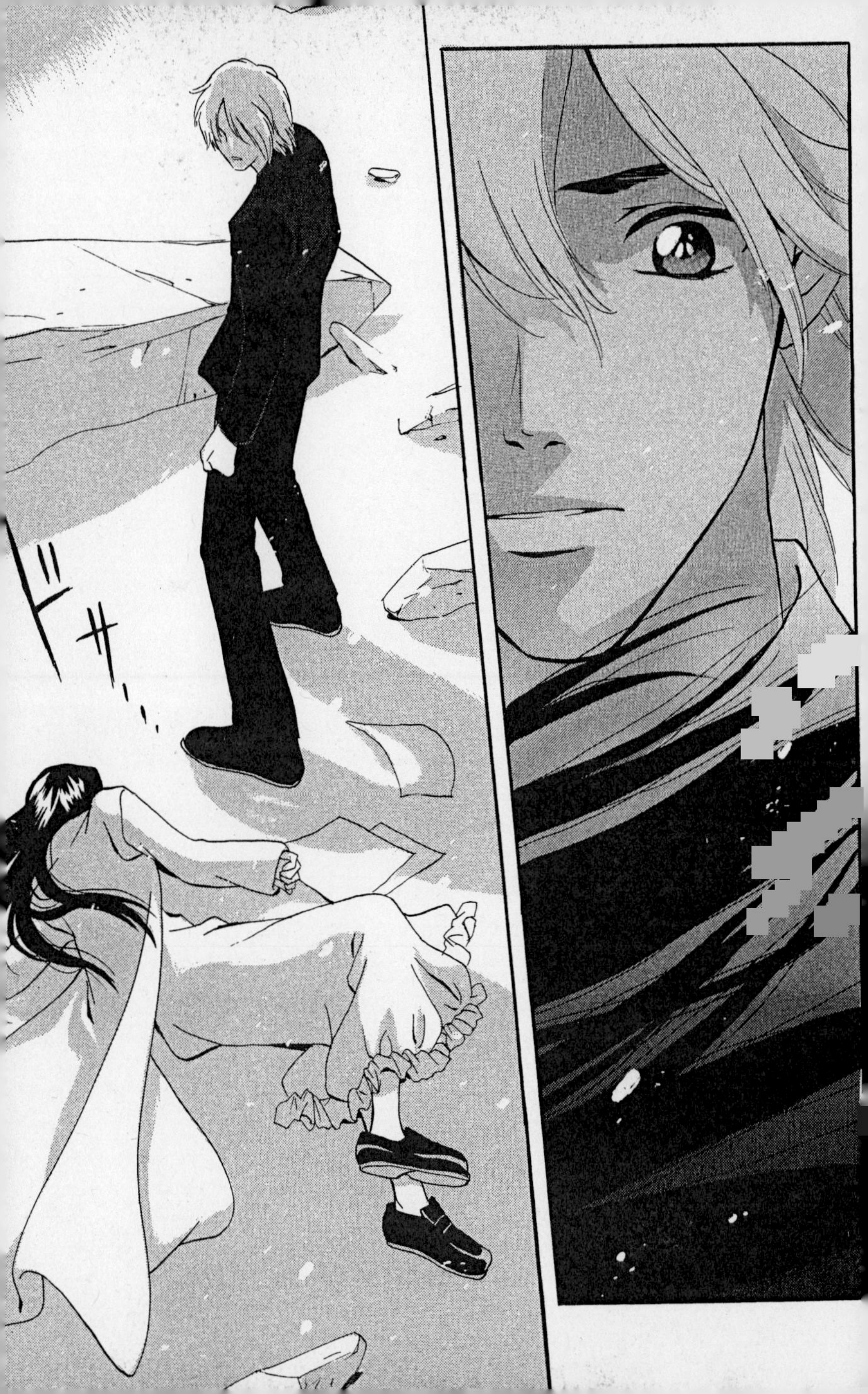

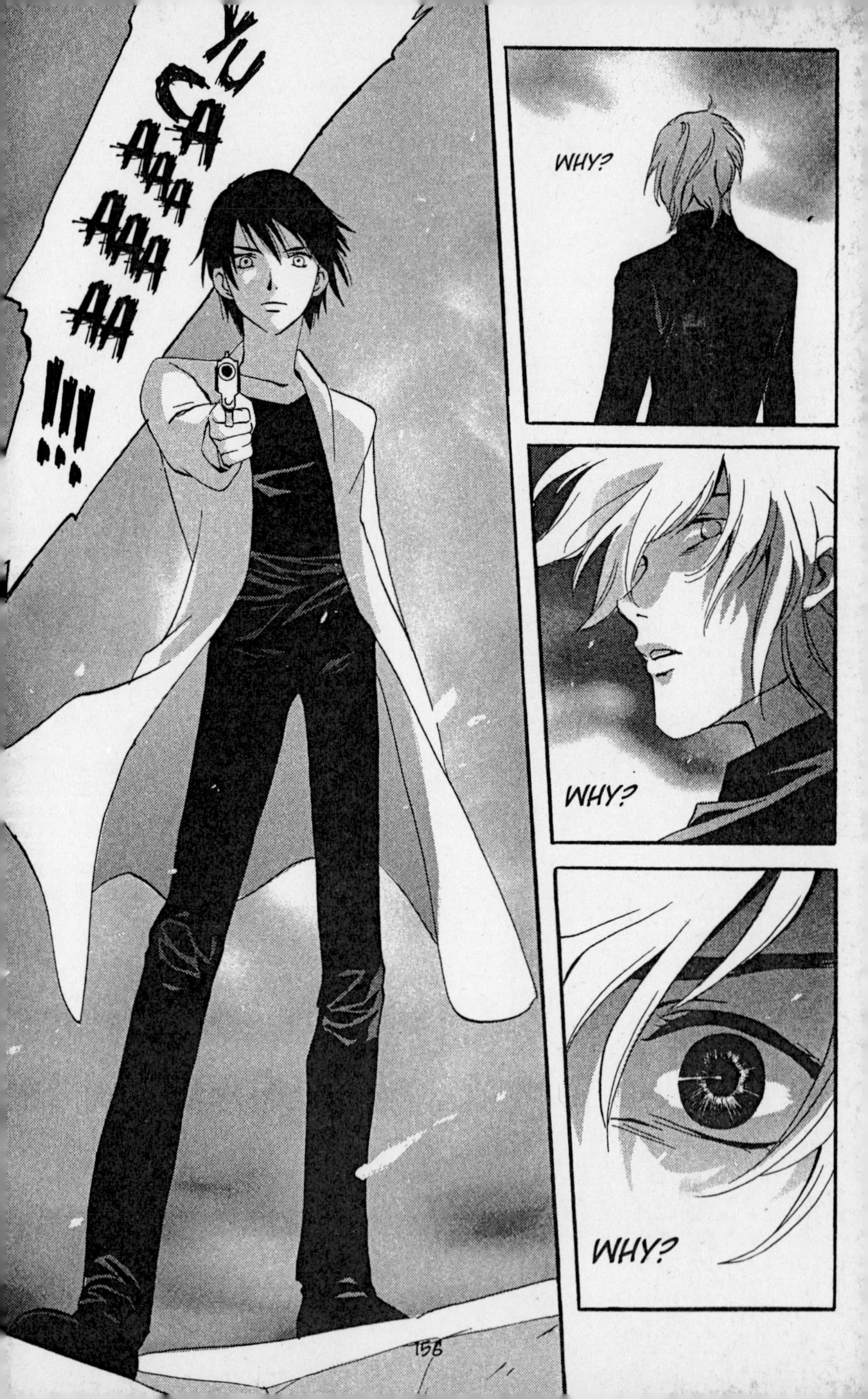
WHY?
WHY?
WHY?
YUCAAAAAAAA!!!

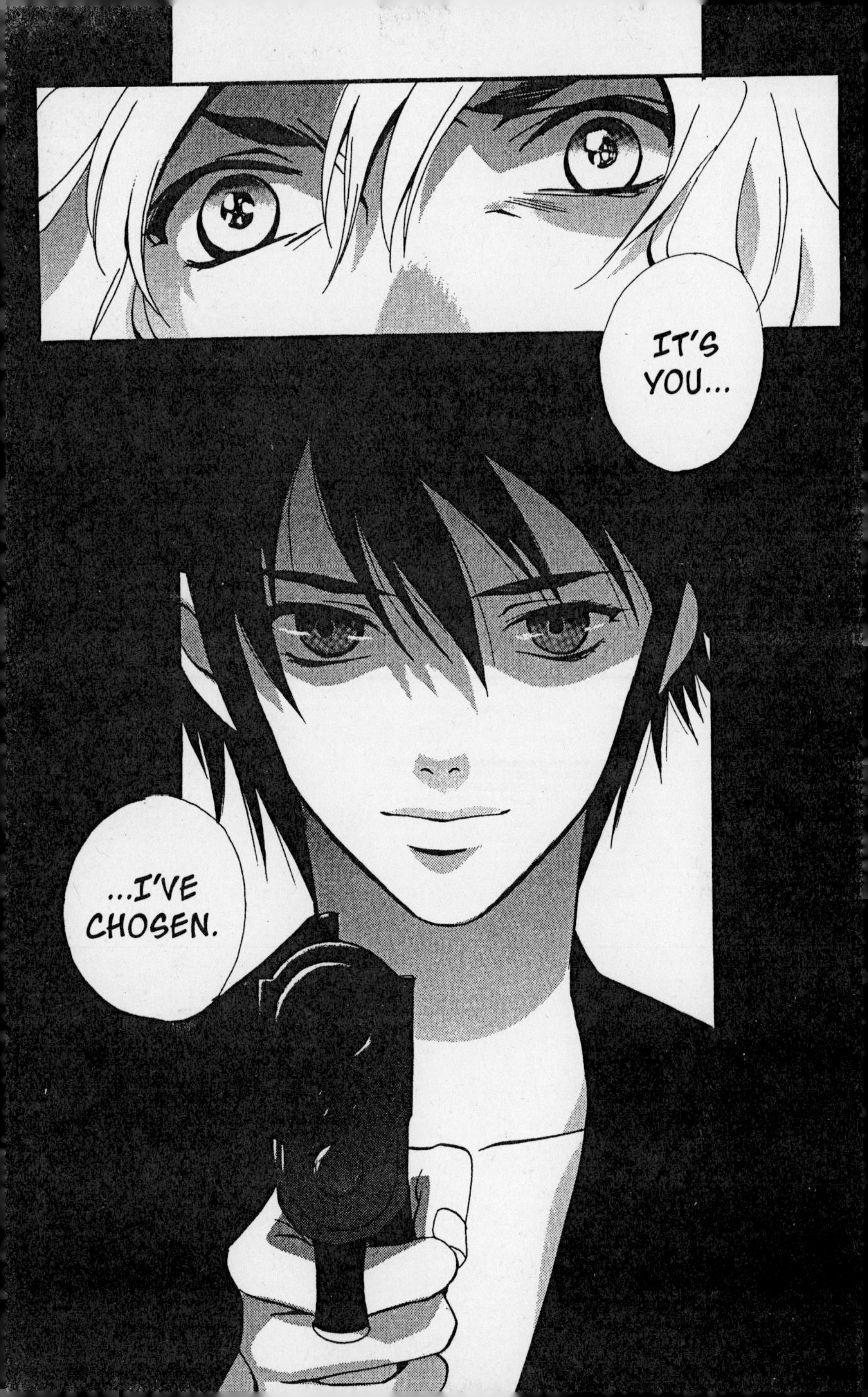
IT'S YOU...
...I'VE CHOSEN.

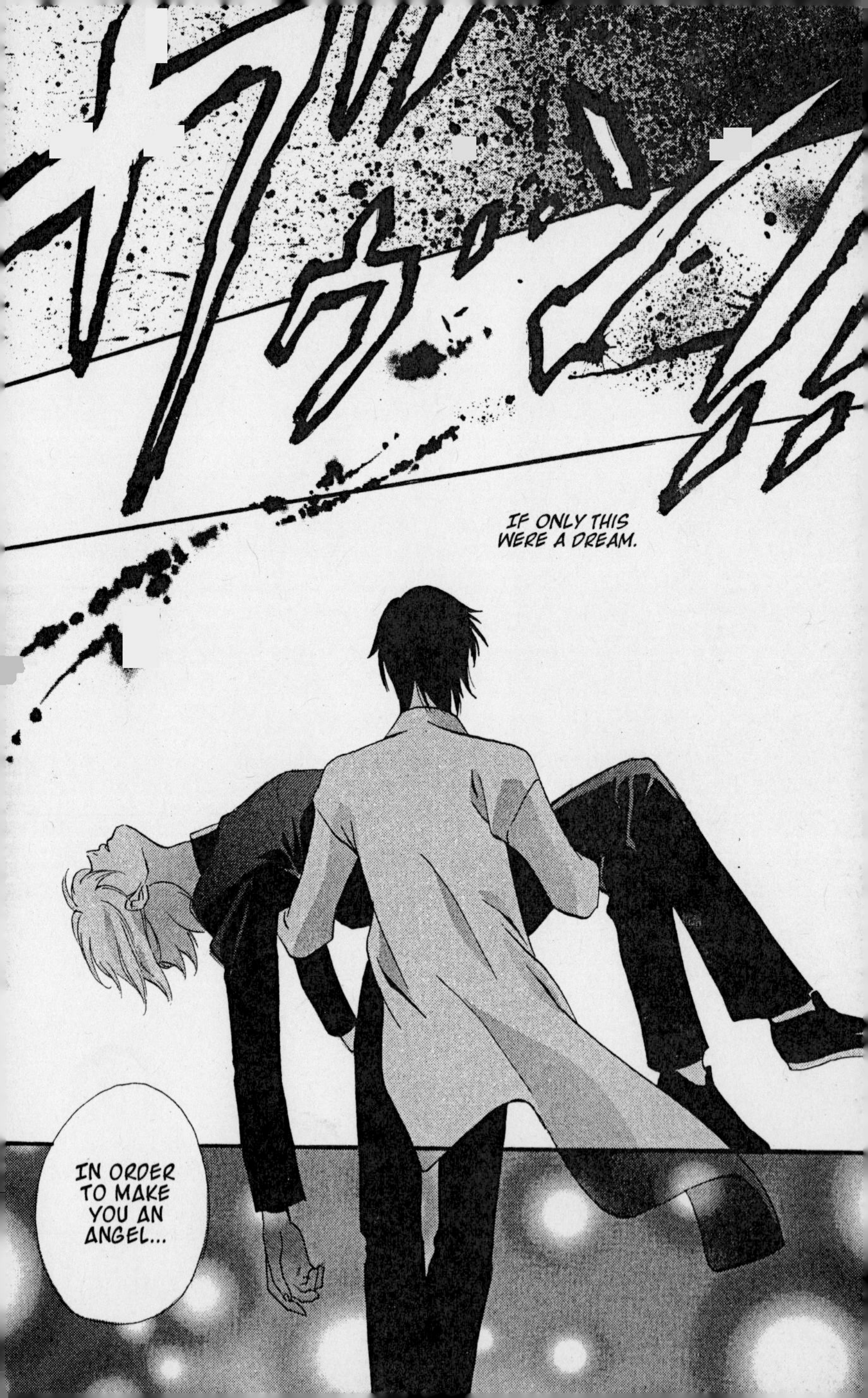
IF ONLY THIS WERE A DREAM.
IN ORDER TO MAKE YOU AN ANGEL...

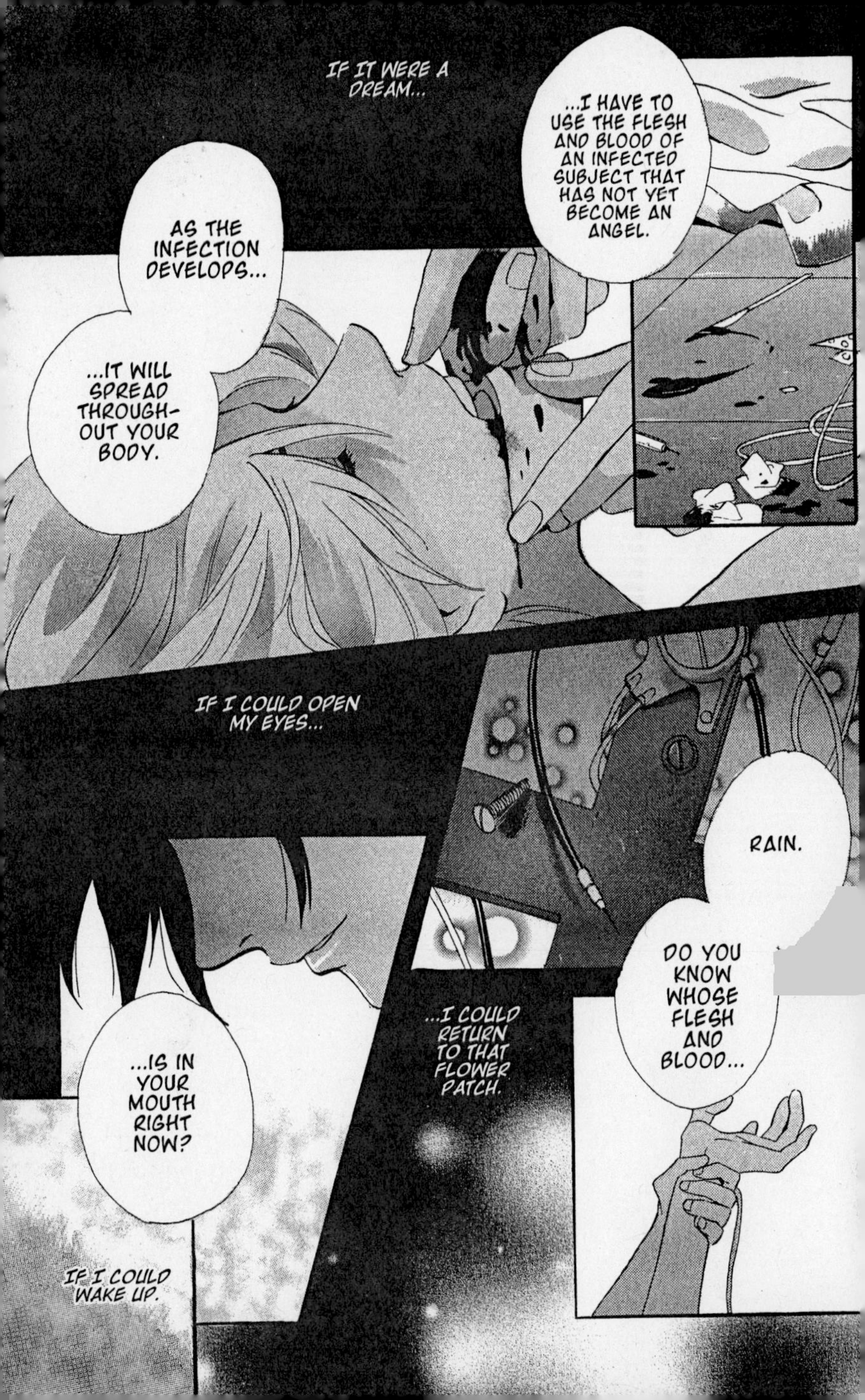

...I HAVE TO USE THE FLESH AND BLOOD OF AN INFECTED SUBJECT THAT HAS NOT YET BECOME AN ANGEL.
IF IT WERE A DREAM...
AS THE INFECTION DEVELOPS...
...IT WILL SPREAD THROUGH-OUT YOUR BODY.
IF I COULD OPEN MY EYES...
RAIN.
DO YOU KNOW WHOSE FLESH AND BLOOD...
...I COULD RETURN TO THAT FLOWER PATCH.
...IS IN YOUR MOUTH RIGHT NOW?
IF I COULD WAKE UP.

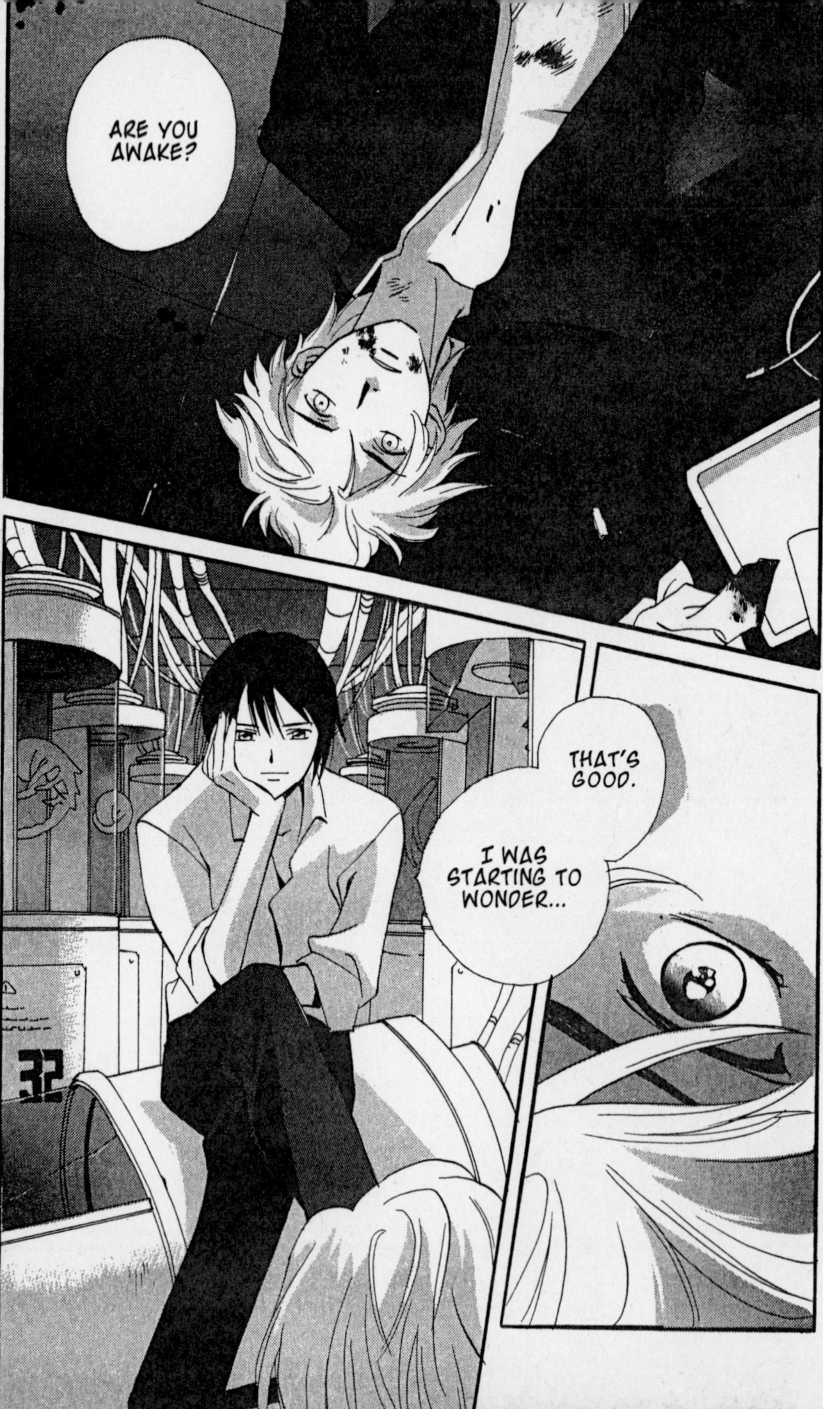
ARE YOU AWAKE?
THAT'S GOOD.
I WAS STARTING TO WONDER...

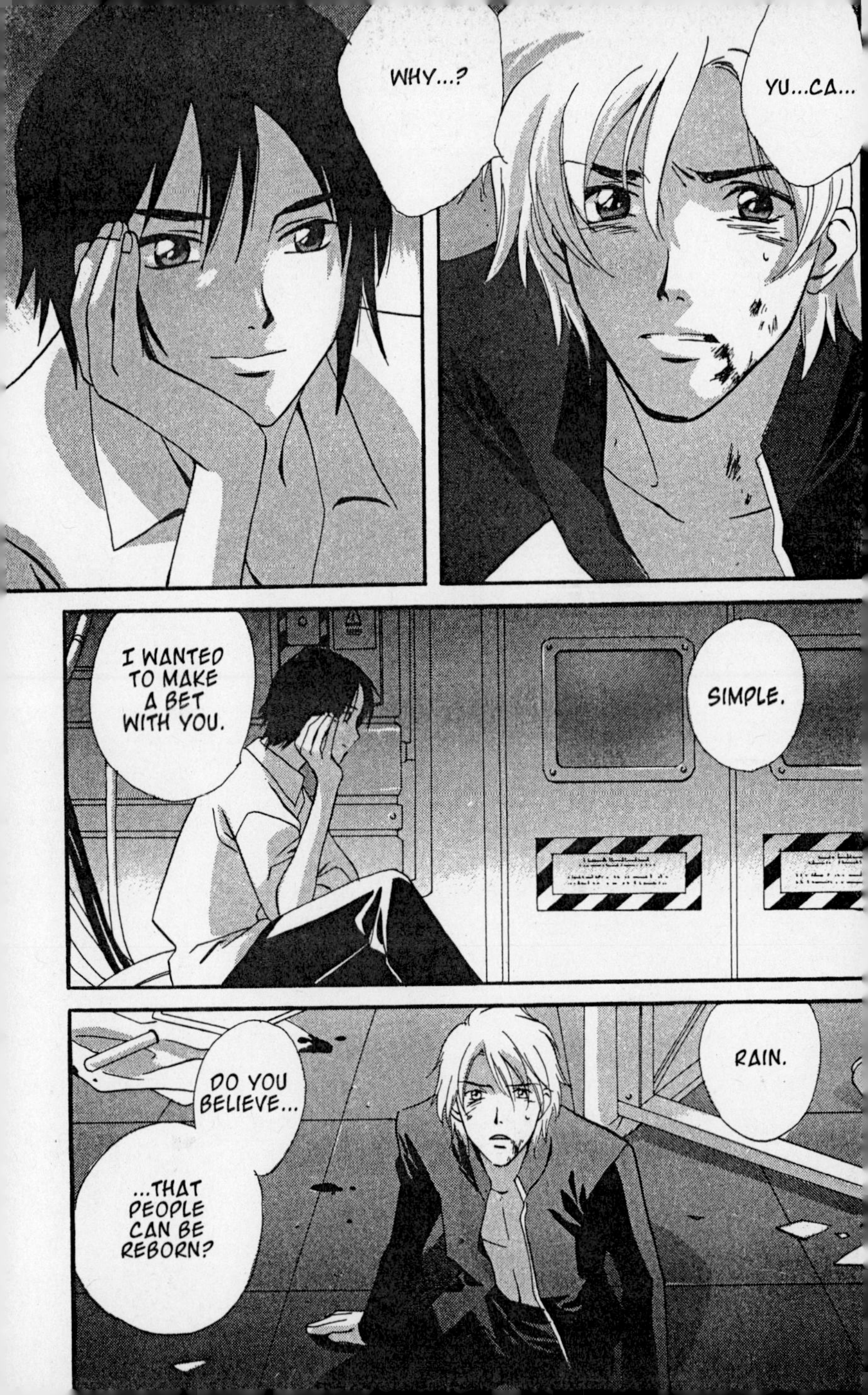
YU...CA...
WHY...?
SIMPLE.
I WANTED TO MAKE A BET WITH YOU.
RAIN.
DO YOU BELIEVE...
...THAT PEOPLE CAN BE REBORN?

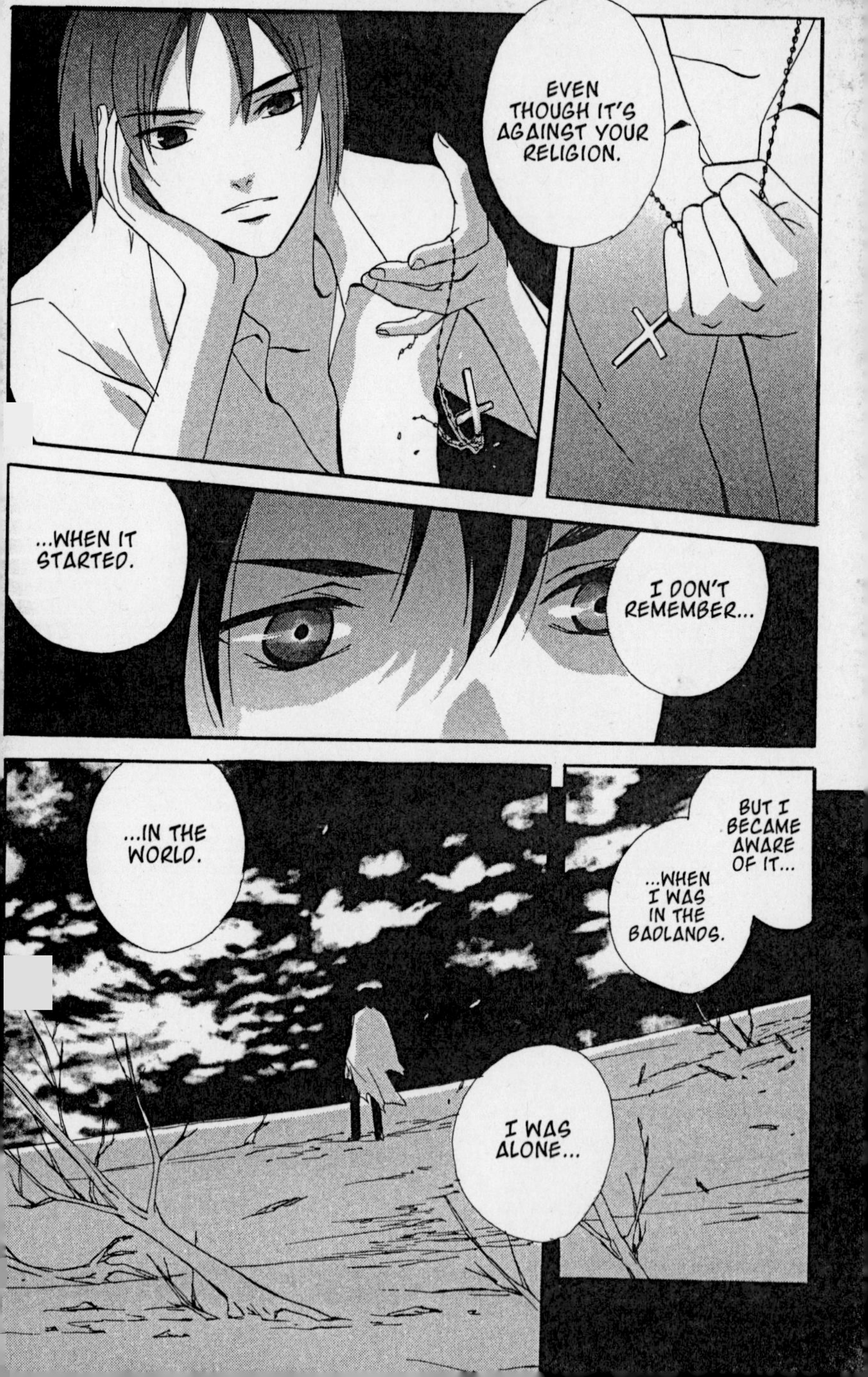
EVEN THOUGH IT'S AGAINST YOUR RELIGION.
I DON'T REMEMBER...
...WHEN IT STARTED.
BUT I BECAME AWARE OF IT...
...WHEN I WAS IN THE BADLANDS.
I WAS ALONE...
...IN THE WORLD.

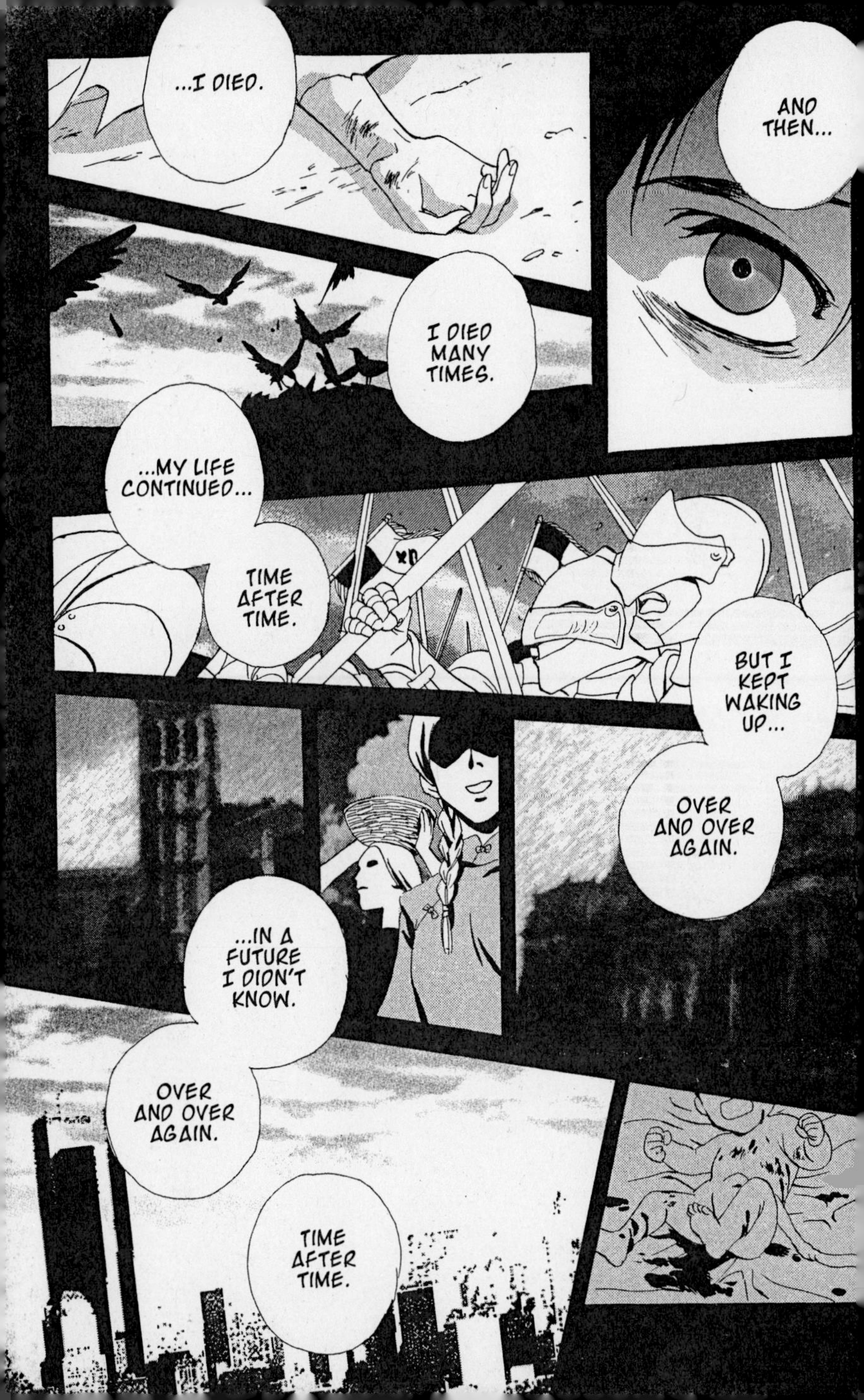
AND THEN...
...I DIED.
I DIED MANY TIMES.
BUT I KEPT WAKING UP...
OVER AND OVER AGAIN.
...MY LIFE CONTINUED...
TIME AFTER TIME.
...IN A FUTURE I DIDN'T KNOW.
OVER AND OVER AGAIN.
TIME AFTER TIME.

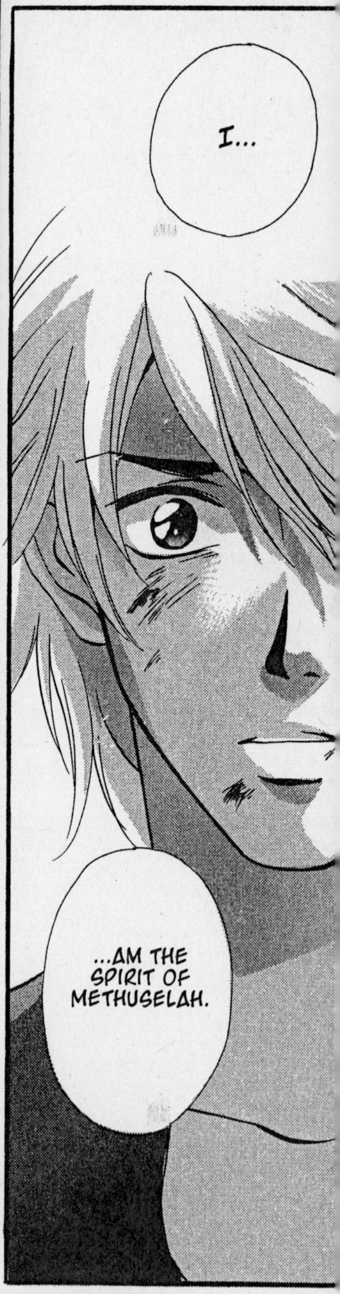
I...
...AM THE SPIRIT OF METHUSELAH.

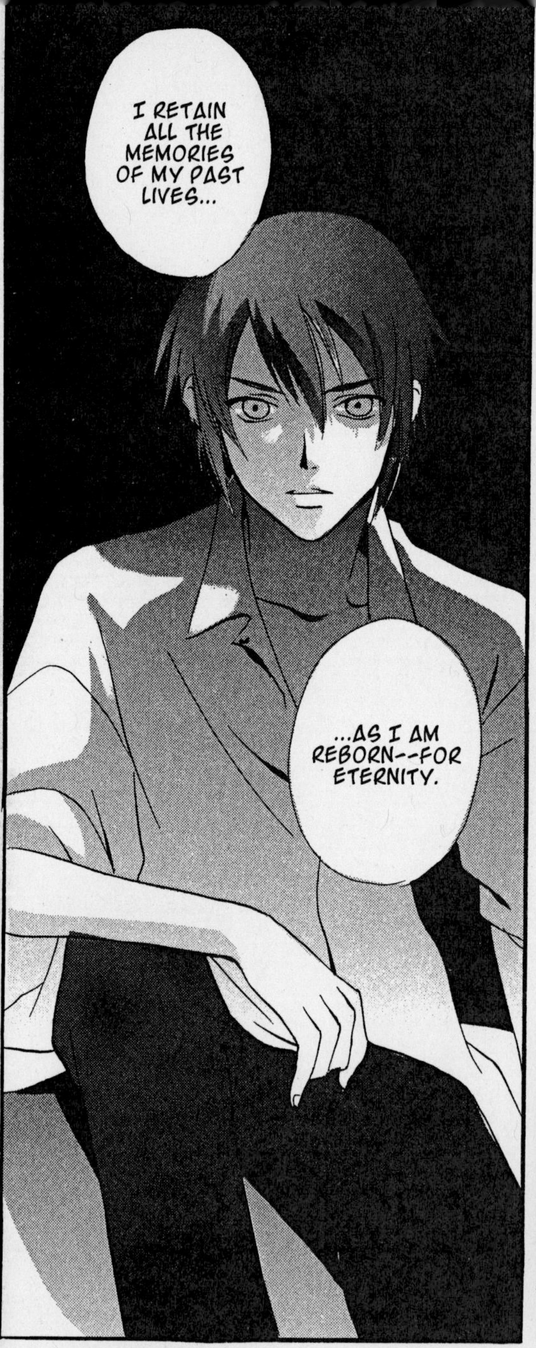
I RETAIN ALL THE MEMORIES OF MY PAST LIVES...
...AS I AM REBORN--FOR ETERNITY.

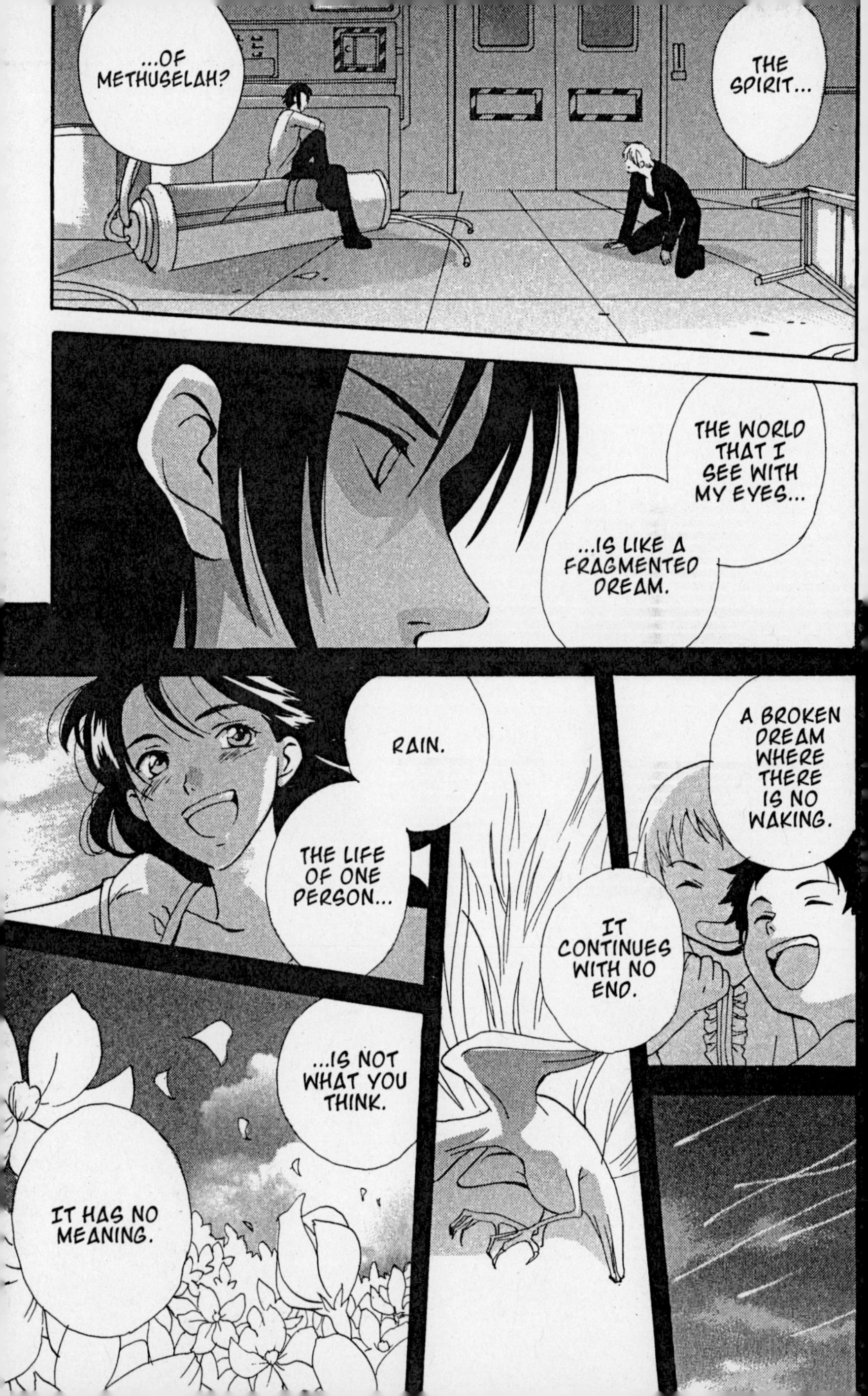
THE SPIRIT...
...OF METHUSELAH?
THE WORLD THAT I SEE WITH MY EYES...
...IS LIKE A FRAGMENTED DREAM.
A BROKEN DREAM WHERE THERE IS NO WAKING.
IT CONTINUES WITH NO END.
RAIN.
THE LIFE OF ONE PERSON...
...IS NOT WHAT YOU THINK.
IT HAS NO MEANING.

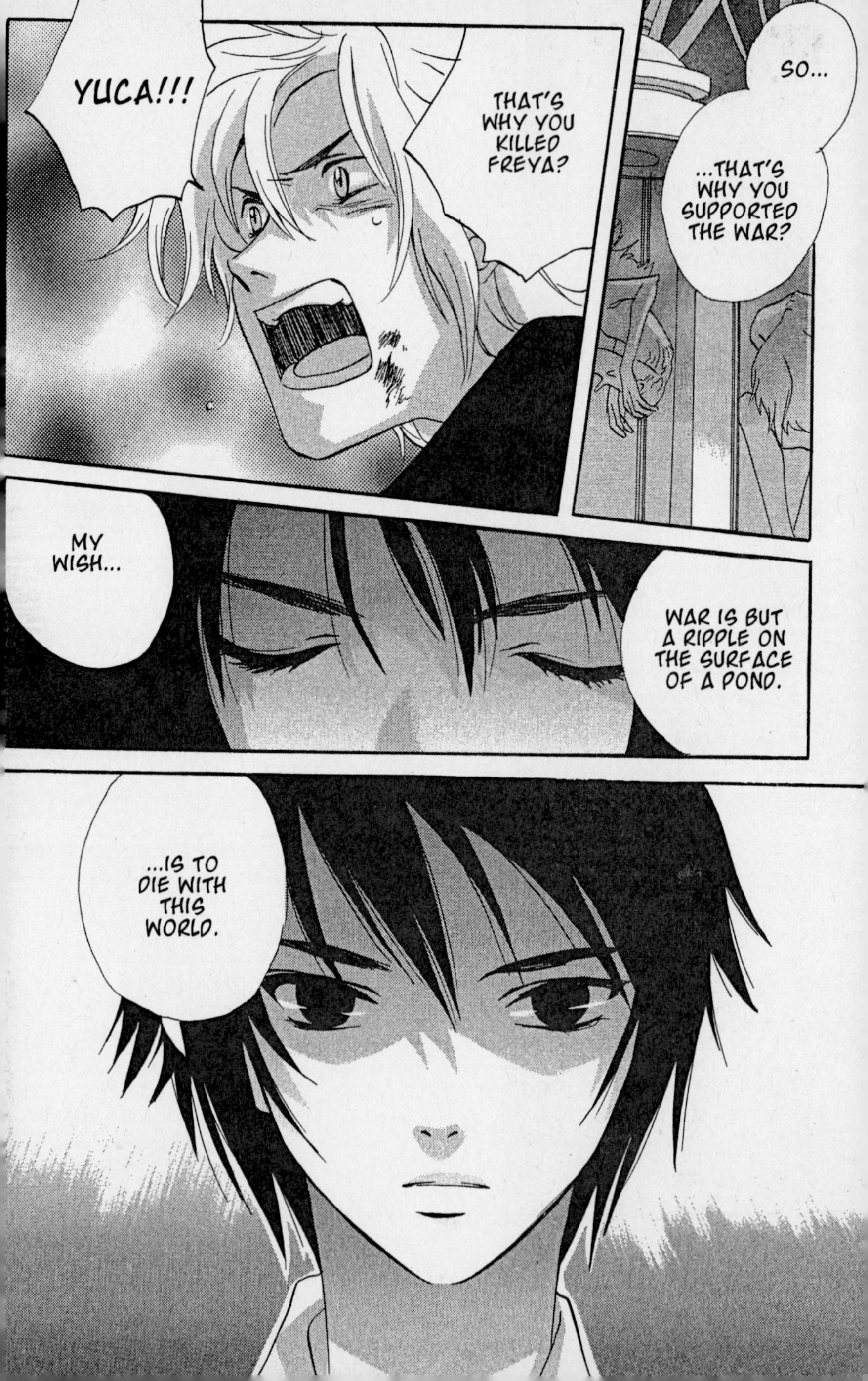
SO...
...THAT'S WHY YOU SUPPORTED THE WAR?
YUCA!!!
THAT'S WHY YOU KILLED FREYA?
WAR IS BUT A RIPPLE ON THE SURFACE OF A POND.
MY WISH...
...IS TO DIE WITH THIS WORLD.

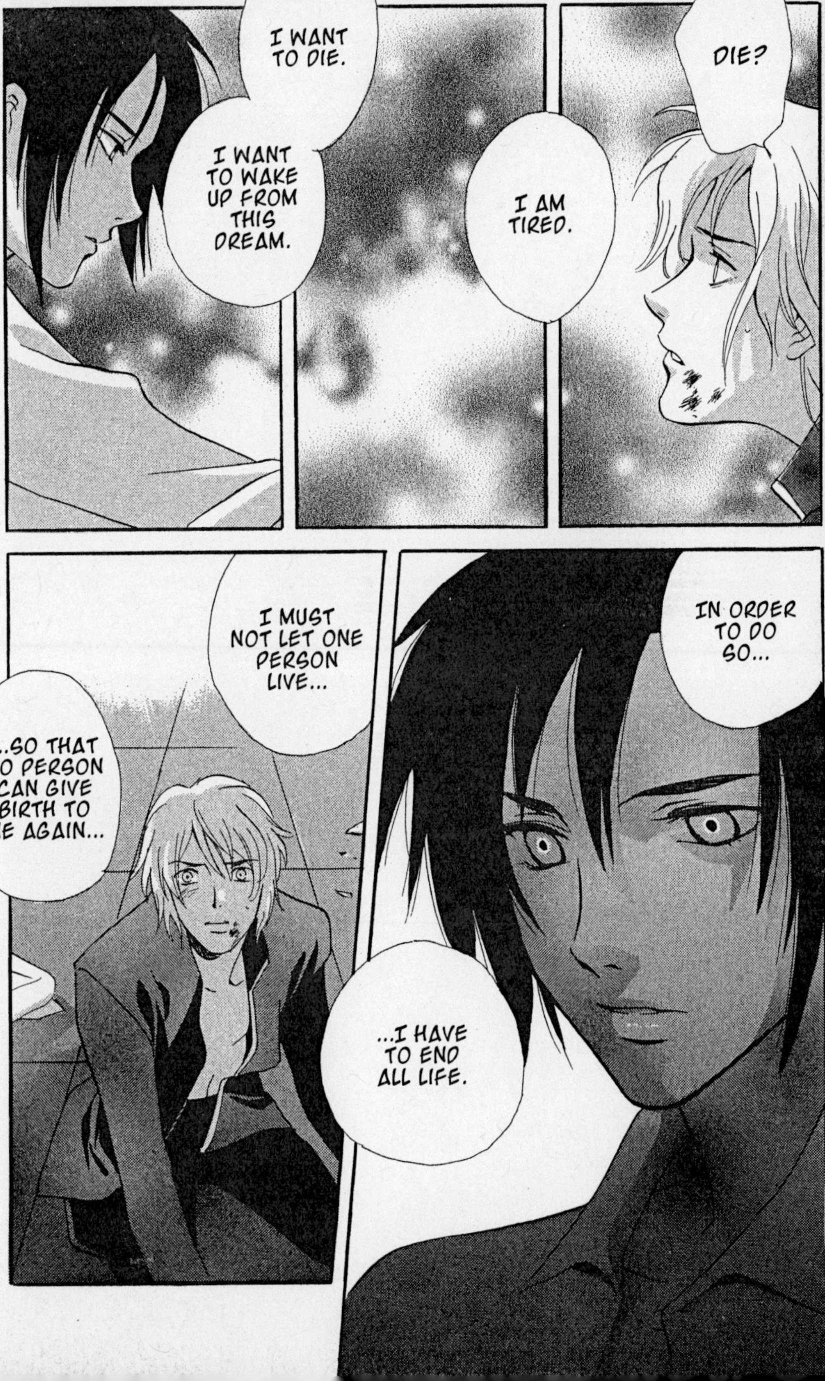
DIE?
I AM TIRED.
I WANT TO DIE.
I WANT TO WAKE UP FROM THIS DREAM.
IN ORDER TO DO SO...
...I HAVE TO END ALL LIFE.
I MUST NOT LET ONE PERSON LIVE...
...SO THAT NO PERSON CAN GIVE BIRTH TO ME AGAIN...

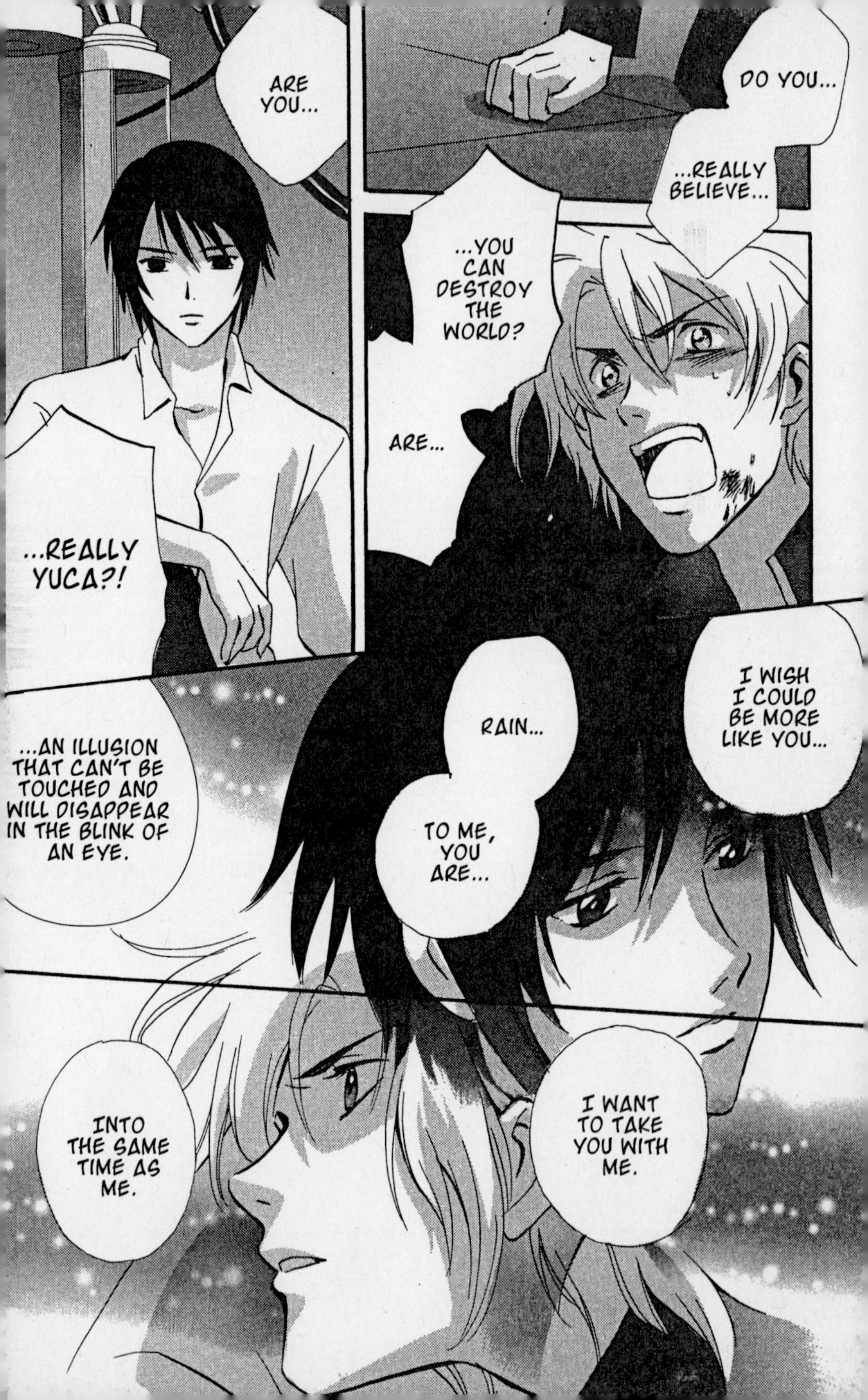
DO YOU...
...REALLY BELIEVE...
...YOU CAN DESTROY THE WORLD?
ARE...
ARE YOU...
...REALLY YUCA?!
I WISH I COULD BE MORE LIKE YOU...
RAIN...
TO ME, YOU ARE...
...AN ILLUSION THAT CAN'T BE TOUCHED AND WILL DISAPPEAR IN THE BLINK OF AN EYE.
I WANT TO TAKE YOU WITH ME.
INTO THE SAME TIME AS ME.

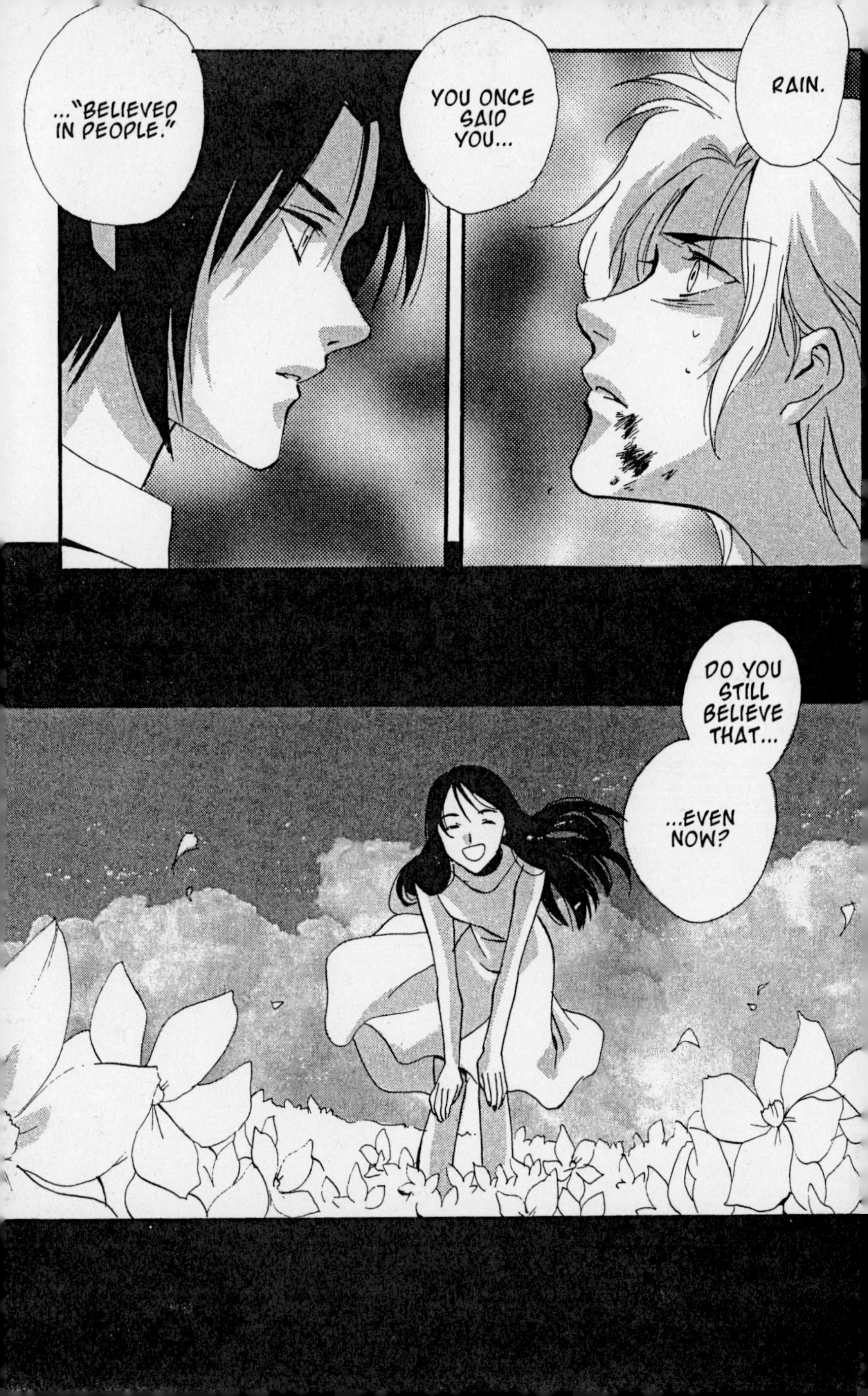
RAIN.
YOU ONCE SAID YOU...
..."BELIEVED IN PEOPLE."
DO YOU STILL BELIEVE THAT...
...EVEN NOW?

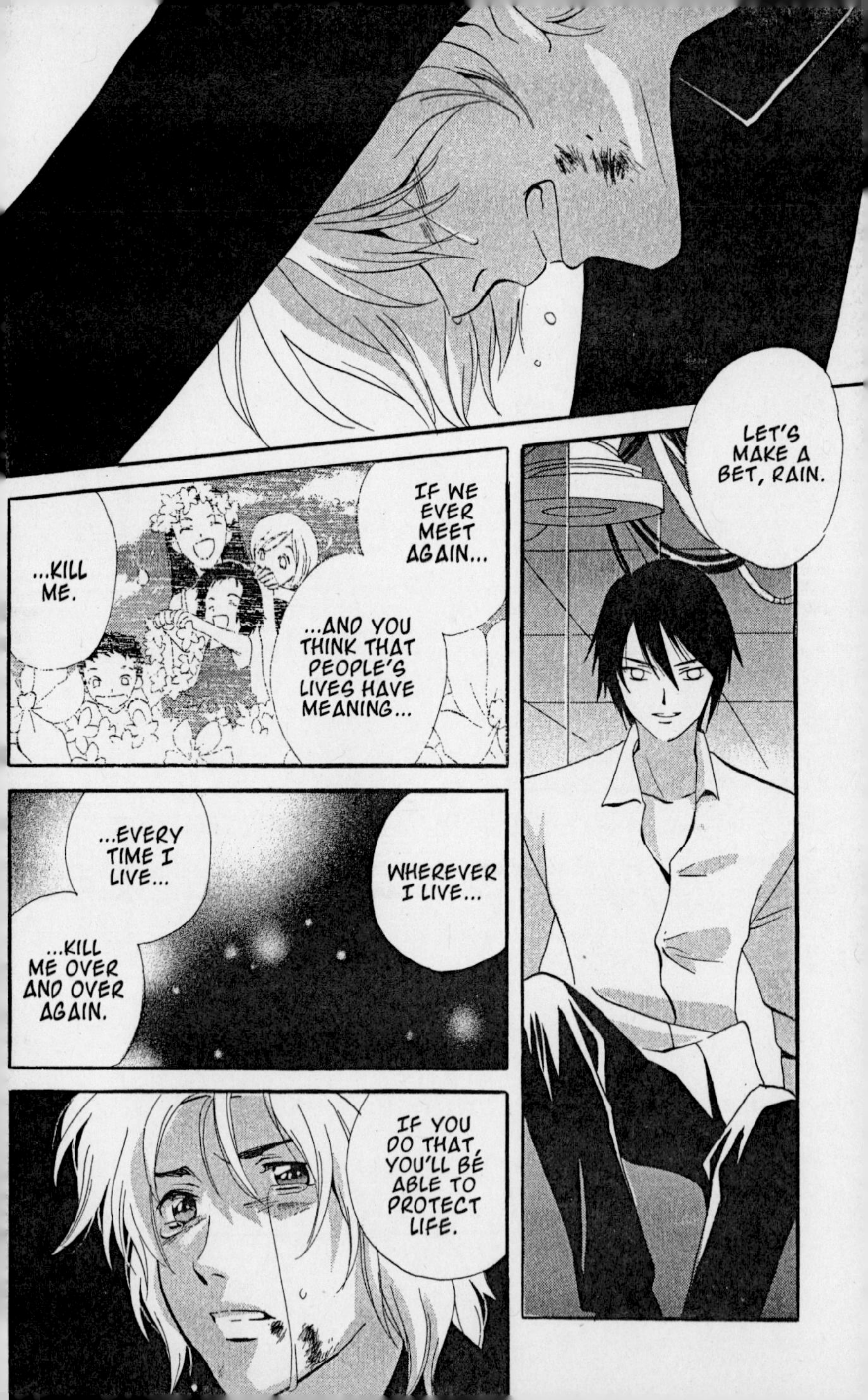
LET'S MAKE A BET, RAIN.
IF WE EVER MEET AGAIN...
...AND YOU THINK THAT PEOPLE'S LIVES HAVE MEANING...
...KILL ME.
WHEREVER I LIVE...
...EVERY TIME I LIVE...
...KILL ME OVER AND OVER AGAIN.
IF YOU DO THAT, YOU'LL BE ABLE TO PROTECT LIFE.

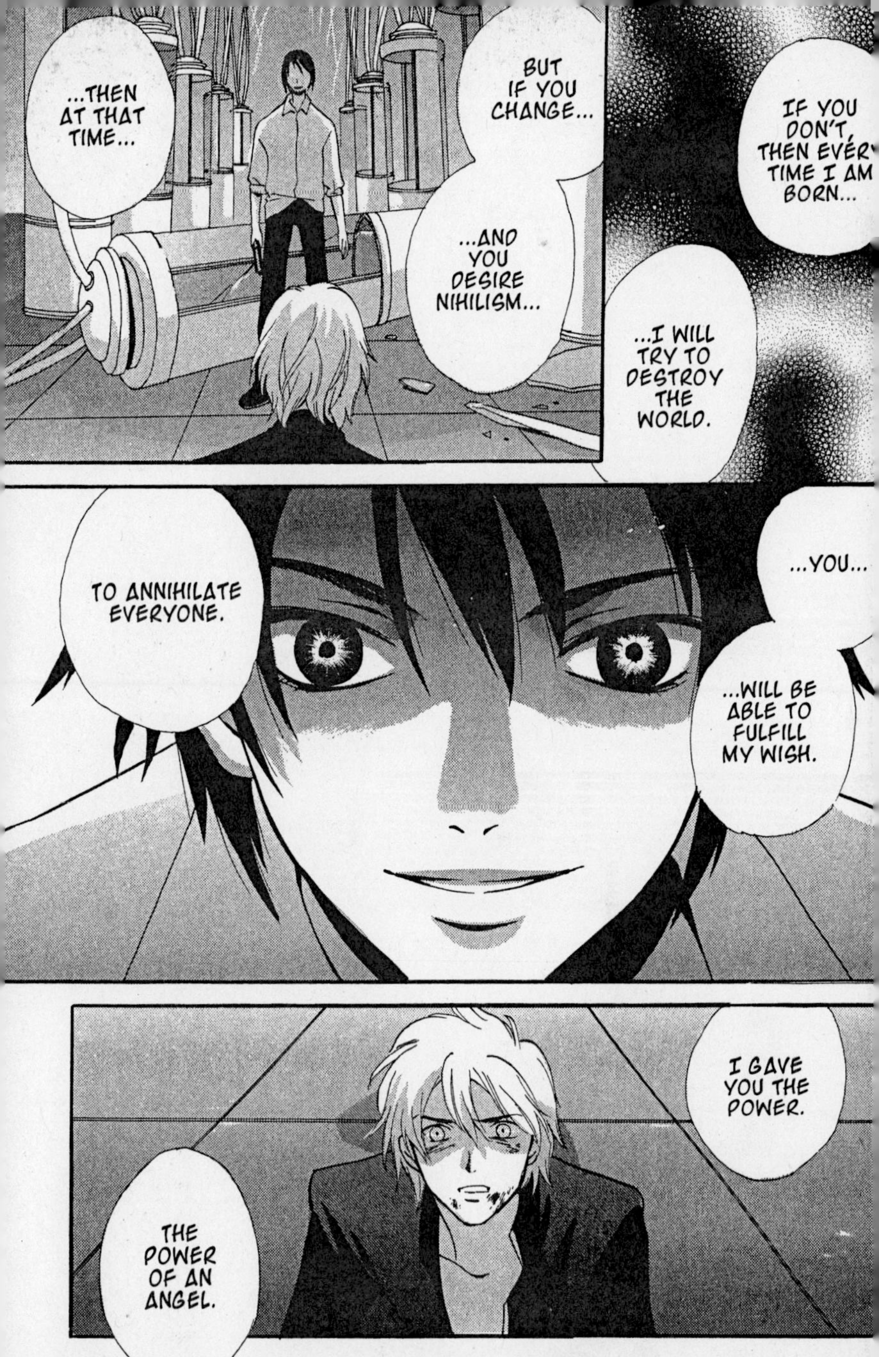
IF YOU DON'T, THEN EVERY TIME I AM BORN...
...I WILL TRY TO DESTROY THE WORLD.
BUT IF YOU CHANGE...
...AND YOU DESIRE NIHILISM...
...THEN AT THAT TIME...
...YOU...
...WILL BE ABLE TO FULFILL MY WISH.
TO ANNIHILATE EVERYONE.
I GAVE YOU THE POWER.
THE POWER OF AN ANGEL.

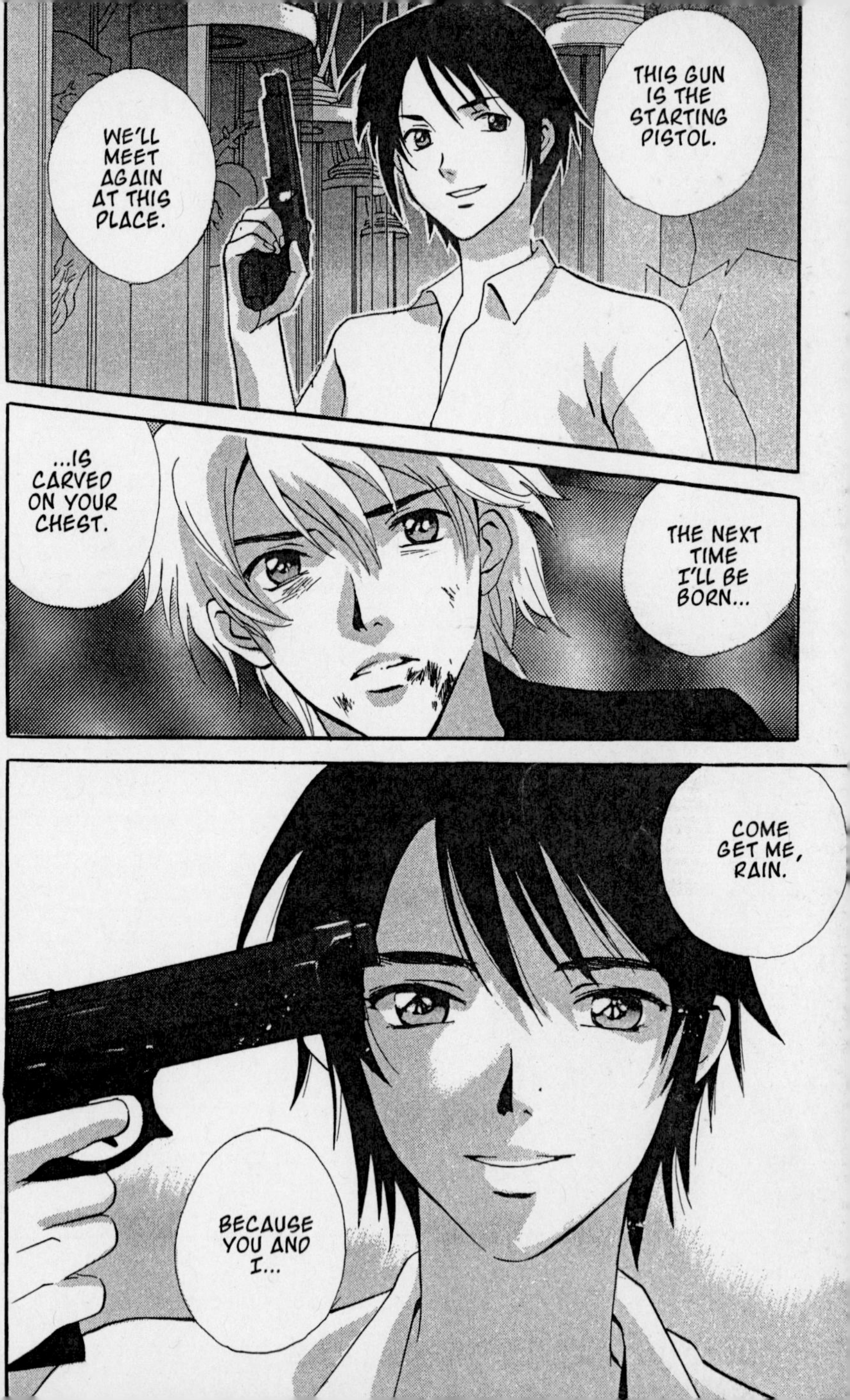
THIS GUN IS THE STARTING PISTOL.
WE'LL MEET AGAIN AT THIS PLACE.
THE NEXT TIME I'LL BE BORN...
...IS CARVED ON YOUR CHEST.
COME GET ME, RAIN.
BECAUSE YOU AND I...

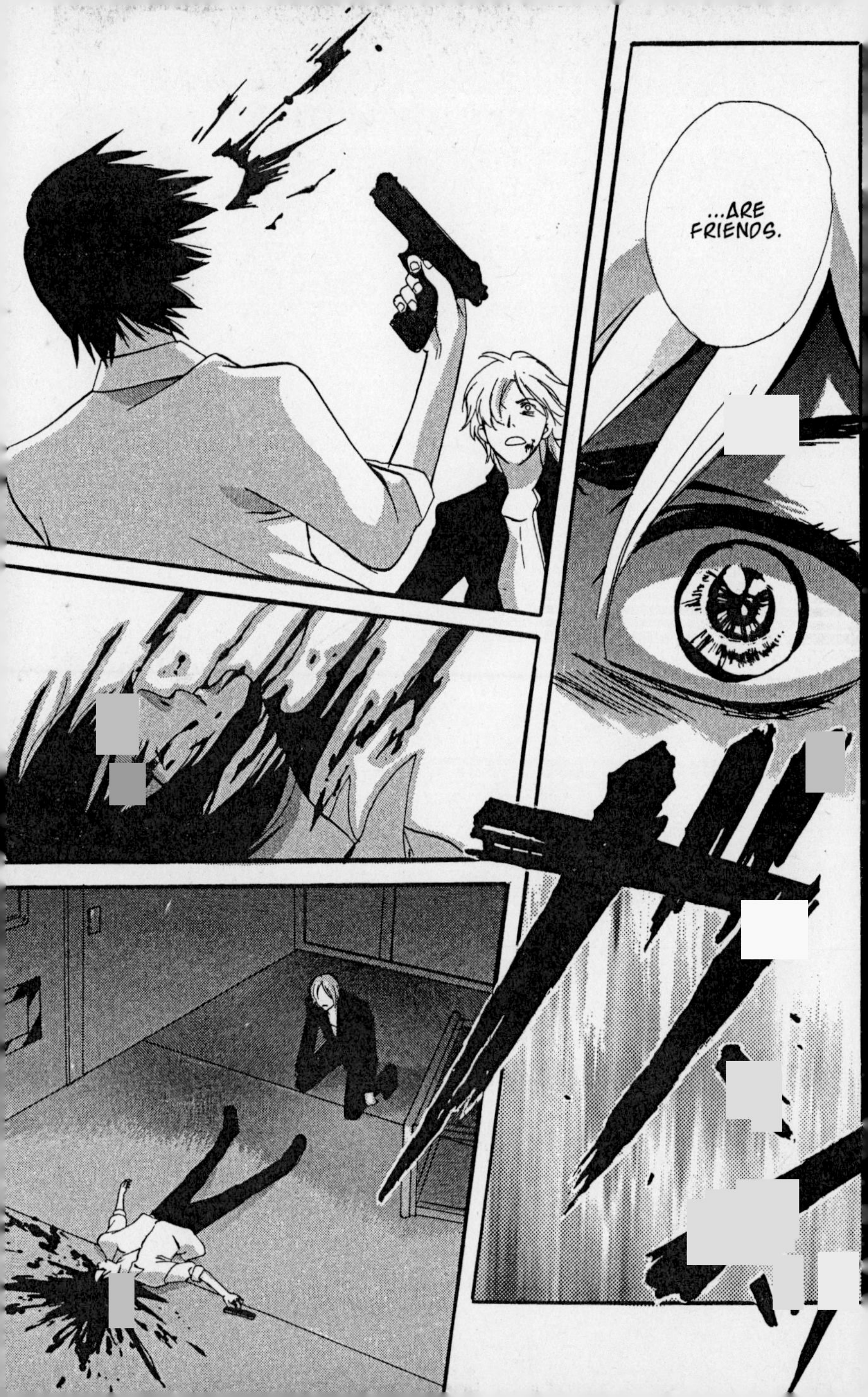
...ARE FRIENDS.

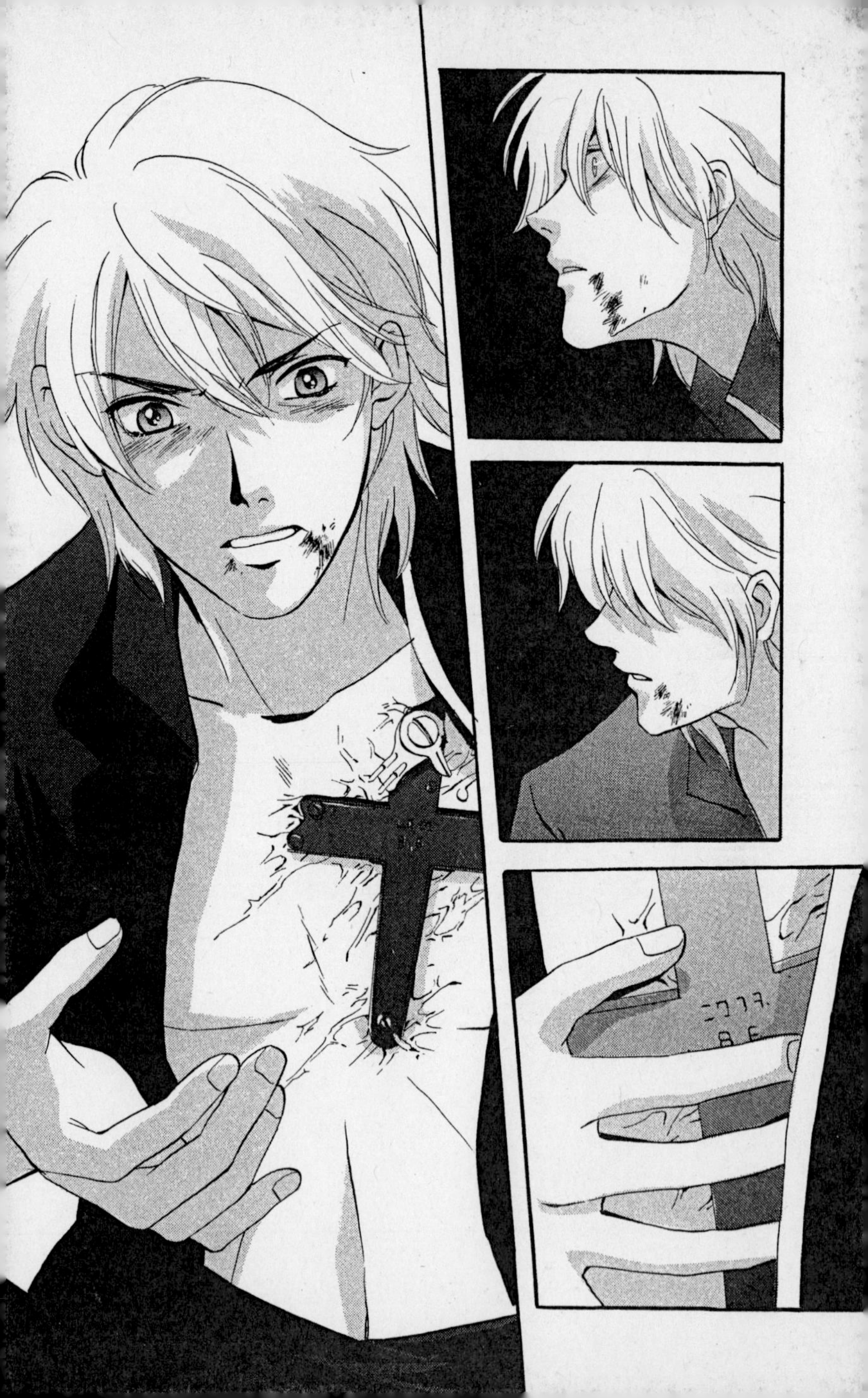

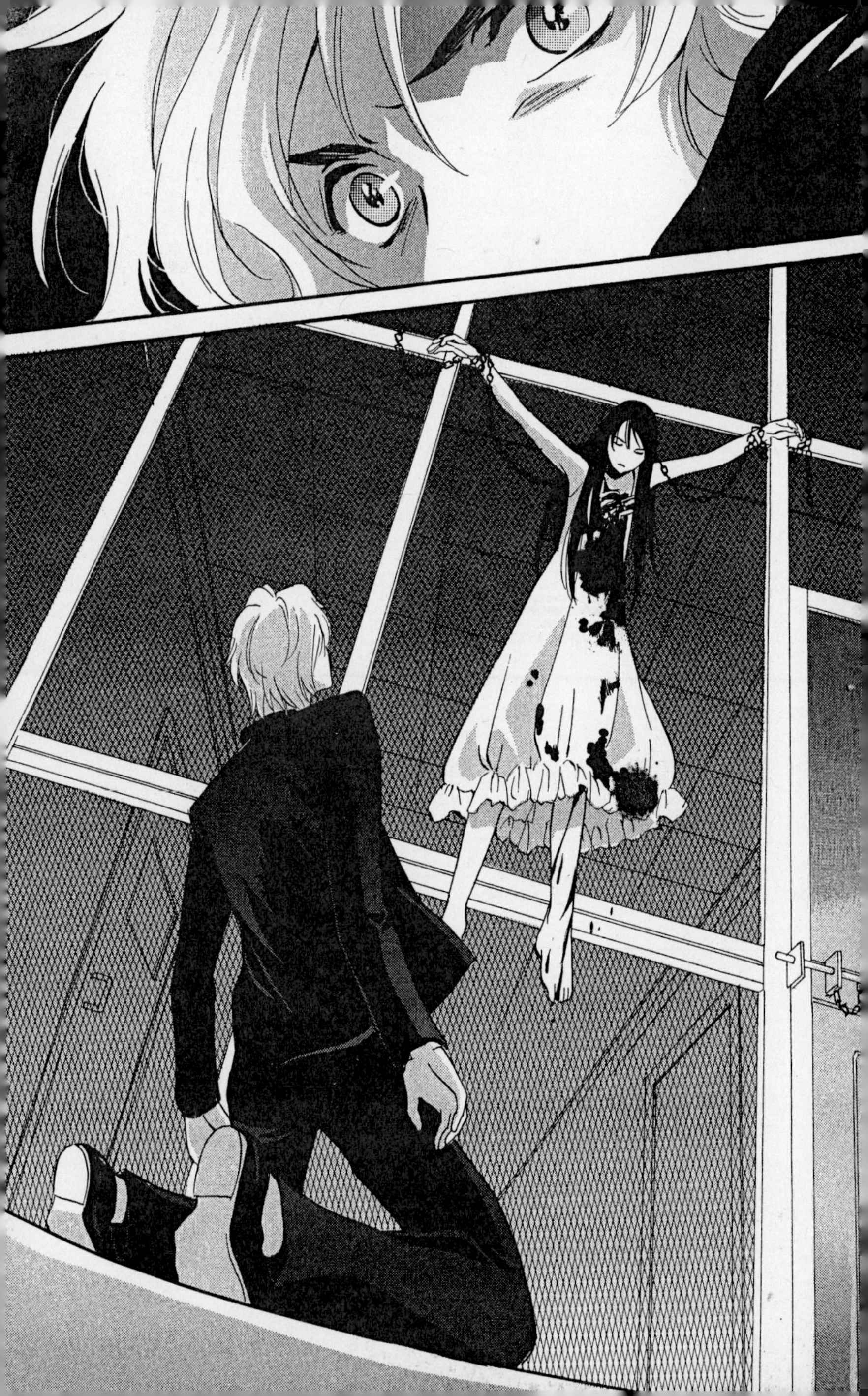

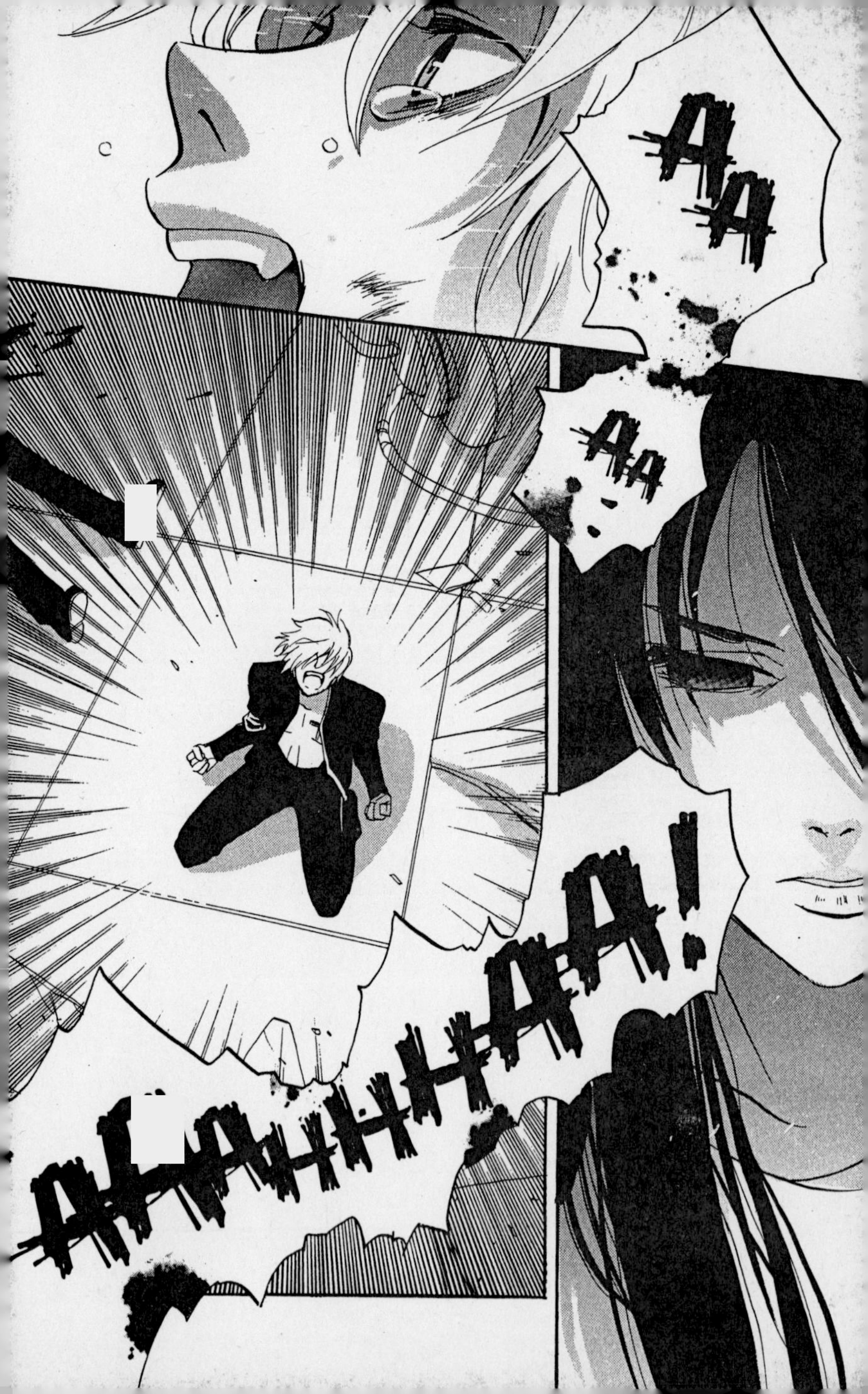
AA
AA
AAHHHHHAA!

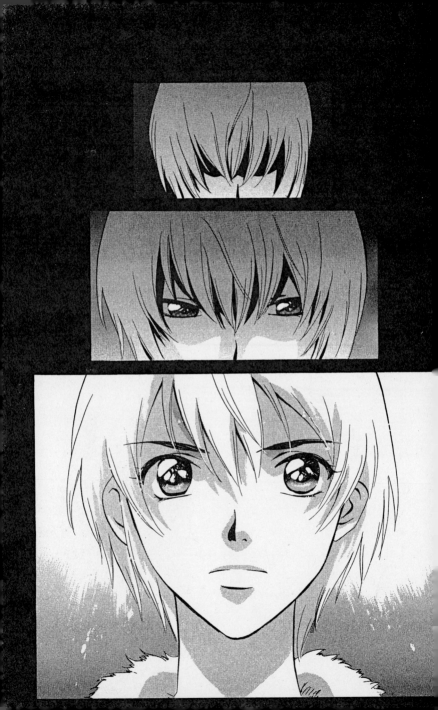

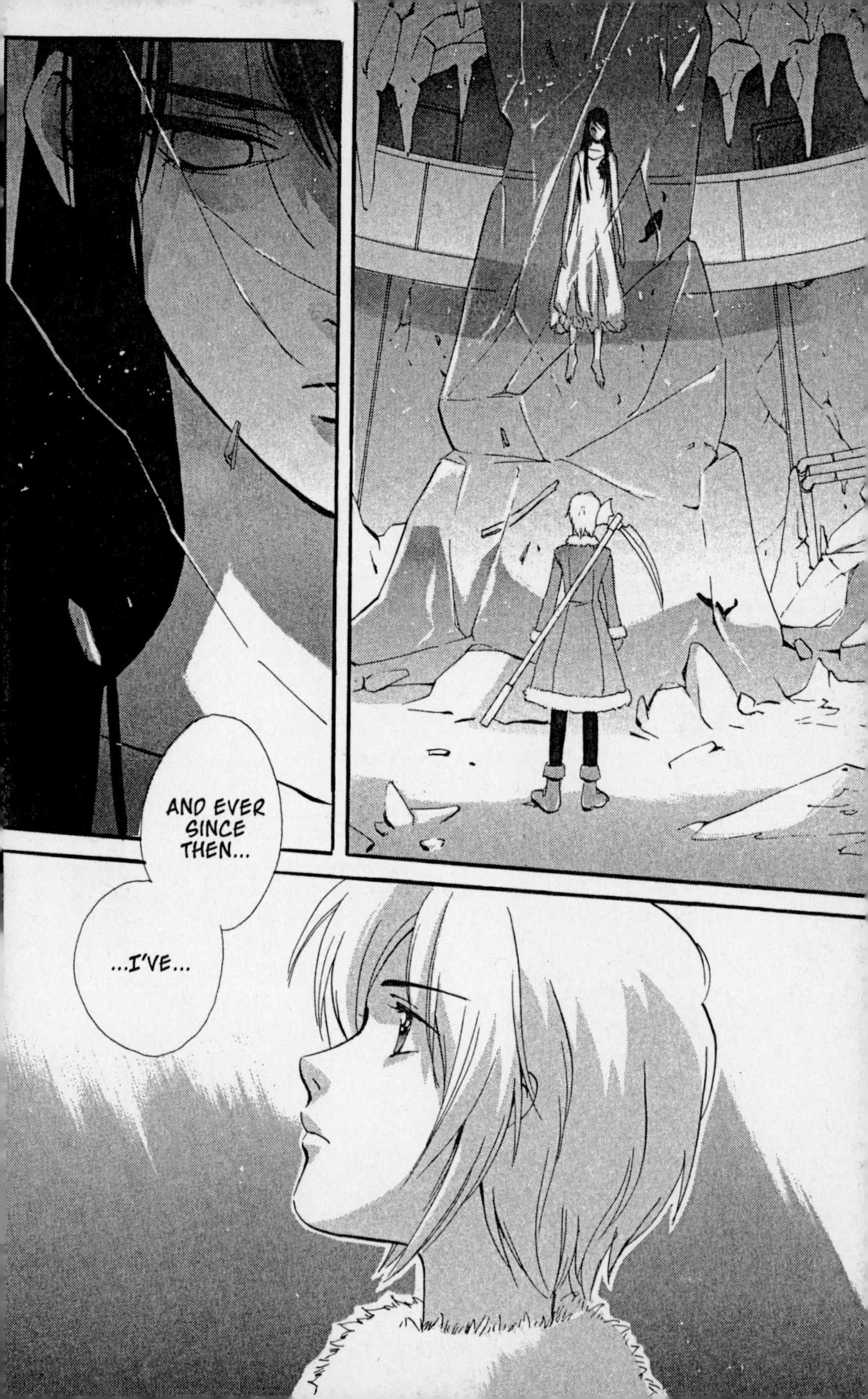
AND EVER SINCE THEN...
...I'VE...

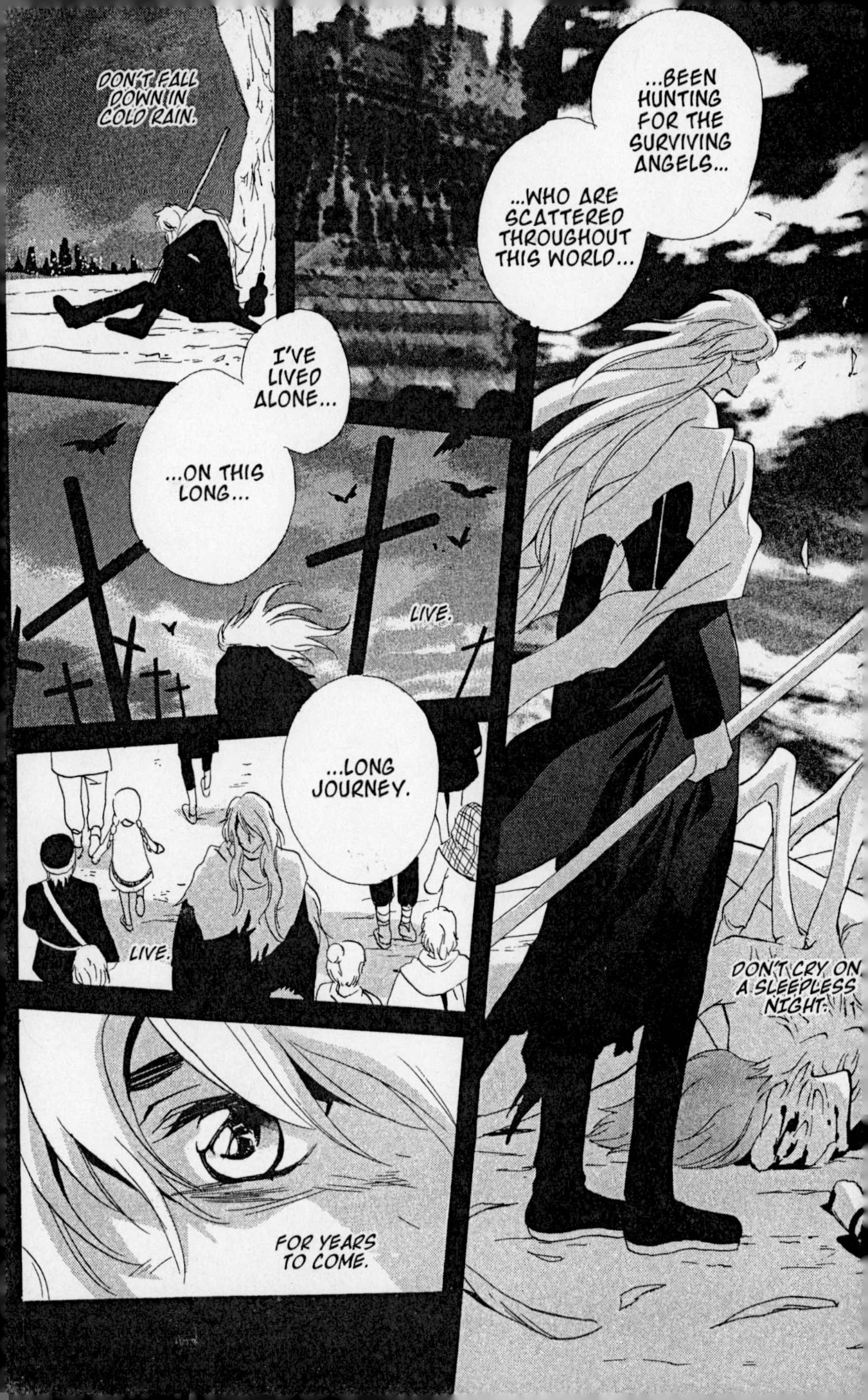
...BEEN HUNTING FOR THE SURVIVING ANGELS...
...WHO ARE SCATTERED THROUGHOUT THIS WORLD...
DON'T CRY ON A SLEEPLESS NIGHT.
I'VE LIVED ALONE...
DON'T FALL DOWN IN COLD RAIN.
...ON THIS LONG...
LIVE.
...LONG JOURNEY.
LIVE.
FOR YEARS TO COME.

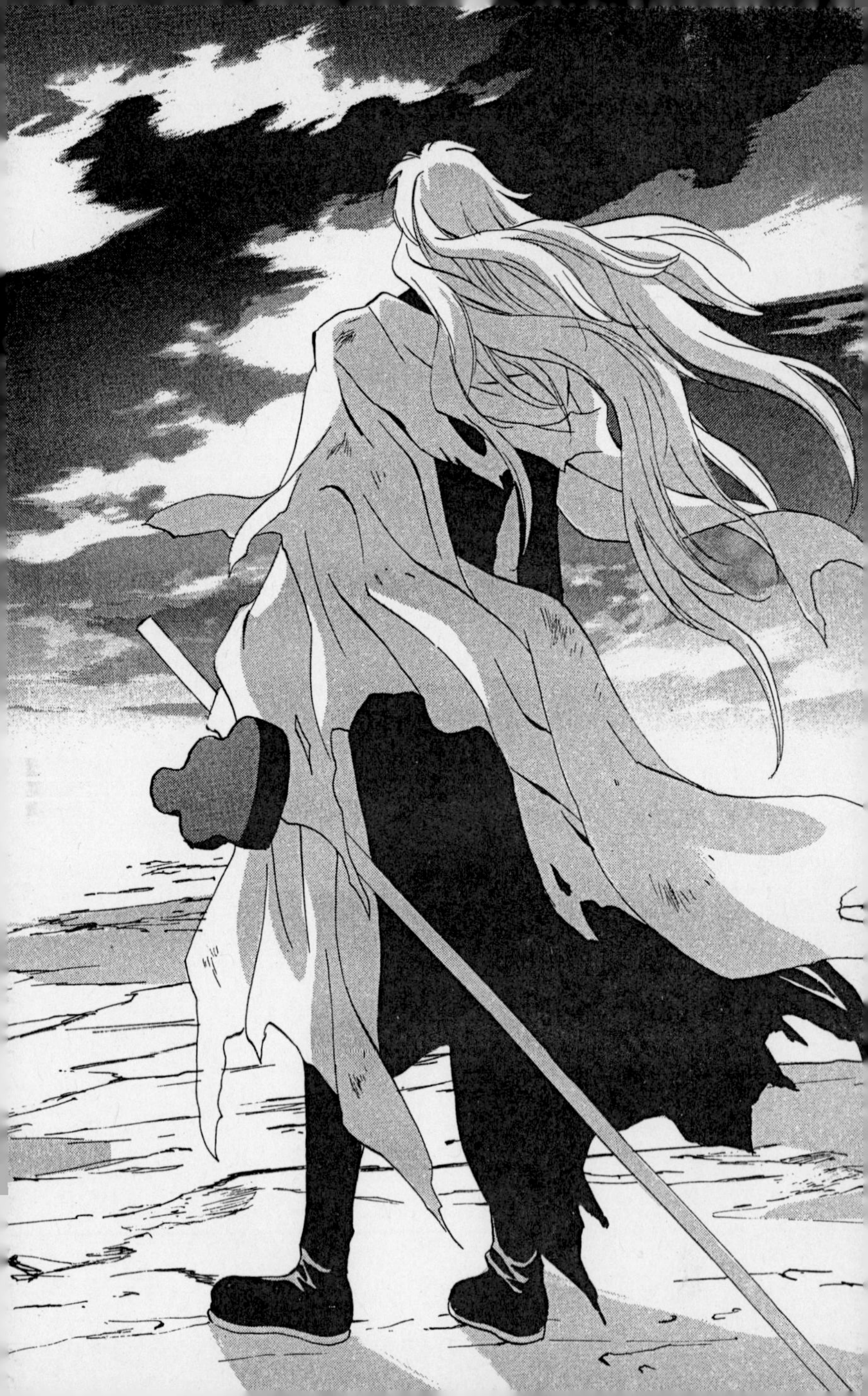

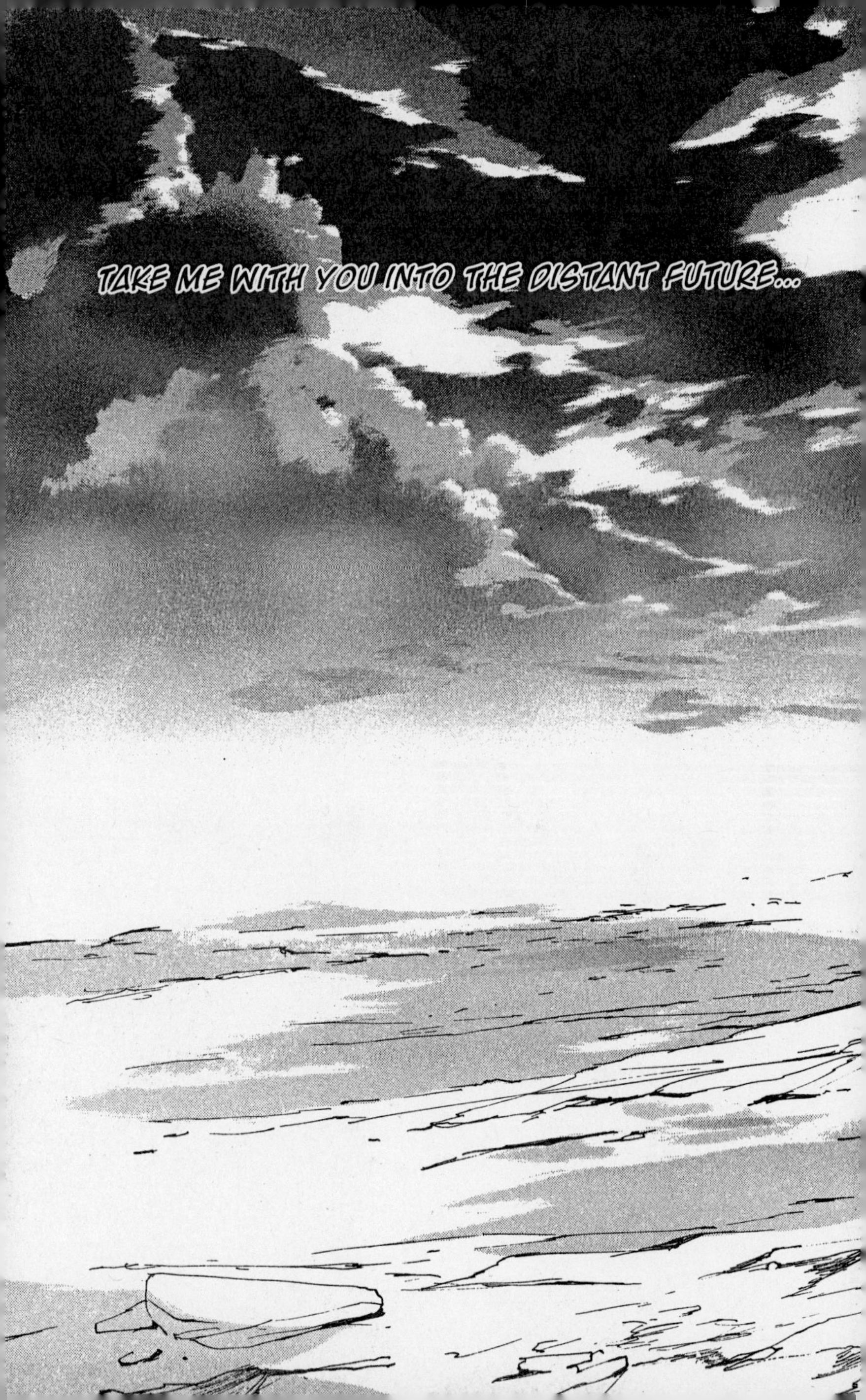
TAKE ME WITH YOU INTO THE DISTANT FUTURE...

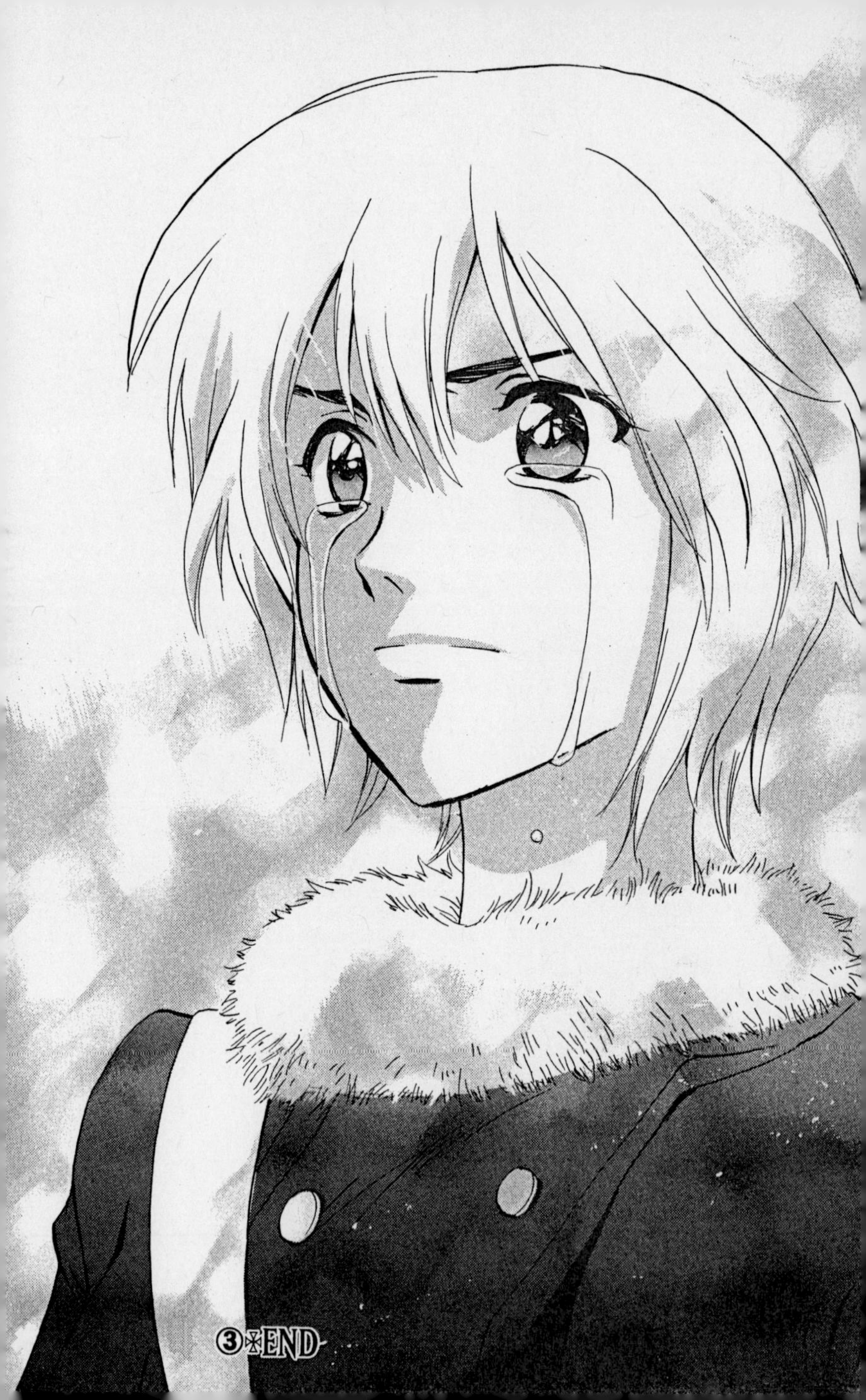
3 END

Yuca Collabell

NO DATA

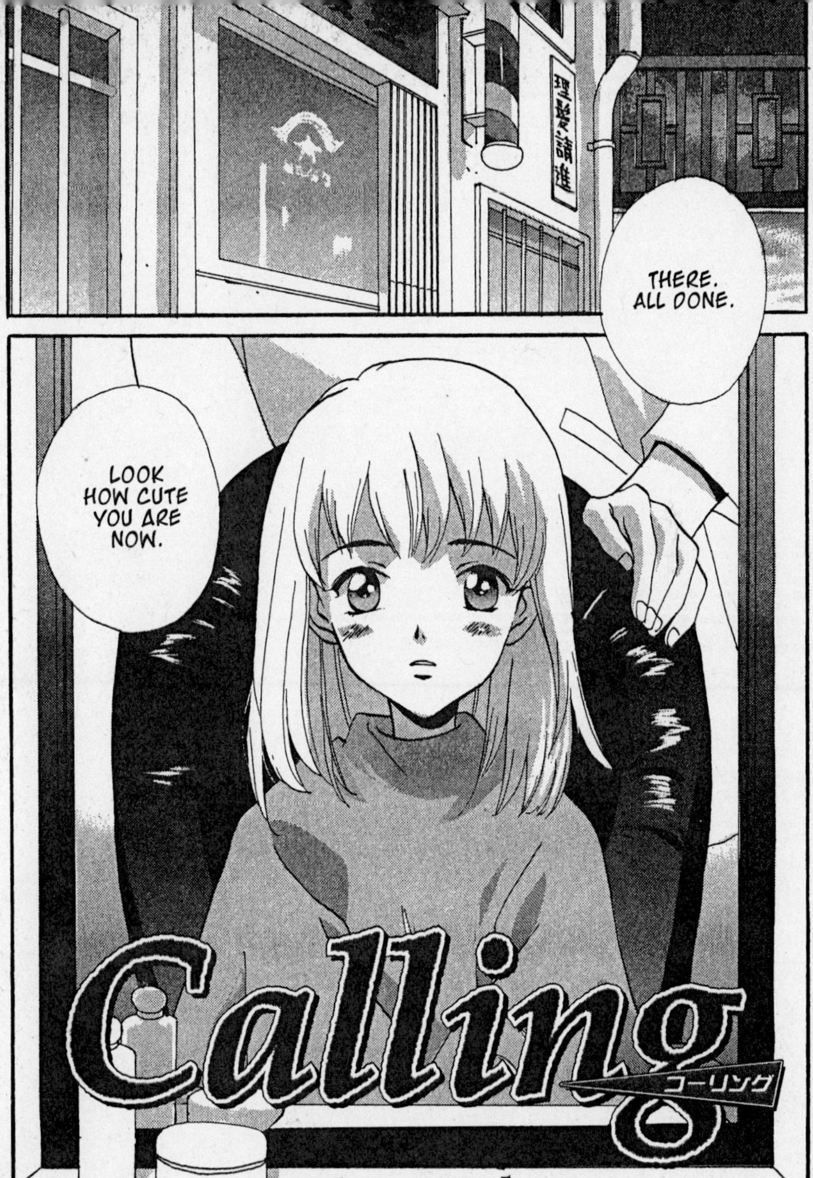
理髮請進
THERE. ALL DONE.
LOOK HOW CUTE YOU ARE NOW.
Calling
コーリング
Immortal Rain Side Story

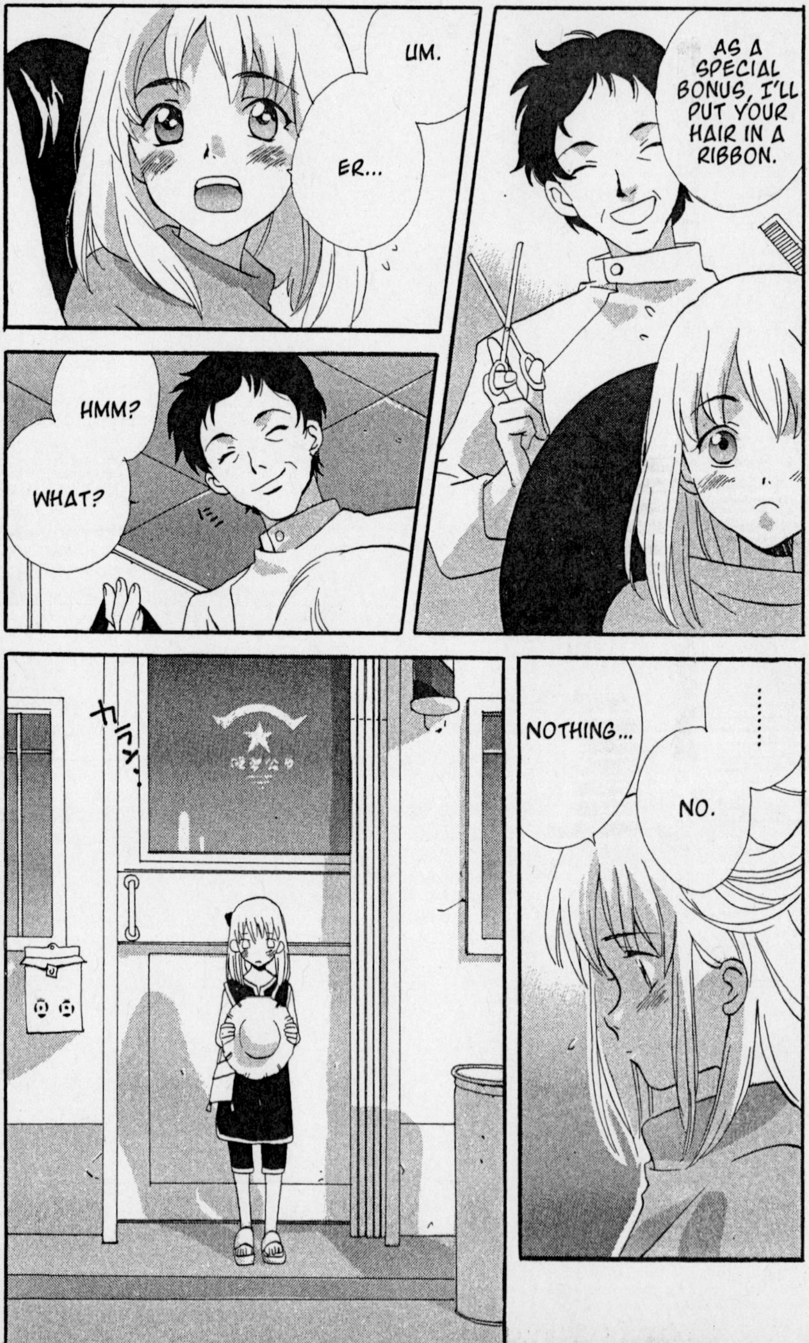
AS A SPECIAL BONUS, I'LL PUT YOUR HAIR IN A RIBBON.
UM.
ER...
HMM?
WHAT?
......
NO.
NOTHING...

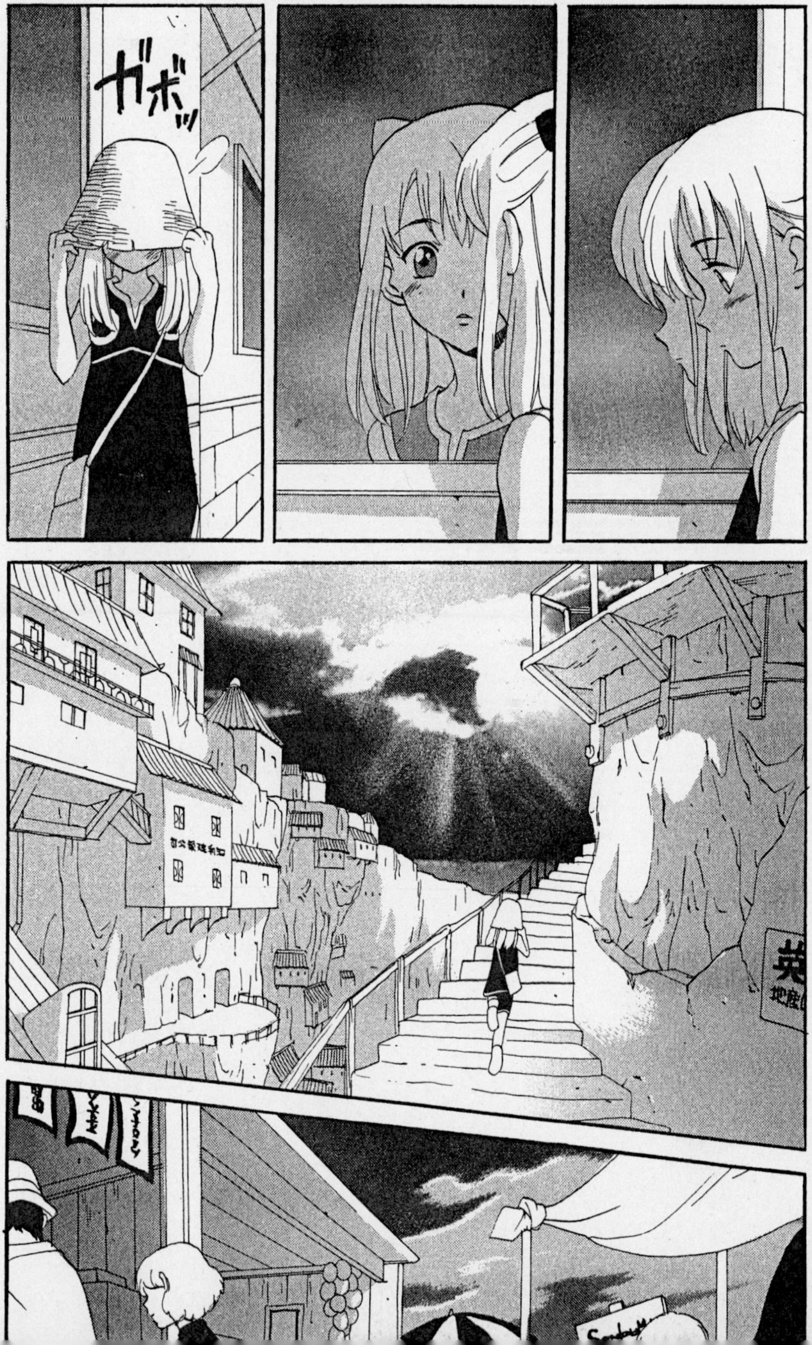
ガボッ

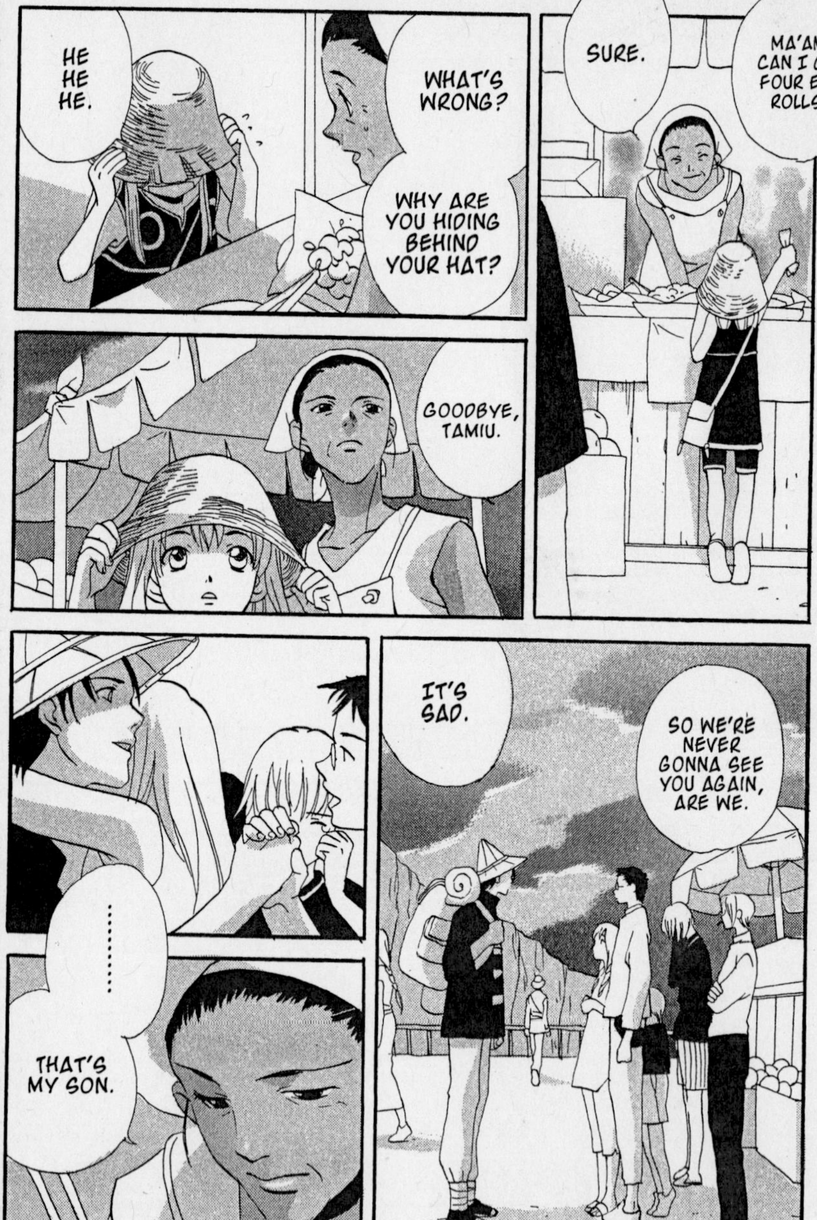
MA'AM, CAN I GET FOUR EGG ROLLS?
SURE.
WHAT'S WRONG?
WHY ARE YOU HIDING BEHIND YOUR HAT?
HE HE HE.
GOODBYE, TAMIU.
SO WE'RE NEVER GONNA SEE YOU AGAIN, ARE WE.
IT'S SAD.
......
THAT'S MY SON.

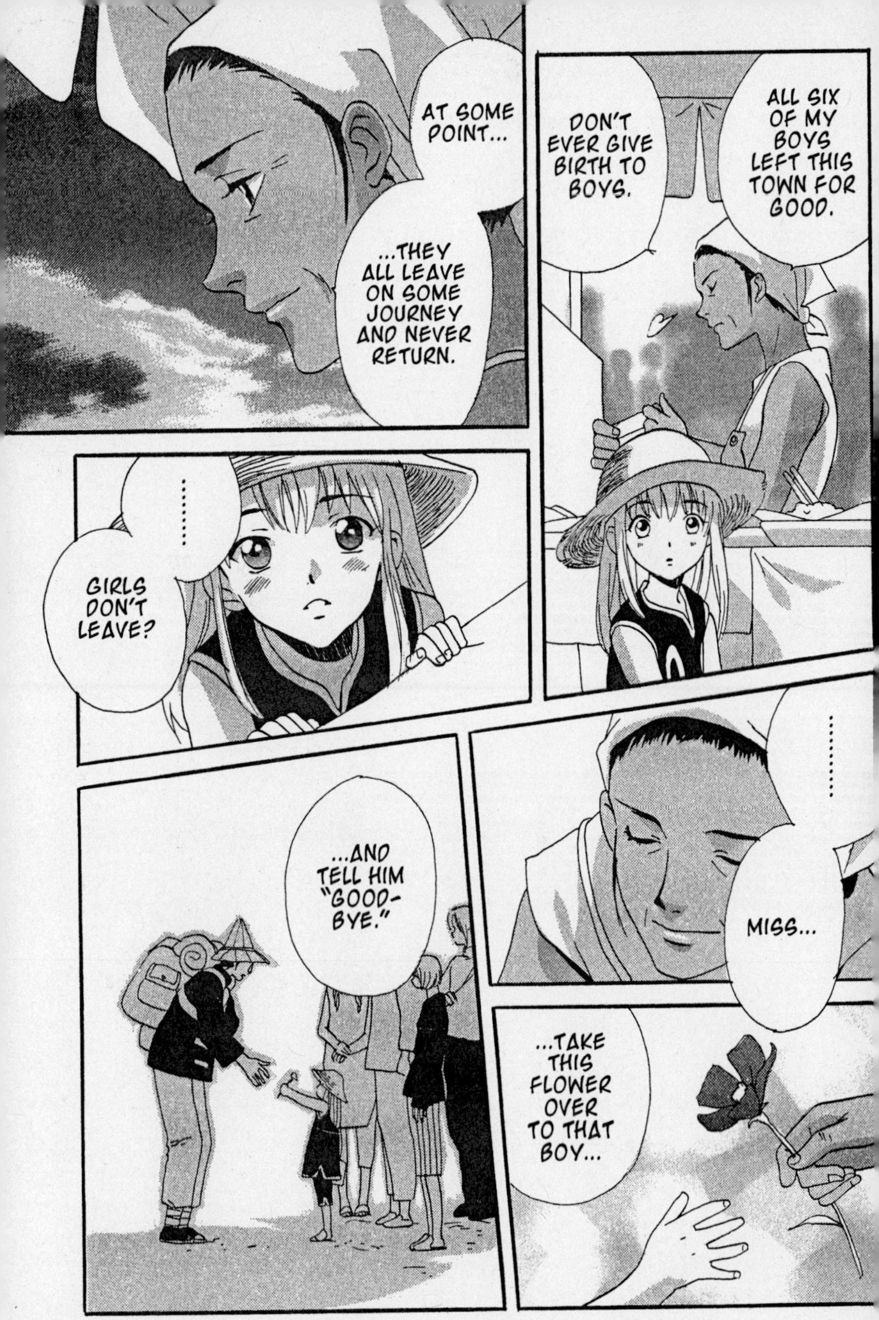
ALL SIX OF MY BOYS LEFT THIS TOWN FOR GOOD.
DON'T EVER GIVE BIRTH TO BOYS.
AT SOME POINT...
...THEY ALL LEAVE ON SOME JOURNEY AND NEVER RETURN.
......
GIRLS DON'T LEAVE?
....
MISS...
...TAKE THIS FLOWER OVER TO THAT BOY...
...AND TELL HIM "GOOD-BYE."

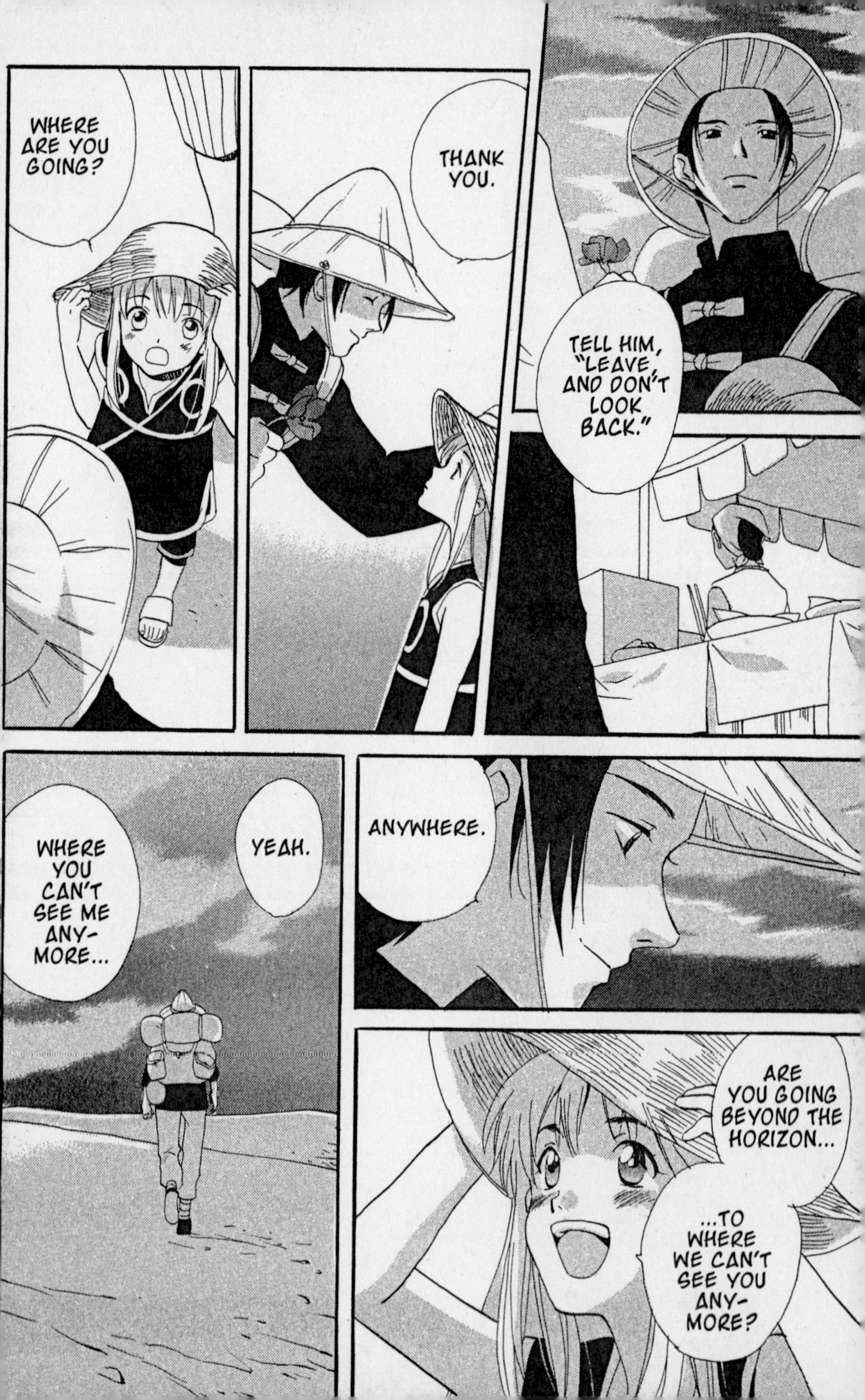
TELL HIM, "LEAVE AND DON'T LOOK BACK."
THANK YOU.
WHERE ARE YOU GOING?
ANYWHERE.
ARE YOU GOING BEYOND THE HORIZON...
...TO WHERE WE CAN'T SEE YOU ANY-MORE?
YEAH.
WHERE YOU CAN'T SEE ME ANY-MORE...

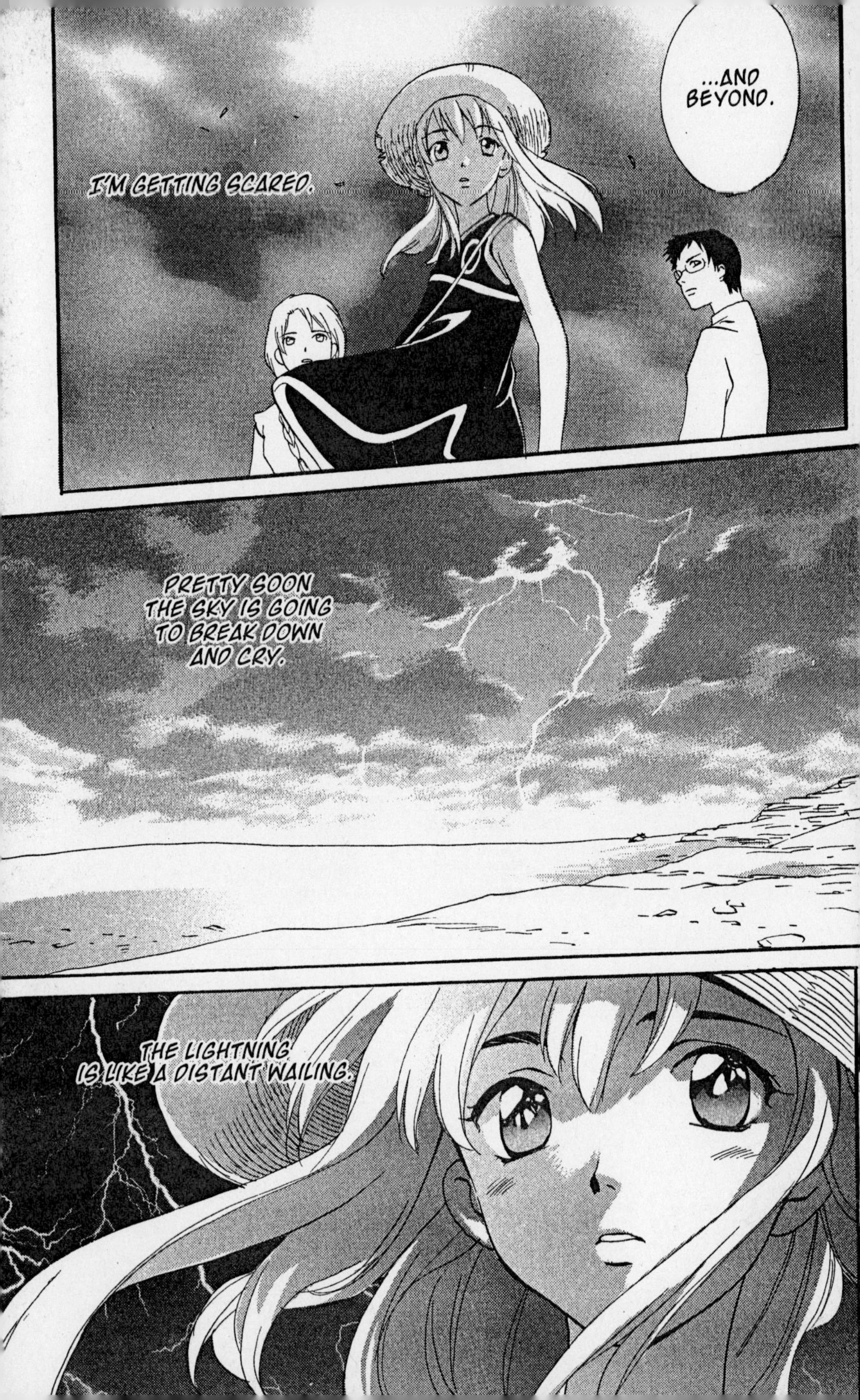
...AND BEYOND.
I'M GETTING SCARED.
PRETTY SOON THE SKY IS GOING TO BREAK DOWN AND CRY.
THE LIGHTNING IS LIKE A DISTANT WAILING.

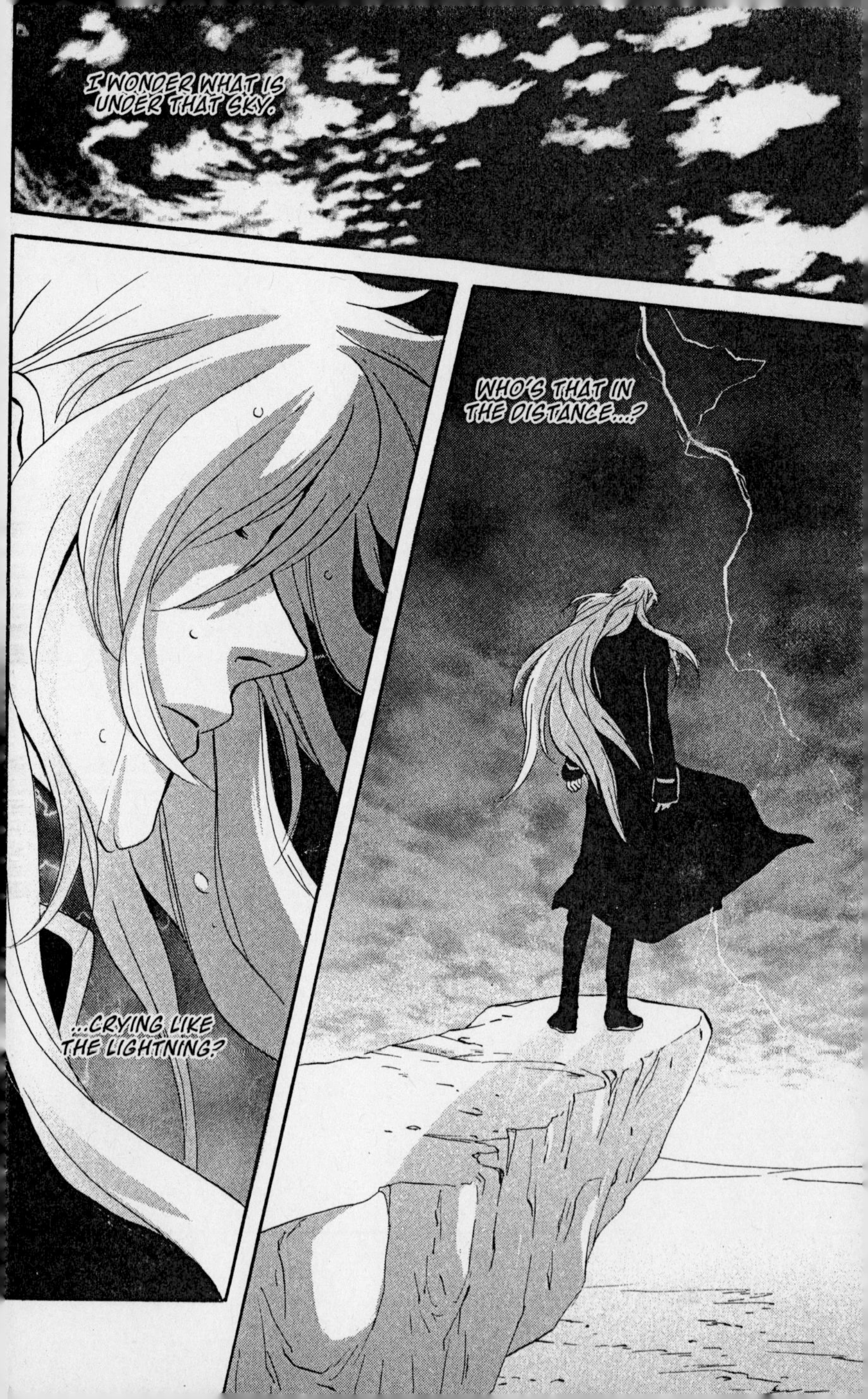
I WONDER WHAT IS UNDER THAT SKY.
WHO'S THAT IN THE DISTANCE...?
...CRYING LIKE THE LIGHTNING?

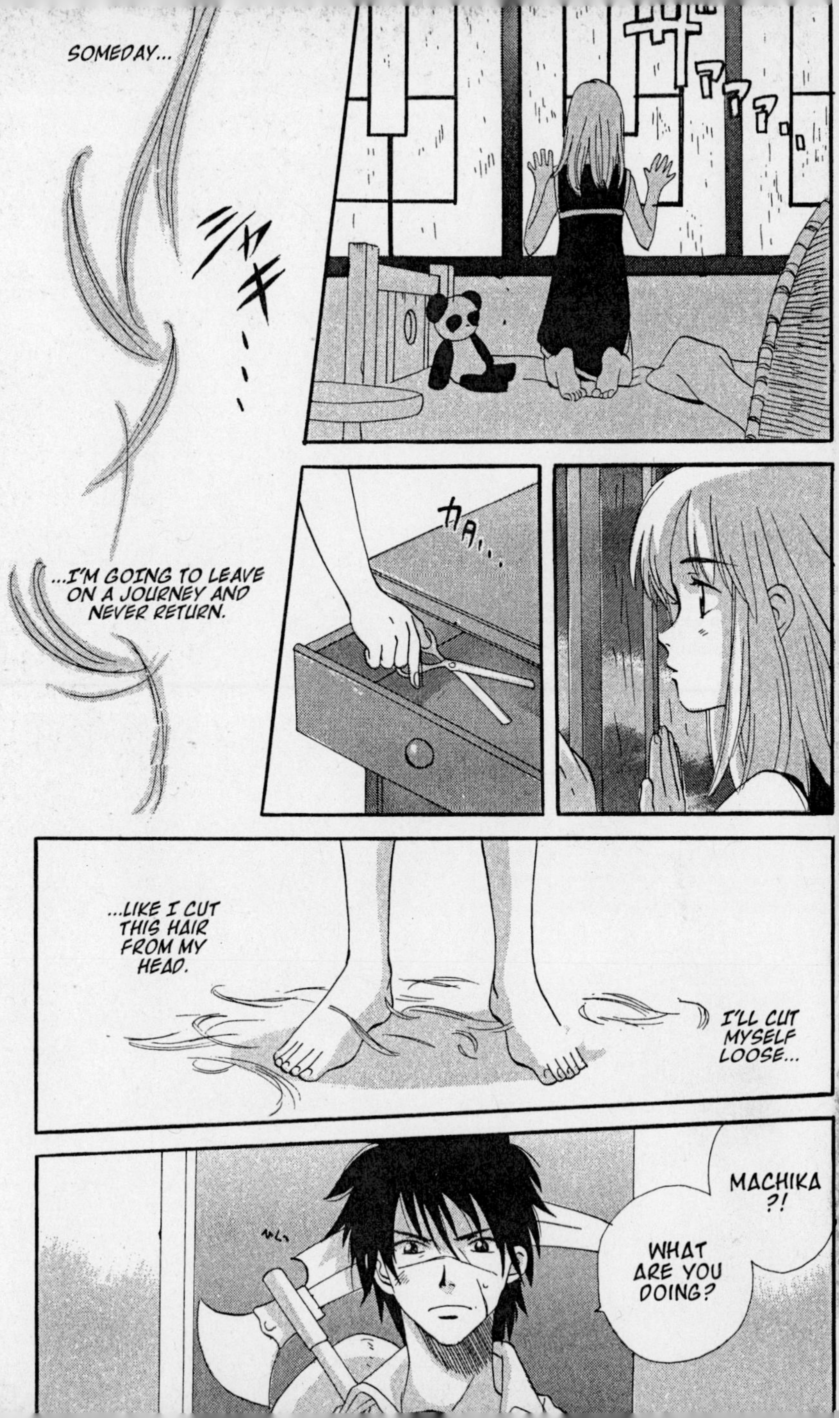
ザァァァ…
SOMEDAY...
シャキ…
カタ...
...I'M GOING TO LEAVE ON A JOURNEY AND NEVER RETURN.
I'LL CUT MYSELF LOOSE...
...LIKE I CUT THIS HAIR FROM MY HEAD.
MACHIKA?!
WHAT ARE YOU DOING?

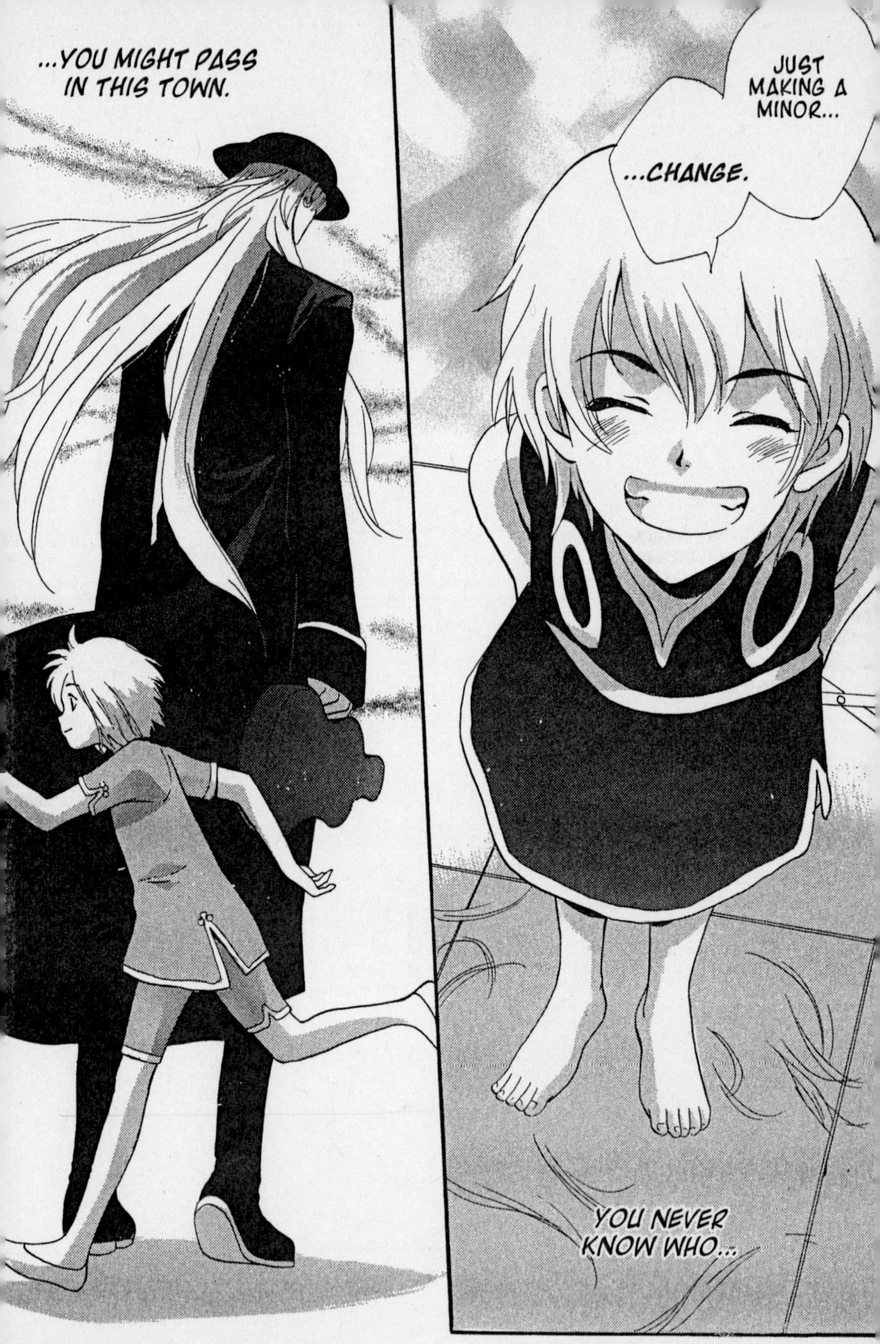
JUST MAKING A MINOR...
...CHANGE.
YOU NEVER KNOW WHO...
...YOU MIGHT PASS IN THIS TOWN.

Calling END

BACK STAGE

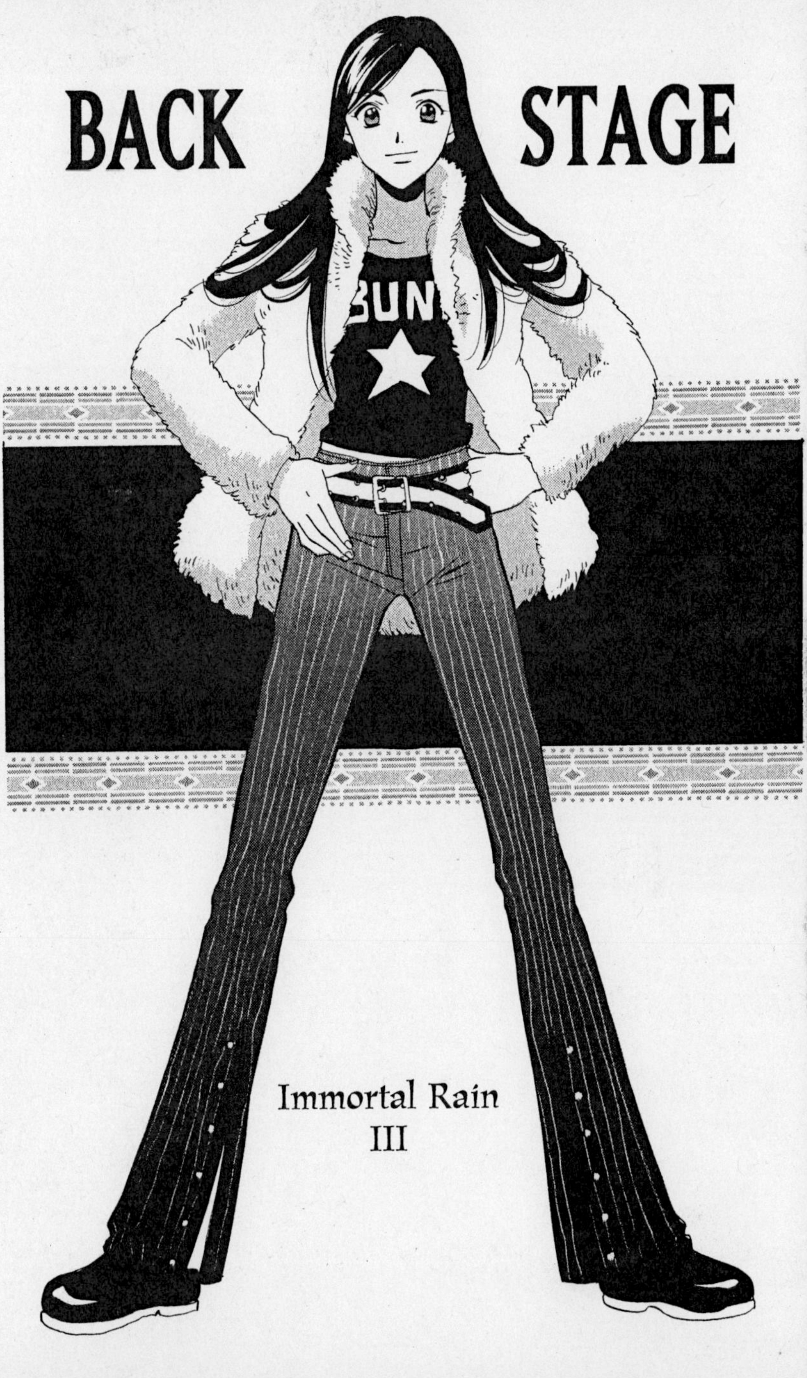

Immortal Rain
III

 HELLO, HOW ARE YOU ALL DOING?
I MADE YOU WAIT SO LONG YET AGAIN.
I NEED TO DO A MOON-SAULT FROM THE SKY AND
END IN A BOW TO MAKE UP FOR IT. BUT THIS IS
REALLY AS FAST AS I CAN WORK.

I REALLY LABORED OVER THE FLASHBACK CHAPTERS.
I WORRIED FOR TWO YEARS. LOTS OF BLOOD FLOWED
WHEN I FINALLY GAVE BIRTH TO THE STORY.

BABY RAIN.

EVERY TIME I DRAW, IT'S SLOW, CLUMSY AND CHOPPY.
ALTHOUGH I'M A MANGA ARTIST, I'M REALLY NOT CUT OUT FOR IT.
EVEN SO, JUST LIKE EATING OR GOING TO THE BATHROOM, MY BASIC FUNCTIONS IN
LIFE INCLUDE DRAWING. I REALLY ADMIRE PEOPLE WHO WERE BORN TO DRAW. AS FOR
ME, I JUST CAN'T LIVE IF I DON'T DRAW. NERD.

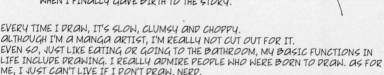

RECENTLY I'VE BEEN READING YOUR COMMENTS ON THE INTERNET.
BUT I REALLY LIKE LETTERS WHERE EVERYONE WRITES BY HAND.
AND BECAUSE OF THAT, I WILL WRITE THIS PAGE BY HAND. BUT IT'S REALLY BAD.

ALL I SEE ON TELEVISION THESE DAYS IS THE TERRORIST ATTACK THAT HAPPENED IN
AMERICA. I STILL HAVE MUCH TO DRAW. BECAUSE THERE IS A MONSTER IN ME. I'M
DEFINITELY STARTING AFTER THIS.

SEPTEMBER 2001,
A WARM
RAINING DAY.
OZAKI KAORI.

IS THAT
REALLY
LEARNING
HOW TO
WRITE?

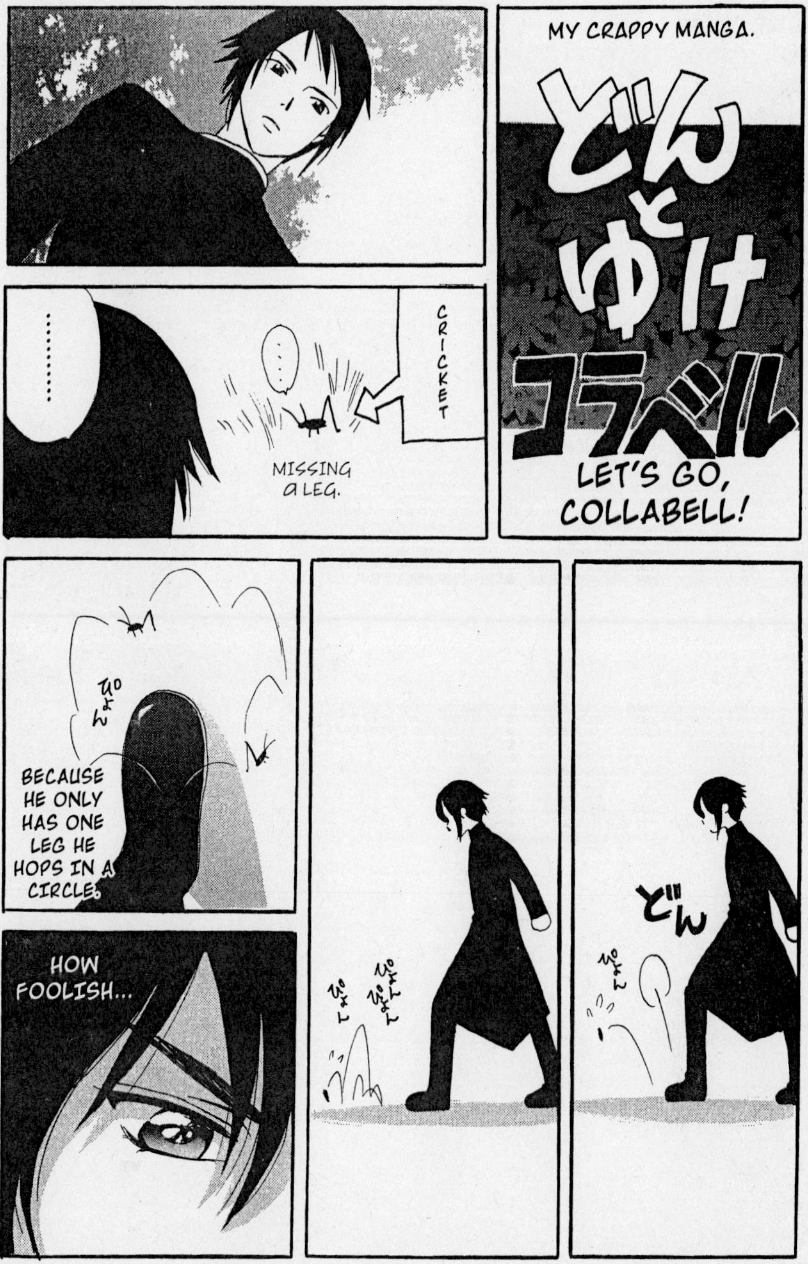
MY CRAPPY MANGA.
どんとゆけコラベル
LET'S GO, COLLABELL!
CRICKET
...
MISSING a LEG.
......
どん
ぴょん
ぴょん ぴょん
ぴょん
ぴょん
BECAUSE HE ONLY HAS ONE LEG HE HOPS IN A CIRCLE.
HOW FOOLISH...

SEE YA.

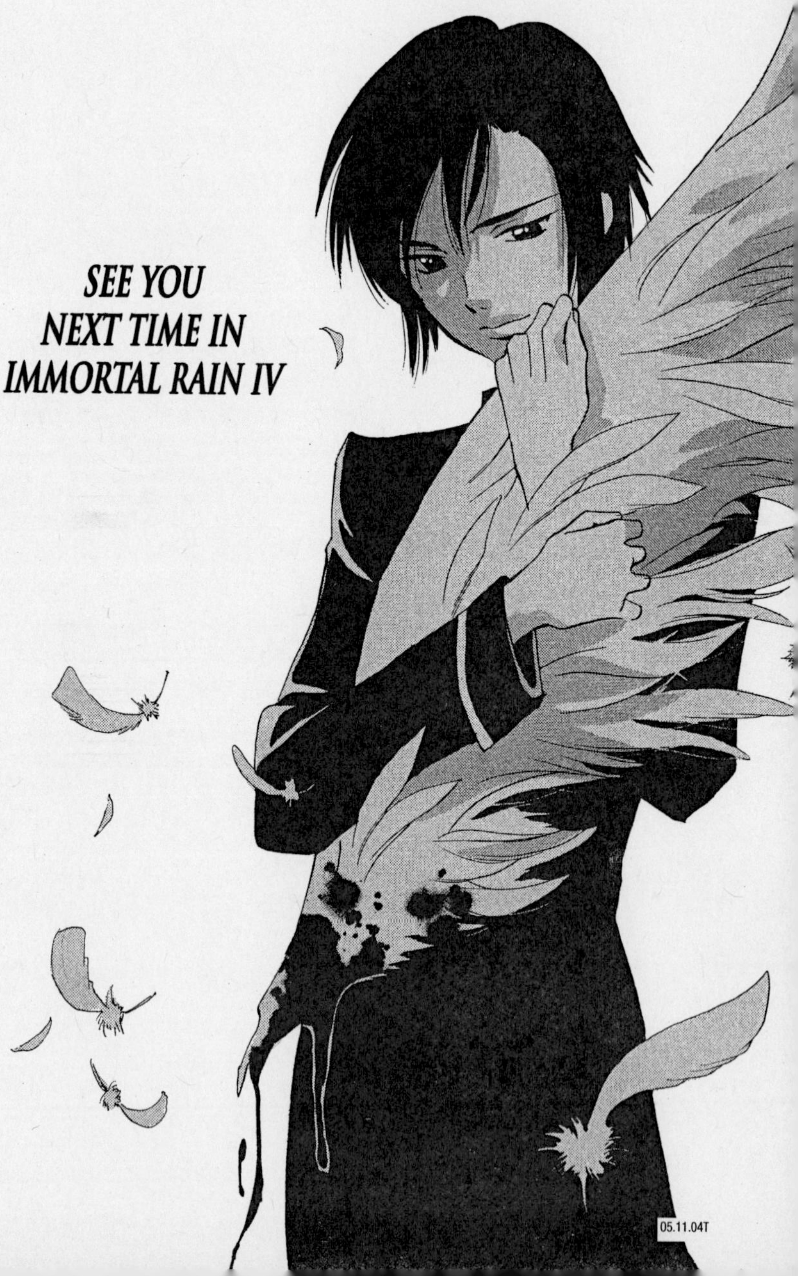
SEE YOU
NEXT TIME IN
IMMORTAL RAIN IV

05.11.04T

IN THE NEXT VOLUME OF

IMMORTAL RAIN

Having related the story of his and Yuca Collabell's mutual past, it's time for the group to move forward, into the future. Unfortunately, that will have to wait, as Eury Evans, Sharem and crew stage a surprise raid on The Angel's Graveyard! It's a battle for survival and a race against time, as the rebirth of Yuca Collabell draws near. Where will Collabell appear next, and how will this affect the schemes of the shadowy Corporation? Find out in Immortal Rain volume 4!

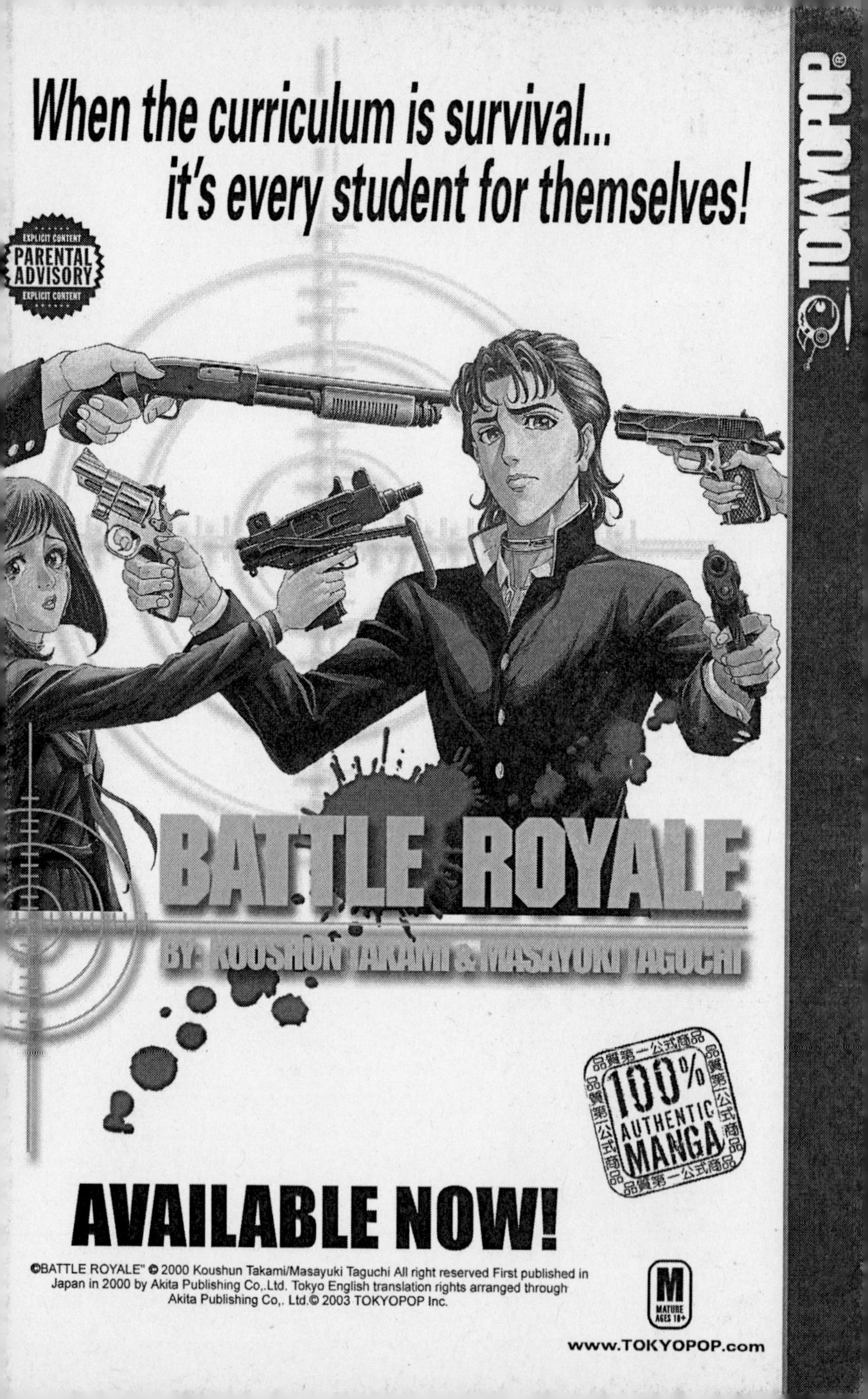

When the curriculum is survival...
it's every student for themselves!
TOKYOPOP®
EXPLICIT CONTENT
PARENTAL ADVISORY
EXPLICIT CONTENT
BATTLE ROYALE
BY: KOUSHUN TAKAMI & MASAYUKI TAGUCHI
品質第一公式商品
100% AUTHENTIC MANGA
AVAILABLE NOW!
©BATTLE ROYALE" © 2000 Koushun Takami/Masayuki Taguchi All right reserved First published in Japan in 2000 by Akita Publishing Co,.Ltd. Tokyo English translation rights arranged through Akita Publishing Co,. Ltd.© 2003 TOKYOPOP Inc.
M MATURE AGES 18+
www.TOKYOPOP.com

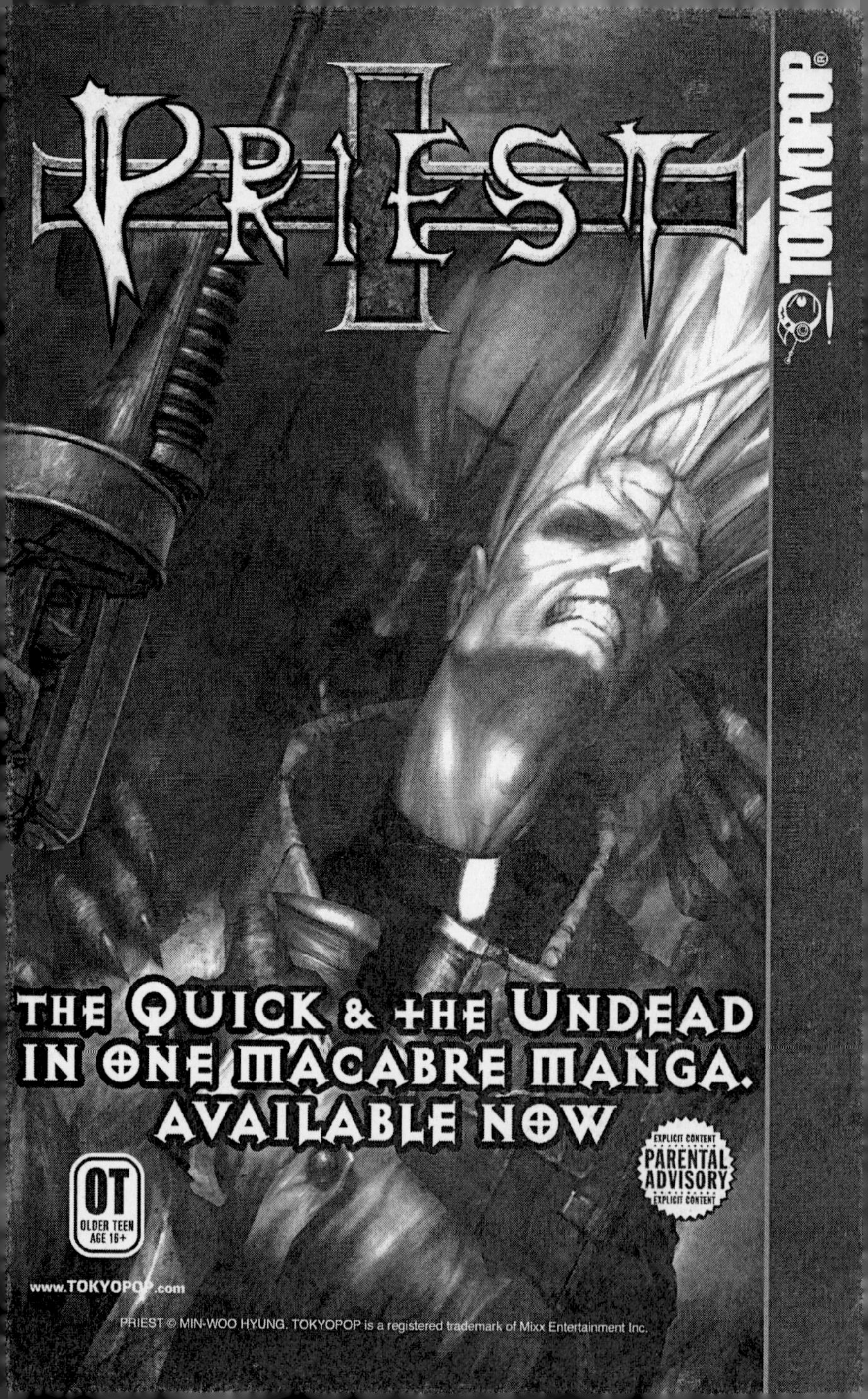
PRIEST
TOKYOPOP
THE QUICK & THE UNDEAD
IN ONE MACABRE MANGA.
AVAILABLE NOW
OT
OLDER TEEN
AGE 16+
EXPLICIT CONTENT
PARENTAL ADVISORY
EXPLICIT CONTENT
www.TOKYOPOP.com
PRIEST © MIN-WOO HYUNG. TOKYOPOP is a registered trademark of Mixx Entertainment Inc.

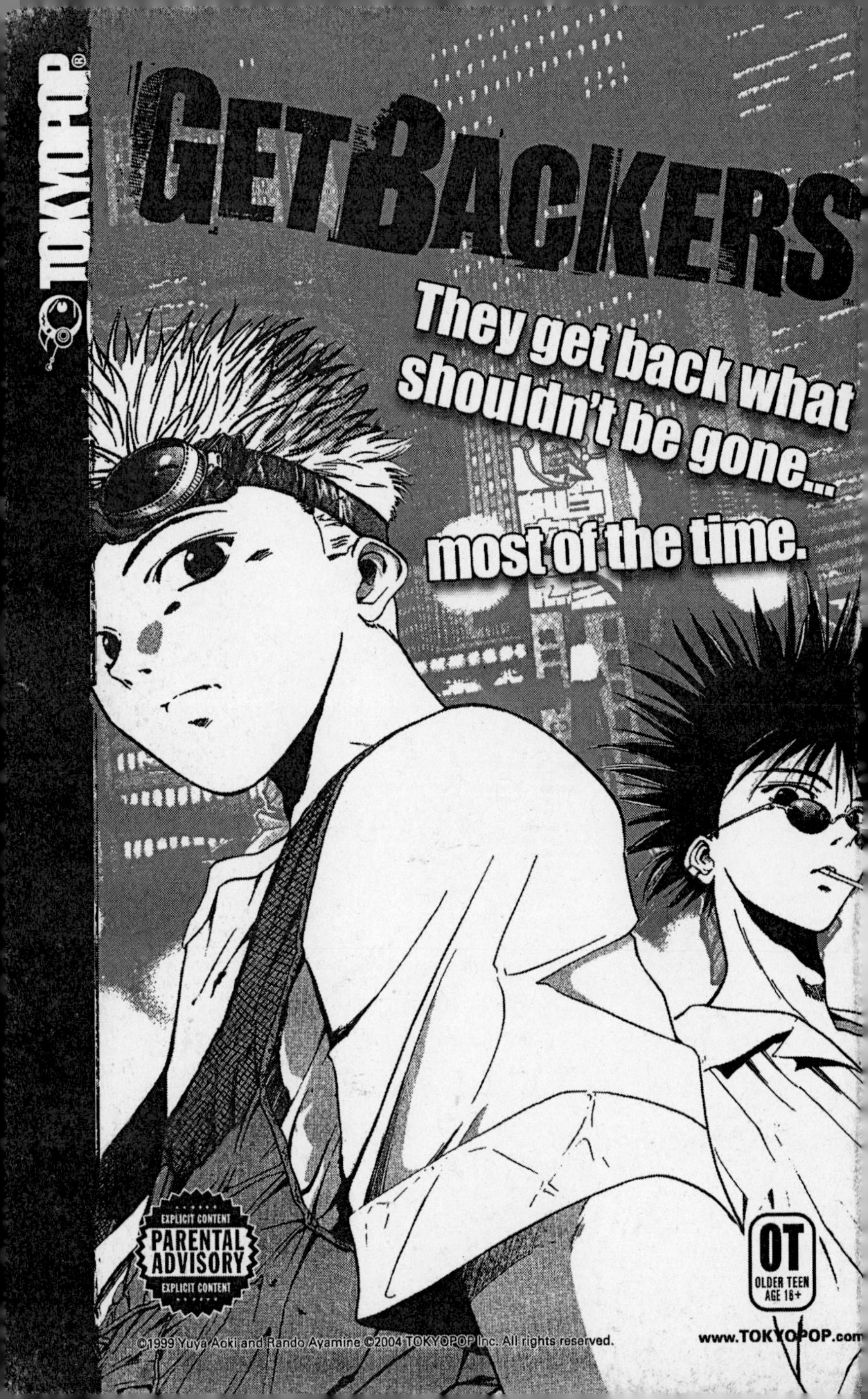
TOKYOPOP
GETBACKERS
They get back what shouldn't be gone... most of the time.
EXPLICIT CONTENT
PARENTAL ADVISORY
EXPLICIT CONTENT
OT
OLDER TEEN AGE 16+
©1999 Yuya Aoki and Rando Ayamine ©2004 TOKYOPOP Inc. All rights reserved.
www.TOKYOPOP.com

ALSO AVAILABLE FROM  TOKYOPOP.

ALSO AVAILABLE FROM ✿TOKYOPOP®

MANGA

.HACK//LEGEND OF THE TWILIGHT
@LARGE
ABENOBASHI: MAGICAL SHOPPING ARCADE
A.I. LOVE YOU
AI YORI AOSHI
ANGELIC LAYER
ARM OF KANNON
BABY BIRTH
BATTLE ROYALE
BATTLE VIXENS
BOYS BE...
BRAIN POWERED
BRIGADOON
B'TX
CANDIDATE FOR GODDESS, THE
CARDCAPTOR SAKURA
CARDCAPTOR SAKURA - MASTER OF THE CLOW
CHOBITS
CHRONICLES OF THE CURSED SWORD
CLAMP SCHOOL DETECTIVES
CLOVER
COMIC PARTY
CONFIDENTIAL CONFESSIONS
CORRECTOR YUI
COWBOY BEBOP
COWBOY BEBOP: SHOOTING STAR
CRAZY LOVE STORY
CRESCENT MOON
CROSS
CULDCEPT
CYBORG 009
D•N•ANGEL
DEMON DIARY
DEMON ORORON, THE
DEUS VITAE
DIABOLO
DIGIMON
DIGIMON TAMERS
DIGIMON ZERO TWO
DOLL
DRAGON HUNTER
DRAGON KNIGHTS
DRAGON VOICE
DREAM SAGA
DUKLYON: CLAMP SCHOOL DEFENDERS
EERIE QUEERIE!
ERICA SAKURAZAWA: COLLECTED WORKS
ET CETERA
ETERNITY
EVIL'S RETURN
FAERIES' LANDING
FAKE
FLCL
FLOWER OF THE DEEP SLEEP, THE
FORBIDDEN DANCE
FRUITS BASKET

G GUNDAM
GATEKEEPERS
GETBACKERS
GIRL GOT GAME
GRAVITATION
GTO
GUNDAM SEED ASTRAY
GUNDAM WING
GUNDAM WING: BATTLEFIELD OF PACIFISTS
GUNDAM WING: ENDLESS WALTZ
GUNDAM WING: THE LAST OUTPOST (G-UNIT)
HANDS OFF!
HAPPY MANIA
HARLEM BEAT
HYPER RUNE
I.N.V.U.
IMMORTAL RAIN
INITIAL D
INSTANT TEEN: JUST ADD NUTS
ISLAND
JING: KING OF BANDITS
JING: KING OF BANDITS - TWILIGHT TALES
JULINE
KARE KANO
KILL ME, KISS ME
KINDAICHI CASE FILES, THE
KING OF HELL
KODOCHA: SANA'S STAGE
LAMENT OF THE LAMB
LEGAL DRUG
LEGEND OF CHUN HYANG, THE
LES BIJOUX
LOVE HINA
LOVE OR MONEY
LUPIN III
LUPIN III: WORLD'S MOST WANTED
MAGIC KNIGHT RAYEARTH I
MAGIC KNIGHT RAYEARTH II
MAHOROMATIC: AUTOMATIC MAIDEN
MAN OF MANY FACES
MARMALADE BOY
MARS
MARS: HORSE WITH NO NAME
MINK
MIRACLE GIRLS
MIYUKI-CHAN IN WONDERLAND
MODEL
MOURYOU KIDEN: LEGEND OF THE NYMPHS
NECK AND NECK
ONE
ONE I LOVE, THE
PARADISE KISS
PARASYTE
PASSION FRUIT
PEACH GIRL
PEACH GIRL: CHANGE OF HEART
PET SHOP OF HORRORS
PITA-TEN

07.15.04T

STOP!

This is the back of the book.
You wouldn't want to spoil a great ending!

This book is printed "manga-style," in the authentic Japanese right-to-left format. Since none of the artwork has been flipped or altered, readers get to experience the story just as the creator intended. You've been asking for it, so TOKYOPOP® delivered: authentic, hot-off-the-press, and far more fun!

DIRECTIONS

If this is your first time reading manga-style, here's a quick guide to help you understand how it works.

It's easy... just start in the top right panel and follow the numbers. Have fun, and look for more 100% authentic manga from TOKYOPOP®!